Miller's
Church History

Vol. 3

Christian Classics Revived

The Publishers endeavor herein to make reaccessible to Researchers, Academics & Libraries worldwide Reproduced Editions of such rare and time-honored publications which continue to stand out for their cultural & historical importance, over the years. In this Series we'll focus on Christian Faith & Living vis-à-vis topics like Literature & Poetry, Indigenous Philosophizing, Ethical response towards Agriculture, Health & Healing, Science & Technology, Ecofeminist Theology, Sociological approach towards Human Rights, Law & Politics, Arts, History of Ideas, Ancient Civilizations, Cultural Contiguity, Religious Cosmologies & Mysticism, Footsteps of famous Theologians, World Peace & Harmony, Global Capitalism, Network Marketing, Cybertheology, Population & Demographics, Epigraphic Studies, Contextualized Education, and many others. We welcome your comments on our this effort and further suggestions for taking up any such scholarly titles, having gone in oblivion, befitting Classic Works of glorious and legendary writers on Christian Studies.

Christian Classics Revived - 12

Miller's Church History

From First to Twentieth Century
(Short Papers on Church History)

By
Andrew Miller

Vol. 3

Christian World Imprints™

© This Reprint in India 2015, by:

Christian World Imprints^{TM}
Christian Publishing & Books from India
H-12 Bali Nagar, **New Delhi-110015**
info@christianworldimprints.com
www.ChristianWorldImprints.com
Phone: +91 11 25465925

ISBN 13: 978-93-5148-072-3 (Set)
ISBN 13: 978-93-5148-073-0 (Vol. 1)
ISBN 13: 978-93-5148-074-7 (Vol. 2)
ISBN 13: 978-93-5148-075-4 (Vol. 3)

ISBN 10: 93-5148-072-0 (Set)
ISBN 10: 93-5148-073-9 (Vol. 1)
ISBN 10: 93-5148-074-7 (Vol. 2)
ISBN 10: 93-5148-075-5 (Vol. 3)

Cataloging in Publication Data--DK
    Courtesy: D.K. Agencies (P) Ltd. <docinfo@dkagencies.com>

Miller, Andrew, 1810-1883, **author.**
    Miller's Church history : from first to twentieth century (short
papers on church history) / Andrew Miller.
    3 volumes   cm. -- (Christian classics revived ; 12)
    Reprint.
    Includes index.
    ISBN 9789351480723 (Set)
    ISBN 9789351480730 (Vol. 1)
    ISBN 9789351480747 (Vol. 2)
    ISBN 9789351480754 (Vol. 3)

    1. Church history.   I. Title.   II. Series: Christian classics
revived ; 12.

DDC 270   23

Printed at Replika Press Pvt. Ltd.

Preface

A S all we know of history comes to us through books, I have
examined, with some care, the authors which are most
esteemed in this country and considered the most reliable.
And although there is frequent reference to volume and page,
this by no means indicates all that has been gathered from those
histories. It would be impossible to say how many thoughts,
words, and sentences, are interwoven with my own. The
references have been generally given, not so much to verify
what has been written, as to induce the reader to study them or
whatever works may now be available as he may have opportunity.
The materials are so varied and abundant, that the difficulty lies
in making a selection, so as to maintain a continued historic line,
and yet leave out what would now be neither profitable nor
interesting.

Some of my earliest and valued friends, such as Greenwood,
Milman, and Craigie Robertson, conclude their histories about
the fourteenth century ; Waddington, D'Aubigne, and Scott,
about the middle of the sixteenth ; and Wylie closes his history of
Protestantism with its establishment under the reign of William
and Mary. Dr. M'Crie's special histories and biographies are
extremely valuable ; and so is the history of Protestantism in
France by Felice, the history of the Reformation in the Low
Countries by Brandt, the brief history of the Middle Ages and
the Reformation by Hardwick, and also Cunningham's history
of the Scotch Church; but good general histories from the early
part of the sixteenth to the present century are indeed scarce.

I have aimed at more than mere history. It has been my
desire to connect with it Christ and His Word, so that the reader
may receive the truth and blessing, through grace, to his soul.
And it will be observed that I commence with the Lord's revealed
purpose concerning His Church in Matthew 16. Other parts of
the New Testament have been carefully examined as to the first
planting of the Church, but its actual history I have endeavoured
to trace in the light of the addresses to the seven Churches in
Asia. This of course must be in a very general way, as I have
been desirous to give the reader as broad a view of ecclesiastical
history as possible, consistently with my plan and brevity.

May the Lord's blessing accompany the volume that now goes
forth.

LONDON   ANDREW MILLER

Contents

		Page
INTRODUCTION		1

The Seven Churches of Asia, 3

CHAPTER I
THE ROCK FOUNDATION ... ... — 7
Foundation of the Church, 8—Opening of the Kingdom of
Heaven, 11—Church Government, 13

CHAPTER II
THE DAY OF PENTECOST ... ... — 18
Resurrection and Ascension of Christ, 19—Descent of the
Holy Ghost, 20—Calling in of the Gentiles, 25—First
Christian Martyr, 27

CHAPTER III
THE DISCIPLES PERSECUTED AND SCATTERED ... ... — 30
Jerusalem and Samaria United by the Gospel, 32—
Conversion of Saul of Tarsus, 35

CHAPTER IV
THE FIRST MISSIONARIES OF THE CROSS ... ... — 40
The Twelve Apostles, 41—Herodian Line of Kings, 46

CHAPTER V
THE APOSTLE PAUL ... ... — 66
First Visit to Jerusalem, 67—First Missionary Journey,
69—First Council of the Church, 73—Visit to Athens, 83

CHAPTER VI
PAUL'S THIRD MISSIONARY JOURNEY ... ... — 91
Departure for Macedonia, 92—Fifth Visit to Jerusalem,
96—Before the Sanhedrin, 103—Martyrdom of Paul, 117

CHAPTER VII
ROME AND HER EARLY RULERS ... ... — 120
First Persecution Under the Emperors, 121—The Real
Cause of Persecution, 129—Persecutions in France, 143

CHAPTER VIII
THE ITERNAL HISTORY OF THE CHURCH ... ... — 150
Apostolic Fathers, 151—Origin of Clergy and Laity, 154—
Origin of Dioceses, 156

CHAPTER IX
FROM COMMODUS TILL THE ACCESSION OF CONSTANTINE ... — 158
Persecution in Africa, 160—Altered Position of Christianity,
163—Final Contest Between Paganism and Christianity,
170—The Condition of the Church, 173

CHAPTER X
CONSTANTINE THE GREAT 182
Church as Constantine Found It, 189—Effects of Royal
Favour, 192—Baptism and Death of Constantine, 195

CHAPTER XI
THE COUNCIL OF NICE 200
The Council of Tyre, 204—The Barbaric Invaders, 213

CHAPTER XII
THE INTERNAL HISTORY OF THE CHURCH 218
Infant Baptism, 223—First Society of Ascetics, 229—
Calamities of Rome, 234

CHAPTER XIII
THE EPISTLE TO THE CHURCH IN THYATIRA 243
Leo the First, Surnamed the Great, 249—Missionary Zeal of
Gregory, 253—Romish Hierarchy in England, 258

CHAPTER XIV
THE SPREAD OF CHRISTIANITY OVER EUROPE 263
First Preachers in Ireland, 263—First Preachers in Scotland,
267—Foreshadowing of the Man of Sin, 278

CHAPTER XV
MOHAMMED, THE FALSE PROPHET OF ARABIA 281
Religion of Islam, 282—Successors of Mohammed, 285—
Second Council of Nice, 294

CHAPTER XVI
THE SILVER LINE OF SOVEREIGN GRACE 296
Origin of the Paulicians, 297—Religious Wars of Charle-
magne, 303—Feudal Hierarchical System, 309

CHAPTER XVII
THE PROPAGATION OF CHRISTIANITY 316
Louis the Pious, 317—The Slavonians Receive the Gospel,
319—England, Scotland, and Ireland, 320

CHAPTER XVIII
THE CHURCH-BUILDING SPIRIT REVIVED 326
Revivals of Letters by the Arabs, 327—Traces of the Sliver
Line of God's Grace, 329

CHAPTER XIX
THE PONTIFICATE OF GREGORY VII 332
Gregory and Clerical Independence, 334—Celibacy and
Simony, 336—The Emperor Deposed by the Pope, 340—
Effects of the Papal Policy, 345—Burning of Ancient Rome,
348

CHAPTER XX
THE CRUSADES 353
The First Crusade, 357—The Second Crusade, 364—The
Third Crusade, 366—The Remainder of the Crusades, 367

CHAPTER XXI

HENRY V AND GREGORY'S SUCCESSORS 371
St. Bernard, Abbot of Clairvaux, 373—The Great Council of
the Lateran, 381—Arnold of Brescia, 385

CHAPTER XXII

THE ENCROACHMENTS OF ROME IN ENGLAND 390
The Introduction of Canon Law into England, 392—Thomas
à Becket and Henry II, 394—The "Constitutions of Claren-
don", 397

CHAPTER XXIII

THE THEOLOGY OF THE CHURCH OF ROME 403
Transubstantiation, 403—Mary-Worship, 405—Saint-Wor-
ship, 407—Relic-Worship, 409—Purgatory, 410—Extreme
Unction, 414—Auricular Confession, 416—Indulgences, 419

CHAPTER XXIV

INNOCENT III AND HIS TIMES 422
Innocent's Views of Popedom, 426—Philip and Otho, 433—
Innocent and England, 442—England Surrendered to Rome,
448

CHAPTER XXV

INNOCENT AND THE SOUTH OF FRANCE 453
Peter Waldo. 457—Raymond a Spiritual Outlaw, 463—The
Real Object of the Catholics, 469

CHAPTER XXVI

THE INQUISITION ESTABLISHED IN LANGUEDOC 484
The Application of Tortue, 488—The *Auto de Fé*, 490—St.
Benedict, 492—New Orders-St. Dominic and St. Francis, 498

CHAPTER XXVII

THE APPROACHING DAWN OF THE REFORMATION ... 509
Christianity in Ireland, 509—Christianity in Scotland, 511—
Popery as a System, 515

CHAPTER XXVIII

THE DECLINE OF PAPAL POWER 522
Gregory IX and Frederick II, 524—The Overruling Hand of
God, 529—The Humiliation of the Pontiff, 531

CHAPTER XXIX

THE FORERUNNERS OF THE REFORMATION 536
Literary Men, 537—The Theologians, 538—The Waldenses,
542—The Dark Year of 1560, 547

CHAPTER XXX

JOHN WYCLIFFE 549
England and the Papacy, 550—Wycliffe and the Bible, 558—
The Lollards, 561

CHAPTER XXXI

THE REFORMATION MOVEMENT IN BOHEMIA 568
The Imprisonment of John Huss, 574—The Arrest and
Imprisonment of Jerome, 582—The United Brethren or
Moravians, 590

CHAPTER XXXII

THE CAPTURE OF CONSTANTINOPLE   593
The First Printed Bible, 595—The Immediate Precursors of
Luther, 598—Reflections on the Life of Savonarola, 600

CHAPTER XXXIII

THE REFORMATION IN GERMANY   608
Popery and Mankind, 609—The First Period of Luther's
Life, 611—Luther's Conversion, 619

CHAPTER XXXIV

THE FIRST PAPAL JUBILEE   628
Luther's Public Appeal, 633—Distinguised Men of the Sixteenth Century, 638—The Diet of Worms, 642

CHAPTER XXXV

LUTHER AT WARTBURG   650
Luther and the German Bible, 652—The Hundred Grievances,
656—The First Diet of Spires, 660

CHAPTER XXXVI

PROTESTANTISM   664
The Lutheran Churches, 671—Meetings of the Protestants,
675

CHAPTER XXXVII

THE SACRAMENTARIAN CONTROVERSY   677
The Conference at Marburg, 683—A Proposal for Toleration
and Unity, 689

CHAPTER XXXVIII

THE COUNCIL AT BOLOGNA   694
The Diet of Augsburg, 695—The Articles of Faith, 708—
The Letters of Melanchthon and Luther, 710

CHAPTER XXXIX

THE POPISH REFUTATION   713
The Final Decree, 717—The League of Smalcald, 723—The
Peace of Ratisbon, 725

CHAPTER XL

THE REFORMATION IN SWITZERLAND   728
Zwingle, Pastor of Glaris, 732—The Rising Storm, 742

CHAPTER XLI

THE LEADERS OF THE REFORMATION IN SWITZERLAND ...   744
The Progress of the Reformation-Zurich, 751—Zwingle and
His Brothers, 755—The Disputations at Zurich, 756

CHAPTER XLII

THE RESULTS OF THE DISPUTATIONS   766
The Answer of Zurich to Lucerne, 769—The Swiss and German Reformation, 771—The Weapons of Rome's Warfare,
774

CHAPTER XLIII
THE GENERAL PROGRESS OF REFORM 781
The Reformation in Berne, 783—The Conference at Baden, 785—The Great Conference at Berne, 788—The Reformation of Basle, 794

CHAPTER XLIV
THE EXTENSION OF REFORM IN SWITZERLAND 801
The Five Cantons and Austria, 802—The Treaty of Cappel, 807—War Declared Against Zurich, 813

CHAPTER XLV
THE REFORMATION IN GERMANY 823
The Great Actors Passing Off the Scene, 826—The Death of Luther, 830—Reflections on the Life of Luther, 832

CHAPTER XLVI
THE OPENING OF THE COUNCIL OF TRENT 842
The Smalcald War, 845—The Treaty of Maurice, 851—The Germans Treated as a Conquered People, 855

CHAPTER XLVII
"THE INTERIM" 857
The Revolution in Germany, 863—The Calamities of the Protestants, 867—The Rise of the Jesuits, 868

CHAPTER XLVIII
THE EFFECT OF THE REFORMATION IN GERMANY ON THE NATIONS OF EUROPE 873
Sweden and Denmark, 873—Italy, 876—Spain, 882—The Netherlands, 888

CHAPTER XLIX
THE REFORMATION IN FRENCH SWITZERLAND 899
William Farel, 901—The Arrival of Calvin in Geneva, 909—Calvin and Calvinism, 921

CHAPTER L
THE REFORMATION IN FRANCE 923
The Bible in French at Meaux, 928—Commencement of Persecution in France, 930—The Year of the Placards, 941

CHAPTER LI
THE GREAT PROGRESS OF THE REFORMATION 947
The First Planting of the Reformed Church in France, 951—The Saint Bartholomew Massacre, 953—The Council of Trent, 961

CHAPTER LII
THE WALDENSES 964
The Wars of Extermination, 965—The Sympathy of England, 971—The Persecution and Expulsion of the Waldenses, 973

CHAPTER LIII

THE REFORMATION IN THE BRITISH ISLES 978
Ireland, 978—Scotland, 983—The Fiery Zeal of Cardinal
Beaton, 990—George Wishart, 995—John Knox, 1000

CHAPTER LIV

THE REFORMATION IN ENGLAND 1009
The Reformation Begun, 1015—The Persecution Begins,
1019—Ridley, Latimer, and Cranmer, 1026

CHAPTER LV

THE REIGN OF ELIZABETH 1029
The Puritans 1029,—John Wesley, 1035—Sunday Schools,
1038—Foreign Missions, 1039

CHAPTER LVI

THE LAST FIFTY YEARS 1041
Evangelical Degeneracy, 1045—The Evangelical Revival,
1051—Conferences and Missions, 1057—A Return to the Word
of God, 1061—The Welsh Revival, 1068

APPENDIX A

ARIUS AND GNOSTICISM 1075

APPENDIX B

THE FESTIVAL OF EASTER 1076

GENERAL INDEX 1077

INDEX TO PERSONS 1085

INDEX OF PLACES 1090

Chapter XXXIX

The Popish Refutation

On the 13th of July, or rather less than three weeks after the reading of the Protestant Confession, the Popish divines presented their **reply to the Emperor.** It consisted of two hundred and eighty pages ; but the style was so abusive and violent that Charles would not allow it to be read in the diet. He was much displeased, and ordered another to be drawn up, shorter and more moderate. The document having been so altered as to suit the mind of the Emperor, he caused it to be read in full diet on the 3rd of August. The first copy was in accordance with the counsels of the Pope, the second with the policy of Charles.

The Count-Palatine, after admitting, in a general way, that many abuses had crept into the Church, and that the Emperor by no means defended them, delivered the following message : " That the Emperor found the articles of this Refutation orthodox, Catholic, and conformable to the Gospels ; that he therefore required the Protestants to abandon their Confession, now refuted, and to adhere to all the articles that had just been set forth ; that, if they refused, the Emperor would remember his office, and would know how to show himself the advocate and defender of the Roman Church."

These words could not be misunderstood by the Protestants. They breathed force and violence. This was the boasted clemency of the Emperor. Each party now stood on its own proper ground. The Protestants had taken their stand on the Word of God ; the Catholics on the word of man—the fathers, the Popes, and the councils. These were, and are, and ever must be, the essential features of divine and human ground, of true religion and false.

The Refutation wholly rejected the doctrine of justification by faith, without the merit of good works. And with respect to the marriage of priests, the Catholics wondered that the Protestants could demand such a thing, seeing it had never been the practice for priests to marry since the days of the apostles (?). With regard to the mass, it was affirmed to be a sacrifice for the living and the dead ; " that Daniel had prophesied long ago, that when Antichrist should come, the daily offering should cease ; but as yet this had not come to pass in the Holy Catholic Church. Nevertheless, in those places where mass was despised, altars destroyed, and images burned, that prophecy was fulfilled." Such were the enlightened arguments of the Popish doctors.

The moment they refer to Scripture, they prove that they are blinded by the god of this world.

Such was the character of the Refutation which Charles invited the Protestant princes to accede to, out of deference to his own authority, as protector of the integrity of the Roman Church, and the religious unity of the empire.

A COPY OF THE REFUTATION REFUSED.

John, the good **Elector of Saxony,** nobly answered for himself and his friends : " That they would do anything for peace which they could do with a safe conscience ; and, if convicted of any error by Scriptural authority, they would readily renounce it. But he desired a copy of the Refutation, that they might consider it at leisure, and show on what points it was not satisfactory to them ; which would be in conformity with the fair and candid discussion to which they had been invited by the edict of convocation." This reasonable request, however, was refused. The Refutation was not published, and no copies of it were given to the Protestants. But they persisted in demanding a copy ; and Charles agreed to give them one on the following conditions, namely, "that the Protestants should not reply ; that they should speedily agree with the Emperor and submit to his decision that no transcript of it should be made ; and that it should not be communicated to any other persons, as the Emperor would have no further debate." On such conditions they declined to receive it, and appealed to God and His truth.

The firmness of the princes greatly irritated the Emperor. They thus refused all that he had proposed to them, even what he considered a favour ; and he had utterly failed, with all the craft of Rome, either to gain or disunite them. "Agitation," says D'Aubigné, " anger, and affright were manifest on every bench of that august assembly. This reply of the evangelicals was war —was rebellion. Duke George of Saxony, the Princes of Bavaria, all the violent adherents of Rome, trembled with indignation. There was a sudden, an impetuous movement, and an explosion of murmurs and hatred." *

PRIVATE NEGOTIATIONS.

So violent was the tumult produced in the diet by the Protestants rejecting the Emperor's proposals, that the Electors of Mayence and Bradenburg interposed, and requested the Emperor to accept their offices for the private and amicable arrangement of the differences. This being agreed to, **mediators were appointed.** They were six in number—all violent enemies of the Reformation—the Elector of Bradenburg, the Archbishop of Saltzburg, the Bishop of Strasburg, Wurtzburg, and Bamberg,

* D'Aubigné, vol. iv., p. 277 ; John Scott, vol. i., p 53.

and Duke George of Saxony. The affair was now placed on new ground, but no nearer a peaceful settlement. Had Charles been left to his own convictions, there would have been little difficulty in coming to peaceful terms with the Reformers. He wanted both money and men from Germany, and could not see the policy of desolating the country, and exterminating his subjects because they refused obedience to the Pope. Besides, it is thought by some historians that the nearer he contemplated the principles of the Reformers the more did they strike a chord in his own spirit. And it is certain that his own sister, Mary, who was married to Christiern, King of Denmark, was a pious princess, and probably a Lutheran. Like Margaret with her brother Francis I she often pleaded with her brother Charles on behalf of the Protestants.

But the Emperor was in a difficulty ; he must play the politician. He was under the most solemn oath to defend the Roman Church and the Pontifical dignity ; he had therefore to assume a position that would be gratifying to the Pope and his party. But as he was slow in his movements, messages were sent from Rome of the most violent character ; and Campeggio redoubled his zeal. " Let the Emperor," said the legate, " conclude a treaty with the Catholic princes of Germany, and if these rebels, equally insensible to threats and promises, obstinately persist in their diabolical course, then let his majesty employ fire and sword, let him take possession of all the property of the heretics and utterly eradicate these poisonous pests. Then let him appoint holy inquisitors, who shall go on the track of the remnant of reform, and proceed against them as in Spain against the Moors." Besides all this, the University of Wittemberg was to be excommunicated ; the heretical books burned, and those who had studied there were to be declared unworthy the favour of Pope or Emperor. " But first of all," said the crafty legate to Charles, " a sweeping confiscation is necessary. Even if your majesty confines yourself to the leaders of the party, you may extract from them a large sum of money, which is at all events indispensable to carry on the war with the Turks." *

Such were the counsels of Rome, and by such the mediators were animated. In the first conference which was held, they addressed the Protestants after the style of their party—repeating to them the mildness of the Emperor, his desire to establish unity, and to correct some abuses which had crept into the Christian Church, in conjunction with the Pope. " But," said the Elector of Bradenburg, " how contrary to the Gospel are the sentiments you have adopted ! Abandon then your errors, do not any longer remain separate from the Church, and sign the

* Ranke's " History of the Popes," vol. i., p. 76.

Refutation without delay. If you refuse, then, through your fault, how many souls will be lost, how much bloodshed, what countries laid waste, what trouble in all the Empire!" And, turning to the Elector of Saxony, he said in plain terms, "that if he did not renounce and anathematize the new-fangled doctrine which he had embraced, the Emperor would by force of arms deprive him of his dignities, his possessions, and his life; that certain ruin would fall upon his subjects, and even upon their wives and children." The prince, now old and infirm, was, for the moment, much affected by such outrageous language, but speedily recovered his wonted resolution. The princes remained firm and unanimous, though surrounded by the imperial guards, and the city almost in a state of siege.

Immediately after the first meeting, the Landgrave of Hesse left Augsburg. His sudden departure caused a good deal of uneasiness to the Emperor, the princes, and the whole diet. His intentions were unknown; but he left a note with his Chancellor for the Elector, in which he assured him of his unalterable constancy in the cause of the Gospel, and his determination rather to shed the last drop of his blood than abandon it. He also exhorted his allies to permit themselves in no manner to be turned aside from the Word of God. His ministers remained in the diet, instructed to give their vigorous support to the Protestant cause.*

Philip, who was a man of a quick and discerning mind, probably saw that the dispute was now placed on more dangerous and more hopeless ground than ever, and, becoming weary of the insolence of the Papists, longed for home. And, as the result, proved, his judgment was right. The whole of the month of August was spent in long conferences, but without effect. The differences did not admit of arrangement; toleration could not be thought of by the Church of Rome, nor could the unreserved submission which the Catholics demanded be thought of by the Protestants. At the end of the month, the controversy was referred back to the Emperor, in the same state in which the Electors had taken it out of his hands.

THE TERMINATION OF THE DIET.

What divines and princes had failed to accomplish, the great Charles, no doubt, thought would soon be done by his personal influence. But he was bitterly disappointed. He probably never understood the real nature of the dispute; at least he could not understand the power of conscience enlightened by the Word of God. It was a new word and a new power to the soldier. His only idea of arrangement was by concessions from both parties, or the entire submission of one. But he soon had to

* Waddington, vol. iii., p. 84.

prove that **conscience** was beyond the reach of his personal influence and the power of his sword.

Finding private means, with all the ingenuity of Papal diplomacy, utterly ineffectual, he sent for the chiefs of the Protestant party, on the 7th of September, to meet him in his audience chamber. Only his brother, and a select number of his confidential advisers were present. The princes and deputies having been introduced, he expressed to them, by the mouth of the Count-Palatine, his surprise and disappointment at their conduct : "That they, who were few in number, should have introduced novelties, contrary to the ancient and most sacred customs of the universal Church ; should have framed to themselves a singular kind of religion, differing from what was professed by the Catholics, by himself, his brother, and all the princes and states of the Empire ; nay, utterly disagreeing with all the kings of the earth, and of their own ancestors. Being desirous, however, of peace, he would use his interest with the Pope and the other princes to procure a general council, as soon as the place could be agreed upon ; but still, on this condition, that they should, in the meantime, follow the same religion which he and the rest of the princes professed." In reply the Protestants most respectfully declined his terms. They "denied that they had stirred up new sects contrary to the holy Scriptures ; thanked him for the proposal of a council, but that nothing could compel them to re-establish in their Churches the abuses which they had condemned in their Confession, nor, even were they so disposed, could force them upon subjects now too enlightened to receive them."

Charles was embarrassed. He did not desire war, and yet how could he avoid it with honour ? "He could not understand how a few princes, inconsiderable in power, should reject the conciliatory and condescending proposals he had made to them. It was their duty to abide by the decision of the majority, and not arrogantly to prefer their own opinion to that of the Church, and their own wisdom to that of the Pope and all the other princes of Christendom." He begged the Protestants to renew the conference, and hoped that the work of concord might be completed in eight more days. But they declined to renew the conference, as only occasioning useless delay ; and on the 9th of September all direct communication between them and Charles terminated.

THE FINAL DECREE.

The Emperor now ordered a committee to be chosen for framing a decree, and required the Elector of Saxony to stay four days longer, that he might hear the draft of it. The commissioners appointed for drawing up this decree were, the Electors of Mayence and Bradenburg, the Archbishop of Saltzburg, the Bishops of Strasburg and Spires, George, Duke of Saxony, William, Duke of Bavaria, and Henry, Duke of Brunswick—comprising all the most violent enemies of the Reformation.

On the 22nd of September the decree was read to the Protestants. It affirmed that the Confession of the Elector and his associates had been publicly heard and confuted ; that in the subsequent conferences those princes had retracted part of their new doctrines, but still retained the rest ; that space was now allowed them, till the 15th of the ensuing April, to return to the doctrine of the Church, at least till the decision of a council ; and that they were to make known their final resolution before that day. Meanwhile they were commanded to live peaceably, to permit no changes in religion, to publish no new religious works, to prevent none of their subjects from returning to the ancient faith, and to join with the other princes of the Empire to suppress the Anabaptists and Sacramentarians ; assuring them that within six months the Emperor would send out his summons for a council, to commence the next year.

The tone of this resolution is extremely moderate, compared with the violent language which we have frequently heard from the Papal party ; but, whatever may have been their object, the Protestants replied with their usual firmness : " That they could never admit that the Confession had been refuted ; on the contrary, they were more than ever convinced that it was conformable to the Word of God, which they would more fully have demonstrated had a copy of the Refutation been allowed them." Here Pontanus presented to the diet an " **Apology for the Confession**," which had been composed in reply to the Refutation, so far at least as the substance of it could be recollected by those who heard it. After referring to their oft-repeated willingness to abandon every opinion not founded on Scripture, and their most profound assurances of loyalty to the Emperor and the Empire, they concluded by requesting a copy of the proposed decree, that they might make up their minds respecting it before it passed.

On the morning of the 23rd of September, the Elector had his audience of leave ; the Emperor then gave his hand to the princes, and allowed them to depart.

The diet continued its sittings for at least a month after the departure of the Protestant princes, chiefly engaged in providing supplies for the Turkish war. The " **Recess**," or final decree, of the diet was published on the 19th of November. After comparing several abstracts of this important document, we think Waddington's the clearest and simplest for modern readers ; it is as follows :

" Those who denied the corporeal presence were proscribed ;

the restoration of the ancient sacraments, rites, and ceremonies, in the places where they had been abolished, was commanded ; so was the degradation of all married priests ; nor were any other to be substituted for them, or instituted anywhere, without the approbation of the bishop. The images, which had been removed, were to be restored ; the freedom of the will was to be asserted, and the opposite doctrine prohibited as insulting to God ; so was the doctrine of justification by faith alone ; obedience to the civil authorities was diligently inculcated ; the preachers were commanded to exhort the people to the invocation of the saints, the observance of feasts and fasts, and attendance at mass ; the monks were to obey the rules of their order ; the clergy to lead a reputable. and decorous life. All who should attempt any change in doctrine or worship were made liable to personal inflictions. The destroyed monasteries were to be rebuilt, and their revenues restored to the monks. The decree was to be executed by military force, wherever it might not find voluntary obedience, and the States of the Empire were to unite their forces with those of the Emperor for that purpose. The ' imperial chamber.' was to pursue the rebels, and the neighbouring States to execute its sentences. The Pope was to be solicited to convoke a council, within six months, to be assembled within a year from the date of convocation."

Two days after the public reading of the Recess, Charles V quitted Augsburg. According to the opinion of .D'Aubigné, he was greatly distressed in his mind, and knew not how to escape from the labyrinth in which he was caught. As the head of the State, he had interfered for the protection of the Church, and the suppression of her enemies. But the opposite had been the result. " If he did not execute his threatenings, his dignity was compromised, and his authority rendered contemptible... The ruler of two worlds had seen all his power baffled by a few Christians ; and he who had entered the imperial city in triumph, now left it gloomy, silent, and dispirited. The mightiest power of earth was broken against the power of God." *

REFLECTIONS ON THE DIET OF AUGSBURG.

No study is dry and barren, and no time is misspent that leads us to a deeper knowledge of God, and to a more intimate acquaintance with His ways. To see His hand guiding and overruling the most complicated affairs of men for the accomplishment of His own gracious purposes is truly refreshing and edifying to the soul. " Whoso is wise, and shall observe these things, even they shall understand the lovingkindness of the Lord." " And we know that all things work together for good to them that love God, to them who are the called according to His purpose "

* D'Aubigné, vol. iv., pp. 132-340 ; Waddington, vol. iii., pp. 43-113 ; Scott's " Continuation," vol. i., pp. 1-99 ; Du Pin, vol. iii., p. 206.

(Psa. 107. 43 ; Rom. 8. 28). Historians may expatiate with wonder and admiration on the results of such a contest—at the triumph of the few over the many, of the weak over the strong ; but while we would seek to speak impartially of each combatant, we would have our eye especially on Him who is " Head over all things to the Church, which is His body, the fulness of Him that filleth all in all."

It must have been observed that the Pontifical ministers, guided by the subtle and experienced Campeggio, and countenanced by the Emperor, completely failed to gain any important advantage over the comparatively rude provincial princes. Like the waves breaking against the rock, their craft, duplicity, and evil counsel fell powerlessly on the Elector and his allies. By faith and constancy in the Word of God, they stood firm against the angry passions and threatenings of their enemies.

The Pope, the Emperor, the legates, the princes, with all their experience in diplomacy, were utterly astonished to perceive how little they could accomplish. "Day after day," says a close observer, "their designs were penetrated, and their artifices eluded, by men of no pretensions to political skill, by Germans, native of obscure provinces, subjects of petty princes, unpractised in the arts of courts, uninstructed even in the rudiments of intrigue. It was in vain that they taxed their ingenuity for some fresh expedient to succeed those that had failed—it was defeated by the same considerate and suspicious sagacity."

In reflecting on the proceedings of the Diet of Augsburg, we are forcibly reminded of the Diet of Worms, and of the great changes which had taken place during those nine years.

1. At that time Luther stood alone as the representative of the Reformation. Not a single prince had then declared for the new doctrines. At Augsburg all is changed. In place of a solitary monk, we see a numerous and well-organised body of princes, nobles, and theologians, and all of them men of weight and respectability. But Rome was not more humble and perplexed by the latter than by the former. She could no more silence the single monk than the host of princes. Such was the manifest power of God in connection with His own Word. Then she sent forth an edict similar to the Recess of Augsburg which she never was able to execute. What could be more convincing, as to the strength of the Reformation, and the weakness of her enemies !

2. The effects, or results, of the Augsburg diet were evidently favourable to the Protestants. The one grand object of the Papal party at this time was to crush and root out, by the sword of Charles, the very seeds of the Reformation from the soil of Germany ; but in place of accomplishing its Satanic design, Protestantism was immensely strengthened, and delivered from

gross misrepresentation. The calm, sober, respectful, and dignified behaviour of the princes led many of the Papists to think more favourably of them, and ultimately to unite with them. " Among the most important converts were Hermann, Archbishop of Cologne ; Frederic, Count Palatine, first minister of the Emperor, and afterwards Elector ; Eric, Duke of Bruns-wick ; the Dukes of Mecklenburg and Pomerania ; Joachim, Prince Elector of Bradenburg, who soon after succeeded his father ; and George Ernest, son of Prince William of Hennenberg. Some free cities, hitherto Papal or neutral, declared in favour of the Reformation ; and even the Emperor and his brother carried away with them a less bigoted aversion for the faith and name of Protestant, than they had imbibed from the lessons of their ecclesiastical counsellors."

3. A considerable **amount of truth** was kept before the mind of that august assembly for nearly six months. This was an immense point gained. Many dignitaries both in Church and State heard the pure truth of God for the first time. Besides the great Confession of the Lutheran Churches, two others were presented to the diet. One was sent by Zwingle, the other was called the Tetrapolitan, deriving its name from having been signed by the deputies of the four imperial cities, Strasburg, Constance, Memmingen, and Lindau. Bucer has the credit of drawing up the Tetrapolitan, as Melanchthon has of the Lutheran Confession. Thus God had ordained that the truth should be established by three noble confessions. They were substantially the same as to the great fundamental truths of the Word of God ; they only differed on the doctrine of the real presence, or, con-cerning the manner in which Christ's body and blood are present in the Eucharist.

4. It would be easy to point out many **blessed truths** in the Word of God which were not referred to in those confessions of faith, but our present object is to speak thankfully of what the Lord enabled those noble men to do, and with so much grace. The truth of God as to the Church, the body of Christ, and her Heavenly relations ; the operations of the Holy Spirit ; the difference between the righteousness of God and the righteousness of the law ; the believer's oneness with an exalted Christ ; the hope of the Lord's coming *for* His saints, and afterwards *with* His saints to reign in Millennial glory, were comparatively, if not altogether, unknown to the Reformers. Nevertheless, they were faithful to what they knew, and held it firmly in the face of every danger. It was by faith that the victory was won.

The history of the Reformation, morally viewed, is now accomplished. There will still be conferences and discussions ; leagues, failures, and desolating wars ; to say nothing of endless persecutions and martyrdoms ; but the emancipating truth of salvation through faith in the Lord Jesus Christ, without the merit of good works has taken so deep a hold of the European mind, that neither the sword of the Empire, the conspiracies of Popery, nor the powers of Hell, shall ever be able to extinguish it.

THE PROVIDENCE OF GOD IN THE AFFAIRS OF CHARLES.

There is nothing more interesting in connection with the history of the Reformation, than the overruling hand of a Divine providence in the midst of its enemies. The persons, the writings, and the testimony of God's chosen witnesses are guarded and protected by means the least thought of and the most remote. He only could convert the disputes of monarchs and the armies of the Turks into instruments for the furtherance of the Gospel of peace. And this He did from the very commencement.

Immediately after the promulgation of the Edict of Worms against the Reformers, **war commenced** between the Emperor and Francis, King of France. "How desirous soever the Emperor might be to put a stop to Luther's progress," says Dr. Robertson, "he was often obliged, during the Diet at Worms, to turn his thoughts to matters still more interesting, and which demanded more immediate attention." The great object of his ambition at this time was to oppose the power of Francis. According to civil history both Charles and Francis laid claim to the duchy of Milan, which had been lost by Louis XII, after he had obtained it by conquest. "For a time Francis was successful; but, about the year 1525, Charles again brought it under his own power. Charles, on his part, laid claim to Artois as part of the Netherlands; while he had to defend Navarre, which his grandfather Ferdinand had taken from France. In addition to which, Francis asserted his right to the two Sicilies." Here we have an explanation of the Emperor's backwardness to commence hostilities against the Germans. But these quarrels and contests between the leading powers of Europe so occupied their attention for many years, that the Reformation was allowed to spread far and wide, and the oft-repeated threatenings of the Papal powers were from time to time diverted and deferred.

Again, the severity of the Edict of Augsburg very naturally excited the most serious apprehensions of all the members of the Protestant body—of all Germany. There was only one expectation throughout the whole country, that of an immediate civil war—the destruction of the Protestants. Such was the outward aspect of affairs; but God had ordained otherwise. The heart, as well as the position of Charles, was unfavourable to persecution at that time. His familiar intercourse with the Protestants for nearly six months had taught him that they were not the dangerous fanatics or the domestic enemies he had understood them to be. He must have been greatly impressed with the fairness and justness of their cause, though he could not understand the civil and religious liberties which they claimed ; yet he saw no reason why he should chastise them as rebels for the pleasure of the Pope. Clement and all his Italian adherents were greatly disappointed that the Emperor had not assumed his proper character as defender of the Church, and had not waged war against the incorrigible heretics. But in the providence of God this was impossible, even if Charles had been as bloodthirsty as Clement.

Despatches from the East greatly perplexed the Emperor, and relieved the Protestants. Solyman had again invaded Hungary at the head of three hundred thousand men, and for the avowed purpose of dethroning Ferdinand and placing another on his throne. Such intelligence drew the thoughts of the Emperor entirely away from Germany. But here we must leave him for a moment, and notice the position of the Protestants.

THE LEAGUE OF SMALCALD.

Immediately after the dissolution of the Diet of Augsburg, and the issuing of its menacing decree, the Elector of Saxony and his associates proceeded to adopt such measures as appeared most likely to avert its effects, and to prepare without delay for the worst extremities. The dread of those calamities falling on the Reformers oppressed the feeble mind of Melanchthon, even to the borders of despair ; but Luther was neither disconcerted nor dismayed. By his letters, written from his seclusion at Coburg, he comforted and encouraged his friends. Convinced that the work was the work of God, he exhorted the princes to stand firm on the ground of eternal truth, to trust in the protection of God, and to concede nothing of the pure Gospel to the enemy.

As early as the month of November, 1530, the Landgrave of Hesse, more impetuous than the rest, and less averse to the doctrines of the Swiss Reformers respecting the Lord's Supper, entered into an alliance for six years with the cantons of Zurich, Berne, and Basle, and the city of Strasburg. On the 22nd of the following month, the Landgrave and the other Protestant leaders met at Smalcald, in Upper Saxony, and laid the foundation of the famous league, known in history as the " Articles of Smalcald." The Landgrave, who had never desisted from his favourite object of union, took great pains to have the Swiss included in the Confederacy ; but Luther and those who followed him absolutely refused to admit them.

The Protestant States of the Empire, in virtue of this league, were now formed into one body for their mutual defence. But Luther, and some others who had written and spoken strongly against any confederacy, even for the defence of their cause had great scruples as to the alliance. The jurists were consulted as well as the divines respecting its legality. The former affirmed "That there were certain cases in which the laws permitted resistance to the imperial authority ; for, by virtue of the compact between the Emperor and the States, the Emperor engaged not to infringe upon the laws of the Empire, and the rights and liberties of the Germanic Church. This compact the Emperor had violated ; and therefore the states had a right to combine together against him." Luther replied, that he had not been aware of this, but, now being persuaded that it was so, he had no objections to make ; for the Gospel did in no respect invalidate civil institutions. Yet he could not approve of any offensive war. Here we may notice in passing that this is the first and fatal downward step of the Protestants. Through fear of the enemy they are taken off the ground of faith. Even Luther falls. In place of conscience and the Word of God, they combine to repel force by force.

An affair, not connected with religion, happened about this time, which furnished the Protestants with a *political* ground of resistance to the Emperor. Charles, whose ambitious views enlarged in proportion to the increase of his power, expressed his desire that his brother Ferdinand should be elected **King of the Romans**. Accordingly the Emperor summoned the electoral college to meet at Cologne for this purpose. The Elector of Saxony refused to be present ; but instructed his eldest son to appear there, and to " protest against the election as informal, illegal, contrary to the articles of the Golden Bull, and subversive of the liberties of the Empire." But the protest was disregarded. The other electors whom Charles had been at great pains to gain, chose Ferdinand King of the Romans, who, a few days after, was crowned at Aix-la-Chapelle.

THE SECOND MEETING AT SMALCALD.

On the 29th of March, 1531, the Protestants opened their second assembly at Smalcald. The league, though at first limited to Protestant electors, princes, and states, was now extended so as to include those, who, whatever might be their religious sentiments, were opposed to the Emperor, and protested against the election of Ferdinand. They also took measures to bring the Kings of France, England, and Denmark, as well as other princes and states, into the Confederacy. The Dukes of Bavaria, and others who had not been present at the first meeting, now joined the league. Regulations were made for the levying of supplies and soldiers to be ready in case of need.

CHARLES SEEKS TO CONCILIATE THE PROTESTANTS.

The warlike aspect of the confederates, and the position of Charles in his Turkish war, led him to court the friendship of the Protestants rather than to provoke hostilities with them.

He greatly needed their assistance, and sent his order for men and money. But they refused to furnish their contingent unless peace were secured to them. They reasonably replied, that it would not be wise in them to place their means of self-defence at the disposal of their persecutors ; accordingly they required, that the hostile proceedings of the Imperial Chamber—the executive council of the Empire—should be stopped. Charles was now in a great difficulty. To make this concession would amount to a virtual repeal of the decree of Augsburg.

After various consultations, the Elector of Mayence and the Prince Palatine interposed as mediators between the parties. They met at Schweinfurt, the following articles being proposed by the mediators : " That the Confession of Augsburg, without further innovation, or any connection with Zwinglians or Anabaptists, should be the doctrine of the Protestants until the decision of a council ; that these should make no attempts to diffuse their tenets in the Catholic states, or to disturb the jurisdiction or ceremonies of the Church ; that they should furnish supplies for the Turkish war ; that they should submit to the imperial decrees and tender their allegiance to the Emperor and to the King of the Romans." The Protestants objected, but chiefly on account of the elevation of Ferdinand. They refused to acknowledge the validity of his title, and on this ground they were supported by some of the Catholic princes and by the Kings of France and England.

THE PEACE OF RATISBON.

The Protestants, now conscious of their own strength, replied to the mediators, " That the Emperor should proclaim forthwith a general religious peace ; that the two parties should be prohibited from offering any sort of insult or molestation to each other ; that the Imperial Chamber should be instructed to suspend the execution of the sentences pronounced on religious matters. If these should be accorded, they promised on their side not in any way to innovate into their confession ; not to interfere with the ecclesiastical jurisdiction in places where it was still established ; to render the most zealous obedience to the Emperor ; and to furnish all possible supplies for the Turkish war." After some discussion, when no agreement seemed possible, the Conference was adjourned to the 3rd of June, 1532, at Nuremberg.

Meanwhile the Turks were advancing nearer to Austria, and the heart of the Empire was in danger. Such was the state of things when the Conference resumed its negotiations at the time appointed. But the discussions and difficulties were speedily disposed of : " The arguments of the diplomatists were silenced by the march of Solyman ; and the conditions proposed by the Protestants were accepted. The Emperor was awaiting the result at Ratisbon, and it is recorded that, when the treaty was at length brought to him, without so much as examining the document, he affixed his signature."—August 2, 1532.

THE OPINIONS OF HISTORIANS.

It may be interesting to notice here, how uniformly historians attribute this great triumph of the Reformers to the direct intervention of God. "It is indeed true," says Waddington, "that it was not by the physical power of the Protestants, still less by the moral authority of their doctrine, but solely by that stronger **providential dispensation,** which converted the very arms of the infidel into an instrument for the revival of the Gospel. Still it was an advantage of most essential importance. The Edicts of Worms and Augsburg were now virtually suspended ; and the interval of their suspension was indefinite." Scultetus calls upon us to admire "the providence of God, which made the Turkish Sultan the great instrument of annulling, or at least suspending the execution of the decrees of Augsburg against the Reformation." Melanchthon says, "By the tacit commandment of God, the Emperor was called away from his designs against the Germans by the Turkish war. The dogs lick the sores of Lazarus. The Turk mitigates the edict of Augsburg. No race of men were ever in greater peril than we were : no party was ever subjected to animosities more bitter than ourselves. There was no aid but from God."

And the testimony of the civil historian, Dr. Robertson, is even more weighty than that of the ecclesiastical historians. He says : "In this treaty it was stipulated, that universal peace be established in Germany, until the meeting of a general council, the convocation of which within six months the Emperor shall endeavour to procure ; that no person shall be molested on account of religion ; that a stop shall be put to all processes begun by the Imperial Chamber against Protestants, and the sentences already passed to their detriment shall be declared void. On their part, the Protestants engaged to assist the Emperor with all their forces in resisting the invasion of the Turks. Thus by their firmness in adhering to their principles, by the unanimity with which they urged all their claims, and by their dexterity in availing themselves of the Emperor's situation, the Protestants obtained terms which amounted almost to a toleration of their religion : *all the concessions were made by Charles—none by them* ; even the favourite point of their approving of his brother's election was not mentioned ; and the Protestants of Germany, who had hitherto been viewed only as a religious sect, came henceforth to be considered as a political body of no small consequence." *

* Waddington, vol. iii., p. 160 ; John Scott, vol. i., p. 112 ; Robertson's "Reign of Charles V.," vol. v., p. 391.

How far their attainment of political importance was conducive to the interests of Christianity is another question, and for our own opinion on that subject we must refer the reader to our exposition of the Epistle to Sardis at the beginning of the volume. The politician and the theologian should never be united in the same person. The Christian's citizenship is in Heaven, the principle of his position here is strangership—that of a pilgrim and a stranger (1 Peter 2. 11 ; Phil. 3. 20).

The princes nobly redeemed their pledge to Charles. They brought forces into the field which exceeded the numbers expected. The Imperial army, by the fresh levies, was increased to ninety thousand well disciplined foot, and thirty thousand horse, besides a prodigious swarm of irregulars. The Emperor took the command in person ; and mankind waited in suspense the issue of a decisive battle between the **two greatest monarchs** in the world. More than half a million men, of nearly all nations, looked each other in the face for a time, and closely watched each other's movements ; but what were the results ? The great Sultan, Solyman the Magnificent, with three hundred thousand men, seemed to have been deprived of energy and decision, or to have been intimidated by this display of power, and quickly withdrew his formidable army without coming to a battle. It is remarkable, that in such a martial age, this was the first time that Charles, who had already carried on such extensive wars, and gained so many victories, appeared at the head of his troops. " In this first essay of his arms," says his able biographer, " to have opposed such a leader as Solyman was no small honour ; to have compelled him to retreat merited very considerable praise."

But who, we think, can fail to see **a higher hand** in this bloodless victory than the young Emperor's ? When the Turk had terrified Charles into submission by his appearance, his work was done. The God who rules over all sent him home. The Empire must still be saved for the sake of the Reformation. Solyman had made great preparations for this campaign, but, unaccountable to all, save to faith, it ended without any memorable event. Charles returned to Spain, to superintend his vast military preparations. The Reformers returned to their peaceful and Christian occupations ; the Church had rest from persecution, and the period of her tranquillity was prolonged for well nigh fifteen years.

The Reformation having now gained, through the Lord's watchful care, a great triumph and a solid footing in Germany, we may turn for a little and examine the rise and progress of the Reform movement in Switzerland.

Chapter XL

The Reformation in Switzerland

In studying the history of the Reformation in Germany, and that of Switzerland, the heart is greatly refreshed in observing the perfect unity of the Spirit's operations in both countries. Nationally, politically, and socially, they were widely different. The great monarchical system of Germany, and the thirteen small republics of Switzerland were contrasts. In the former, the Reformation had to struggle with the imperial power, in the latter with the democratic. But, as if by concert, the great work of God's Spirit commenced in both places about the same time, and with precisely the same character of truth. This was clearly of God, and demonstrates the Divine origin of the Reformation. "I began to preach the Gospel," says Zwingle, "in the year of grace, 1516, that is to say, at a time when Luther's name had never been heard in this country. It is not from Luther than I learnt the doctrine of Christ, but from the Word of God. If Luther preaches Christ, he does what I am doing; and that is all."

D'Aubigné is the only historian—so far as we know—who takes particular notice of this interesting fact in its Divine aspect. And as he has now gone to his rest and his reward, it gives us unfeigned pleasure to bear testimony to the piety of the historian who could thus walk with God in the midst of his abundant labours.

The ways of God in government as well as in grace are truly edifying if we study them in communion with Himself. But the most spiritual subjects will prove barren if He fills not our thoughts. Thus D'Aubigné writes : " Zwingle had no communication with Luther. There was, no doubt, a connecting link between these two men : but we must not look for it on earth ; it was above. He who from Heaven gave the truth to Luther, gave it to Zwingle also. Their bond of union was God." *

But although the Reformation in both places—and in other states of Europe—derived a striking unity from the One Spirit, the national features of each are not difficult to discern ! In Germany the person of Luther, as of lofty stature, towers above all his fellow-reformers. He is seen, he is heard, he is prominent everywhere and on all occasions. Nothing can be done, nothing can be settled without him. He is the acknowledged head of a party. But in Switzerland there was no such leader. It pleased God to reveal His truth, and to exercise many minds in different

* D'Aubigné, vol. ii., p. 382.

cantons at the same time. A number of noble names, resembling a republican senate, stood forth as champions of the faith: Justus, Wittenbach, Zwingle, Leo Juda, Capito, Haller, Farel, Œcolampadius, Oswald Myconius, and Calvin. But though none of them assumed the command, one name rises above all the others—Ulric Zwingle.

As the great branch of the professing Church, commonly called " **The Reformed Churches**," originated in the Swiss Reformation, it demands a careful and distinct notice, though comparatively brief. The Church histories best known in the families of this country are Mosheim's and Milner's ; but in neither is there any history of the Reformation in Switzerland. Mosheim, a Lutheran divine, almost ignores it ; Milner merely remarks on some of the leading men in passing. But before we attempt to trace the history of the Reformation, it may be well to renew our acquaintance with the religious condition of Switzerland previous to that great moral revolution.

CHRISTIANITY INTRODUCED INTO SWITZERLAND.

Christianity was first introduced into that country of mountains and lakes in the seventh century, by **St. Gall,** a native of Ireland, and a follower of the great abbot Columbanus.* After the death of Gallus, or St. Gall, his disciples and other missionaries from Ireland, continued to labour for the conversion of the Swiss, for the founding of monasteries, and for the propagation of the Gospel. A Helvetian Church was formed, strictly Romanist in its character, and yielding submission to Papal power. About the middle of the eleventh century two hermits found their way from St. Gall to a distant valley on the Lake of Zurich. By degrees the valley was peopled around their cells, and on an elevation of two thousand feet above the level of the lake a Church was built, and afterwards the village of Wildhaus. The bailiff or magistrate of this parish, about the end of the fifteenth century, was a man named Zwingle, the father of our Reformer. Thus we can trace the light of truth from Ireland to the continent, indeed throughout Europe and throughout Christendom.

The position of Switzerland in the bosom of its own mountains, in the very heart of Europe, has been compared to a military school, through which the surrounding nations learnt to perfect themselves in the art of war. The reputation of the Swiss soldiers for courage and endurance, led to the ruinous habit of enlisting extensively in the service of foreign countries. Though strongly attached to their native mountains and their native liberty, the charms of foreign gold induced many to quit their Alpine pastures for the service of strangers.

See " Short Papers," vol. i., p. 267.

This practice became a **great national evil.** Husbandry was neglected, families were bereaved of father and son, thousands who left never returned, and those who did were demoralised, so that the ancient simplicity of the people was gradually disappearing. But sad to relate—though recorded by all chroniclers that we know—the great foster-father of this national calamity was the Roman Pontiff. In his contentions with other nations he frequently found it necessary to solicit that help from the cantons, which his own subjects, either from a want of courage or fidelity, refused to give him. The apostolical treasury supplied the sinews of war, and the poor but brave Swiss often determined the fortunes of the Pope on the battlefield of northern Italy. The priests, stationed in various parts of Switzerland, were instructed to prepare the people for this form of obedience to the holy father. "The deluded mountaineers were taught that it was a holy thing to gird their loins for battle, and a glorious martyrdom to fall in the service of the Church." But such was the growing benality of the Swiss, that the highest bidders for their services were sure to obtain them. This led the Pope to great liberality in the distribution of indulgences and benefices ; which naturally resulted in the moral corruption and degradation of both priests and people. From this time the intense reverence which the Swiss Church had so long entertained for the See of Rome rapidly diminished.

"At the commencement of the sixteenth century the Church of Rome had attained such a height of grandeur and power, that it seemed impossible that it should be disturbed. Especially in Switzerland any change of religion appeared hopeless, on account both of the *strict alliance which existed with the Pope,* and of the extreme ignorance and corruption which prevailed. But it is in such circumstances that God is pleased to work, that all the glory may be given to Him. His righteousness could not permit Him longer to tolerate the *frightful excess* of disorder which reigned in the Churches of Europe.... But God must have His true worshippers, who shall *worship Him in spirit and in truth.*" *

Such was the state of things in general as the new day began to dawn in the valleys of the Alps. Ulric Zwingle has been styled the apostle of the Swiss Reformation. He was no doubt the chief instrument in commencing and carrying on this great work, though some had been in the field before him. He was possessed of a strong and clear judgment, an ardent lover of the truth, earnest in its propagation, and animated with a noble zeal for the glory of God and the good of His Church. In many things he was mistaken, as the best of the Lord's servants may

* Abraham Ruchat, of Lausanne, as quoted by Scott, vol. ii., p. 328 ; Gardner's " Faiths of the World," vol. ii., p. 19.

be, but he is well-fitted to rank with such men as Luther and Calvin, or the most illustrious names in ecclesiastical history.

THE BIRTH AND EDUCATION OF ZWINGLE.

The family of the Zwingles was ancient, respectable, and at this time in great esteem in the county of **Tockenburg**—a small district of lofty mountains and narrow valleys, covered with wood and pasturage. Ulric was the third son ; he had five brothers and a sister. He was born on the New Year's day, 1484, in an obscure village on the Lake of Zurich, which, from its mountainous situation, was called Wildhaus, or the Wildhouse.

The father and sons were chiefly engaged with their flocks and herds—the chief riches of the district. And beyond the narrow sphere of Tockenburg, Ulric might never have stepped, had not the promising dispositions of his childhood determined his father to consecrate him to the Church. Before he was ten years of age he was placed under the care of his uncle, the dean of Wesen. His uncle gave such an account of his abilities to his father, that with his sanction and assistance he studied successfully at Basle, Berne, Vienna, and then again at Basle. From the remarkable progress which he made in his studies and the promising dispositions he displayed, he was a great favourite with all his masters. While at Berne, the Dominicans had observed the beautiful voice of the young mountaineer, and hearing of his precocious understanding, prevailed upon him to come and reside in their convent. When the father heard of this step, he strongly expressed his disapproval, and ordered his son forthwith to leave Berne and proceed to Vienna. The unsuspecting youth thus escaped from those monastic walls within which Luther suffered so much, and from the moral effects of which he suffered all his life.

During Zwingle's second visit to **Basle,** he studied theology under the justly celebrated Thomas Wittenbach. From this able theologian, who did not conceal from his pupils the errors of the Church of Rome, Zwingle seems to have learnt, what Luther about the same time learnt from Staupitz, the great doctrine of justification by faith. " The hour is not far distant," said Wittenbach, " in which the scholastic theology will be set aside, and the old doctrines of the Church revived." He assured those earnest young men who flocked around him, " that the death of Christ was the only ransom for their souls." The warm heart of Zwingle drank in the truth, and like his master and some of his fellow-students, eagerly rushed into the new field of conflict.*

Here, too, he formed some of his warmest friendships, which continued through life, and which death itself could not destroy

* D'Aubigné, vol. ii., p. 399 ; Waddington, vol. ii., p. 268 ; " The Faiths of the World," vol. ii., p. 20.

Leo Juda, the son of an Alsatian priest, and Capito, were now the intimate friends of Ulric. Like the mountaineers in general, and like his compeer, Luther, Zwingle was a musician, and could play on several instruments : the lute, harp, violin, flute, dulcimer, and hunting horn, were familiar to him, and were often applied to in hours of heaviness, or as a relaxation from severer studies.

ZWINGLE, PASTOR OF GLARIS.

After having gone through his course of theology, and taken the degree of Master of Arts, he was chosen—the same year, A.D. 1506—by the community of **Glaris** to be their pastor. There he remained for ten years, faithfully discharging his professional duties while diligently studying the Holy Scriptures. During this time he seems to have acquired in knowledge and experience the needed preparation for his future services to the Lord and to His Church. " A most interesting manuscript," says one of his biographers, " still exists in the library of Zurich—a copy of all St. Paul's epistles in the original Greek, with numerous annotations from the principal fathers, which Zwingle wrote with his own hand, and then committed entire to memory." At the end of the MS. is written, " Copied by Ulric Zwingle, 1514." He also studied the Latin classics, and collected from the writings of the fathers—especially from Origen, Ambrose, Jerome, Augustine, and Chrysostom—the doctrines and practices of the early Church. " I study the doctors," he said, " not as authorities, but with the same end as when we ask a friend : How do you understand this passage ? " The writings of Wycliffe and Huss he also knew, but like all students of his age, he devoured the writings of Erasmus as they successively appeared.

From this time, the ecclesiastical abuses which Rome had introduced became obvious to his mind ; and, while expounding the Scriptures from the pulpit, he faithfully and fearlessly exposed the innovations and corruptions of the Romanistic system. This was the **dawn of the Reformation in Switzerland.** Zwingle was maintaining the absolute authority of the truth of God and denouncing the falsehoods of Rome.

While thus engaged, he was obliged to leave his more sacred duties, and accompany the confederate army on an Italian expedition. Threatened by Francis I, who vowed to avenge in Italy the honour of the French name, the Pope, in great consternation, entreated the cantons to come to his aid. It was then the custom in Switzerland for the *Landamman*, or chief magistrate of the canton, and the pastor of the parish, to take the field with the troops on such campaigns. In the years 1513 and 1515, Zwingle was compelled to follow the banner of his parish to the plains of Italy. On the former of these occasions the French were defeated by the confederates at Novara ; and monks and priests proclaimed from their pulpits that the Swiss were the people of God, who avenged the bride of the Lord on her enemies. But, on the latter occasion he witnessed a signal defeat of his countrymen on the fatal field of Marignan. There, says history, the flower of the Helvetian youth perished. And Zwingle, who had been unable to prevent the great disaster, overcome by his national feelings and patriotism, seized a sword and threw himself into the midst of danger. This was natural, and in those times it was considered noble, but it was not Christian. He forgot for the moment that as a minister of Christ he should fight only with the sword of the Spirit, which is the Word of God. "For the weapons of our warfare are not carnal," says the apostle, "but mighty through God to the pulling down of strongholds ; casting down imaginations, and every high thing that exalteth itself against the knowledge of God, and bringing into captivity every thought to the obedience of Christ ' (2 Cor. 10. 4, 5).

Zwingle now felt more keenly than ever the necessity of reform in both Church and State. He had seen the consequences of the practice long prevalent among his people, of letting out their soldiers to fight the battles of other nations, and to settle quarrels which did not belong to them. The sight of so many of his brave countrymen being slaughtered beyond the Alps in defence of a faithless and ambitious Pope, filled him with indignation. He raised his voice against the practice ; and, through his means, it was given up by several of the cantons. He also saw when in Italy, as Luther had seen, the pride and luxury of the prelates, and avarice and ignorance of the priests, and the licentiousness and dissipation of the monks. His future course was decided. He ascended the pulpit with a holier determination to preach the Word of God more clearly, more fully, comparing Scripture with Scripture ; and soon a fresh spirit of inquiry began to breathe on the mountains and in the valleys of Switzerland.

The question of *priority* between Zwingle and his Saxon ally, as to their aggressions on the Papacy, has been raised by some historians. Both seem to have received the truth about the same time, especially the knowledge of salvation by grace through faith alone ; but as a Reformer, Luther evidently was first in the field. When Zwingle was preaching the Gospel in a comparatively quiet way, Luther was publicly raising the standard of truth against the dominion of error, and causing his voice to be heard in all parts of Christendom.

ZWINGLE AT EINSIDLEN.

In the autumn of 1516, Zwingle received an invitation from the governors of the Benedictine monastery of **Einsidlen,** in the canton of Schweitz, to be pastor and preacher in the Church of the Virgo Eremitana—"Our Lady of the Hermitage." The hand of the Lord in bringing His servant to Einsidlen is very manifest. It was the grand resort of superstition for all Switzerland, for nearly all Christendom. "It may be called," says Ruchat, "the Ephesian Diana, or the Loretto of Switzerland." Legends of the most marvellous kind crowd its early history. Here the great Reformer was to have a nearer view of the idolatrous worship of Rome. The great object of attraction was an image of the virgin, carefully preserved in the monastery, and which had, it was said, the power of working miracles. Crowds of pilgrims flocked to Einsidlen from every part of Christendom, to pay their devotions and present their offerings.

Over the gate of this abbey the blasphemous inscription was engraven on a tablet, and supported by the figure of an angel : "Here a plenary remission of sins may be obtained." This delusion brought pilgrims from all quarters to merit this grace by their pilgrimage, at the festival of the virgin. "The Church, the abbey, and all the valley were filled with her devout worshippers. But it was particularly at the great feast of 'the consecration of the angels' that the crowd thronged the Hermitage. Many thousand individuals of both sexes climbed in long files the slopes of the mountain leading to the oratory, singing hymns or counting their beads. Such was then, and is even to the present day, the scenes at 'our Lady of the Hermitage.' It is computed that not less than a hundred thousand poor deluded votaries visit this place yearly. Such is Popery, even in the present hour, where it is dominant ; and that in a free country, surrounded by an enlightened population, and within sight of Protestant establishments." *

After what we have said of the extraordinary sanctity of this monastery, the reader may be surprised to find that the abbot, Conrad of Rechburg, was the most celebrated huntsman and breeder of horses in the whole country. He was greatly averse to superstition, therefore he preferred his stud and the field to the Hermitage. When urged by the visitors of the convent on one occasion to celebrate the sacrifice of the mass, he replied : "If Jesus Christ is really present in the host, I am unworthy to look upon Him, much less to offer Him in sacrifice to the Father ; and, if He is not there present, woe unto me if I present bread to the people as the object of their worship instead of God . . . I can only cry with David, ' *Have mercy upon me, O God, according to Thy loving kindness, and enter not into judgment with Thy servant.*' I desire to know nothing more."

The manager of the temporalities of the abbey, Baron Geroldseck, was a man of another order. He is represented as mild

* Scott, vol. ii., p. 344 ; D'Aubigné, vol. ii., p. 426.

in character, sincere in piety, and a zealous patron of learning. His favourite habit was to invite learned men to his convent, and, influenced by the fame of Zwingle's learning and piety, he had invited him to accept the office of minister of the Abbey Church. In this seclusion the young Reformer enjoyed rest, leisure, the advantages of a library, and congenial friends. The eloquence of the new preacher and the character of the governor, drew a number of learned men to Einsidlen. He soon acquired the confidence of the admirers of Reuchlin and Erasmus, and contracted some of the most intimate and tender friendships. On this page of his history we find the names of Francis Zingk, Michael Sander, John Œxlin, Capito, and Hedio—men whose names are famous in the history of the Reformation. But although he greatly enjoyed reading the Scriptures, the fathers, Reuchlin and Erasmus, with these intelligent men, his real work was *Reformation*, and, in as far as he then understood it, he honestly pursued it.

ZWINGLE AND REFORM AT EINSIDLEN.

He began with the governor. "Study the Scriptures," said Zwingle to Geroldseck : " a time may soon come when Christians will not set great store either by St. Jerome or any other doctor, but solely by the Word of God." He acted on the prophetic words of the Reformer himself, and also permitted the nuns in the convent to read the Bible in the vulgar tongue. And so great was his esteem and affection for Zwingle, that he followed him to **Zurich,** and died with him on the field of Cappel, October 11, 1531. The hunting abbot, too, appears to have profited by the ministrations of the new preacher. He banished almost all superstitious observances from his abbey, and died in 1526, confessing that he had confidence in nothing but the mercy of God. Zwingle's faithful and energetic preaching drew crowds to the Abbey Church, and made a great impression on their minds. He endeavoured to lead them away from the worship of images to faith in Christ ; from human inventions and traditions to the pure doctrine of the Gospel. " Seek the pardon of your sins," he cried, " not from the blessed Virgin, but in the merits and intercession of the Lord Jesus Christ."

What Luther learnt from his visit to Rome, Zwingle learnt from his residence at Einsidlen. His whole soul was stirred within him when he saw thousands of pilgrims from the most distant parts of Europe, coming there to merit the forgiveness of their sins by presenting their offerings to the patroness of the Hermitage. He did not hesitate between his conscience and his interests, or the interests of the monastery, but boldly raised his voice against the delusion. He struck at the very root of the evil, by proclaiming a free salvation through faith in Christ, without the merit of pilgrimages, indulgences, vows, and penances. He appealed to the multitudes on two grand fundamental truths more especially—*that God is the source of salvation, and that He is the same everywhere.* " Do not imagine," said he from the pulpit, " that God is in this temple more than in any other part of creation. He is as ready to hear prayers at your own homes as at Einsidlen. Can long pilgrimages, offerings, images, the invocation of the Virgin, or of the saints, secure for you the grace of God ? What avails the multitude of words with which we embody our prayers ? What efficacy has a glossy cowl, a smooth shorn head, a long and flowing robe, or gold embroidered slippers ? . . . God looks on the heart, but, alas ! our hearts are far from Him."

At the same time he preached the doctrine of reconciliation through faith in the precious sacrifice of Christ once offered on Calvary. " Now then we are ambassadors for Christ, as though God did beseech you by us ; we pray you in Christ's stead, be ye reconciled to God. For He hath made Him to be sin for us, who knew no sin, that we might be made the righteousness of God in Him " (2 Cor. 5. 21).

THE EFFECT OF ZWINGLE'S PREACHING.

Admiring friends might have given a somewhat embellished representation of **Zwingle's discourses** but the effects produced, according to the record of the times, plainly proved his great power over the multitudes of pilgrims. " Language so unexpected produced impressions difficult to describe. Admiration and indignation were painted alternately on every face while Zwingle was preaching ; and, when at length the orator had concluded his discourse, a confused murmur betrayed the deep emotions he had excited. Their expression was restrained at first by the holiness of the place ; but, as soon as they could be freely vented, some, guided by prejudice and personal interest, declared themselves against this new doctrine ; others felt a fresh light breaking in upon them, and applauded what they had heard with transport . . . Many," it is said, " were brought to Jesus, who was earnestly preached to them as the only Saviour of the lost ; and many carried back with them the tapers and offerings which they had brought to present to the Virgin. The grand motto of the preacher to the pilgrims : ' *Christ alone saves, and He saves everywhere,*' was remembered by many, and carried to their homes. Often did whole bands, amazed at these reports, turn back without completing their pilgrimage, and Mary's worshippers diminished in number daily." *

But although Zwingle thus uncompromisingly attacked the superstitions of the crowd that surrounded him, his orthodoxy

* Scott, vol. ii., p. 348 ; D'Aubigné, vol. ii., p. 428.

was still unsuspected by the Papal party. They saw the power which such a man would have in a republican state, and their plan was to gain him ; they had gained Erasmus by pensions and honours, why not Zwingle ? Besides, the court of Rome was always politic enough to allow considerable latitude to eminent men, provided they recognised the supremacy of the Pontiff. Just about this time—1518—Zwingle was flattered by the avowed estimation in which he was held by Pope Leo X, who sent him a diploma, constituting him a chaplain of the Holy See ; and for two years after this he received his pension from Rome. Both Luther and Zwingle were long in learning that the Church of Rome could not be reformed, that it was corrupt, root and branch, and that the voice of God to His people always is, " Come out of her, My people, that ye be not partakers of her sins, and that ye receive not of her plagues." When the Christian finds himself in a wrong position ecclesiastically, the first thing he has to do is to leave it, trusting the Lord for further light and future guidance (Rev. 18. 4 ; Isa. 1. 16, 17 ; Rom. 12. 9).

ZWINGLE REMOVES TO ZURICH.

After remaining nearly three years in Einsidlen, Zwingle received an invitation from the provost and canons of the Cathedral Church of **Zurich** to become their pastor and preacher. During his residence at Einsidlen he had become known to many persons of great consideration, and the number of his friends had greatly increased. But he had no friend more devoted than Oswald Myconius, master of the public school at Zurich, and in high esteem there for his piety, learning, and intelligence. In answer to this call, and the earnest entreaties of Myconius, Zwingle went to Zurich to talk over the matter, and weigh it well in the presence of the Lord. Some of the canons, fearing the effects of the innovating spirit of so bold a preacher, objected to his appointment. But his personal appearance, as well as his reputation, was in his favour. He was a man of the most graceful form and manners, his countenance agreeable beyond expression, mild and gentle in his general bearing, pleasing in conversation, and celebrated throughout the whole country for his eloquence, seriousness, and discretion. He was elected by a large majority and removed to Zurich.

On the first day of January, 1519, being his thirty-fifth birthday, Zwingle entered upon his new office. The Divine Master had been educating His servant during his residence at the Hermitage for this central sphere of labour. He who had chosen the new University of Wittemberg for the Saxon Reformer, selected for the Swiss the Cathedral Church of Zurich. The Lord was overruling all things for the good of His Church and the progress of the Reformation. The city of Zurich was regarded

as the head of the Confederation.   Here the Reformer would be
in communication with the most intelligent and energetic people
in Switzerland, and still more with all the cantons that collected
around this ancient and powerful state.   The new and earnest
style of Zwingle's preaching attracted great crowds to the
Church, and produced a strong impression on their minds.
Soon after his arrival he was reminded by the administrator of
the temporalities that he must make every exertion to collect
the revenues of the Chapter, and to exhort the faithful, both
from the pulpit and the confessional, to pay all tithes and dues,
and to show by their offerings their affection for the Church
But Zwingle was happily delivered from the spirit of the rapacious
priests, and bent all his energies in another direction.

ZWINGLE AND THE GOSPEL.

Before accepting the office, he had stipulated that he should
not be confined in his preaching to the lessons publicly read, or
to certain passages appropriated to the festivals and different
Sundays in the year ; but that he should be allowed to explain
every part of the Bible.   He saw that the habit of preaching from
a few detached portions year after year necessarily limits the
people's knowledge of the Word of God.   He commenced with
the Gospel of St. Matthew.   "The life of Christ," said he to the
Chapter, "has been too long hidden from the people.   I shall
preach upon the whole of the Gospel of St. Matthew, chapter
after chapter, according to the inspiration of the Holy Ghost,
without human commentaries, drawing solely from the fountain
of Scripture, sounding its depths, comparing one passage with
another, and seeking for understanding by constant and earnest
prayer.   It is to God's glory, to the praise of His only Son, to the
real salvation of souls, and to their edification in the true faith,
that I shall consecrate my ministry."   Thus did Zwingle nobly
abandon the exclusive use of the mere scraps of the Gospels which
had been the text-book of the Papal preachers since the time of
Charlemagne.

Language so novel so bold, but obviously so consistent for a
minister of the New Testament, made a deep impression on the
college of canons.   "This way of preaching," exclaimed some,
"is an innovation ; one innovation will lead to another ; and
where shall we stop ? "   "It is not a new manner," replied
Zwingle, "It is the old custom.   Call to mind the homilies of
Chrysostom on St. Matthew, and of Augustine on St. John."
Unlike Luther, he did not shock men's minds by his rough and
stormy replies ; he was mild and courteous in his intercourse
with the heads of the Church.   But in the pulpit—his own
province—he proclaimed the glad tidings of salvation with
unmeasured heart and voice, and thundered against the abuses

of the times. He everywhere enforced the necessity of an undivided and unreserved adherence to the written Word of God as the only standard of faith and duty. And so great was the impression which he had made on the Zurichers, that in little more than a year after his settlement there, the Supreme Council published an edict, enjoining all preachers and persons having the care of souls, to teach nothing which they could not prove from the Scriptures; and to pass over in silence the mere " doctrines and ordinances of men."

Like John the Baptist, he called most earnestly upon all classes to repent. He attacked the prevailing errors and vices among his people—idleness, intemperance, luxury, the oppression of the poor, and foreign services. " He spared no one in the pulpit," says Myconius, " neither Pope, prelate, Emperor, kings, dukes, princes, lords, nor even the confederates themselves. Never had they heard a man speak with such authority. All the strength and all the delight of his heart was in God : and accordingly he exhorted all the city of Zurich to trust solely in Him." His labours were attended with the most encouraging success. At the close of his first year he could reckon upon as many as two thousand persons who had embraced his opinions, and professed to be converted to the Gospel which he preached. There we leave them. God will judge the heart. But what a moment for Zurich, for the souls of men ! The Lord who is Head over all things to His Church, was sustaining and protecting His servant, and His Spirit was at work in the hearts and consciences of the people.

Such was God's chief instrument in the work of Reformation in Switzerland. His rejection of the errors of the Papal system and his experience of the power of truth, was produced and sustained solely by the instrumentality of the New Testament, which he diligently perused with earnest prayer for the teaching of the Holy Spirit. From day-break until ten o'clock he used to read, write, and translate. After dinner he listened to those who required his advice ; he then would walk out and visit his flock. He resumed his studies in the afternoon ; took a short walk after supper, and then wrote his letters, which often occupied him till midnight. He always worked standing, and never permitted himself to be disturbed except for some important matter." *

ZWINGLE AND THE SALE OF INDULGENCES.

In the month of August, 1518, the bull of Pope Leo X for the **sale of indulgences** throughout Christendom, was published in Switzerland. One Bernardin Samson, a Franciscan monk of Milan, to whom the Pope gave his commission, crossed the

* See D'Aubigné, vol. iii., p. 450 ; Scott, vol. ii. p. 355 ; " Universal History,", vol. vii., p. 73.

Italian Alps with his long procession of attendants. He executed the disgraceful traffic entrusted to him by " his holiness " with the same blasphemous pretensions, and the same clamorous effrontery as the notorious Tetzel of Germany. Zwingle was at that time pastor of the Hermitage, and fearlessly testified against the imposture and against the personal conduct of Samson. Through the opposition thus offered by our Reformer, Samson had little success within the Canton of Schweitz. He thence proceeded to Zug, Lucerne, and Unterwalden, where he had many purchasers. But being chiefly poor people, they could not give more than a few pence for an indulgence. This did not suit Samson's money chest, and he prepared to proceed. " After crossing," says the Genevese historian—whose pardonable love of his native land leads him to embrace every opportunity to speak of its grandeur—" after crossing fertile mountains and rich valleys, skirting the everlasting snows of the Overland, and displaying their Romish merchandise in these most beautiful portions of Switzerland, they arrived in the neighbourhood of Berne."

Here Samson was received with some reluctance ; but eventually he succeeded in gaining admission. He entered the town with a splendid retinue, under banners displaying jointly the arms of the Pope and of the cantons. He set up his stall in St. Vincent's Church, and began to bawl out his indulgences, varying in price from a few pence to the sum of five hundred ducats. " Here," said he to the rich, " are indulgences on parchment for a crown." " There," said he to the poor, " are absolutions on common paper for two batz "—three halfpence. Such were the shameless impositions which the emissaries of the Romish Church were permitted, and even commissioned by the Pope himself, to practise upon the pitiable ignorance of its credulous devotees.

From Baden, where his traffic was turned into ridicule by the wits, he entered the diocese of the Bishop of Constance. Acting solely on the authority of the Pontifical bulls, he omitted to present his credentials to the bishop or to ask his sanction. The bishop was offended at this disrespectful conduct, and immediately directed Zwingle as the chief pastor of Zurich, and the other pastors of his diocese to exclude the stranger from their Churches. The bishop was not sorry to have so good a reason for rejecting the intruder. He was regarded as invading the rights of bishop, parish priest, and confessor ; for they were left short of their dues by this exciting trade.

In obedience to this mandate, **Henry Bullinger,** rural dean of Bremgarten, and the father of the illustrious Reformer of the same name, refused to receive the Pope's agent. After a severe altercation which ended in the excommunication of the dean,

Samson proceeded to Zurich. Meanwhile Zwingle had been engaged for about two months—seeing the enemy gradually approaching—in arousing the indignation of the people against the Pope's pardons. He knew in his own soul, and on the authority of Scripture, the sweetness of God's forgiveness, through faith in the precious sacrifice of Christ. Like Luther, he often trembled because of his sinfulness, but he found in the grace of the Lord Jesus a deliverance from all his fears. " When Satan would frighten me," he said, " by crying out, You have not done this or that which God commands ! forthwith the gentle voice of the Gospel consoles me by saying, That thou canst not do—and certainly thou canst do nothing Christ has done perfectly. Yes, when my heart is troubled because of my help-lessness and the weakness of my flesh, my spirit is revived at the sound of the glad tidings, Christ is thy sanctification ! Christ is thy righteousness ! Christ is thy salvation ! Thou art nothing, thou canst do nothing ! Christ is the Alpha and Omega ; Christ is the first and the last ; Christ is all things ; He can do all things. All created things will forsake and deceive thee, but Christ, the holy and righteous One, will receive and justify thee . . . Yes ! " exclaimed the enlightened, the happy, the humble, but firm Reformer ; " Yes ! it is Christ who is our righteousness, and the righteousness of all those who shall ever appear justified before the throne of God."

In the knowledge, enjoyment, and proclamation of such soul-emancipating truths, the Zurichers in general were prepared to shut their gates against the impostor. When he reached the suburbs, a deputation was appointed to meet him outside the walls, who informed him that he would be allowed to retire unmolested on condition of his revoking the excommunication of Bullinger. The legate, seeing the strong feeling that was against him, speedily obeyed and retired. Slowly he moved off with the wagon drawn by three horses, and laden with the money that his falsehoods had drained from the poor, he turned towards Italy and repassed the mountains. The diet im-mediately addressed a strong remonstrance to the Pope, in which they denounced the disgraceful conduct of his legate, and recommended his holiness to recall him. Leo replied in about two months—April, 1519—with mildness and address. His experience of the Saxon revolution no doubt led him to hope that by timely concessions he might prevent a second in the Swiss cantons.

" **The Helvetic Diet,**" says D'Aubigné, " showed more resolu-tion than the German. That was because neither the bishops nor the cardinals had a seat in it. And hence the Pope, deprived of these supporters, acted more mildly towards Switzerland than towards Germany. But the affair of the indulgences, which played so important a part in the German, was merely an episode in the Swiss Reformation."

THE RISING STORM.

The zeal of Zwingle, in assailing and expelling the vendors of indulgences from the diocese of the Bishop of Constance, was much applauded by that prelate. And **John Faber**, his vicar, then the warm friend of Zwingle, wrote to him in terms of kindness and esteem, exhorting him " resolutely to prosecute what he had auspiciously begun, and promising him the bishop's support." Encouraged by such commendations, and in the hope that the bishop was disposed to further the work which lay so near his heart, he invited him both by public and private solicitations, to give his support to the evangelical truth, and to permit the free preaching of the Gospel throughout his diocese. " I failed not," says Zwingle, " with all reverence and humility, publicly and privately, by written addresses to urge him to countenance the light of the Gospel, which he now saw bursting forth so that no human power could avail to stifle or suppress it." But the Reformer soon found that a change had taken place in the mind of the bishop and his vicar since the indulgence seller had left the country. " They," he adds, " who had lately excited me by their reiterated exhortations, now deigned me no answer beyond these public and official documents ; yet the vicar in the first instance, expressly assured me, both by word of mouth and by letter, that his bishop could no longer endure the insolence and unjust arrogance of the Roman Pontiff."

John Faber—whom we have seen at Augsburg, in association with Eck and Cochlæus—after this break with Zwingle, became one of the most persevering enemies of the Reformation. The Reformer, from the commencement of his ministry at Zurich, had laboured unweariedly to instruct the people in the meaning, object, and character of the Gospel, and at the same time to impress upon them the importance of being guided in all their religious duties by the Scriptures of truth only. " All Scripture is given by inspiration of God, and is profitable for doctrine, for reproof, for correction, for instruction in righteousness ; that the man of God may be perfect, thoroughly furnished unto all good works " (2 Tim. 3. 16, 16). Nothing can be a " good work " for the performance of which, Scripture gives us no information. Such views and such teaching Zwingle had soon to prove, could not long be approved by the dignitaries of the Papal hierarchy. But by the blessing of God, from this time henceforward, he was to place all his hopes and expectations on a surer foundation. **Antonio Pucci**, the Pope's legate, endeavoured to seduce him, but in vain. " He conferred with me four times," says Zwingle, " and made me many splendid promises ; but I told him that from that time forward I should devote myself, by the Divine grace, to the preaching of the Word, as the effectual means of shaking the power of the Papacy."

Thus prepared to proceed inflexibly on his course, **Zwingle resigned** in the year 1520 a pension which he received from Rome for the purchase of books, and as chaplain of the Holy See. "Formerly," he says, "I thought myself permitted to enjoy the liberality of the Pope, so long as I could maintain with a pure and pious conscience his religion and his doctrines ; but after the knowledge of the Son had grown up in me, I renounced for ever both the Pontiff and his presents."

The effect of Zwingle's preaching upon the minds of the people, and the influence of his presence in Zurich, were first displayed about this time. Many of the ceremonies of the Roman Church were disregarded and fell into disuse. The fast of Lent, which had hitherto been kept with the utmost strictness, was neglected by the townspeople. The civil authorities became alarmed, and on the complaint of several priests some were thrown into prison. The people maintained that in their liberty as Christians they had given up such distinctions of meats. The Bishop of Constance, hearing of the unsettled state of things, instantly issued an edict against the innovations and the innovators, exhorting the people by his agents to remain steadfast to the Church, at least till after the decision of the council—the usual salvo. The monks, who had been ordered by an edict of the senate to preach the Word of God only, were confounded. Most of them had never read it. This decree became the signal for the most violent opposition from every order of monks and priests. Plots began to be formed against the head pastor of Zurich ; his life was threatened. Sometimes it was considered necessary to place a patrol in the street to protect the Reformer and his friends.

Zwingle now saw the storm gathering in all quarters, and well he knew against whom its fury would be directed. But this only aroused his zeal, and led him to write pamphlets in vindication of the truth and his friends, and to send them broadcast over the land. The principles of the Reformation now made such progress throughout Switzerland, that Erasmus, in a letter which he wrote in 1522 to the president of the court of Mechlin, declared that "the spirit of Reform had so much increased in the Helvetic Confederacy that there were two hundred thousand who abhorred the See of Rome, and were to a great extent adherents of Luther."

Seeing that the work of Reformation is thus hopefully commencing in other parts of the Helvetic republic, we may here pause for a little, and briefly notice some of these positions, and some of the principal men with whom we shall become better acquainted as we proceed.

CHAPTER XLI

The Leaders of the Reformation in Switzerland

HAVING rapidly traced the course of proceedings in the successive scenes of Zwingle's labours in the three cantons, Glaris, Schweitz, and Zurich, we will now pass on to other scenes and make ourselves acquainted with some of those devoted men whom God raised up and fitted for the same blessed work of His sovereign grace and power in Switzerland.

John Hausschein, which in Greek is ŒCOLAMPADIUS, was born in the year 1482, at Winsperg, in Franconia, about a year before Zwingle and Luther. He was descended from a respectable family which had come from Basle. His father at first destined him to business or the legal profession ; but his pious mother desired to consecrate him to God and His Church ; and to this end she watched over him like Monica over Augustine. He was of a mild and peaceful disposition, of excellent character, and from early life he was distinguished above his contemporaries for his progress in learning. He was sent to Heidelberg, and thence to Bologna, where he studied jurisprudence ; but as this study was contrary to his own inclination and the desire of his mother, his father was willing that he should devote himself to theology.

In accordance with the wish of his parents he commenced his ministry in his native place ; but from an over-sensitive mind, he was persuaded that he was not qualified for such a charge, and in a short time left for Basle. He was appointed to the principal Church there, and two years afterwards he was promoted by the University to the dignity of doctor on theology. He was a sincere Christian, an earnest and an eloquent preacher of Christ. He was greatly loved and admired by his hearers, not only for his public ministrations, but for his humility, meekness, and piety. Meanwhile he made such unusual proficiency in the three languages of religion as to attract the attention of Erasmus. Basle was then the great city of learning and of the printing press. " Erasmus was at this time engaged in preparing his first edition of the New Testament, and obtained the assistance of Œcolampadius in comparing the quotations from the Old Testament, which are found in the New, with the Hebrew original. Œcolampadius soon became enthusiastically attached to Erasmus, and might have suffered seriously in his soul from his ideas of a half-way Reformation ; but the Lord in His good providence called him away for a time to the quiet retreat of his native place. Erasmus seems to have been equally fond of the youthful preacher He thus acknowledges the important service he rendered him : " In this part I have received no little aid from the subsidiary labours of a man eminent not for his piety only, but for his knowledge of the three languages, which constitutes a true theologian. I mean John Œcolampadius ; for I had not myself made sufficient progress in Hebrew to authorise me to pronounce on those passages."

From Basle he removed to **Augsburg,** having received an invitation from the canons of the Cathedral Church to become preacher there. Here he had the opportunity of preaching Christ to large numbers of the people, but again his timidity of mind pursued him and induced him to resign. Though a Christian, he had not found perfect rest for his soul in the finished work of Christ. Peace with God is the only remedy for such uneasy, restless souls. It gives stability and consistency to the mind even in the ordinary affairs of this life. We can look at things more calmly, weigh them up in the presence of God, and estimate them in the light which makes manifest the nature and reality of everything. " I have set the Lord always before me," says the Psalmist, and what are the consequences ? " He is at my right hand, I shall not be moved, my heart is glad, my glory rejoiceth." These are the unfailing consequences of having the Lord always before us as our one object : at our right hand, the place of strength ; hence follow—stability of mind, gladness of heart, always rejoicing. But like thousands more, and in all ages, Œcolampadius had not left the corrupt system in which he found himself. In place of ceasing to do evil, and then learning to do well (as exhorted in the Old Testament) or abhorring that which is evil, then cleaving to that which is good (as in the New Testament), he remained in Rome and vainly desired a purification of Romanism. Disappointed and despairing, as every sincere heart must be that tries to patch the old garment in place of accepting the new one, he threw himself into a monastery, proposing to spend his future days in retirement and study.

There he remained for nearly two years, and there he became acquainted, like Luther, with that monastic life which is the highest expression of the Papal system. After leaving the cloister of Saint Bridget, he found a refuge in the castle of the celebrated Francis Sickingen, then the resort of so many learned men ; after his death he returned to Basle, where he engaged in good earnest in the work of the Reformation, and where he spent the remainder of his days.

Leo Juda is represented by historians as a man of small stature, but of an heroic mind ; as full of love for the poor, and of zeal against false doctrine ; indeed, it was said of Leo Juda, that whatever constitutes a good man was not only found, but abounded in him. He was born in the year 1482, and was descended from a family of some rank in Alsace. After studying for a time at Schlestadt, he removed in 1505 to Basle, and there became the fellow-student of Zwingle under the excellent Wittenbach. His first pastoral charge, like Œcolampadius, was in his own province, but like him also, he very soon left it and returned to Basle. Having preached for some time in the Church of St. Theodore, he succeeded Zwingle at Einsidlen, in 1518, and from thence he removed to Zurich, in 1523, to occupy the station of pastor of Saint Peter's; and to become a true yoke-fellow to Zwingle in the work of the Reformation. Besides being an earnest preacher of the Gospel, he was a diligent student of the writings of Reuchlin, Erasmus, and Luther. He translated into the German language a paraphrase of the New Testament by Erasmus; which was considered at the time of great importance, as scarcely any exposition of the Scriptures in the vernacular tongue was then in circulation. He also employed his knowledge of the Hebrew in the production of valuable translations of the sacred writings into the German and Latin languages.

Conrad Kirsner, or PELLICAN, was also a native of Alsace, and born in the year 1478. He was celebrated for his acquaintance with Hebrew and other Oriental literature, which he consecrated to the illustration of Divine truth. Much against the wishes of his friends he entered upon the monastic life at the age of sixteen. At the age of twenty-four his learning and piety recommended him to the office of professor of theology at Basle; and two years afterwards he received the degree of doctor in divinity by a bull from the Pope. He was taken ill at Milan on his way to Italy—where he was to be crowned with higher honours—but he returned to Basle, and was employed by the bishop to draw up a summary of the chief points of Christian doctrine, directly from the Sacred Scriptures. His fame, influence, and honours rapidly advanced, but with them a great and salutary change of mind. He had now begun to distrust the reigning doctrines and figments of Popery—indulgences, confessions, Purgatory, and the Pope's supremacy. The writings of Luther began at this time to be spread abroad; and ninety-five theses which that Reformer had published were put into his hand, with which he agreed in the main, but hoped that Luther would explain himself more fully. After this Pellican gradually prepared to renounce his monastic cowl, and his prospects of advancement; he laboured to disseminate the pure truth of God for some time at Basle, and in the year 1526 removed to Zurich, where he continued till his death in 1556.

Wolfgang Fabricus Koefflin, or CAPITO, was the son of an Alsatian senator. His mother was of noble family. He was born at Haguenau, in the year 1478. Thus the province of

Alsace has the honour of being the birthplace of three most distinguished men and zealous Reformers. Capito's own inclination was the Church, but as his father had a strong dislike to the character of the clergy and the theology of the times, he applied himself to medicine ; indeed he successively studied physics, divinity, and canon-law, and gained the degree of doctor in each ; but after his father's death he confined himself to his original choice of the clerical profession.

His career may be briefly stated. He was professor of philosophy for a short time at Friburg, then preacher at Spires for three years ; when on a visit to Heidelberg he formed an acquaintance with Œcolampadius which was interrupted only by the death of the latter. In 1513 he found his way to Basle. On the invitation of the senate, he accepted the office of minister of the Cathedral Church of their city. Erasmus speaks of him as " a profound theologian, a man eminently skilled in the three languages, and of the utmost piety and sanctity." When settled at Basle, he persuaded his friend Œcolampadius to join him there. This was the dawn of the Reformation in that place. These two devoted men laboured abundantly in the Gospel and in the ministry of the Word. Much good seed was sown, which produced a rich harvest in the salvation of souls to the glory of God the Father.

For five years, ending with 1520, Capito had been happily engaged in expounding the Scriptures, especially the Gospel of Matthew, to large congregations ; and he thus announced, in that year, his progressive success : " Here matters are constantly improving. The theologians and monks are with us. A very large audience attends my lectures on Matthew. There are some indeed who threaten dreadful things against Luther ; but the doctrine is too deeply rooted to be torn up by violence. Some accuse me of favouring Lutheranism ; but I carefully conceal from them my inclination." This smooth state of things did not long continue. He was charged with the heresy of Luther ; a conspiracy of priests and monks was formed against him ; and, being at that time solicited by Albert, Archbishop of Mentz, to become his chancellor, he accepted the invitation and left the place. The people hearing of this were greatly excited, their indignation was roused against the priests and the monks, and a violent commotion broke out in the city.

The fame of Capito as a man of learning and piety was now so great that Leo X, unsolicited, conferred on him a provostship. The Emperor, Charles V, raised him to the rank of a noble ; and Albert, the first prince of the German Empire, gave him the appointment of ecclesiastical counsellor and chancellor. But these high positions and honours did not suit the spirit of his mind or the real desire of his heart, though at that time he little understood the great work for which the Lord was preparing him. Gradually his eyes were opening to the discovery of the truth ; the mass became offensive to his conscience, and he refused to celebrate it any more. After being about three years at the court of the cardinal archbishop, he resigned, and joined Bucer at Strasburg as a humble preacher of the Gospel, where he continued till his death in 1541. This was the work in which his soul delighted. He began to urge the necessity of a reformation, and of vigorously prosecuting the work in dependence upon the living God. He and Pellican, as early as 1512, were of one mind as to the Lord's Supper being a memorial or remembrance of Christ. This was long before the doctrine was taught publicly by the Swiss Reformers.

Caspar Hedio was a native of the Marquisate of Baden, in Suabia. He was educated and graduated at Basle. He laboured long and successfully in the Gospel, first at Mayence, and then at Strasburg. When Capito left Basle, Hedio was chosen as his successor. The Papal party objected. "The truth stings," says the indefatigable preacher, "it is not safe now to wound tender ears by preaching it ; but it matters not ! Nothing shall make me swerve from the straight path." The monks redoubled their efforts. "He is Capito's disciple," they cried, and the general disturbance increased. "I shall be almost alone," wrote Hedio to Zwingle about this time, "left in my weakness to struggle with these pestilent monsters. Learning and Christianity are now between the hammer and the anvil. Luther had just been condemned by the Universities of Louvain and Cologne. If ever the Church was in imminent danger, it is now." He seems to have retired some time after this to Strasburg, where his labours were less interrupted. He was a man of a mild and moderate temper.

Berthold Haller, the Reformer of Berne, was born at Aldingen, in Wurtemberg, about the year 1492. He studied at Pforzheim, where Simmler was his teacher, and Melanchthon his fellow student The Bernese, who had been hostile to the new opinions, and incensed at Zurich for the countenance it had given to what they called *Lutheranism*, began to relax in their prejudices under the gentle but evangelical preaching of Berthold Haller. In the year 1520, he was appointed to a canonry and preachership in the Cathedral. He was joined in his labours by *Sebastian Meyer*, a Franciscan, who had been a Papist, but was now a zealous preacher of the Gospel of the grace of God. Haller was possessed of considerable learning and eloquence, and his powers as a preacher gained him great influence with the citizens. By the united efforts of these two Reformers, the state of religious feeling in a short time was such as to call for the interference of the Government.

Naturally timid and diffident, he applied to Zwingle for counsel in his troubles, and confided to him all his trials ; and Zwingle was well fitted to inspire him with courage. "My soul is overwhelmed," said he one day to Zwingle, "I cannot support such unjust treatment. I am determined to resign my pulpit and retire to Basle, to employ myself wholly, in Wittenbach's society, in the study of sacred learning." "Alas !" replied Zwingle, "and I, too, feel discouragement creep over me when I see myself unjustly assailed ; but Christ awakens my conscience by the powerful stimulus of His threatenings and promises. He alarms me by saying, ' *Whosoever shall be ashamed of Me before men, of him shall I be ashamed before My Father* ; ' and He restores me to tranquillity by adding, ' *Whosoever shall confess Me before men, him also will I confess before My Father.*' Oh ! my dear Berthold, take courage ! Our names are written in imperishable characters in the annals of the citizens on high. I am ready to die for Christ . . . Oh ! that your fierce bear-cubs would hear the doctrine of Jesus Christ, then would they grow tame. But you must undertake this work with great gentleness, lest they should turn round furiously and rend you in pieces." Berthold's courage greatly revived. The flame that burned so brightly in Zwingle's bosom rekindled that of Haller's. He preached with increasing zeal and power, and by the blessing of God, the pure Gospel was restored to the republic of Berne, whence it had so long been exiled.

Oswald Myconius—to be distinguished from Frederick Myconius, the disciple of Luther—was a native of Lucerne, and born in 1488. He studied at Basle, where he became known to many learned men who then formed the circle of Erasmus, but more especially to Zwingle. He presided over the public school, first at Basle, then at Zurich, and afterwards in his native town of Lucerne. From the strong military spirit which prevailed in this canton, the preacher of the Gospel of peace, who ventured to condemn the practice of foreign service, or who sought to restrain their warlike habits, was instantly met by the most determined and violent opposition. "He is a Lutheran," was the cry ; "and Luther must be burned, and the schoolmaster with him." He was summoned to appear before the council, and forbidden to read Luther's works to his pupils, or ever to mention him before them, or even to think of them. "But need has anyone to introduce Luther," he answered, "who has the Gospels and the writings of the New Testament to draw from ? " His naturally gentle spirit was wounded and depressed. "Every one is against me," he exclaimed, "assailed by so many tempests, whither shall I turn, or how shall I escape them ? If Christ were not with me, I should long ago have fallen beneath their blows." In the year 1523, he was expelled from Lucerne, and after several changes he became the successor of Œcolampadius at Basle, both in his professorship and his pulpit ; and continued in that situation till his death in 1552. He laboured much to disseminate the truth, and his services to the cause of reform were great and valuable.

Joachim von Walt, or VADIAN, was a distinguished layman, a native of St. Gall, where he was eight times raised to the consulate. He was intimately acquainted with almost every kind of learning ; but at an early period his mind became affected by the great question of Reform, and, by the grace of God, he steadily, zealously, and with great wisdom and prudence promoted the cause of the Reformation. He more than once presided at the great public disputations by which the good work was so materially advanced in Switzerland.

Thomas and Andrew Blaurer were of a noble family at Constance, and both laboured early in the cause of the Reformation. The latter, in particular, is distinguished as the Reformer of his native city. This city, so famous in the history of Papal persecution and Christian steadfastness, was also favoured with the devoted labours of Sebastian Hoffmeister and John Wauner. They nobly maintained the doctrines of the Reformation in that celebrated city, though they suffered for so doing.*

REFLECTIONS OF THE DAWNING OF THE SWISS REFORMATION.

Who could fail to see and adore the good providence and sovereign grace of God in this noble array of witnesses for Christ and His Gospel ! So many different men, in so many different places—as if by concert—all studying the same truths, from the same motives, with the same desires, and persuaded of the same results, and yet, for a time, without the knowledge of each other, and independently of the same character of movement in Germany. We have avoided bringing down the history of these pioneers to a later period than about 1520—a year before the Diet of Worms—when the name and writings of Luther were beginning to find their way into other lands.

The attentive reader must have noticed that most of the leaders we have named were men of high character, of great learning and ability, with the most flattering prospects as to preferments and honours ; all of which they willingly sacrificed that they might devote themselves entirely to the Lord Jesus Christ and the service of His Gospel. And God—who never forgets to honour them that honour His Son—accepted the willing sacrifice, and consecrated their learning, talents, and character to the accomplishment of His own great work. He

* The dates and facts of the foregoing sketches have been taken chiefly from Scott's " History," where the reader will find many details which we have omitted. Vol. ii., pp. 366-384.

made their moral weight to be felt by their most prejudiced enemies. Here it may be truly said, " The Lord gave the Word ; great was the company of those that published it " (Psa. 68. 11). And it has been remarked, that these eminent men were like *brethren dwelling together in unity* ; that they were all firm and faithful friends, even unto death ; and not a discordant note was heard among them.

The heart of faith leaps with joy to see so manifestly the hand and power of God working for the glory of His Son, and the emancipation of His Church from the thraldom of Popery. There is nothing more wonderful in this world than the triumphs of truth when the Spirit of God is working. What have we before us now ? As at the beginning, a few men, by the force of truth alone, engage to change the religious views, feelings, and ways of their contemporaries. The veneration of mankind for antiquity, for the religion of their ancestors, and a thousand different interests arise to arrest its progress ; the kings of the earth and their armies, the Pontiff and his emissaries, combine to oppose the new doctrines and to silence the witnesses by death ; but this work is of no avail unless it be to purify the motives and deepen the zeal of the Reformers. To the natural eye the obstacles must appeear invincible ; yet the cause of truth prevails, every obstacle is surmounted, and without any visible means, save the preaching of the Word and prayer.

In proceeding with our history we shall see the truth of this. Whole nations, obedient to the voice of the Reformers, abandon the worship of their fathers, destroy their idols, and overthrow in one day the usages of many generations. That which at first appeared to be a dispute, only interesting to theologians, pro- duced a great moral revolution, the influence of which extended over the civilised world.*

PROGRESS OF THE REFORMATION—ZURICH.
A.D. 1522.

It was in the course of the year 1520—as we have already seen—that the civil authorities of Zurich first interfered with the work of the Reformation. The effect produced upon the middle and lower classes by the preaching of Zwingle then began to display itself. In addition to the subject of Lent, which then came before the senate, through the edict of the Bishop of Constance, Zwingle called the attention of the Zurichers to the gross licentiousness which prevailed in Switzerland through the celibacy of the clergy ; and in a private letter to the bishop he entreated him not to promulgate any edict injurious to the Gospel, nor any longer to tolerate fornication, nor to enforce the celibacy of the priesthood. " In some of the cantons the priests

---

* Preface, " Life of Zwingle," by J. G. Hess. Translated by Lucy Alkin.

were *required* to keep concubines, and everywhere that practice was permitted for money." Instead, however, of listening to the needed and respectful remonstrance of the Reformer, the bishop began to persecute several of the clergy who were known to have embraced the new opinions. They were branded as **Lutheran heretics**, and denounced as holding opinions hostile to the See of Rome. Until this time the Swiss Reformers had not met with any public or systematic opposition ; but now the Church implored the State to interfere and arrest their progress everywhere.

But under the good providence of God, the opposition which now arose in so many quarters was overruled for the deepening and the extension of the work. The controversies and the public disputations were eminently used in Switzerland for the furtherance of the Reformation. The wind of persecution but scattered the good seed of the kingdom, and caused it to take root all over the land. " The priests stood up," says the Swiss historian, " as in the days of the apostles, against the new doctrines. Without these attacks, it would probably have remained hidden and obscure in a few faithful souls. But God was watching the hour to manifest it to the world. Opposition opened new roads for it, launched it on a new career, and fixed the eyes of the nations upon it. The tree that was destined to shelter the people of Switzerland had been deeply planted in her valleys, but storms were necessary to strengthen its roots and extend its branches. The partisans of the Papacy, seeing the fire already smouldering in Zurich, rushed forward to extinguish it, but they only made the conflagration fiercer and more extensive."*

THE MONKS CONSPIRE AGAINST ZWINGLE.

In the year 1522 the new doctrine had made such progress at Zurich as not only to cause the bishop but the senate considerable anxiety. The divisions and confusion that had prevailed for some time in the city were evidently on the increase. And the monks, encouraged by their superiors, raised the accustomed cry of heresy, sedition, and infidelity. There were three orders of monks in the city—**Dominicans, Franciscans,** and **Augustinians.** These formed a conspiracy against Zwingle, and charged him before the magistrates with " incessantly attacking their orders, and exposing them in his discourses to the contempt and ridicule of the people." They petitioned the senate to silence the preacher, and to repeal the edict of 1520 ; or at least to allow them to draw their sermons from Aquinas and Scotus. The authorities not only refused the petition, but renewed the order—" that nothing should be introduced into the pulpit which could not be clearly proved from the written Word

* D'Aubigné, vol. ii., p. 502.

of God." The exasperated monks were no longer careful to conceal their intentions, but vowed that if Zwingle did not restrain his hostilities, they would be driven to adopt more violent measures.

The bishop, about the same time, made his second and great appeal to the senate. He laid before that body many and heavy charges against Zwingle. And long exhortation was addressed to the clergy and magistrates of his diocese, and also to the provost and chapter of the city. These exhortations were accompanied by copies of the Pope's bull, with the edict of Worms against Luther, and all were entrusted to three ecclesiastical deputies.

When Zwingle stood up and replied to the various accusations of the bishop, his adversaries were completely silenced. But he was so distressed, so grieved in spirit, by the presence of his accusers, who were once his intimate friends, and also by the general state of matters, that he respectfully requested that a public conference should be held, at which he might have an opportunity of defending himself and his doctrines. Meanwhile he employed his pen with all diligence that he might make more widely known the truths which he held and taught, and the errors and abuses against which he testified.

THE PUBLICATIONS OF ZWINGLE.

In July, 1522, he addressed to the members of the Helvetic Confederation at large, a " **Pious and Friendly Exhortation**," entreating them " not to obstruct the preaching of the Gospel, or discountenance the marriage of the clergy." " Fear nothing," he said to the heads of the cantons, "from granting us this liberty ; there are certain signs by which every one may know the truly evangelical preachers. He who, neglecting his own private interest, spares neither pains nor labour to cause the will of God to be known and revered, to bring back sinners to repentance, and give consolation to the afflicted, is undoubtedly in unison with Christ. But when you see teachers daily offering new saints to the veneration of the people, whose favour must be gained by offerings, and when the same teachers continually hold forth the extent of sacerdotal power, and the authority of the Pope, you may believe that they think much more of their own profit than of the care of the souls entrusted to them."

" If such men counsel you to put a stop to the preaching of the Gospel by public decrees, shut your ears against their insinuations, and be certain that it is their aim to prevent any attacks from being made upon their benefices and honours ; say that if this work cometh of men, it will perish of itself, but that if it cometh of God, in vain would all the powers of the earth league together against it."*

* Hess, pp. 130-138.

After explaining the nature of the Gospel, and showing that all salutary doctrine is to be drawn from the Scriptures alone, he touches on the immorality that prevailed among the ecclesiastics as one great prejudice to the cause of Christianity ; he pleads most earnestly against the prohibition of marriage to the clergy—proving that it is a modern device, for the purpose of aggrandising the Church, by breaking the ties which should attach the ministers of religion to the people, by rendering them strangers to the domestic affections, and thus concentrating all their zeal upon the interests of the particular body, or order, to which they belong, and the upholding of the Papal system.

He addressed a similar remonstrance about the same time to the Bishop of Constance ; " in which," says Hess, " he conjured the bishop to put himself at the head of those who were labouring to accomplish a Reform in the Church, and to permit *to be demolished with precaution and prudence, what had been built up with temerity.*" These two petitions were signed by Zwingle and other ten of the most zealous advocates of the Reformation in Switzerland.

The exhortation, or mandate, of the bishop to the chapter of Zurich, drew forth from Zwingle another work which he called his " **Archeteles**," a word which signifies " the beginning and the end ; " it was a summary of the main points at issue between the Reformers and their adversaries. " This work," says Gerder, " exhibits a true picture of the Zwinglian Reformation—very different from what it has been represented by many writers." It obtained more celebrity than his previous pamphlets, and was highly esteemed, not only in Switzerland, but in foreign countries, as proving the author to be " mighty in the Scriptures," and one who united an intrepid courage with true Christian moderation.*

While these things were taking place in connection with Zurich, the bishop, now distrusting his own power to repress the growing dissensions, appealed to the national assembly held at Baden, and claimed the interference of the entire Helvetic body for the execution of his decrees. But the seeds of the Reformation were springing up there as strongly as at Zurich, at least among the pastors, for they had come to the unanimous resolution of preaching no doctrine which they could not prove from Scripture. " This appeal of the bishop," says Waddington, " ended in the persecution of a single and humble delinquent." One Urban Wyss, pastor of Visisbach, in the County of Baden, boldly preached against the invocation of saints ; he was seized and delivered over to the prelate ; and a long imprisonment, which he endured at Constance, has dintinguished him as the **first of the Swiss Reformers** who suffered for the truth's sake.

* Scott's quotation from Gerdes, or Gerdesius, Professor of Divinity at Groningen, and from A. Ruchat, vol. ii., p. 406.

ZWINGLE AND HIS BROTHERS.

As we mentioned in connection with the early days of our Reformer, that he had five brothers, it may be interesting to notice, that they were all alive at this period of his history, and, hearing such reports concerning Ulrich's apostasy, they manifested great uneasiness about their brother, and wished to see and confer with him on the subject. Although their anxiety seems to have been more for the respectability of their family than for the salvation of his soul, it gave him an opportunity of writing most fully and freely on the great subject of the Gospel, and of expressing the deep Christian feelings of his heart.

After expressing his most sincere affection for his brothers, and the deep interest he always feels in their welfare, he assures them that he will never cease to discharge faithfully and diligently the duties of a Christian pastor, unmoved by the fear of the world or the powerful tyrants that rule in it. " With respect to myself," he says, " I am not at all solicitous ; for I have long since committed myself and all that concerns me to the hands of God . . . Be assured there is no kind of evil which can befall me, that I have not fully taken into my account, and that I am not prepared to meet. I know indeed that my strength is perfect in weakness. I know also the power of those with whom I have undertaken to contend. But as St. Paul says concerning himself, *I can do all things through Christ that strengtheneth me* . . . But you—' What a disgrace would it be, and with what infamy would it brand our whole family, should you be brought to the stake as a heretic, or otherwise suffer an ignominious death ? And what profit could result from it ? ' My dearest brothers, hear my answer, Christ the Saviour and Lord of all, whose soldier I am, hath said, ' Blessed are ye, when men shall hate you, and when they shall separate you from their company, and shall reproach you, and cast out your name as evil, for the Son of Man's sake. Rejoice ye in that day, and leap for joy ; for, behold, your reward is great in Heaven ' (Luke 6. 22. 23). Hence learn, that the more my name is branded with infamy in this world for the Lord's sake, the more will it be had in honour in the sight of God Himself . . . Christ the Son of God condescended to shed His blood for our salvation : *he,* therefore, is a cowardly soldier of His, and unworthy the name, who would not willingly sacrifice his life for the glory of his commander ; but rather, like one who, basely casting away his shield, contemplates disgraceful flight . . .

" You are my own brothers, and as such I acknowledge you ; but if you will not be my brothers in Christ, I must grieve over you with the deepest pain and sorrow ; for the Word of the Lord requires us to forsake even father and mother if they would draw away our hearts from Him. Rely on the Word of God with an unhesitating and assured mind. Carry all your sorrows and complaints to Christ, pour out your prayers before Him ; seek from Him alone grace, peace, and the remission of your sins. Finally, be joined to Christ by such an intimate tie and bond of union, that He may be one with you, and you one with Him. God grant, that being received under His guardian care, you may be led by His Spirit, and under His teaching ! Amen. I will never cease to be your faithful brother, if only you will be the brethren of Christ.—At Zurich, in great haste, in the year of Christ, 1522."

These deep breathings of the innermost soul of Zwingle must command the grateful praise of every renewed heart to the God of all grace. What devotion to Christ, to His Gospel, to His Church, to his own relatives, to his country, to mankind ! How evidently, how wonderfully taught of God ! His knowledge of the way of salvation, and his deeper entrance into the grand rest-giving truth of the believer's *identification with Christ*, fill our hearts with admiring delight. True, he did not understand deliverance *through death* from sin, Satan, and the world, as taught in Romans 6 and similar portions ; nor could he have known the teaching of Scripture on the subject of the Church as the body of Christ, according to that Word. " For by one Spirit are we all baptised into one body, whether we be Jews or Gentiles, whether we be bond or free ; and have been all made to drink into one Spirit " (1 Cor. 12. 13). But he understood that there was communion in grace and blessing *through faith* in Christ's precious sacrifice. Had he been more under " the power of his resurrection " he would have been less of what his biographers call " the Christian patriot, the Christian hero." Not that he would have loved his neighbour, his kindred, or mankind less, but he would have manifested his love more in accordance with the spirit of one who is not only dead, but risen in Christ, and joined unto the Lord by one Spirit—the indwelling of the Holy Spirit. Like Luther, he held that justification by faith alone is the key-stone of Christianity ; though, evidently, he was less under the power of prejudice, and had a much broader view of Divine truth than the Saxon Reformer, and a more elevated style of expressing it.

THE DISPUTATIONS AT ZURICH.

In compliance with the request of Zwingle, already noticed, the senate of Zurich proclaimed a conference for the discussion, or the composing, of religious differences, to be held on January 29th, 1523. This was the first of those public disputations which, under the overruling providence of God, so rapidly advanced the progress of the Reformation. An invitation was given to all persons who had anything to allege against the chief pastor to come forward publicly and state their charges.

One noble stipulation, however, was announced by the senate— "that all appeals must be made to the Scriptures, as the sole rule of judgment, and not to mere custom or the traditions of men." The clergy of the canton were invited, and the bishop was especially entreated to appear in person, or, if that were impossible, to send competent representatives.

That all parties might be well informed as to the subjects proposed for discussion, and that none might plead that they were taken by surprise, Zwingle published some time before, **sixty-seven propositions,** embodying the chief doctrines he had preached, and which he was prepared to maintain. These he had extensively distributed in good time.

THE THESES OF ZWINGLE.

As the theses of Zwingle may be considered the creed of the Swiss Reformers, it will be satisfactory to the reader, briefly to state the most important of these propositions.

"That the Gospel is the only rule of faith, and the assertion erroneous that it is nothing without the approbation of the Church of Rome ; that Christ is the only Head of the Church ; that all traditions are to be rejected ; that the attempt of the clergy to justify their pomp, their riches, honours, and dignities, is the cause of the divisions in the Church ; that penances are the dictates of tradition alone, and do not avail to salvation ; that the mass is not a sacrifice, but simply the *commemoration* of the sacrifice of Christ ; that meats are indifferent ; that God has not forbidden marriage to any class of Christians, and consequently it is wrong to interdict it to priests, whose celibacy has become the cause of great licentiousness of manners. To give absolution for money is to be guilty of simony ; that God alone has power to forgive sins—the Word of God says nothing of Purgatory. The assertion that grace is necessarily derived from receiving the sacraments is a doctrine of modern invention ; that no person ought to be molested for his opinions, as it is for the magistrate to stop the progress of those which tend to disturb the public peace."*

THE MEETING AT ZURICH.

At an early hour on the morning of the 29th, great numbers, say the chroniclers, thronged the hall of conference. All the clergy of the city and canton, with many others from distant parts, were present, and a numerous company of citizens, scholars, men of rank, and other persons of various descriptions. The consul of the Republic, Mark Reust, a man of high character, opened the deliberations. He referred to the sixty-seven propositions of Zwingle, and called upon any who dissent from them to state their objections without fear. The grand master of

* Hess. p. 148.

the Episcopal court, and the vicar-general Faber, with several theologians, were present as the bishop's representatives. All supposed that Faber would have attempted a confutation of Zwingle's theses, and a defence of the established system ; but Faber knew his opponent too well, and refused to discuss any one of the articles. Zwingle pressed him to the disputation, but in vain. " I was not sent here to dispute," said Faber ; " but to listen ; besides, this is not the place for so great an argument ; that it was more decorous to await the decision of a general council, which was the only legitimate tribunal in doctrinal matters and which would shortly be convoked ; meanwhile, that he was commanded to offer his mediation for the removal of the differences which distracted the city."

Zwingle, who was urgent to have his doctrines subjected to the severest examination, was deeply pained by the evasive courtier-like style of Faber. " What ! " he exclaimed, standing in front of a table on which a Bible lay ; " is not this vast and learned meeting as good as any council ? We have only to defend the Word of God." After making this appeal—which produced a solemn silence in the assembly—he addressed the meeting at some length. " He complained of the calumnious charges with which his doctrines were continually assailed ; he challenged his slanderers to come forward on that public occasion, appointed for that express purpose, and discuss with him the articles in question." But the Reformer found that those who were most prompt to accuse and defame him in secret preserved an obstinate silence in public. But he had an upright conscience, and he wished to give an account of his doctrine, publicly, before the senate of his country, before his diocesan, and before the whole Church of God, and to hear whatever could be alleged against him. Thankful to be corrected if he were in error, but prepared to maintain what he believed to be the truth of God.

Faber still refused to dispute with Zwingle before the great council, but promised to publish a written refutation of his errors.

As no other opponent appeared, the president then said : " If there be any one here who has anything to say against Zwingle or his doctrines, let him come forward." This was repeated three times, but as no one presented himself, the senate declared that the evangelical propositions had gained an undisputed triumph, and immediately published an edict to the following effect : " That since Master Ulric Zwingle had publicly and repeatedly challenged the adversaries of his doctrine to confute them by Scriptural arguments, and since, notwithstanding, no one had undertaken to do so, he should continue to announce and preach the Word of God, just as heretofore. Likewise that all other ministers of religion, whether resident in the city or country, should abstain from teaching any tenet which they could not prove from Scripture ; that they should refrain, too, from making charges of heresy and other scandalous allegations, on pain of severe punishment."

On hearing the decree, Zwingle could not refrain from publicly expressing his heartfelt joy. "We give thanks to Thee, O Lord, who willest that Thy most holy Word should reign alike in Heaven and on earth." Faber, on hearing this, could not restrain his indignation. "The theses of Master Ulric," said he, "are contrary to the honour of the Church and the doctrine of Christ, and I will prove it." "Do so," said Zwingle, "but I will have no other judge than the Gospel."

Leo Juda, Hoffmann, Meyer, and others, endeavoured as well as Zwingle, to draw the Papal party into a discussion, but beyond the slightest skirmishing respecting the invocation of the saints, nothing passed between them.

THE EFFECTS OF THE DECREE.

The promulgation of this decree, according to Hess, gave a powerful impulse to the progress of the Reformation in Switzerland. And the effects of **Zwingle's address** in the hall was most favourable to himself and his doctrines. "His simplicity, firmness, and gentleness inspired his audience with great veneration ; his eloquence and knowledge carried away those who were hesitating between the two parties ; and the silence of his adversaries, being regarded as a tacit proof of their weakness, served his cause almost as much as his own arguments. From this time the friends of Reform multiplied rapidly in all classes of society." Considering that the times were still Papal, the decree was most just and reasonable. It ordained no pains, no penalties, on religious grounds. Zwingle, and all the pastors, were merely to be protected in going on to preach the Word of God as heretofore ; and by that Word the preachers were to stand or fall. A breach of the peace, or what directly tended to it, was to be punished by the authorities.

Faber, soon after the conference, writing to a friend at Mayence, expressed in the following terms his apprehensions of Zwingle : " I have no news for you, except that a second Luther has arisen at Zurich, who is the more dangerous, as he has an austerer people to deal with. Contend with him, whether I will or not, I must ; I do it with the greatest reluctance, but I am compelled. You will presently learn this, when I publish my book to prove the mass to be a sacrifice."*

But in proportion to the triumph of the Reformers and the confirmation of their principles, was the vexation and disappointment of their opponents. The most skilful advocates of the

* Waddington, vol. ii., p. 284.

Papacy had been silent before the great council of their country—
The Two Hundred. They were evidently afraid to enter into
debate with Zwingle. But unscrupulous Rome had other
weapons. It is stated by the most reliable historians, that the
Pope's legate, Ennius, and the Bishop of Constance, employed
emissaries to take the life of Zwingle, if the opportunity could be
found without too great a risk. "Snares surround you on every
side," wrote a secret friend to Zwingle, " a deadly poison has
been prepared to take away your life. I am your friend ; you
shall know me hereafter." "Leave Zwingle's house forthwith ;
a catastrophe is at hand," said another to a chaplain who lived
with him. But the man of God was calm and peaceful,
trusting in Him. "I fear my enemies," said he, " as a lofty
rock fears the roaring waves, with the help of God." But
though both the poison and the poignard failed to accomplish
the foul deed, Rome had not exhausted her means ; now she
tries flattery.

Soon after the decree was issued, Hadrian, who then filled the
Papal chair, appeared to take no interest in the controversy at
Zurich, though he was thundering his anathemas in Saxony
He despatched a most flattering letter to Zwingle, called him
" his beloved son," and assured him of his " special favour."
" And what has the Pope commissioned you to offer him ? "
said Myconius to the bearer of the Papal brief. " Every thing
except the chair of St. Peter." Mitre, crosier, or cardinal's hat
were at his will. But Rome was greatly mistaken with the
Reformer of Zurich in this respect. All her proposals were
unavailing. Even D'Aubingé admits, "that in Zwingle the
Romish Church had a still more uncompromising enemy than
Luther." He had never been a monk ; his conscience was less
perplexed, his judgment less enthralled by Popish dogmas, and
altogether he cared less for the ceremonies of former ages than
the Saxon Reformer. It was enough for his Swiss ally if any
custom, however innocent in itself, were not warranted by
Scripture, he fell violently upon it. His jealous care for the
dignity, sufficiency, and authority of Scripture was remarkable.
" The Word of God," he used to say, " should stand alone."
" Yet these convictions," it has been said, " were attained
through fewer struggles, and burnt with less violence, than in
the heart of Luther." This we can only see to be true in the
case of one doctrine—justification by faith alone. All will
readily admit, that although the Swiss Reformer believed this
truth, as sincerely as the Saxon, it never was to the former
what it was to the latter. As a Divine truth, it was the source
of Luther's convictions, strength, comfort, vitality, and energy.
The two men had been led of God by different paths, and were
differently furnished for their great work.

THE ZEAL OF ZWINGLE AND LEO JUDA.

Notwithstanding the immense power and popularity which Zwingle gained by the result of the conference in January, he was in no haste to promote alterations. His great object was to instruct the people, remove their prejudices, and bring them to oneness of mind before recommending any great changes. He therefore devoted himself to the preaching of the Word with greater zeal and boldness than ever ; and he was ably assisted by his friend, **Leo Juda,** who had lately been elected a minister of Zurich. It is not certain that Faber's promised book on the mass ever appeared, but Zwingle produced one in the same year, " On the Canon of the Mass," arguing with great force against that corner-stone of the Papal system. About the same time a priest, named Louis Hetzer, published a treatise entitled, " The Judgment of God Against Images," which produced a great sensation, and engrossed the thoughts of the people.

The citizens of Zurich had now become warm friends of the Reformation ; and in their zeal some of the more ardent spirits expressed a determination to purge the city of idols. Outside the city gates stood a crucifix elaborately carved and richly ornamented. The superstition and idolatry to which this image gave rise moved the people to give vent to their indignation. Some of the lower class, having at their head an artisan named Nicholas Hottinger—" a worthy man," says Bullinger, " and well read in the Holy Scriptures "—assembled and ignominiously threw down this favourite idol. This daring and unlawful act spread dismay on every side. " They are guilty of sacrilege ! They deserve to be put to death ! " exclaimed the friends of Rome. The authorities were obliged to interfere, and caused the leaders of this outbreak to be apprehended ; but when sentence was to be pronounced upon them, the council was divided. What some regarded as a crime worthy of death, others considered to be a good work, but done in a wrong way from inconsiderate zeal. During the debates upon this sentence, Zwingle maintained in public that the law of Moses expressly forbade images to be the objects of religious worship, and concluded that those who had pulled down the crucifix could not be accused of sacrilege ; but he pronounced them deserving of punishment for open resistance to the authorities.

The language of Zwingle increased the embarrassment of the magistrates ; the whole city was much divided ; and the council again determined to submit the question to a discussion, in the meantime retaining the prisoners in custody.

Thus we see that, in the good providence of God, even such acts of insubordination by the rude undisciplined children of the Reformation, were the means of bringing to light not only the dark shades of Popery, but the truth of God on subjects of vital importance, and of securing fresh triumphs and greater liberty to the Reformers.

THE SECOND DISPUTATION AT ZURICH.

The 26th of October, 1523, was the day fixed for the second disputation ; and the subjects to be discussed were—" whether the worship of images was authorised by the Gospel, and whether the mass ought to be preserved or abolished." The assembly was much more numerous than the preceding ; above nine hundred persons were present, from every part of Switzerland, including the grand council of Two Hundred, and about three hundred and fifty ecclesiastics. Invitations had been sent to the Bishops of Constance, Coire, and Basle, to the University of the latter city, and to the twelve cantons, requesting them to send deputies to Zurich. But the bishops declined the invitations. The humiliation of their deputies in January was fresh in their mind, and they were not disposed to risk a second defeat. Only the towns of Schaffhausen and St. Gall sent delegates, and these, Vadian of St. Gall, and Hoffmann of Schaffhausen were chosen presidents. The edict of convocation having been read, and the object of the meeting stated, Zwingle and Leo Juda were requested to answer all who defended the worship of images and the mass as a sacrifice.

With a devotion and 'piety, ever prominent in the spirit of Zwingle, he proposed that the deliberations should be opened with prayer. He reminded the friends of the promise of Christ, that " where two or three are gathered together in My Name, there am I in the midst of them " (Matt. 18. 20). After prayer, and a few words from the president, enjoining upon all who spoke to draw their argument only from Scripture, Zwingle was desired to commence the proceedings.

Before speaking on the first proposition—the worship of images—he begged to offer a few remarks on the Scriptural usage of the word Church ; since on that depended the right and authority of their present deliberations. He rejected the exhorbitant claims of the Church of Rome, which asserted that nothing was valid in the whole Christian world but what was done with her sanction. According to his view, the term " the Church," designated, first, the universal body of the faithful ; secondly, any portion of that body meeting in the same province or city ; such as the Church of Ephesus, of Corinth, the Churches of Galatia, or the Church of Zurich. He denied that the term could be restricted to a convention, consisting of the Pope, cardinals, bishops, and other ecclesiastics exclusively. His object was to overthrow the objections urged by the Roman Catholics against the authority of such assemblies as the present ; and to show that every assembly, united together by faith in

Christ, and by the Gospel, as the only rule of faith and practice, possessed the perfect right to discuss and settle their affairs. Zwingle was thus withdrawing the Church of Zurich from the jurisdiction of the Bishop of Constance, and separating it from the Latin hierarchy.

Here Zwingle paused ; and an invitation was given to all who had anything to object to his positions, to come forward and express their sentiments without fear. The Reformers sought publicity, and feared not fair discussion. One, **Conrad Hoffmann,** a canon of Zurich, attempted a reply, but as he spoke only of the authority of the Pope's bull, the Emperor's edict, the canons, and the impropriety of all such discussions, without any reference to Scripture, he was given to understand that he was not observing the rule of the assembly. The Prior of the Augustinians, a famous preacher, and much attached to the ancient orthodoxy, confessed that he could not refute the propositions of Zwingle, unless he were allowed to have recourse to the canon law. Zwingle immediately referred to a passage in the canon law, which showed that the Scriptures alone were to be relied upon. The monk thus silenced, resumed his seat, muttering to himself, " The Pope has decided ; I abide by his decisions, and leave others to argue."

Leo Juda, to whom was entrusted the subject of the **images,** addressed the assembly at some length, proving from the Scriptures, " that images are forbidden by the Word of God ; and that Christians ought not to make them, set them up, or pay them any homage." On the second day of the Conference, Zwingle introduced the subject of **the mass,** showing from the words of the institution, and from other portions of the New Testament that the mass is not a sacrifice, that no one man can offer to God a sacrifice for another ; and that the mode of celebrating the Eucharist in the Church of Rome is quite different from the institution of the Saviour. The few feeble attempts that were made to sustain the established practice and doctrine, were immediately confuted by the two champions of the Reformation to the entire satisfaction of the Council.

THE WORD OF GOD PREVAILS.

A deep and salutary impression was produced on the assembly. " Until this hour," exclaimed Schmidt, the commander of Kussnacht, " ye have all gone after idols. The dwellers in the plains have run to the mountains, and those of the mountains have gone to the plains ; the French to Germany, and the Germans to France. Now ye know whither ye ought to go. God has combined all things in Christ. ·Ye noble citizens of Zurich, go to the true source ; and may Christ at length re-enter your territory, and there resume His ancient empire." The aged warrior, Reust, turning to the Council, gravely said, though in military language : " Now, then, . . . let us grasp the sword of God's Word, and may the Lord prosper His work." With such expressions of sympathy Zwingle was completely overcome. " God is with us," he said, with deep feeling, " He will defend His own cause. Let us go forward in the Name of the Lord." Here his emotion was too great for utterance ; he burst into tears, and many mingled their tears with his.

Thus the colloquy ended ; it lasted three days. It was decisive in favour of the Reformation. The victory was undisputed. The presidents rose ; Vadian of St. Gall, speaking on behalf of those who had presided with him, observed, " that no definite sentence was to be pronounced as the decision of the meeting. They had heard the testimony of God's Word in support of the two propositions, and likewise what could be urged against them ; each person must judge for himself what was the conclusion to be formed, and must follow the dictates of his own conscience." Reust joined in the exhortation, and " entreated all present to take the Word of God for their only guide, and to follow it, fearing nothing." The meeting then closed.

REFLECTIONS ON THE CHARACTER OF THE CONFERENCE.

All who know something of the value of the Word of God must reflect with supreme satisfaction on the rule by which these disputations were governed. We can never be too thankful for such an appreciation of the Holy Scriptures. In this respect Zwingle did a great and noble work. He **restored the Bible** to its true place, and the people to their true privileges. Perfect freedom of discussion was allowed to both parties, with this stipulation, " that all arguments were to be derived directly from Scripture, the sole standard of judgment ; that all merely verbal disputes, and vain contentious subtleties, were to be instantly repressed." And this, let us bear in mind, this noble assertion of the authority and sufficiency of Scripture was publicly made at a time when nearly all classes were only beginning to hear of the errors of Popery, and of the character, if not of the existence of the Bible. Many of the priests even had never seen one, and scarcely any of them had read it.

It required more than the commanding presence of Zwingle— more than his brilliant talents, his high cultivation, his natural eloquence, to maintain such a position. Nothing less than faith in the living God, and in the Divine presence, could have sustained him at such a moment. Mere cleverness and superstition could then give, as they can give now, a thousand reasons why the dogmas of the Papacy should be held supreme ; but faith did then—as it must now—assail the whole system of Popery as the imposture of Satan, and in direct opposition to the truth of God. In the face of nine hundred members of the Roman Catholic Church, lay and clerical, Zwingle, Leo, Juda, and others maintained that the pure Word of God, which should be in the hands of the people, was the only standard of faith and morals, and that all the time-honoured customs and traditions of Romanism, though sanctioned by the credulity of ages, and backed by the display of worldly power, were the mere inventions of priestcraft, and ruinous to the souls of men.

This was bold work, and at such a time ; but when Christ has His right place in the heart, His strength is made perfect in our weakness. The Word of God, we know, is the Sword of the Spirit, by which all questions should be settled, and to which alone all Christians should appeal. One line of Scripture far outweighs ten thousand reasons. But how far, we may ask, is this rule observed by Christians in the present day ? Where shall we find such inflexible adherence to the plain truth of God ? We know not where to look for it. But we hear on all sides of questions being raised as to the plenary inspiration of the Scriptures ; and that, as it is capable of various interpretations by the learned, it cannot be appealed to as decisive. Such, alas ! alas ! is the growing infidelity of our own day, which will tend to the increase of Romanism, and to the final apostasy of Christendom. Meanwhile let all who love the Lord hold fast His Word as unchanged and unchangeable. For He hath " magnified His Word above all His Name." And it still holds true that, " them that honour Me I will honour, and they that despise Me shall be lightly esteemed." The Lord give us grace to honour His Name by faithfully keeping His Word, and, like the Master, may be able to say as to all our religious observances : " Thus saith the Lord," . . . " It is written," " It is written " (Rev. 3. 8 ; Psa. 138. 2 ; 1 Sam. 2. 30 ; Matt. 4).

CHAPTER XLII

The Results of the Disputations

THE authorities, though convinced that neither the mass nor the use of images could be justified by the Word of God, did not think it expedient to abolish by law either the one or the other at that moment. Zwingle prudently recommended great caution and moderation. " God knows," he said to the council, " that I am inclined to build up, and not to throw down. I am aware there are timid souls who ought to be conciliated. The people generally are not yet sufficiently enlightened to receive with unanimity such extensive alterations." The magistrates, following his advice, allowed every minister to say mass or decline it, as he thought proper ; reserving to themselves the right of ordaining at a future time what they should judge proper.

During this delay, the friends of the Reformation petitioned the council to release the persons imprisoned for throwing down the crucifix. All were set at liberty with the exception of **Hottinger,** who, because of the leading part he had taken in the commotion, was banished for two years from the canton of Zurich. This slight sentence, contrary to the intentions of those who passed it, was soon followed by a violent and cruel death.

THE FIRST MARTYR OF THE SWISS REFORMATION.

In proportion as the cause of the Reformation advanced, the rage of its adversaries increased. At a diet held at Lucerne, in the month of January, 1524, all the cantons were represented with the exception of Zurich and Schaffhausen. The clergy present endeavoured to excite the council against the new doctrines and those who had promulgated them. Alarmed at what might be the consequences of the changes which were taking place at Zurich, they were determined to be silent spectators no longer. Through the influence of the partisans of Rome in the council, an edict was passed, " forbidding the people to preach, or to repeat any new or Lutheran doctrine in private or public, or to talk or dispute about such things in taverns or at feasts ; that whatever laws the Bishop of Constance enacted respecting religion should be observed ; that every one, whether man or woman, old or young, who saw or heard anything done, preached or spoken, contrary to this edict, should give immediate information of the same to the proper authorities." Thus was the snare laid, through the subtlety of Satan, for the feet of the Reformers ; and, the council being national, it was spread over all Switzerland. Hottinger was the first to be caught in its toils.

When banished from Zurich, he repaired to the county of Baden, where he lived by the labour of his hands. He neither sought nor avoided occasions of speaking about his religion. When asked what the new doctrines were which the Zurich pastors preached, he frankly conversed on the subject. He was now narrowly watched, and reported to have said, " That Christ was sacrificed once for all Christians ; and that by this one sacrifice, as St. Paul says, He hath perfected for ever them that are sanctified ; therefore the mass is no sacrifice ; and that the invocation of saints and the adoration of images are contrary to the Word of God." This was more than enough to condemn the unsuspecting man. He was denounced for his impiety to the grand bailiff, and very soon arrested. When questioned as to his religious belief, he did not conceal his convictions, and professed himself ready to justify what he had stated. He was convicted before the tribunal of having contravened an ordinance of the sovereign power, which forbade all discussions on the subject of religion. He was then removed to Lucerne, when he was condemned by the deputies of seven cantons to be **beheaded.**

When informed of his sentence, he calmly answered : " **The will of the Lord be done !** May He be pleased to pardon all who have contributed to my death." . . . That will do," said one of his judges, " we do not sit here to listen to sermons ; you can have your talk some other time." " He must have his head off this once," said another of his judges, " but if he should ever get it on again, we will then be of his religion." " To Jesus also it was said," he replied, " ' *Let Him now come down from the Cross, and we will believe Him.*' " A monk presented a crufix to his lips, but he put it from him saying, " It is by faith that we must embrace Christ crucified in our hearts." He was greatly strengthened by the presence of the Lord when on his way to the place of execution. Many followed him in tears. " Weep not for me," he said, " I am on my way to eternal happiness." He preached the Gospel to the people as one so near his end would, entreating them to look to the Lord Jesus Christ, in whom alone pardon and salvation could be found. His last words on the scaffold were : " Into Thy hands I commit my spirit, O my Lord and Saviour Jesus Christ." In a few moments he was absent from the body and present with the Lord.

The tranquillity, courage, and wisdom which Hottinger showed before his judges, and on his way to the scaffold, give him a high place among those who died for the cause of the Reformation. Calmly and firmly in his last moments he prayed for the mercy of God in favour of his judges, and that their eyes might be opened to the truth. Then turning to the people, he said : " If I have offended anyone among you, let him forgive me as I have forgiven my enemies. Pray to God to support my faith to the last moment. When I shall have undergone my sentence, your prayers will be useless to me."*

THE BLOOD OF HOTTINGER INFLAMES THE ZEAL OF THE PAPISTS.

The council of Zurich had protested against the irregularity of its allies in the condemnation of a fellow-citizen ; but in place of listening to remonstrance, their persecuting zeal was evidently inflamed by the execution of Hottinger ; for scarcely was the blood of that innocent man cold when the diet determined on more vigorous efforts to crush the Reformation itself. They immediately resolved that a deputation should be sent to Zurich, the seat of the mischief, calling upon the council and the citizens to renounce their new opinions.

In accordance with this resolution an embassy was sent to Zurich, on the 21st of March, 1524, in which all the cantons represented at Lucerne united, with the single exception of Schaffhausen. The deputies, in the most specious style of address, lamented that the unity of the ancient Christian faith should be broken, and that universal sorrow should be occasioned by the unhappy changes which had lately been introduced ; the delightful repose of Church and State, transmitted from all antiquity, had been thus violently interrupted. " **Confederates of Zurich**," said the delegates, "join your efforts to ours ; let us stifle this new faith ; it had been well if this growing evil had been stopped in the beginning, and if, after the example of our ancestors, we had vindicated the honour of God, the blessed Virgin, and all the saints, at the expense of our lives and fortunes : the fruits of the doctrine of Luther are everywhere apparent in the menacing aspect of the people, who show themselves ripe for rebellion." Thus the deputation appealed to the Zurichers, and entreated them to dismiss Zwingle and Leo Juda, the instruments of communicating this contagion to the Swiss. That there were abuses in the ecclesiastical system, they readily admitted. " They were all oppressed by the Pope, and his train of cardinals, bishops, and agents, who, by their usurpation, simony, and indulgences, exhausted the wealth of the country. They were willing to co-operate in any scheme for the correction of these evils and such as these ; but the states in assembly could no longer endure the innovations which were sheltered and nourished by the Senate of Zurich."

Thus spoke the adversaries of the Reformation ; and what reply can the council give to such fair speeches from so large a

* Hess, p. 168.

portion of the Helvetic body ? The answer was immediate, firm, and noble. The death of Hottinger had not discouraged them, but rather raised their indignation against the states which had perpetrated it.

THE ANSWER OF ZURICH TO LUCERNE.

"We can make no concessions," said the Zurichers, "in what concerns the Word of God. For five years past we have been listening to the sacred instructions of our ministers. At first their doctrine did seem new to us, as we had heard nothing of the like before. But when we understood and clearly perceived that this was its end and scope—to make manifest Jesus Christ as the author and finisher of our salvation ; who died on the Cross as the Saviour of mankind, and shed His precious Blood to cleanse our sins away ; who is now in Heaven as the only Advocate and Mediator between God and man—when we heard so salutary a message we could not refrain from embracing it with great eagerness." They then proceeded to reply at some length to the representations of the delegates, to expose the abuses of the Church of Rome, and to assert that all blessing to their souls and all harmony in the states must spring from obedience to the Word of God. They reasserted that the single weapon for overthrowing the power, usurpations, and rapacity of the Papists is the preaching of the pure Word of God.

How interesting to the Christian reader of the present day to find that statesmen, warriors, and political bodies, so openly and with such wondrous faith, referred to the Word of God in those times. It was their only standard of appeal and their sole rule in practice. It is too much taken for granted now that all are secretly governed by it, therefore there is no reference to it in our public assemblies. "There is nothing," said the senate in conclusion, "that we desire more ardently, than the universal prevalence of peace, nor will we in any respect violate our laws and treaties of alliance. But in this affair, which involves our eternal safety, we cannot act otherwise than we do, unless we should be first convicted of error. We therefore again exhort you, as we have already done, if you think our doctrine opposed to Scripture, to point it out, and prove it against us ; but we must entreat you not to delay the attempt beyond the close of the month of May ; till that time we shall expect an answer from you and from the bishops, and from the University of Basle."

THE DOWNFALL OF THE IMAGES.

The appointed interval had elapsed, and as no reply was received from the Roman Catholic cantons, the council of Zurich determined to proceed in the work of Reformation. The decree for the demolition of images was passed in January, but the authorities were in no haste to have it executed. There is nothing more to be admired at this moment of our history, than the patient and considerate way in which this delicate matter was conducted by the magistrates. They delayed in the expectation that the work would be accomplished by the general consent, and not by the open violence of the people.

At the request of the three pastors, Zwingle, Leo Juda, and Engelhardt, the council published an order to the effect that, honour being due to God only, the images should be removed from all the Churches of the canton, and their ornaments sold for the benefit of the poor ; that the council prohibit all private persons from destroying any image, without public authority, except such as are their own property ; that every separate Church may destroy its images after a prescribed method ; that those persons whose families had erected images in the Churches must have them removed within a limited time, or they will be destroyed by public authority. By these prudent and moderate measures, of which Zwingle was the counsellor, civil dissension was entirely avoided, and the work proceeded as if by the unanimous determination of the citizens.

The appointed officers, consisting of twelve councillors, the three pastors, the city architect, masons, carpenters, and other necessary assistants, went into the various churches, and, having closed the doors, took down the crosses, defaced the frescoes, whitewashed the walls, burned the pictures, and broke in pieces or otherwise destroyed every idol, to prevent their ever becoming again the objects of idolatrous worship. The country Churches following the example of the capital, displayed even greater zeal in destroying their ancient decorations and the objects of their recent adoration. Zwingle speaks with a little playfulness of a famous **stone statue of the Virgin** among the nuns in Altenbach, held in great reverence, and of much miraculous celebrity. The monks affirmed that it could never be removed from its place, or at least it could never be kept from its venerated station. It had been repeatedly taken away, firmly fixed and fastened elsewhere, and even locked up, but it always reappeared the following morning on its former basis. But alas ! it failed to vindicate the prediction of the monks ; it quietly submitted to be roughly removed, and returned no more to its ancient position. Thus the idol lost credit with the people.

" I rejoice then," exclaims Zwingle, " and bid all others to rejoice with me, that this most iniquitous imposture was at length removed from the eyes of men ; for, when this was once accomplished, all the other figments of Popery were overthrown more easily. To God, through whose power and grace all this has been accomplished, be praise and glory for ever, Amen."

THE SWISS AND GERMAN REFORMATION.

Here, in the presence of such a mighty work of God's Spirit, it may be well to pause for a moment and contemplate the difference between the two great leaders of the Reformation, the character of their principles and action, and the consequent results. The difference has often arrested us, and sometimes we have referred to it, and as D'Aubigné, the warm-hearted champion of Luther, has noticed the difference we refer to, we may draw attention to it the more freely.

That which completely ruled Zwingle's mind, and all his teaching and actings as a Reformer, was his supreme regard for the Holy Scriptures. All religious observances that could not be found in, or proved by, the Word of God, he boldly maintained should be abolished. His Hebrew Bible and His Greek New Testament lay on the table before him in the halls of discussion, and he would own no standard but these. Luther's principle of dealing with the old religion was of a widely different character. He desired to maintain in the Church all that was not *directly* or *expressly contrary* to the Scriptures. This is by no means a safe or a sound principle. It might be difficult to prove that certain things are *expressly* forbidden in the Word of God, though it might be still more difficult to prove that they had any place in Scripture. Truth is definite and positive, this dogma is loose and uncertain.

Even D'Aubigné admits that Luther rose up against those that had violently broken the images in the Churches of Wittemberg, while the idols fell in the temples of Zurich by Zwingle's own direction. The **German Reformer** wished to remain united to the Church of Rome, and would have been content to purify it of all that was opposed to the Word of God. The **Zurich Reformer** passed over the middle ages entirely, and reckoned nothing of absolute authority that had been written or invented since the days of the apostles. Restoration to the primitive simplicity of the Church was his idea of a Reformation. There was therefore greater completeness in the mind of Zwingle as a Reformer.

Primitive Christianity had been transformed in its early days by the self-righteousness of Judaism and the paganism of the Greeks into the confusion of Roman Catholicism. The Jewish element prevailed in that part of her doctrine which relates to man—to salvation by works of human merit, or to trading in the salvation of the souls of men, as by indulgences. The pagan element prevailed especially in that which relates to God—to the innumerable false gods of Popery ; to the long reign of images, symbols, and ceremonies ; to the dethroning of the infinitely blessed and all gracious God. "The German Reformer proclaimed the great doctrine of justification by faith, and with it inflicted a death-blow on the *self-righteousness* of Rome. The Reformer of Switzerland unquestionably did the same ; the inability of man to save himself forms the basis of the work of all the Reformers. But Zwingle did something more : he established the sovereign, universal, and exclusive supremacy of God, and thus inflicted a deadly blow on the *pagan worship* of Rome."*

THE MARRIAGE OF ZWINGLE.

Of the many innovations which were now introduced, none gave a greater scandal to the Papal party than the **marriage of the clergy.** It was setting at defiance all ecclesiastical discipline, and by those who were naturally expected to be its guardians. To live, as if married, was overlooked, if not sanctioned, by the ecclesiastical authorities ; but to marry was a mortal sin. Such was the morality of Popery. But the Spirit of God was now working, and the eyes of many were being opened to the truth. One of the pastors in the city of Strasburg, who had been living like many others at that time, was led to see his sin and married immediately. The bishop, because it had been done publicly, could not overlook the offence, and caused a great stir to be made both in the Church and in the senate. The time, however, was past for the bishop to have all his own way : numbers approved of the new doctrine, following the example of the pastor ; and the magistrates refused to interfere.

In the month of April, 1524, Zwingle availed himself of the privilege which he had so often claimed for all the priesthood. His nuptials with **Anna Reinhart,** widow of John Meyer, lord of Weiningen, in the county of Baden, were publicly proclaimed, thereby setting a good example to his brethren. Only two of several children survived him ; Ulric, who became a canon and Archdeacon of Zurich ; and Regula, who was married to Rudolph Gaulter, a divine of eminence. The following year Luther was married to **Catherine of Bora.** These events gave occasion to great calumnies ; but as Zwingle had not been a monk, or his bride a nun, the scandal was not so enormous as in the case of Luther and Catherine.

THE PROGRESS OF REFORM.

The Lord greatly blessed the labours of the Reformers in Zurich at this time, and stayed the cruel hand of their enemies. The Word of the Lord had found its right place in their hearts, and, through them, in the hearts of the people. And God never fails to bless the people or the nation that honours His Word. It is ever the certain pathway to the richest blessings. He still says, " Them that honour Me I will honour " (1 Sam. 2. 30).

The downfall of the images was immediately followed by the

* D'Aubigné, vol. iii., pp. 356-359.

voluntary dissolution of the two most important religious institutions in Zurich. The first was that of an ancient and wealthy **abbey,** of royal foundation, known by the name of Frauen-Münster, and used for the reception of ladies of quality. It was distinguished not only by very high antiquity, but also by various immunities and privileges, and the possession of splendid revenues. This extraordinary society of females exercised the sovereign right of coining all the money circulated, and of nominating the persons who should preside in the tribunals of justice. The lady-abbess, of her own accord, surrendered all the rights and possessions of the institution into the hands of the government, on the understanding that the funds should be applied to pious and charitable purposes, with a due respect to vested rights. The abbess, Catherine Cimmern, retired on an honourable pension and soon after married. In consequence of this change, the city of Zurich, in the year 1526, for the first time coined money and established courts of justice in its own name.

The chapter of canons also, of which Zwingle was a member, after arranging with the government respecting their rights and revenues, followed the example of the opulent nuns. The few remaining monks of the three orders were collected into one monastery ; the young to be taught some useful trade, the aged to end their days in peace.

The news of these triumphs of the Word of God rapidly spread over the mountains and valleys of Switzerland. The Roman Catholic cantons were exasperated. Facts were distorted ; falsehoods were circulated ; diets were assembled unknown to the senate of Zurich, and the deputies of the cantons bound themselves never to permit the establishment of the new opinion in Switzerland.

Meanwhile the Pontiffs were not indifferent spectators. Clement VII addressed a brief to the Helvetic Republic generally, which he saluted with the most profuse expressions of respect and benevolence. He also addressed himself in the most flattering terms to all—lay and clerical—who had exerted themselves in support of the Catholic faith. Their zeal was " more glorious than all the victories and military achievements of their brave country ; " and he further exhorted them to persevere in their laudable course, until they had extirpated the " Lutheran doctrines " from the soil of Switzerland.

Animated by this artful address, and aroused by the proceedings at Zurich, the ten cantons, which had not avowed the reformed faith, assembled at Zug, in the month of July, and sent a deputation to Zurich, Schaffhausen, and Appenzel. The delegates were commissioned to acquaint these states with the firm resolve of the diet to **crush the new doctrines** ; and to prosecute its adherents to the forfeiture of their goods, of their honours, and even of their lives. Zurich could not hear such threatenings without deep emotion ; but she was ready with her usual reply : " In matters of faith the Word of God alone must be obeyed." On receiving this answer, the Catholic cantons trembled with rage. Lucerne, Uri, Schweitz, Zug, Unterwalden, and Friburg, declared to the citizens of Zurich, that they would never again sit with them in diet unless they renounced their novel dogmas. The federal unity was thus broken by the partisans of Rome ; and, in spite of their oaths and alliances, they determined to arrest the progress of truth by the sword of persecution.

THE WEAPONS OF ROME'S WARFARE.

Matters now began to assume a more alarming aspect. An event soon occurred which increased the misunderstanding of the confederates, and gave Rome the opportunity of showing with what weapons she was prepared to fight for the ancient faith.

The village of **Stamheim,** situated on the frontiers of Thurgau, was dependent upon Zurich ; except for its criminal jurisdiction, which was vested in the bailiff of Thurgau. This village possessed a chapel dedicated to St. Anne, and enriched by the gifts of a multitude of pilgrims. But, notwithstanding these great advantages to the inhabitants, they were inclined to abandon their idolatrous practices and gains, and embrace the principles of Reform. Stamheim was at that time governed by a vice-bailiff, named John Writh, a worthy man, and an ancient Reformer. He had two sons, young priests, John and Adrian, who had been stationed there by the council of Zurich for the instruction of the people. Full of piety and courage, and zealous preachers of the Gospel, the citizens were taught to regard the honours which were offered to the patroness of their village as dishonouring to God and contrary to His Holy Word ; and having received the edict of the council of Zurich on the subject of images, they burned the votive pictures that attested the miracles of St. Anne, and removed the images which had been placed in the public situations of Stamheim.

For the moment the popular feeling was in favour of Reform, but there were many still who clung to their idols with a tenacity peculiar to idolatry, and murmured deeply for the blood of their destroyers. Such carried their complaints to the grand-bailiff of Thurgau, named Joseph Amberg. This unhappy man was at one time inclined to the opinions of Zwingle ; but when a candidate for the office of grand-bailiff, in order to obtain the suffrages of his fellow-citizens, all zealous Catholics, he promised to use his utmost power to suppress **the new sect** in Thurgau. He would gladly have seized and imprisoned the offenders, but

Stamheim was beyond his jurisdiction. His violent hatred, however, of the bailiff Writh and his sons he took no pains to conceal, nor of his purpose to be avenged because of the dishonour done to the images.

THE ILLEGAL ARREST OF ŒXLIN.

The evil genius of Rome came to the assistance of Amberg. He saw that the minds of men were in that state of excitement which indicates a readiness for tumult and violence. This was his snare, and a fatal one it proved. **Œxlin,** a great friend of Zwingle's, and the principal apostle of the Reformation in Thurgau, was arrested in the hope of stopping its progress. At midnight, on the 7th of July, 1524, the learned and pious minister of Burg was seized by the bailiff's soldiers and carried off, in defiance of his cries and in contempt of the privileges of his position. The inhabitants, hearing the disturbance, rushed into the streets, and the village soon became the scene of a frightful uproar; but their pastor was not rescued, the soldiers were off, and the night was dark. According to the custom of those times, the tocsin was rung—the alarm-bell; and the inhabitants of the adjacent villages were soon on the move and inquiring of one another what was the matter.

When John Writh and his sons heard that their friend and brother had been violently carried off, they hastened to join the pursuers. But they were too late; the soldiers, hearing the alarm, redoubled their speed, and soon placed the river Thur between themselves and the pursuing party. Application was made to Amberg for the release of Œxlin on bail, but their terms were refused. Unhappily, a number of unprincipled, turbulent spirits, who always make their appearance in such tumults, became unruly. They applied for some refreshment at the convent of Ittingen, but not content with what they received, they began to pillage and drank to excess. Writh and his sons did their utmost to restrain them, but without success. It was believed by the populace that the inmates had encouraged the tyranny of Amberg, and that they should be revenged on the monks of Ittingen. While revelling in the store-rooms and cellars, a fire broke out, and the monastery was burned to the ground.

THE WRITHS FALSELY ACCUSED.

This was enough for the evil purposes of the adversary. The grand-bailiff, in giving an account to his government of the fatal event, blamed the inhabitants of Stein and Stamheim, and above all, the bailiff Writh and his sons, whom he accused of causing the tocsin to be sounded; of being the authors of the excesses committed at Ittingen: of having profaned the host, and burned the monastery.

50

In a few days the deputies of the cantons assembled at Zug. So great was their indignation, that they would have marched instantly with flying banners on Stein and Stamheim, and put the inhabitants to the sword. " If any one is guilty," said the deputies of Zurich with more reason, " he must be punished, but according to the laws of justice, and not by violence." They also represented to the deputies of the cantons, that the grand-bailiff had provoked the commotion, by violating the privileges of the town of Stein in the illegal arrest of the pastor Œxlin. In the meantime the Council of Zurich sent one of its members, with an escort of soldiers to Stamheim—whose subjects they were—to seize the persons accused. Several consulted their safety by flight ; but Writh and his sons, who had returned before the monastery was burned, and were living quietly at Stamheim, refused to fly, depending upon their own innocence and the justice of their government. When the soldiers made their appearance, the worthy bailiff said to them : " My lords of Zurich might have spared themselves all this trouble. If they had sent a child, I should have obeyed their summons." The three Wriths, with their friend, Burchard Ruteman, bailiff of Nussbaum—a man of the same spirit—were taken prisoners, and carried to Zurich.

After a three weeks' imprisonment, they were brought up for examination. They acknowledged that they had gone out at the sound of the tocsin, and that they had followed the crowd to Ittingen ; but they proved that, instead of exciting the peasants to disorder, they had endeavoured to dissuade them from it, and that they had returned home immediately they knew that the grand-bailiff refused to set Œxlin at liberty. Nothing could be proved against them ; they had only acted according to the republican principles of their country, in turning out at the sound of the alarm-bell. They were pronounced, after a full examination, to be entirely innocent.

THE ASSEMBLY OF BADEN.

These proceedings were communicated to the cantons then assembled at Baden, but they were not satisfied. Jezebel's thirst for blood had been whetted by having her prey so near her grasp, and she determined on lengthening her arm, and making it secure. Contrary to the established customs of the Confederation, she demanded the prisoners to be given up, in order to be judged at Baden. The Zurichers refused on the ground that to them belonged the right to judge their own subjects, and that the diet had no right over the persons accused. On hearing this, the deputies trembled with rage. " We will do ourselves justice," they exclaimed, " if the accused are not delivered up to us immediately ; we will march our troops to

Zurich and carry them off by force of arms." Knowing the
state of feeling against Zurich because Zwingle and the Reforma-
mation, and dreading the calamities of a civil war, the resolution
of the Senate was shaken.

Unhappy moment for the honour of Zurich ! " To yield to
threats," said Zwingle, " to renounce your just rights when the
life of a subject is at stake, is a criminal weakness, from which
none but the most fatal consequences can be expected. If the
persons accused were guilty, I should be far from wishing to
save them from the sword of justice, but since they have been
judged innocent, why deliver them up to a tribunal, determined
before hand to make the whole weight of its hatred against the
Reformation fall upon their heads ? " The whole town was
in agitation ; opinions were divided. At last it was supposed
that a middle course had been found. The prisoners were to be
delivered to the diet, on condition that they would only be
examined with regard to the affair of Ittingen, and not as to their
faith. The diet agreed to this, and on Friday, 18th August,
the three Wriths and their friends, accompanied by four councillors of state, and several armed men, quitted Zurich.

" A deep concern," says the historian, " was felt by all the
city at the prospect of the fate which awaited the two youths
and their aged companions. Sobbing alone was heard as they
passed along. What a mournful procession ! exclaimed one.
God will punish us for delivering them up, cried another. Let
us pray Him to impart His grace to these poor prisoners, and to
strengthen them in their faith." The Churches were all filled.
Zwingle and others lifted up their voices ; and who, we may ask,
did not bathe with their tears those firstfruits to God of the
Reformation in Switzerland ?

THE WRITHS AND RUTEMAN FALSELY CONDEMNED.

When the prisoners reached **Baden,** they were thrown into a
dungeon. The *form* of an examination began the following day ;
the bailiff Writh was first brought in. The Catholics, acting
upon their old motto, " that it is wrong to keep faith with heretics," immediately questioned the bailiff concerning the removal
of the images at Stamheim, and other points affecting his religion.
The deputies of Zurich protested, reminding the diet that this
was a gross violation of the conditions on which the prisoners were
allowed to appear. But expostulations were of no avail now.
The Zurichers and their appeals were treated with derision.
The prisoners were put to the torture, in the hope of extorting
from them some confessions which might give a colour of justice
to the sentence which was already determined to be pronounced
upon them.

The most cruel tortures were inflicted on the father, without regard to his character or his age ; but he persisted in declaring his innocence of the pillage and burning of Ittingen. From morning till noon they practised their cruelties on the old man. His pitiful cries to God to sustain and comfort him, only called forth the impiety of his tormenters. "Where is your Christ now ? " said one of the deputies, " Bid Him come to your relief." His intrepid son, John, was treated with still greater barbarity. But nothing could move his constancy in Christ. He seems to have triumphed in his sufferings, and gloried in his cross. Adrian was threatened with having his veins opened one after another, unless he made a confession of his guilt. But he could only confess to having preached the Gospel of Christ, and been married. When wearied with their work of torture, they sent back the faithful confessors of Christ to a loathsome dungeon ; their bodies wellnigh racked to pieces, themselves strong in the consciousness of their innocence, and sustained by the presence and power of their Lord and Master, Christ Jesus.

The **bailiff's wife,** Hannah Writh, and the mother of the two young priests, hastened to Baden, carrying an infant child in her arms, to implore the mercy of the judges. With floods of tears she pleaded for mercy to her husband and her sons ; she pleaded her large family, her husband's past services to the state and his country ; but all in vain. Her entreaties, such as only a wife and a mother could pour forth, instead of softening the judges, irritated them more and more, and betrayed that Satanic hatred to the truth which was the real cause of all their cruelties. One of the judges, the deputy for Zug, was led in the providence of God to give the most wonderful testimony to the character of Writh, and the treachery of his judges. " You know the bailiff Writh," said a friend of the distressed wife to him. " I do," he replied, " I have been twice bailiff of Thurgau, I never knew a more innocent, upright, and hospitable man than John Writh. His house was open to all who stood in need of his assistance ; in fact, his house was a convent, an inn, and an hospital ; and I cannot imagine what demon can have drawn him into this tumult. If he had plundered, robbed, or even murdered, I would willingly have made every exertion to obtain his pardon ; but seeing he has burned the image of the blessed St. Anne, the mother of the Virgin, he must die ; there can be no mercy shown him." The court broke up, the deputies returned to their cantons, the prisoners to their cells, and did not meet again till that day month.

THE MARTYRDOM OF THE WRITHS AND RUTEMAN.

At length those dreary four weeks passed away, and the deputies assembled to deliberate on the sentence. In solemn mockery of all justice, and with closed doors, the **sentence of**

death was passed on the bailiff Writh ; on his son John—who was the strongest in the faith, and who had led away others— and on the bailiff Ruteman. Adrian—it may have been to colour over the cruelty and injustice of this sentence—was given back to his mother's tears with a show of mercy.

The officers proceeded to the tower to bring the prisoners into court. On hearing the sentence, Adrian burst into tears. His father calmly embraced the brief interval, to exact from him a promise, that he would never, in any way, attempt to avenge their death. " My brother," said John to Adrian, " the cross of Christ must always follow His Word. Do not then weep, my brother ; resume your courage, preach the Gospel of Christ, be constant in the cause of Christ. I can render thanks to my Lord this day, that He has honoured me by calling me to suffer and die for His truth. Blessed be His holy Name for ever ! His holy will be done ! "

They were next conducted to the scaffold. The sufferings of these faithful men from their long detention in unwholesome dungeons, and from the tortures that were inflicted on them, made death a welcome messenger of peace. But that noble son— to be remembered with admiration and gratitude for ever— whose heart was filled with the tenderest anxiety for his father, sought in every way to comfort and sustain him. Floods of tears fell from all spectators, as he embraced his father, and bade him **farewell on the scaffold**. " My dearly beloved father, hence-forward you shall be no longer my father, nor I your son. We are brethren in Christ Jesus, for the love of whom we are about to die. But we are going to Him who is our Father, and the Father of all the faithful ; and in His presence we shall enjoy eternal life. Let us fear nothing ! " " Amen," replied the father, "may God be glorified, my dearly beloved son and brother in Christ." The bailiff Ruteman prayed in silence.

All three knelt down together in the Name of the Lord Jesus Christ ; and in another moment their heads fell on the scaffold, and their happy souls had found their home and rest in the blooming Paradise of God.

The crowd gave loud utterance to their lamentations. The two bailiffs left twenty-two children, and forty-five grand-children. Hannah had brought up a large family in the fear of the Lord, and was greatly respected for her virtues throughout the whole district. But she had not yet drained the cup of her bitter anguish. She was condemned to pay *twelve crowns to the executioner* who had beheaded her husband and her son. Let the reader note the refined barbarity, the ignoble littleness, the cowardly persecution, the wanton cruelty, that delights in lacerating an already sorely wounded woman's heart. " O my soul come not thou into their secret ; unto their assembly, mine honour, be not thou united " (Genesis. 49. 6).

Adrian Writh was released, with orders to make a public confession of his crime at Einsidlen ; but he escaped to Zurich, where he found an asylum, became pastor of Altorf, and was the father of the celebrated Rudolph or Ralph, Hospinian, author of the Sacramentarian history. Œxlin was released, after having been put to the torture at Lucerne. He likewise found a refuge in the canton of Zurich, and became a pastor there.*

* For more lengthy details, see " Life of Zwingle," by Hess, 178-194 ; D'Aubigné, vol. i., chap. 5 ; Scott, vol. ii., pp. 494-501.

CHAPTER XLIII

The General Progress of Reform

THE Reformation in Switzerland had now been baptised in blood—the blood of the martyrs of Jesus. The adversary of the Gospel had done his work—his cruel work ; but it made all men thoughtful. The violence of the blow was felt by all classes throughout Switzerland. The power of Rome was weakened, the triumphs of the Reformation were accelerated. Even the heads of the Catholic cantons, notwithstanding their hatred against the Reformers, could not conceal from themselves that the general corruption of manners, and the glaring immoralities of the clergy, rendered some reform absolutely indispensable. And seeing the indifference of the ecclesiastical authorities to all such matters, they resolved to provide for the wants of the Church, and for the tranquillity of their common country. But the plan of the deputies was opposed by the whole clerical influence, and they had neither energy nor authority to press it. The future general council, so often demanded, so long promised, was again spoken of as the only hope of pacifying Christendom.

While these things were agitating the heads of the Catholic cantons, those favourable to the Reformation were drawing closer together. Zurich, Berne, Glaris, Schaffhausen, and Appenzell, formed an alliance for the more effectual spread of the truth, and for the protection of their rights and liberties. Such were the favourable results of the martyrdom of the Wriths. " Every time," says D'Aubigné, " that Rome erects a scaffold, and that heads roll upon it, the Reformation will exalt the holy Word of God, and throw down some abuses. When Hottinger was executed, Zurich suppressed images, and now that the heads of the Wriths have fallen, Zurich will reply by the abolition of the mass."

Ever since the decision of the **two conferences,** the Council of Zurich had been resolved to abolish the superstitious rites of the mass ; but it was thought desirable to delay until the public mind should appear to be prepared for the change. The mass was therefore allowed to remain untouched after the removal of the images, but no priest was compelled to say it, nor any layman to hear it. It became generally neglected, and day by day it fell more and more into disrepute, so that the proper time for its total abolition seemed to have arrived.

THE ABOLITION OF THE MASS.

On the 11th of April, 1525, the pastors, Zwingle, Leo Juda, and Engelhardt, accompanied by Megander, chaplain of the hospital, and Myconius, preacher in the Abbey Church, presented themselves before the council, and recommended the immediate abolition of the sacrifice of the altar. One advocate alone presented himself to defend the established opinion. **Englehardt,** formerly a doctor of Pontifical law, explained the difference between the service in the Latin Church and the Eucharist according to the institution of Christ and the apostolic practice. All felt the solemnity and importance of the resolution which the council was called upon to take, and thought it well to adjourn the debate till the following day. And then, after some further conference between the divines and the senators, a decree was published to the following effect : " Henceforward, by the will of God, celebrate the Eucharist according to the institution of Christ, and the apostolic practice. Be it permitted to those infirm, and yet rude in faith, to continue the ancient practice for this time only. Let the mass be universally abolished, laid aside, and antiquated, so as not to be repeated even to-morrow." The altars were accordingly removed from the Churches, and replaced by communion tables ; the great body of the people communicated according to the new form ; those who attended mass were even less numerous than the Reformers expected. Thus fell that mystery of iniquity, which had deeply impressed for centuries the feelings and the credulity of mankind. Mass had been celebrated in the Latin Church from an early period ; but prostration at the elevation of the host, and other ceremonies, were of a later date.

THE CELEBRATION OF THE LORD'S SUPPER.

Zwingle, first of all, preached from the words : " It is the Lord's passover." After the conclusion of the sermon a table was covered with a white cloth, unleavened bread, and cups filled with wine, to recall the remembrance of the last supper of our Lord with His disciples. The minister then approached the table. The words of institution from the Epistle to the Corinthians, and other portions were read aloud by the deacons. The crowd was so great, and the services so prolonged, that several ministers and deacons assisted. After prayer, and exhorting the people to self-examination, the minister lifted the bread, and, with a loud voice, repeated the institution of the Lord's Supper. He then delivered the bread, and afterwards the cup, to the deacons, to present them to the people, and for the people to distribute them to each other. While the elements were passing round, one of the ministers read from the Gospel of St. John those ever fresh and ever blessed discourses, held by the Lord with His disciples, immediately following the feast of the Passover in chapter 13. After the Supper the congregation all knelt down, and offered up their grateful adorations and thanksgivings ;

then hymns, full of the expression of love and praise to their Saviour and Lord, terminated this solemn and affecting scene— the first celebration of the Lord's Supper by the Reformers in Switzerland. It occupied three days—Thursday in Passion Week, Good Friday, and Easter Sunday.

For the establishment of the good work in Zurich, and for the spread of the truth elsewhere, Zwingle, Leo Juda, and other learned men, published about this time, several useful works on the Holy Scriptures ; such as the Pentateuch, and other historical books of the Old Testament, besides an able commentary on " True and False Religion."

We may now leave Zurich for a time. Having given a some-what minute account of the work of God's Spirit there, we must be brief with the other places, as many fields still lie before us. Besides, there is a great similarity in the work in the different places.

THE REFORMATION IN BERNE.

Berne was one of the most influential states in the confedera-tion. It numbered many powerful friends of the Gospel, and many formidable adversaries. For the first few years after the appearance of Luther and Zwingle, a strong opposition was manifested to the new opinions. Nowhere was the struggle likely to be more severe. But under the evangelical preaching of **Haller and Meyer** the more violent prejudices began to soften down.

By the blessing of God on the labours of these devoted, earnest, and consistent men, the cause of truth, prospered, and from an act of the government in 1523, we may conclude that the balance inclined to the side of the Reformation. It was decreed, " That as conflicting doctrines were delivered to the people,. and the preachers thundered against each other, they should all of them thenceforward preach the same Gospel, namely the doctrine revealed by God, and illustrated by the prophetical and apos-tolical writings ; that they should propound nothing contrary to Holy Writ, whether on Luther's or on any other authority, and avoid every discourse of a seditious tendency."

By this decision of the senate, the preaching of the Gospel in all its fulness and simplicity was encouraged, and the Word of God was established as the only standard of appeal in discussion, the only test of truth. Thus was the foundation surely laid of a true Reformation, and under the sanction of the Government. But these advantages, intentional or unintentional, were sufficient to alarm the Papists, and to drive them to their favourite weapons of intrigue, treachery, and violence. The two faithful witnesses in Berne, Haller and Meyer, must be silenced by fair means or foul. They were falsely accused, together with the famous Wittenbach, of having spoken to some nuns with the view of

inducing them to leave their conventual life, and were sentenced
to banishment from Berne. But when the plot was discovered,
the opposition on the part of the people was so great, that the
matter was carried before the Great Council, which reversed the
decision of the Smaller Council, and discharged the ministers,
with an exhortation to confine themselves to their pulpits, and
not to meddle with cloisters. This was all that these devoted
men wanted—their pulpits. Thus the Reformation gained a
fresh victory, and her enemies were covered with disgrace.

THE NUNS OF KÖNIGSFELDT.

A few months after this occurrence, the principles of the
Reformation were greatly strengthened by the conversion of the
nuns of Konigsfeldt. This was a wonderful triumph of the
Gospel. The monastery stood near the castle of Hapsburg, and
was surrounded with all the magnificence of the Middle Ages.
From the family of Hapsburg the imperial house of Austria
sprang in the seventh century, and gave, in after years, many
Emperors to Germany. Here the daughters of the nobles in
Switzerland and Swabia used to take the veil. Beatrice of
Laudenberg, sister to the Bishop of Constance, was one of the
inmates. But the truth of God, which the bishop was seeking
with all his power to suppress, was the means of the conversion
of many of the nuns in this imperial monastery. The writings
of Luther and Zwingle, and the Holy Scriptures, had found their
way into this institution, and the saving change was accomplished. Nor need we wonder. God was working by His Holy
Spirit, and the strongest prejudices and the greatest difficulties
were overcome. The following letter, written by Margaret
Watteville, a youthful nun, and sister to the provost of Berne,
will furnish a better idea of the fruits of the Reformation, and of
the Christian spirit that existed in these pious women, than any
explanation we could give. She writes to Zwingle :
" May grace and peace in the Lord Jesus be given and multiplied towards you always by God our heavenly Father. Most
learned, reverend, and dear sir, I entreat you to take in good part
the letter I now address to you. The love which is in Christ
constrains me to do so, especially since I have learnt that the
doctrine of salvation is spreading day by day through your
preaching of the Word of God. For this reason I give praise to
the everlasting God for enlightening us anew, and sending us
by His Holy Spirit so many heralds of His blessed Word ; and at
the same time I offer up my ardent prayers that He will clothe
with His strength both you and all those who proclaim His glad
tidings, and that, arming you against all the enemies of the truth,
He will cause His Divine Word to grow in all men. Very learned
sir, I venture to send your reverence this trifling mark of my

affection : do not despise it ; it is an offering of Christian charity. If this electuary does you any good, and you should desire more, pray let me know ; for it would be a great pleasure to me to do anything that was agreeable to you ; and it is not I only who think thus, but all those who love the Gospel in our convent at Königsfeldt. They salute your reverence in Jesus Christ, and we all commend you without ceasing to His almighty protection. —*Saturday before Lœtare.*"

These pious ladies, believing that they could better serve the Lord outside than inside the walls of a convent, petitioned the Government for permission to leave it. The council, in alarm at this strange proceeding, endeavoured to induce them to remain, promising that the discipline of the convent would be relaxed, and their allowance increased. " It is not the liberty of the flesh that we require," said they to the council, " it is the liberty of the Spirit." As they persisted in their petition, the Government found it necessary at length to yield. And the decree which restored them to liberty contained a general provision for the liberation of all who, with the consent of their parents, might desire it. The convent gates were now thrown open, which greatly weakened the credit and power of Rome, and manifested the triumphs of the Reformation, for many of those ladies were in a short time honourably married.

THE CONFERENCE AT BADEN.

But although the principles of the Reformation were gaining ground rapidly, the Roman Catholic party was still very powerful and very active. A more decisive battle must be fought before victory can be declared.

Ever since the first conference held at Zurich, the Bishop of Constance, or rather **John Faber,** his grand vicar, had been constantly deliberating by what means he could most effectually arrest the progress of the Reformation. Experience had proved that bishops' charges were little regarded ; that writing books was hopeless, as the Reformers surpassed their adversaries in learning and talents ; indeed, success seemed utterly hopeless unless the destruction of Zwingle could be accomplished. His popularity and influence were increasing day by day.

A political event which happened about this time yet further impressed upon the Romanists the necessity of some instant and vigorous measure. The battle of Pavia, fought between the French and the Imperialists, threw a dark shadow over Switzerland, but shed a bright gleam on the wisdom, patriotism, and Christianity of Zwingle. More than ten thousand Swiss mercenaries had fought on that field so fatal to France. Between five and six thousand swelled the number of the slain ; and five thousand were made prisoners. When these were released and sent home, their maimed and emaciated forms were like so many spectacles of horror wandering over the land, and were every-where met by the wailings of the widows and the orphans of the slain. The people now remembered how often Zwingle had thundered against these foreign enlistments from the pulpit; and spoke of him as the truest patriot and their best friend.

The Romanists now saw that the general feeling was in favour of Zwingle, and that some means must be taken to check his growing influence. But how is this to be done? Who can solve the problem? We must go wisely to work. Jezebel, long in practice, came to their aid; and thus, we may say, she coun-selled. The first thing to be done is to induce Zwingle to leave Zurich. Of course he will come to the conference. Once out of the territory of that state, he would be in your power. You could seize him and burn him, and the death of the champion would be the death of the whole movement. The plan was approved, victory was certain. "The torrent once stemmed, the waters of heresy will retreat to the abyss whence they issued, and the ' everlasting hills ' of the old faith, which the deluge threatened to overtop, will once more lift up their heads stable and majestic as ever." Faber communicated his plan to Dr. Eck, vice-chancellor of Ingolstadt, who had acquired great reputation with his party by combating the opinions of Luther at Leipsic ; and it was agreed that he should take charge of the plot.

This notorious and unscrupulous advocate of the Papacy addressed a letter to the cantons, filled with invectives against Zwingle, and offering to convince him publicly of his errors, if they would furnish him with a favourable opportunity. " I am full of confidence," he said, " that I shall, with little trouble, maintain our old true Christian faith and customs, against Zwingle, who has no doubt milked more cows than he has read books." A diet was at length fixed to be held at Baden—a Romish city, in May, 1526.

Zwingle and the other divines of Zurich were invited to attend ; but the senate refused compliance. To send Zwingle to Baden, said the council, would be to send him not to dispute, but to die. There the blood of the Wriths was shed, and there the Popish cantons were all-powerful ; they had burned his books at Friburg and his effigy at Lucerne, and they were only thirsting to burn himself. Indeed the Papal party took no pains to conceal their intentions towards Zwingle, whom they denounced in their public manifesto as a rebel, a heretic, and a perverter of Scrip-ture. With these threatenings before them, the council of Zurich decreed that Zwingle should not go to Baden. They also protested against the resolutions that might be taken by the diet, but offered Eck full security if he would come and confer with the Reformer at Zurich. This offer was rejected, and the conference took place without the presence of Zwingle.

THE OPENING OF THE DIET.

Faber, Eck, and Murner, accompanied by prelates, magistrates, and doctors, robed in garments of silk and damask, and adorned with chains, rings, and crosses, repaired to the Church. Œcolampadius and Haller, two quiet timid men, were the only Reformers who appeared in the discussion. The same dogmas which had been replied to over and over again, were brought forward by Eck. The following are his **seven propositions,** as given by the learned and candid Roman Catholic historian, Du Pin. They will also place before the reader the figments of Popery for which the Papists were fighting, and for which they were ready to shed the blood, not only of their best citizens, but of the saints of God. 1, That the real body and blood of Christ are present in the sacrament of the altar. 2, That they are truly offered in the sacrifice of the mass for the living and the dead. 3, That we ought to call on the blessed Virgin and the saints, as our intercessors. 4, That the images of Jesus Christ, and His saints, ought not to be taken down. 5, That there is a Purgatory after this life. 6, That infants are born in original sin. 7, That baptism takes away that sin.*

Eck alone spoke in defence of the Popish doctrines ; but the absence of Zwingle greatly disconcerted him, and nullified the chief object of the diet. " I thank God," wrote Œcolampadius to Zwingle, " that you are not here. The turn that matters take makes me clearly perceive that, had you been here, we should neither of us have escaped the stake. How impatiently they listen to me ! But God will not forsake His glory, and that is all we seek." The assembly, being entirely governed by Eck, pronounced an excommunication against Zwingle and all his adherents, and particularly required of the senate of Basle to deprive Œcolampadius of his office, and to banish him. It also strictly prohibited the sale of the books of Luther and Zwingle, and forbade all innovations—all change in worship or doctrine, under severe penalties.

The Papal party affected to make much of their victory at Baden ; but victory was only in appearance. Œcolampadius was received with open arms at Basle, and Haller was retained in the exercise of his functions, notwithstanding the excommunications launched against him. The cantons of Zurich, Berne, Basle, and Schaffhausen, demanded permission to inspect the acts of the assembly, but they were not allowed to see them : on which account they refused all further concern with the official decision of the diet.

* Du Pin, folio ed., vol. iii., p. 201 Hess ,pp. 240-250.

A dispute, which immediately followed on the return of Haller and the deputies from Baden, fairly tested the strength of both parties. For six months preceding the conference, the Reformer had suspended the celebration of mass in Berne. The smaller senate, influenced by the decrees of Baden, insisted on his restoring it. He firmly but respectfully refused, and appealed to the larger senate. They no doubt felt the difficulty of their position. Will they annul the generous edict of 1523, and confirm the persecuting mandate of 1526 ? The populace came to their help. The people, by whom Haller was much loved, assembled in multitudes, and expressed their determination not to be deprived of their Christian pastor. The senate, yielding to the popular commotion, decreed : That he should resign his dignity, but continue in his ministerial functions, and that the celebration of mass should not be required of him. The day was evidently past for communities to be governed by Papal edicts or alarmed by Church censures. The strength of public feeling, embittered by religious strife, was far beyond their reach. The breach which separated the Papal and the Protestant parties was widening day by day, and the spirit and position of each becoming more and more hostile.

The Catholic cantons, or those most firmly attached to the faith of their fathers, Lucerne, Uri, Schweitz, Unterwalden, and Zug, which are frequently spoken of as *the five*, perceiving the instability of Berne in the case of Haller, offered to the authorities to send deputies to assist in the maintenance of the old religion. This message, fortunately, offended the pride of Berne—a military state. The government replied : "That the embassy proposed was quite unnecessary, since the people of Berne were sufficient for the management of their own affairs, and the care of their religion was of all others most especially their own." They now revoked any engagement they had come under at Baden by their deputies ; they confirmed the edict of 1523 ; and decreed that a public disputation should be held in their city during the winter following, for the final decision of the disputed questions.

THE GREAT CONFERENCE AT BERNE.

The Bishops of Constance, Basle, Zion, and Lausanne, together with all their most eminent theologians, were summoned to appear at this great conference, on pain of forfeiting such of their possessions as lay in the Bernese territory. They commanded all their own divines to be present, and stated that the Holy Scriptures would be the only standard of appeal. At the same time they published **ten articles,** to be maintained by the advocates of the Reformed Churches, and to be the subject of the conference.

1, That the Church, of which Jesus Christ is the only Head, sprang from the Word of God, and subsists by the same Word. 2, That the Church ought to observe no other laws, and is not subject to the traditions of men. 3, That the death of Christ on the Cross is a sufficient expiation for the sins of the whole world, and they that seek salvation in any other way deny Jesus Christ. 4, That it cannot be proved by any testimony of Scripture, that the body and blood of Jesus Christ is corporeally received in the sacrament. 5, That the sacrifice of the mass is opposed to Scripture, and derogates from the sacrifice of Christ. 6, That Christ is the only intercessor and advocate for His people with God the Father. 7, That the existence of a Purgatory cannot be proved from Scripture; therefore, the prayers, ceremonies, and annual services for the dead are useless. 8, That the worship of images, statues, and pictures, is contrary to the Word of God. 9, That marriage is not forbidden to any order of men. 10, That all lewd persons ought to be put out of the communion of the Church, as the Scriptures teach us; for nothing is more unbecoming the order of priesthood than a lewd and unchaste celibacy.*

Haller, the real author of the ten articles, naturally turned to Zwingle for help in their defence. "If you do not stretch out your hands to me," he wrote, "I fear all is over." The contest seemed unequal. On the one side the Roman hierarchy, with the sanction of ages, the prejudices of mankind, and backed by the authority of the civil powers; and on the other side, Berthold Haller, a modest, timid preacher of the Gospel. But the sword of the Spirit was invincible. Nevertheless the servant of the Lord had to prove, through deep exercise of soul, his own weakness and where his great strength lay. Zwingle, as well as Œcolampadius, promised their assistance. The decisive moment was at hand. The success of the Reformation throughout the whole of Switzerland was involved in the approaching assembly.

THE OPPOSITION OF ROME.

The Catholic party, apprehending the results of the conference, made great efforts to prevent it. They assembled at Lucerne, and strongly opposed the meeting, referring the Bernese to the disputation of Baden as having sufficiently decided the questions at issue. The Catholics of Germany also addressed a strong remonstrance to the government of Berne, dissuasive of the conference. "They implored them not to be seduced unto those novelties by the influence of a few foreigners, but to adhere to the religion of their fathers and forefathers, under the shadow of which they had achieved so many glorious victories, and extended so widely the boundaries of their dominions." To this plausible appeal the senate of Berne nobly replied: "That

* Waddington, vol. ii., pp. 327-336; Scott, vol. iii., pp. 1-25; D'Aubigné, vol. iv., pp 361-385; Hess, pp. 250-258.

the religion of Christ, that the salvation of souls, that the peace of the republic, were at stake ; and that from a resolution thus grounded no reasons could possibly move them." Other means of persuasion and intimidation were then attempted. The Friburgers even endeavoured to excite the people of Berne to rise against their rulers. Passports were refused to the evangelical ministers ; and all persons were forbidden to pass through the territories of the Catholic cantons to the meeting. Nor did the Emperor suffer his numerous engagements to prevent his writing to the government of Berne, urging them to change their mind and refer the whole question to a general council.

The reader must draw his own conclusions as to the motives of the Catholics in uniting all their energies to prevent the proposed assembly. They dreaded the light of plain Scripture. Roman Catholicism can only exist in gross darkness as to the truth of God. But their remonstrances and menaces were all in vain. The senate was firm ; and the evangelical principles had made such manifest progress among all classes of the inhabitants, that any attempt to arrest the cause of Reform would have immediately ended in a popular commotion and bloodshed.

THE OPENING OF THE CONFERENCE.

On the 7th of January, 1528, the **great conference** was opened. None of the prelates, and very few of the higher powers who had been invited were present ; yet a great number of ecclesiastics and learned men assembled from all parts of Switzerland and the surrounding countries. As many as a hundred evangelical teachers from Glaris, Schaffhausen, St. Gall, Constance, Ulm, Lindau, Isenach, Augsburg, Strasburg, and other places proceeded first to Zurich, in order to go in a body with Zwingle. But so suspicious were the Zurichers of Papal treachery, and so anxious about the safety of their own Reformer, that the magistrates sent forward his party under a strong military escort.

More than three hundred and fifty ministers of the Gospel were present at the disputation. Many of those worthy men deserve a place in our history for the Lord's sake ; but we can only give the names of a few. Haller was supported by Zwingle, Œcolampadius, Capito, and Bucer, the flower of the Swiss and Strasburg Reformation ; there were also Pellican, Bullinger, Blaurer, Hoffmeister, Megunder, Zingk, Schmidt, the burgomaster Reust, and Vadian, consul of St. Gall. On the side of the Papacy the cause was left, says Waddington, " to the feeble protection of men without talents or learning, or any sort of reputation or authority not comparable to Eck and Faber— Alexius Grad, Tregarius, Buchstab, Edidius—names which appear on no other occasion on the page of history. But the positions of Haller were defended with much solid erudition and great and practised talents." If we accept a few feeble attempts by the Papal party to disturb the unanimity of the Reformers, there was no feature of any remarkable interest in the whole assembly, at least to readers in our day.

THE REGULATIONS OF THE CONFERENCE.

Four presidents were appointed ; and, that everything might be recorded with unimpeachable fidelity, four secretaries were chosen—two by each of the two parties—and sworn to give a faithful account of the proceedings. The meeting took place in the Church of the Franciscans, and lasted from the 7th till the 28th of January. Two sessions were held daily, and each session was opened with prayer. Perfect freedom of debate was allowed to both parties, with this one condition, " That no proof should be admitted but from Scripture, nor any explanation of the proofs which was not also supported by Scripture—no judge being allowed but Scripture explained by itself, that is, by the comparison of more obscure parts with those which are more clear." The ten theses composed by Haller were successively discussed. Zwingle, Œcolampadius, Capito, Bucer, and Haller defended them alternately with so much success, that a great majority of the clergy of Berne, together with the canons the prior and sub-prior of the Dominicans, signed the ten articles, declaring that they judged them in perfect accordance with the sacred Scriptures. The presidents of the assembly then exhorted the magistrates to adopt such measures for the interest of religion as they should deem wise and practicable.

THE RESULTS OF THE CONFERENCE.

The authorities proceeded immediately to act upon the advice of the presidents. The altars were removed from the Churches, and the images were destroyed, yet without disorder and bloodshed. They published a decree, with the concurrence of the citizens, proclaiming the ten articles as the creed of all. They further, by this decree, deprived the four bishops of all spiritual jurisdiction within their territories, ordering the removal of all such rural deans as opposed the Reformation, and the abolition of the mass and images at Berne for ever. Thus was the downfall of the Papacy throughout that extensive canton completely accomplished, and the idols which had reigned for twelve hundred years were overthrown and destroyed in one day !

When **Constantine** made the profession of Christianity a pathway to worldly preferment, his heathen soldiers and senators eagerly rushed into the Church. But alas ! they brought their idolatries with them. It was then that statues, images, paintings, pomps, festivals, vestments, and the demigods of paganism were introduced into the professing Church ; and all this, that

51

she might enjoy the favour of princes. From the fourth till the sixteenth century, idolatry was supreme, and the Word of God was degraded and rejected by the dominant Church. But now we see a greater than Constantine—son of a herdsman in the valley of the Tockenburg—the humble pastor of Zurich ; standing before us, through grace, as the noblest champion of the Word of God, and the most uncompromising enemy of the Judaism and the paganism of Rome, that the sixteenth century has furnished us with. Luther was a great Reformer as to doctrine, but feeble as to idolatry. Zwingle was valiant in both. Here, all praise be to the God of all grace, and the power of His Holy Spirit, Zwingle restores the long banished Bible to its right place, and purifies the Church of its inveterate abuses.

Before leaving Berne, he went to the Cathedral, where twenty-five altars and a great many images had been thrown down, and finding his way through these "eloquent ruins," he ascended the pulpit in the midst of an immense crowd. In great emotion he said : "Victory has declared for the truth, but perseverance alone can complete the triumph. Christ persevered even until death. Stand fast, my brethren, in the liberty wherewith Christ has made you free, and be not entangled again with the yoke of bondage. Fear not ! That God who has enlightened you, will enlighten your confederates also, and Switzerland, regenerated by the Holy Spirit, shall flourish in righteousness and peace."

The work was severely complete. "The citizens were commanded without exception, to withdraw their obedience from the Episcopal authorities ; deacons, pastors, and all other ministers of the Church, were absolved from their oaths of allegiance to the bishop ; altars, images, and masses were abolished throughout the territory, together with the long list of Pontifical observances and ceremonies, such as anniversaries of the saints, dedications of Churches, the use of sacred vestments, fast-days and feast-days." The capital adopted the new form of worship, and in the space of a few months all the municipalities of the canton followed the example.

THE MERCY OF THE GOSPEL.

How seldom it has been our lot to witness a great victory celebrated by acts of mercy ! Alas ! this is a new thing in Christendom. It has never been so in the reign of Jezebel. Her disobedient children have either been drowned in blood or consumed in fire. But the principles of the Papacy are essentially opposed to the mercy of the Gospel. Fire and sword are the arguments of the one, love and mercy of the other.

At Berne, we find that the great triumph of the truth was celebrated by public rejoicings and deeds of mercy. The magistrates opened the prison doors ; two men condemned to death were pardoned ; others who had been banished from the republic were recalled—her exiles returned to their homes. Thus charity followed in the footsteps of faith and victory. "A great cry resounded far and wide," writes Bullinger, "in one day **Rome had fallen** throughout the country, without treachery, violence, or seduction, by the strength of the truth alone." The monks resigned their monasteries into the hands of the magistrates : the funds were appropriated for benevolent and educational purposes, and the religious houses were converted into schools and hospitals. And now we find the princely monastery of Königsfeldt was also devoted to the same useful purposes. "If a king or emperor," said the citizens, "in alliance with us, were to enter our city, would not we remit offences, and show favour to the poor ? And now the King of kings, the Prince of Peace, the Son of God, the Saviour of mankind, has visited us, and brings with Him the pardon of our sins, who only deserve eternal banishment from His presence. And can we better celebrate the advent of Him to our city than by forgiving those who have trespassed against us ? "

In the same strain followed a moral and political regeneration, which was not among the least honourable or merciful accompaniments of the Reformation. All mercenary service to foreign powers was prohibited, and foreign pensions abolished.

At Easter, the Lord's Supper was celebrated for the first time according to the institution of the blessed Lord, and the practice of the apostles. As to Zurich, it was a time of great solemnity and deep interest. The citizens and their wives, in quiet sober dress, gathered round the table of the Lord, which recalled the ancient Swiss simplicity. The heads of the state, and the people mingled together, and each one felt that the Lord was present with them. "How can the adversaries of the Word refuse to embrace the truth at last," said Hoffmeister, "seeing that God Himself renders it so striking a testimony ? "

Thus was the Reformation established at Berne, and thus it has continued until the present day. If the disputation at Baden gave a temporary ascendency to the Papal party, it was more than counteracted at Berne. "The citizens of Constance, Schaffhausen, St. Gall, Glaris, Tockenburg, and other places, in which the struggle was till that time undecided, now boldly declared their adherence to the Reformation, and gave the customary proofs of their evangelical zeal by abolishing images, altars, and the mass."*

* For lengthy details of the great crisis, see Scott, vol. iii. He quotes from Bucer's account of the meeting, and from Munster's. He also quotes from Gerdes, Ruchat, and others. Du Pin, in apologising for the absence of the four bishops, says, " that disputes about matters of faith ought not to be determined by Scripture alone, because every one would explain it according to his own humour . . . that the law of God had provided another way to decide all doubts in religion, which is, to apply themselves to the Pope, and acquiesce in his determination." Such is the blindness of Rome's most reasonable, learned, and devout members.

THE REFORMATION OF BASLE.

According to all history, the triumphs of the Gospel in Berne produced a most sensible effect on several cantons, but more especially on those where the Reformed doctrines had previously found an entrance. Indeed, some venture to say that **all Switzerland was moved** by the decided part which that powerful canton had taken in the Reform movement. "It gave new life," says Wylie, "to the Protestant cause in every part of the country. On the west, it opened the door for the entrance of the Protestant faith into French-speaking Switzerland. On the east, in German Helvetia, the movement, quickened by the impulse communicated from Berne, was consummated in those towns and villages, where for some time it had been in progress. From the Grisons, on the Italian frontier, to the borders of the Black Forest, where Basle is washed by the waters of the Rhine, the influence was felt, and the movement quickened. The great mountains in the centre of the land where the glaciers have their seat, and the great rivers their birth-place, were alone unmoved : yet not altogether unmoved, for the victory of Berne sent a thrill of surprise and horror through the oberland."*

But the Reformation of the learned city of Basle was the most important consequence of the decisive step of the warlike Berne. In importance, it was next to Zurich and Berne in the Swiss Confederacy. We have already spoken of Basle in connection with the early days of Zwingle and Leo Juda, when they sat at the feet of the famous Wittenbach—the first to sow the good seed of the Gospel in Helvetia. Capito and Hedio successively watered that precious seed by their prayers, and the public expositions of the Gospel of the grace of God. And these were followed in 1522 by a yet greater evangelist, Œcolampadius. And here, too, the writings of Luther were printed by the famous Froben, and scattered over Switzerland and other lands.

THE PEOPLE IN ADVANCE OF THE GOVERNMENT.

For about six years the Gospel had been faithfully preached by the meek and pious Œcolampadius ; but with all his scholarly accomplishments he was wanting in decision and courage. It has been said by some that what Melanchthon was to the dogmatic Luther, Œcolampadius was to the prompt and courageous Zwingle. But the middle classes had been so taught by their pastor, that they were more in favour of a change of religion than the ruling powers. "There was," says D'Aubigné, " a **triple aristocracy**—the superior clergy, the nobles, and the university—which checked the expansion of Christian convictions." And these authorities, failing to discern the exact

* " History of Protestantism," vol. ii., p. 70.

moment for concession to popular opinion, were compelled to yield to the demands of the citizens, and to act according to their dictation ; that which ought to have been characterised as a peaceful Reformation, was accomplished (through the temporising of the magistrates) by a violent revolution.

A few years previous to this fresh excitement in 1528, the senate issued an edict : " That there should be an uniformity in the religious worship, and that on some future day a public disputation should be held on the subject of the mass, and the question of its continuance decided by vote." By this decree, the council flattered themselves that they had laid the foundation of public peace ; but, like all half measures in troublous times, it entirely failed of its object. Both the Roman Catholics and the Reformers continued to assail each other in public and private ; but from the boldness and bitterness of the Popish preachers, and their increasing violence, the citizens began to fear that they had their secret supporters among the leading men in the senate. This suspicion aroused the Protestants. They began to assemble in large numbers. But first of all they sent deputies to remind the senate of the obligation of their decree.

This was perfectly legal, and consistent with republican principles. But the friends of Popery, who resided for the most part in Little Basle, which lay on the other bank of the Rhine, assembled in arms, and brandishing their swords and lances, endeavoured to obstruct the passage of the petitioners to the town hall. Meltinger, the burgomaster, and an intrepid leader of the Papists, had great influence in the senate, and haughtily refused the petition. Meyer, who was also burgomaster, and an equally zealous friend of the Reformation, had with him the majority of the people. A collision became inevitable. " The fatal hour approaches," said Œcolampadius, " terrible for the enemies of God." Much debate ensued with no good results. The council affected to be neutral ; trial was made of soft words ; both parties were advised to retire to their homes ; but it was too late, the tumult was gradually rising into a tempest. The deputies not only stood firm, but proceeded to demand " that those senators who encouraged the Papal preachings, in contempt of the decree, and to the promotion of disorder and discord, should be deprived of their dignity." This, the senate altogether refused ; and from this moment the agitation increased. Basle soon wore the appearance of a military camp, which an accidental blow might have changed into that of a battle-field.

BASLE IN A STATE OF SIEGE.

On the night of the 25th of December, the partisans of the bishop, alarmed at the appearance of affairs, met under arms, and raised the cry that an Austrian army was coming to their aid. This was the first formal departure from the legal course. The Protestants hearing this terrible cry, hastily arose from their beds, seized their arms, and repaired to the Gardeners' Hall, the rendezvous of their party. The news of what was going on in Basle brought many deputies from both Reformed and Catholic cantons, to express their sympathy and offer their mediation. But the Reformed citizens were anxiously awaiting the decision of the magistrates. Both parties remained under arms for several days and nights. All the gates of the city, except two, were closed ; and strong guards were posted in every quarter. The senate continued its sittings ; one edict after another was issued, but so temporising, that they increased rather than appeased the violence of the crisis. The Protestants, considering what was due to the glory of Christ to public justice, and to the welfare of their posterity, repeated their remonstrances to the council, and demanded an immediate answer.

On the 8th of February, 1529, the senate replied, " That those senators whose removal was required should refrain from voting on religious questions, but should retain their seats and voices upon all others." The citizens began to fear from the delays required, and the half-measures proposed, that some evil design was thereby concealed, and that their liberties were in danger as well as their religion. This so incensed the citizens, that they took military possession of the gates and towers of the city, and demanded the removal of the suspected members without delay. However contrary such proceedings were, and ever must be, to the Gospel of peace, we must bear in mind what the principles of a popular government are, what the education of those men had been, and that they were only emerging from the darkness of Popery. But a merciful providence so overruled this great commotion that no blood was shed, though a great victory was gained.

For fifteen days the patience of the townspeople had been sorely tried by the halting policy of the council. Basle was on the eve of a civil war, and, what is worse, " a war of hearths." The senate was suspected of treachery. " The mass, the mass— or to arms ! to arms ! " was the Catholic cry, accompanied with a storm of insults, invectives, and sanguinary menaces. The Protestants replied, " No mass, no mass—not even a single one more : we will die sooner ! " The senate was embarrassed. Œcolampadius retired to his pulpit, and preached meekness and patience with such unction that the people were melted to tears. Prayer was offered up to God that He would direct them to those measures that would be for His glory and the deliverance of His people from the superstitions of Rome. Sincerely believing that they were contending for their civil and religious liberties, they resolved not to yield. Twelve hundred men, all well armed, appeared before the senate house.   " We must have your reply to-night," said they.   It was nine of the evening. " To-morrow," said the council, " we will give you an answer," and begged the citizens to retire in peace to their homes. " No eyes shall be closed to-night in Basle," was the substance of their reply.   The Protestants resolved not to separate, and once more, and for the last time, they demanded the answer of the council that very night.   The lords of Basle began to think they had trifled long enough ; some concession must be made.

When near midnight, they sent a messenger to say : " That all members of senate who were relatives of priests would be excluded from that body, and as to the rest of their demands, all things touching religion and policy would be regulated according to their wishes."   This reply was so far satisfactory, but the citizens viewed it as little better than a further compromise, that their enemies might gain time ; so they agreed not to separate nor to relax their vigilance.

THE IDOLS DESTROYED.

While both parties were thus deliberating as to the future, an apparent accident speedily brought the whole matter to an issue.   Those who had been appointed to patrol the streets, and to inspect all the posts in the city, entered the Cathedral Church of St. Peter.   One of the men, urged by curiosity, opened a side door with his halberd, where a number of idols had been stowed away.   One of them falling on the stone pavement was broken to pieces.   The curiosity of the spectators was further moved by the sight of the fragments, and they began turning out the images one after another that were concealed in this closet. The floor was soon covered with heads, trunks, and broken limbs ; the priests, who were not far off, raised a great outcry, and attempted resistance, but this only hastened the work of destruction.   The rumour of a disturbance in the Church flew rapidly through the city.   Hundreds of armed burgers were immediately on the spot.   The hour of religious fury had arrived. " Why should we spare the idols that light up the flames of discord ? " cried the Protestants ; and the Cathedral was swept as by a hurricane.   The altars were demolished, the pictures were torn down, the idols were overturned, and the fragments piled up and set on fire in the public squares.

The priests, trembling with fear, hastened to conceal themselves from public view.   The senate came together in amazement, and attempted to interpose their authority, and appease the tumult, but it was too late.   They had failed in the first requisite in the art of popular government—the wisdom to discern the right time to meet the popular demand.   The citizens were long patient, but their determination gradually increased, and the senate was blinded by the influence of a small faction within it ; and now they must listen to the haughty reply of the people. "We are doing in one hour that on which you have been deliberating for those three years, whether it should be done or not." While the iconoclasts respected all kinds of private property, no symbol of idolatry was spared. Under the blows of these zealous burgers all the idols in all the Churches fell, and were cast into the flames, so that they lighted up the darkness of the night, and warmed the chilly and excited crowds.

The people carried the day ; the senate submitted. Twelve members—opposed to the Reformation—were dismissed to an honourable obscurity, and the demands of the citizens were granted. "They decreed : 1, That the citizens should vote in the election of the members of the two councils ; 2, That from this day the idols and mass should be abolished in the city and the canton, and the Churches provided with good ministers to preach the Word of God ; 3, That in all matters appertaining to religion and the commonwealth, two hundred and sixty of the members of the guilds should be admitted to deliberate with the senate."*

Such were the triumphs of these two eventful days. They had secured the establishment of the Reformed religion ; and gained, what were in their estimation, great civil advantages, and all without shedding one drop of blood. The two objects, civil and religious, were generally combined in the **Swiss Reformation.** "The commencement of the Reformation in Basle," says Ruchat, "was not a little tumultuous, but its issue was happy, and all the troubles that arose about religion were terminated without injury to a single citizen in his life or goods." All the trades met on the 12th of February, and took the oath, guild by guild, of fidelity to the new order of things. The following Sunday the Reformed worship was introduced in all the Churches of Basle, with the singing of the Psalms in German ; and in the course of the week a general amnesty was proclaimed, covering all offences.

THE RESULTS OF THE REVOLUTION.

Everything was now changed in Basle. The leaders of the Papal party, priests, scholars, and monks, prepared to leave it. Not, however, from any fear of bodily harm, but from their dislike to the Protestant faith. Many of them were courteously entreated to remain ; **Erasmus** especially—the most eminent person who withdrew from Basle at this time. In writing to his friend Pirkheimer, a little before his departure, he says : "Œcolampadius made me the offer of his sincere friendship ; which I accepted on condition that he would allow me to differ

* Wylie's " History of Protestantism," vol. ii., p. 75.

from him on certain points. He would have persuaded me not to leave Basle. I told him that it was with reluctance I quitted the city, which, on so many accounts, was highly agreeable to me ; but I could not longer support the odium to which a continuance there would expose me, as I should be thought to approve the public proceedings of the place." Soon after this friendly interview he took his departure and removed to Friburg. His salaries, his credit with the great, with the Pope and the Papal party, were in danger if he remained any longer in that polluted residence. But so prone was this great man of letters to sarcasm and jesting, that he could not restrain his wit against the superstition of his own party. "So many were the insults heaped upon the images and crucifixes," he says, "as to make it strange, that those holy saints, who had been wont to display such prodigies of power on very slight offences, should have refrained, in this important emergency, from the display of their miraculous energies."

New professors, to supply the place of Erasmus and others, were invited to fill the vacant chairs in the University, and in particular, Myconius, Phyrgio, Munster, and Grynæus. At the same time an ecclesiastical order, or confession of faith, was published, which is considered one of the most precious documents of this epoch.*

THE SACRAMENTAL DISPUTE.

About the period at which we have now arrived, one of the most grievous sources of discouragement to the Reformers, both in Germany and Switzerland, was the dispute which arose about the sacrament of the Supper, commonly called **the sacramentarian controversy.** Luther, it will be remembered,† whom God used to raze to the ground almost every part of the Romish system, retained to the end of his days a superstitious reverence for a certain materialism in the supper which he called *consubstantiation* ; that is, "he believed in the presence of the flesh and blood of Christ with, in, or under, the bread and wine." He did not believe, like the Romanist, that the Lord's Supper was a sacrifice, or that the body of Christ in the elements should be worshipped ; but he maintained that the body was there, and received, not merely by faith, but corporeally by the communicant. Zwingle, on the other hand, was extremely simple in his views of the sacred Supper. He maintained that its grand design was a *memorial* or *commemoration.* "This do in remembrance of Me." At the same time he affirmed that it can only be properly commemorated *in faith.* We show the Lord's death— His death for us, the blood shed by which our sins are washed

---

* Scott, vol. III., p. 40 ; Waddington, vol. ii., p. 321 ; D'Aubigné, vol. iv., p. 416.
† See details, vol, ii., pp. 677-693.

away.   We thus rest in faith upon His death as the sure ground
of our eternal life, and joyfully feed on the rich spoils of accomplished redemption.

> " His precious Blood was shed,
> His body bruised for sin ;
> Remembering this, we break the bread,
> And, thankful, drink the wine."

But as we have already described the conference of Marburg,
we return and take up the thread of our history.

CHAPTER XLIV

The Extension of Reform in Switzerland

THE Reformation was now established in the three principal cantons, Zurich, Berne, and Basle. The example of these powerful states greatly influenced a considerable part of **German Switzerland.** In many places the citizens, who had been inclined to the Reformation but were undecided, now boldly declared their faith in the new doctrine. Schaffhausen, St. Gall, Glarus, Bienne, Thurgau, Bremgarten, Tockenburg, Wesen, and other parts of less consideration, were entirely or partially reformed. The effect of the discussions, followed by the zeal of those great centres, was also felt in **French Switzerland,** "lying at the foot of the Jura, or scattered amid the pine-forests of its elevated valleys, and which up to this time had shown the most absolute devotion to the Roman Pontiff."

THE MINGLING OF SPIRITUAL AND POLITICAL AFFAIRS.

But here we must pause for a moment and draw attention to the great and **common mistake of Protestantism** from the beginning—that of looking to the secular arm for protection, in place of simply witnessing for the truth, and trusting in the living God. No sooner had the Reformers broken with Rome than they, as if terrified by her remaining power, stretched out their hands to the civil governments and sought the shelter of their armies.

Luther, it is true, objected to the force of arms in the furtherance of the truth, and looked for the triumphs of the Gospel through the faithfulness of its friends ; yet, as we have seen, he agreed to the princes assuming the entire control over ecclesiastical and spiritual affairs from an early period of the Reformation. But Zwingle went much farther in this dangerous course. When troubles arose, and dangers beset the vessel of the Reformation, through the treachery of the Catholic cantons, he thought it his duty, like a true republican or a Christian patriot, to examine federal questions, to counsel the senate, and to sanction an appeal to arms. But the end of these unscriptural proceedings, as we shall soon painfully see, was the inglorious death of the illustrious Reformer, and an almost fatal blow to the evangelical cause in Switzerland.

From the time that the Reformed states assumed, or rather

usurped the functions of the Church, and the ministers of the Gospel interfered with politics, the clouds began to lower and the storm to gather. Desirous no doubt of strengthening the good work within their cantons, and of extending it without, the magistrates of Zurich and Berne published several edicts, prohibiting their subjects from attending mass and from speaking unfavourably of the recent changes, and ordered a better attendance on evangelical services ; and also, for the purification of morals, they issued a general proclamation against festivities, drunkenness, and blasphemy. But while the civil authorities were thus enforcing their religion by edicts, Zwingle descended from his sacred vocation to that of a political diplomatist. From this time the almighty arm of a divine providence, which had sheltered the great Reformer and the Swiss Reformation, seemed to be withdrawn ; and the council of Zurich, though for a time boastful, was smitten with indecision, weakness, and folly.

THE FIRST FALSE STEP—"CONFEDERACY."

Influenced, or rather misled, as we believe, by his republican education, Zwingle thought it but right for the Reformers and the Reformation to form **a league of self-defence.** Having long foreseen that the Reform movement would eventually divide his beloved country into two camps, he thought himself perfectly justified in promoting an alliance with the evangelical states. In the year 1527 he proposed what was called a *Christian Co-Burghery*, in which all the professors of the Gospel might be united in a new Reformed confederation. Constance was the first to intimate her approval of the new league ; Berne, St. Gall, Mulhausen, Basle, Schaffhausen, and Strasburg followed. "But this Christian Co-Burghery," says D'Aubigné, "which might become the germ of a new confederation, immediately raised up numerous adversaries against Zwingle, even among the partisans of the Reformation." The pastor of Zurich was now on dangerous ground, which the end too speedily proved. As a citizen he had been taught to consider the regeneration of his country as a part of his religion, and the Church in which he was cradled had for centuries wielded two swords. Even in the present day we are surprised to find how much Continental Christians are governed by what is national.

Luther, who was an imperialist, was entirely opposed to the policy of carnal resistance. "Christians," he said, "ought not to resist the Emperor, and if he requires them to die they are to yield up their lives."

THE FIVE CANTONS FORM A LEAGUE WITH AUSTRIA.

The Roman Catholics, on hearing of this new alliance of the Protestants, were filled with alarm and indignation. The five, or forest cantons, Lucerne, Zug, Schweitz, Uri, and Unterwalden, remained firm in their fidelity to Rome. The herdsmen of those mountains, long wedded to their habits, their traditions, and their religion, heard with grief and dismay of the terrible wickedness of the heretics in the plains below. As priests and monks arrived in the Oberland from those scenes of daring impiety, and told their wondrous stories to the excited mountaineers, they were inflamed to madness. This cannot be borne with, this pestilent heresy must be exterminated by fire and sword, was their first thought; and they burned with desire to light the faggots.

Almost entirely ignorant of the meaning of the word **Reform,** we can easily imagine their feelings when messenger after messenger came running to tell them that the altars at which their fathers had worshipped were being cast to the ground, that the images were ignominiously burnt in the public squares, that mass was abolished, and that the holy priests and monks were driven into exile. Their fanatical zeal being thus raised to the highest pitch, and fanned by the artful monks, they were ready for anything desperate; and they were only restrained from proceeding immediately to open violence by the superiority, both in numbers and power, of the Protestant cantons. The Bishop of Constance also appealed to them by letter, entreating them to act with firmness, or all Switzerland would embrace the Reform.

What is to be done? was now the important question. We can sit still no longer! To form an alliance with a foreign power without the consent of all the other cantons would be a violation of the fundamental principles of the Helvetic Confederation, and of the league of brotherhood. Nevertheless, allies we must have, and the claims of the Church are higher far than fidelity to the nation. And knowing that Ferdinand, brother of Charles V, and Archduke of Austria, was distinguished for his hatred of the Protestants, they entered into an alliance with this prince for the extirpation of Reform, and the maintenance of Romanism.

This was unconstitutional, unnatural, and cruel. Austria was the ancient oppressor and the natural enemy of the Swiss nation—the last quarter from which a Swiss canton might have been expected to seek help. "Had they forgotten," exclaims the modern writer, "the grievous yoke that Austria made them bear in other days? Had they forgotten the blood it cost their fathers to break that yoke? Were they now to throw away what they had fought for in the gory fields of Morgarten and Sempach? They were prepared to do this. Religious antipathy overcame national hatred. Terror of Protestantism suspended their dread of their traditional foe."* The alliance was so contrary to all national feeling and prejudice, that the

* Wylie's " History of Protestantism " vol. ii., p. 76.

Austrians had some difficulty in believing it to be in good faith. "Take hostages," said the mountaineers, "write the articles of treaty with your own hands ; command, and we will obey ! " The league was concluded, and sworn to on both sides, the 23rd of April, 1529, at Waldshut. It decreed, "that all attempts at forming new sects in the five cantons should be punished with death. And in case of emergency, Austria shall send into Switzerland six thousand foot soldiers, and four hundred horse, with all requisite artillery. And if necessary, the Reformed cantons shall be blockaded, and all provisions intercepted."

The report of these negotiations excited great distrust and alarm even among the enemies of the Reformation. By leagueing themselves thus with a foreign power, it was said, they were compromising the independence of Switzerland, and, instead of an ally, they would find a master. But these feelings, as the first blush of their patriotism, were soon extinguished by their hatred of the Zwinglians. The men of Unterwalden and Uri, in their fanatical zeal, suspended the arms of Austria with their own, and decorated their hats with peacock's feathers—the badge of Austria. This gave rise to the following lines which expressed the national feeling :

> " Wail, Helvetians, wail,
>   For the peacock's plume of pride
> To the Forest-canton's savage bull
>   In friendship is allied."

The eight cantons not included in this alliance, with the exception of Friburg, united in sending deputies to their mountain confederates, with a view to reconciliation. But they were everywhere disrespectfully treated. Feeling that they had the imperial army to fall back upon, the Papists offered every kind of insult to the doctrines and persons of the Reformers. "No sermon, no sermon ! " they cried ; " would to God that your new faith was buried for ever ! " The deputies, retiring in astonishment, were still further shocked in passing the door of the Secretary of State, where they saw the arms of Zurich, Berne, Basle, and Strasburg hanging from a lofty gibbet.

THE ROMISH CANTONS PERSECUTE THE REFORMED.

Thus **war seemed inevitable.** All things were tending to an open and immediate rupture. The men of the mountains became violent. In order to defend the religion of their fathers, and to exclude the new doctrines from their subjects, they began to fine, imprison, torture and put to death the professors of the Reformed faith. One of these cases, however, was so atrocious, that it roused the feelings of mankind, and speedily brought matters to a crisis.

James Keyser, a pastor of the canton of Zurich, and a father of a family, was making his way on Saturday, 22nd May, to Oberkirk, in the parish of Gaster, where he was to preach on the Sunday. When quietly and confidently walking along a woody part of the road, which he had often gone before, he was suddenly seized by six men, posted there to surprise him, and carry him off to Schweitz. He was brought before the magistrates, tried, and condemned to be burnt alive, on no other pretence than that he was an evangelical minister. The remonstrance of Zurich, to whose territory he belonged, was treated with derision, and the barbarous sentence was carried into execution. When first the pious man heard his sentence, he burst into tears ; but before the hour of his martyrdom arrived, the grace of God had so revived his courage and filled him with joy that he walked cheerfully to the stake, fully confessed his faith, and thanked the Lord Jesus in the midst of the flames, even to his latest breath, that He had counted Him worthy to die for the Gospel. " Go," said one of the Schweitz magistrates, with a sarcastic smile, to the Zurich deputies, " Go and tell them at Zurich how he thanks us ! " This was a defiant challenge to the men of Zurich, and so they understood it.

WAR DECLARED.

The Zurichers, exasperated at this outrageous conduct and regarding it as an affront to themselves, declared war against the five cantons. While it is the duty of the magistrates to defend the oppressed against the oppressor, it is the duty of the minister of Christ, to abide by his sacred calling, and only bring into the field the sword of the Spirit which is the Word of God. But here, alas ! impartial history has recorded the sad departure of the great Reformer from the gracious precepts of his Master, of which he ought to have been a living witness. The burning pile of his brother minister kindled the strongest passions of his soul as a citizen and a patriot. He raised a cry against the bigotry and intolerance of the forest cantons which resounded through all the confederation.

He called for the most energetic measures on the part of the authorities. In the council, in the pulpit, he exhorted them to take up arms, to be firm and fear not. Identifying himself with the army, of which he was chaplain, he exclaimed : " We thirst for no man's blood, but we will clip the wings of the Oligarchy ; if we shun it, the truth of the Gospel and the lives of ministers will never be secure among us. We must trust in God alone ; but when we have a just cause, we must also know how to defend it, and, like Joshua and Gideon, shed blood on behalf of our country and our God."

Had Zwingle been a magistrate in the council, or a general in the army, his appeals would have been consistent and inspiring ;

but he had forgotten that he was a minister of the Prince of Peace, and that the weapons of his warfare were not to be carnal, but spiritual, and mighty through the power of God. At the same time we must remember that it was against political abuses, and not against a difference of faith, that he called for force. " As for the mass, rites, idols, and superstitions," he said, " let no one be forced to abandon them. It is for the Word of God alone to scatter with its powerful breath all this idle dust. Let us propose to the five cantons to allow the free preaching of the Word of the Lord, to renounce their wicked alliances, and to punish the abettors of foreign service."*

MILITARY PREPARATIONS.

Meanwhile the Popish cantons were not idle. They knew what they had done, and what they had to expect. The war of religion was begun. The sound of the war-horn re-echoed in the mountains and the valleys. Men were arming in every direction ; messengers were sent off in haste to Austria ; but Ferdinand, having been attacked by the Turks, could not furnish them with the troops he had promised. Nevertheless, firmly united among themselves, the men of the five cantons marched under the great **banner of Lucerne**, on the 8th of June, to join the battle with the Reformers. Zurich saw there was not a moment to be lost. Four thousand men, on the 9th of June, well armed, issued from the gates of Zurich to meet the foe. The walls and towers were crowded with spectators to witness the departure, among whom was Anna, the wife of Zwingle. At nine in the evening they arrived at Cappel, a village on the frontiers of Zurich and Zug. At daybreak, on the morning of the 10th, the Zurich warriors sent a herald with a formal declaration of war, and of the rupture of the alliance. Immediately the small town of Zug was filled with cries and alarm. The sudden march of the Zurichers had taken them by surprise ; great consternation prevailed : men hastening to put on their armour, and women and children in tears.

But just as the first division of the Zurich army, consisting of two thousand men, was preparing to cross the frontier, a horseman was observed spurring his steed up the hill at full gallop. It was Œlbi, Landamman of Glaris. " Halt ! " he cried, with great emotion ; " I am come from our confederates. The five cantons are prepared, but I have prevailed upon them to halt if you will do the same. For this reason I entreat my lords and the people of Zurich, for the love of God and the safety of the Confederation, to suspend their march at the present moment. In a few hours I shall be back again. I hope, with God's grace, to obtain an honourable peace, and to prevent our cottages from being filled with widows and orphans."†

* D'Aubigné, vol. iv., p. 477.   † D'Aubigné, vol. iv., p. 480 ; Wylie, vol. ii., p. 82.

Œlbi was thought to be an honourable man, and friendly to the Gospel ; therefore the Zurich captains suspended their march. Many believed his embassy to be peace, but Zwingle suspected treachery. Troubled and uneasy in his camp, he beheld in Œlbi's intervention the subtlety of Satan. Unable to obtain assistance from Austria at that moment, they feigned a desire for peace in order to gain time. With something like a prophetic vision, Zwingle went up to Œlbi, whom he knew well, and earnestly whispered in his ear : " Godson Amman, you will have to answer to God for this mediation. Our adversaries are in our power ; this is why they give us sweet words. By and by they will fall upon us unawares, and there will be none to deliver us." No prophecy was ever more literally fulfilled, as we shall soon see. " My dear godfather," replied Œlbi, " let us act for the best, and trust in God that all will be well." So saying, he rode off to Zug, leaving Zwingle in deep thought, anticipating a dark and terrible future. " To-day they beg and entreat," said he, " and in a month, when we have laid down our arms, they will crush us."

THE TREATY OF CAPPEL.

The deputies of Zurich and of the Romanists, with the exertions of the neutral cantons, were sixteen days in drawing up and agreeing to the articles of peace. During this time the soldiers of both armies behaved in the most orderly and friendly manner. They seemed to remember only that they were all Swiss. In the **camp of Zurich,** Zwingle, or some other minister, preached every day. " No oath or dispute was heard ; prayers were offered up before and after meals ; and each man obeyed his superiors. There were no dice, no cards, no games calculated to excite quarrels ; but Psalms, hymns, national songs, and bodily exercise, were the military recreations of the Zurichers. At length a treaty was concluded on June 26th, 1529, which, as Zwingle thought, was only a suspension of the storm. The warriors now struck their tents and returned to their homes."

The terms of this treaty, though not all that the Protestants desired, were nevertheless favourable to Reform, yet not unfavourable to the Catholics. It was agreed that the forest cantons should abandon their alliance with Austria ; that liberty of conscience should be guaranteed to all subjects ; and that the smaller parishes should decide by a majority of votes which religion they would profess. The people of Zurich—not Zwingle —were elated with the success which had crowned their warlike demonstration. The Bernese, who had contributed nothing towards this bloodless victory, were becoming jealous of the growing influence of Zurich, and, unhappily, a spirit of disunion sprang up between those powerful states, which led to the great catastrophe of 1531.

ZWINGLE'S CHRISTIAN CONFEDERATION.

Just at this time when the mind of Zwingle was too much occupied with politics, he fell into the snare of the enemy. Satan knew his weak points as a Christian, and tempted him with grand ideas of the unity of all Switzerland, and of the Reformed Christendom, by a unity of faith. His motives, no doubt, were of the purest and loftiest character. Meditating day and night how he might advance the Reformation, and overthrow that terrible power which had held the nations of Europe so long in bondage, the idea of a holy confederation, consisting of all the Protestant states and nations of Europe, filled his active mind. All Christendom was under his eye. No man of his day had such a comprehensive grasp of its condition—political, military, and religious. But not seeing the difference between the principle of law in the Old Testament, and of grace in the New, he honestly thought that it was the duty of the Protestant states to put forth their military power in defence of the Gospel. "Why should not," he said, "all the Protestant powers unite in a holy confederation for the purpose of frustrating the plans which the Pope and the Emperor are now concocting for the violent suppression of the Reformation?"*

This colossal **scheme of the Reformer** led him into many negotiations to which we need not refer. While they would have done honour to a statesman, they were a reproach to a Christian minister. But whatever were his projects, or whatever his mistakes, his object was one, and a noble one—the spread and establishment of the pure Gospel all over his native land. This to Zwingle was dearer far than life; and the Master knows how to give His servant credit for a good motive, even though He cannot approve of his work. Besides, it is positively affirmed that Zwingle never abated for a moment his pastoral labours; that he was present on all occasions when his duty called him.

THE FIVE CANTONS VIOLATE THE TREATY.

The Popish cantons, enraged at the progress of the Reformation, and its near approach to their own gates, were eager to find some pretext for ridding themselves of the Treaty of Cappel. This was not difficult to find. They had never really kept it. What was called in the treaty "liberty of conscience," or what was beginning to be called by the Protestants "the rights of conscience," the Catholics never acknowledged. They knew no distinction between religious and civil obedience. With this fundamental position of the Protestants, the Catholics never could for a moment agree. It necessarily became a principal matter of contention, and the source of innumerable local jealousies and controversies, which daily increased the irritation,

* Wylie, vol. ii., p. 86.

and determined the mountaineers openly to violate the treaty.

The cup of **Catholic indignation** was at length full. Blood! blood! was the cry. Nothing but the blood of living Christians could atone for the destruction of the dumb idols; nothing but the burning piles of God's saints could answer for the ashes of their altars and images. O Rome! Rome! when wilt thou be satisfied with the blood of God's redeemed? Thy thirst is unquenchable. The oceans which thou hast shed have only inflamed it. On every possible occasion during thy usurped dominion we see thee thirsting for blood. But what will it be when thy reign is ended, and no more blood to shed? That awful word "remember" will throw thee back over the past and fill thee with visions of blood, visions of the dungeons of the Inquisition, and of the flames of thy innocent but helpless victims. Then all will be changed. Unmingled, unending blessedness, shall be their happy portion; but what of that place where the flames shall never be quenched, where the worm shall never die, where the visions of the past shall ceaselessly flit before thy sleepless, restless soul, and where one drop of cold water shall never be procured to cool thy burning tongue? There we must leave thee to the fruitfulness of thy memory, the accusations of thy conscience, and the upbraidings of those whom thou didst deceive by thy sorceries, and drag down by thy delusions to those regions of endless woe.

THE FLAMES OF PERSECUTION REKINDLED.

Switzerland was now divided into two camps, and the gulf which separated them was daily widening. The Forest-cantons, backed by the Emperor and his brother Ferdinand, recommenced the persecution of the Protestants with more fury than ever. They indulged in the most atrocious barbarities. The preachers and the professors of the Reformed faith, wherever they could find them, they imprisoned, confiscated their goods, cut out their tongues, beheaded, and burned them alive. Those who escaped their intolerance implored the protection of Zurich. Under these circumstances, Zwingle thought it his duty to raise his voice and arouse the confederate cantons. He visited many places in person, addressed large assemblies, appealed to everything that could stimulate the zeal of the people, for the defence of the Gospel and the liberty of the subject. "These are Swiss," said he "whom a faction is attempting to deprive of a portion of their liberty transmitted to them from their ancestors. If it would be unjust to attempt to force our adversaries to abolish the Romish religion from among them, it is no less so to imprison, to banish, and to deprive citizens of their property, because their consciences impel them to embrace opinions which are obnoxious to their oppressors."

On the 5th of September, 1530, the principal ministers of Zurich, Berne, Basle, and Strasburg—Œcolampadius, Capito, Megander, Leo Juda, and Myconius, assembled at Zurich, and addressed to their Popish confederates an earnest and Christian remonstrance, but it was utterly disregarded. In a general diet held the following April at Baden, the disputes were renewed with more than their former violence. In vain did the mediating cantons entreat the two parties to banish every cause of discord. The Papal party, having made ample preparations, were now determined to make open war. The Zurichers were importunate in their complaints, and even called for a direct appeal to arms. Zwingle thought this the speediest way to bring the mountaineers to reasonable terms. The men of Berne were more temperate ; while they admitted that the five cantons had broken the Treaty of Cappel, and shamefully violated their own promises, they urged that a milder expedient should be tried.

THE BLOCADE.

" Let us **close our markets** against the five cantons," said the Bernese, " let us refuse them corn, wine, salt, steel, and iron ; we shall thus impart authority to the friends of peace among them, and innocent blood shall be spared." This resolution was adopted, duly published, and rigorously carried out. Situated, as these cantons were, on the mountainous part of Switzerland, the measure was one of extreme severity. From the nature of their country, the greater part of the people had little native produce besides their flocks. They were dependent for their daily supplies upon the harvest and markets of the plains. But now those markets were closed, and roads leading to the towns were blockaded. The consequences of this pitiless decree were most disastrous. Bread, wine, and salt suddenly failed from the chalets of the poor. Famine, with its invariable attendant, disease, spread dismay and death among the inhabitants. The cry of distress which arose from the mountains moved many hearts, and many voices were raised against the interdict, both within the confederate cities and outside the limits of Switzerland ; but it roused those who suffered from it to the highest pitch of indignation and resentment.

ZWINGLE'S POLICY.

As the part which Zwingle took in the political affairs of Zurich at this time has been much criticised by historians, and, we think, severely so by D'Aubigné, we quote the opinion of Dean Waddington, who will not be suspected of any leaning towards republicanism.

" It must here be mentioned that Zwingle expressed his decided opposition to these measures. Doubtless he, too, maintained that just principle, so constantly asserted by Luther, that the cause of reason and truth, when contending with proscriptive oppression, has no enemy so dangerous as the sword. He even ascended the pulpit and preached against the publication of the interdict. He argued that the insulting slanders of the Papists ought to be endured with Christian forbearance ; that an example of that great evangelical virtue was especially required from those who professed the Gospel. But his fellow-citizens closed their ears for once against his admonitions, and hastened whither their inauspicious passion led them."*

As a **matter of policy,** Zwingle maintained that, if the Catholic cantons were to be punished as evil-doers, the means apparently the most violent, were nevertheless the surest to bring them to a more submissive and reasonable temper, and the most humane in the end. But to reduce a whole population to famine would fill the land with the wail of suffering, and the cry of indignation. He also clearly saw that delay would be ruinous to Zurich. " By this measure," he said, " we give the five cantons time to arm themselves, and to fall upon us first. Let us take care that the Emperor does not attack us on one side, while our ancient confederates attack us on the other ; a just war is not in opposition to the Word of God ; but this is contrary to it—taking the bread from the mouths of the innocent as well as the guilty ; straitening by hunger the sick, the aged, children, and all who are deeply afflicted by the injustice of our adversaries. We should beware of exciting by this means the anger of the poor, and transforming into enemies many who at the present time are our friends and our brothers ! " † But notwithstanding these truthful and powerful appeals of the Reformer, the cantons, Berne in particular, were immovable.

The indignant mountaineers, on seeing themselves surrounded by a formidable power, alone with barrenness and famine between their lakes and their mountains, determined on violent measures. " They block up our roads," said they, " but we will make a way with out swords." They first had recourse to the observances of their religion. Prayers were directed to be offered up, pilgrimages to be made, paternosters repeated, and hymns to be sung. War would immediately have broken out had not the Catholic leaders found their advantage in delay. They knew that the Protestants were not agreed among themselves, and by delaying the attack they hoped to widen their divisions.

THE MEDIATORS RENEW THEIR EXERTIONS.

Several attempts were made at **reconciliation,** but without effect. Zurich and Berne demanded that the preaching of the Word of God should be permitted, not only in the common

* " History of the Reformation," vol. iii., p. 236.   † D'Aubigné, vol. iv., p. 536.

parishes, but also in the five cantons. This was asking too much under the circumstances ; and as they persisted in their demands, they only exasperated the proud and inflexible Catholics.

" No," they replied, " we will not listen to any proposition before the raising of the blockade." Deputies from all the cantons met on five different occasions between June 14th and August 23rd. The neutral cantons continued their exertions, with the assistance of ambassadors from foreign powers, until all the expedients that prudence and humanity could suggest were exhausted, yet they were unable to advance the parties a single step towards reconciliation.

The situation of the Reformer was becoming every day more painful and perplexing. It is impossible to contemplate his position at this moment without sharing the agonies of his broken heart. But alas ! he was off the direct line of the Word of God, and without His Divine guidance. In the troubled state of affairs, as the senate could not move without him, he allowed his natural feelings as a citizen to displace those of the Christian and the Reformer. But however well intentioned these services may have been, they were inconsistent with his high and holy calling. The unnatural union of Church and State, which had corrupted Christianity from the age of Constantine, was spreading confusion everywhere, and hastening the ruin of the Reformation. The tendency of Zwingle's policy, without doubt, was to weld them together ; still the Word of the Lord remains the same : " Be ye not unequally yoked together with unbelievers." And if this Divine precept, this ever-abiding Christian principle, be neglected, we may have to reap the bitter fruits of disappointment and disaster. So it was with this great and noble man. He mixed the Reformation with the strife of politics, and it was now far beyond his power to avert the fearful consequences.

THE POSITION OF ZURICH AND THE REFORMATION.

Zwingle was anxious, disquieted, and filled with the most painful forebodings as to the future. He saw the storm gathering on all sides. Those who had been his friends turned against him ; his enemies, taking courage from the ebbing tide of affairs, beset and torment him ; for there were many at Zurich whose hearts still clung to the hereditary despotism, though they had professed some zeal for the principles of Reform. The partisans of the monks, the friends of foreign service, pensioners, and the malcontents of every class, united in pointing out Zwingle as the author of all the sufferings of the people. Seeing his actions were misrepresented, and the measures he had counselled were rejected, he felt he had only to withdraw from public life.

The magistrates were dismayed. Both **Zurich and the Reformation are in danger** if Zwingle cease to pilot the ship ;

they were now in the same vessel, and on the stormy waters of religious contention. Immediately the council sent to him a deputation of honour, and entreated him not to forsake them at so critical a moment. Three days and three nights he spent in prayer, earnestly seeking Divine guidance. All the tenderness of friendship, and all the ardour of patriotism were employed in vain by the deputies ; but when they represented to him the blow that the Reformation would sustain if he left Zurich, he yielded, and consented to retain his post.

By thus consenting to remain at the head of affairs he had thought to recover all his former influence and restore harmony and courage to Zurich ; but he was bitterly disappointed. A strange infatuation seemed to possess both rulers and people. They daily became more and more indisposed towards the war which they at first so importunately demanded, and identified themselves with the passive policy of Berne. But as the Conference still professing pacific objects was held at Bremgarten, Zwingle, attended by two ecclesiastics, secretly repaired thither. He endeavoured to persuade his friends to raise the blockade ; representing to them the many evils which it had occasioned, and the fatal catastrophe in which it was likely to terminate. But his pleadings, though with tears and anguish of heart, were all in vain. On this occasion he took a mournful and last farewell of his young friend Bullinger, the pastor of the place, and commended to his charge the tottering Church of God.

WAR DECLARED AGAINST ZURICH.

During the course of the negotiations the Forest-cantons remained intractable and warlike. Indeed the final proposals of the mediators would probably have been received by the Protestants, but they were decidedly rejected by the Catholics. Matters were now so much involved that war became inevitable. The preparations of the five cantons being completed, they took the field on the 6th of October, 1531. They were **the first in arms.** The defence of the Church and the Holy See were their real objects for waging war, though the interdiction of commerce was the ostensible grievance. The chiefs were closely united together, and the people, burning with indignation against those who had taken away their food, and were seeking to take away their religion, powerfully supported them. Their common faith and sufferings, united them, as by one spirit for one object, which could not fail to impart resolution and courage in action. But no alarm had yet been given. Zurich was asleep. All the passes were seized, all communication between Zurich and the five cantons had been rendered impossible. "The terrible avelanche," says our Swiss historian, " was about to slip from the icy summits of the mountain, and to roll over the valleys, even to the gates of Zurich, overthrowing everything in its passage, without the least forewarning of its fall."

In the hope of dividing the Reformed, the Catholics declared war, not against the body of the Reformers, but against Zurich only. The eye of Jezebel was set upon the blood of Zwingle. Whoever may be saved, he must be slain. So long as he lives there can be no peace for holy Mother Church in Switzerland. Let the battle be against the arch-heretic. Thus inspired by the Papal demon of war, the mountain warriors assembled in their chapels, heard mass, and then, to the number of eight thousand, began their march towards the Protestant frontier. A Papal army, twelve thousand strong, marched into the free parishes. The soldiers having entered the deserted Churches, and seeing the images and the altars broken down, their anger was kindled to madness. They spread like a torrent over the whole country, inflicting all the horrors of war wherever they came. The country people, terrified, and running from chalet to chalet, calling aloud for help, failed to arouse the bewitched Zurichers ; yet in four days was the ruin of Zurich accomplished.

THE INFATUATION OF THE COUNCIL OF ZURICH.

On the evening of the 9th, the council was called together by the assurance that war was begun. Only a small number assembled ; and instead of sounding the tocsin, or calling the people to arms, they despatched two councillors to Cappel and Bremgarten to ascertain what was going on. " The five cantons" said they, " are making a little noise to frighten us, and to make us raise the blockade." But at daybreak, on the morning of the 10th, they were aroused from their slumbers by the positive intelligence that the enemy had crossed the frontier and seized upon Hytzkilch. Still the council was but partially aroused. The day was spent in making speeches and lengthened, tedious debates. A vanguard of six hundred men with artillery was sent on to Cappel to oppose the invaders ; the main body was to follow. At seven in the evening the tocsin was sounded in all the country districts.

It was a fearful night, as if nature herself shuddered at the blood that was about to be shed. " The sun went down behind the Albis," says Wylie ; " the city, the lake, and the canton were wrapped in darkness ; with the darkness came trembling and terror. The bells were rung to summon to arms. They had hardly begun to toll when a tempest burst forth, and swept in terrific fury over Zurich and the surrounding country. The howling of the wind, the lashing of the waves of the lake, the pealing of the steeple-bells, the mustering of the landsturm, and the earthquake, which about nine o'clock shook the city and canton, formed a scene of horror such as had seldom been witnessed. Few eyes were that night closed in sleep. In the dwellings of Zurich there were tears, and loud wailings, and hasty and bitter partings of those who felt that they embraced probably for the last time."*

THE EVIL FOREBODINGS OF THE PEOPLE.

This dreadful night was to be followed by a still **more dreadful day.** The morning came, the tempest was past, but a bright dawn could not dispel the gloom that had settled in the hearts of the Zurichers. The sound of trumpets, and the beating of drums, were calling the inhabitants to arms ; but hours passed away before a few hundred soldiers could be mustered. " The irresolution of the council," says Hess, " filled the citizens with uneasiness, and lessened their submission ; for the vacillation of a government destroys all confidence, and orders given with hesitation are ill obeyed." Instead of an army of four thousand men, which the council had decreed should march to Cappel, only seven hundred were under arms at ten o'clock, and these were disorderly and agitated, without uniform and inefficiently armed. Zwingle, at the command of the council, and in conformity with the customs of his country, accompanied the army as chaplain. With a broken and a bleeding heart he embraced his beloved wife and his beloved children for the last time on earth. " I know," he said, " what all this means—it is all about me—all this comes to pass in order that I may die." He did not deceive himself as to the issue of the expedition, but he thought it his duty to obey the orders of his superiors, without urging any objections. Calm himself in the midst of friends who trembled for his life, he endeavoured to comfort them. " Our cause is good," said he, " but ill defended. It will cost my life, and that of a number of excellent men who would wish to restore Christianity to its primitive simplicity, and our country to its manners. No matter ! God will not abandon His servants ; He will come to their assistance when you think all lost. My confidence rests upon God alone, and not upon men. I submit myself to His sovereign will."

THE BATTLE OF CAPPEL.

At noon, under the drooping banner of Zurich, only seven hundred passed through the gates. The affectionate Anna was seen on the ramparts following her husband with her eyes so long as he was visible. But she had also in that ill-omened army, a son, a brother, a great number of near relations, and many intimate friends, of whose return she had no hope. She shared the forebodings of her husband, and like him, believed that it was for the holy cause of God and His truth that they thus

* " History of Protestantism," vol. ii., p. 93 ; see also D'Aubigné, vol. iv., p. 568.

exposed themselves to danger and to death—it was martyrdom.

Zwingle was observed to fall behind his troops. Those who were near him could hear that he was engaged in prayer. He thus rode mournfully alone, praying for the welfare of the Church of God, until he reached Mount Albis.

Cappel is only three leagues from Zurich, but the road crosses Mount Albis. On its summit they halted ; and some proposed that they should wait for reinforcements ; but the roaring of distant cannon announced that the battle had begun. This sound awoke the native feeling of Zwingle. " Hear ye not the roar of the cannon beneath us ? " he exclaimed, " they are fighting at Cappel ; let us hasten forward to the aid of our brethren." The words of Zwingle prevailed with the leaders, filled them with enthusiasm, and they pushed forward.

Early on the morning of that day the soldiers of the five cantons attended divine service, heard mass, the host was offered up for the sins of the people, and the army, eight thousand strong, began their march at nine o'clock. The division posted at Cappel was attacked by this army at one o'clock, but being ignorant of their force, contented themselves with keeping up a constant fire of artillery. In two hours the Zurichers bearing the "great banner," reached their comrades and joined in battle.

The Catholics, not knowing the extent of this reinforcement, would not hazard a general engagement. The artillery of the Zurichers being advantageously posted and well served, greatly disconcerted the Catholics, who were spread out on a morass beneath them. It was four o'clock ; the sun was sinking rapidly. Loud murmurs were heard in the ranks of the Catholics because of the tardiness of the chiefs. During this altercation, an experienced and brave warrior of the canton of Uri, at the head of three hundred volunteers, silently entered a wood on the left flank of the Zurich army, which they had neglected to occupy, and perceiving the weakness of the Protestant army, he immediately resolved to attack them. The mountaineers coming to the knowledge of this oversight, climbed the hill, and under cover of the beech-trees, opened a deadly fire on the men of Zurich. They were within a short distance of them, and ordered to pick out the men they desired to bring down. Having discharged their fire, they rushed out of the wood, sword in hand, and furiously charged the bewildered Zurichers, crying, " Heretics ! image-breakers ! we have you at last ! "

THE DEATH OF ZWINGLE.

The weakness manifested and the errors committed by the Zurich leaders, can only be accounted for on the principle of judicial blindness. They had gone far away from the narrow path of the Word of God, and He was no longer with them. The Church had become the state, and the state the Church, and the present army was composed of congregations and their ministers rather than of Swiss soldiers. This was failure which God must judge ; and the Catholics were the rod in His hand to chastise the children of His love. But what a moral ! What a lesson for Christians in all ages !

Finding themselves ensnared and surrounded, the men of Zurich fought desperately ; but, being only as one to eight, they were overpowered. And to increase the confusion, some of the enemies' spies joined the rear-guard and raised the cry of *treachery*, which ended in a general flight ; but all those who fought in the first ranks, being thus deserted, were cut down. The carnage was great ; the Alps were echoing and re-echoing the wild roar of battle, when the curtain of night fell, closed the scene of blood, and more than five hundred of the flower of Zurich slept the sleep of death. " The wisest of its councillors, the most Christian of its citizens, and the ablest of its pastors, were left on that fatal field."

But it is with shame and sorrow that we have to record the melancholy fact, that among the slain there were **twenty-five Christian ministers,** who had marched at the head of their flocks. In this respect, we doubt not, the battle of Cappel stands alone in the history of battles. Surely this was expression enough of God's sore displeasure against the unholy mixture of the Church and the world, of the theologians and the politicians, which obtained to such an extent in the Swiss Reformation.

But there was one death which affected Zurich and the Reformation in Switzerland more than all the others—the **death of Ulrich Zwingle.** Scarcely had the action begun, when, stooping to console a dying man, he received a wound on the head and fell to the earth. He attempted to rise, but he was thrice overthrown in the press, and received several wounds. He had not drawn his sword, but he had raised his voice, which was heard above all the uproar, to inspire the troops with courage, and to prevent confusion. Exhausted, he lay with clasped hands in the attitude of prayer, and was heard, to say, " Alas, what a calamity is this ! Well, they can indeed kill the body, but they cannot touch the soul." These were his last words.

THE CAMP FOLLOWERS.

When the field of Cappel was in the possession of the Catholics, the camp-followers, with lighted torches, began to prowl over the battlefield. In turning over the bodies—for the purpose of stripping or robbing them—when they found any who were still sensible, they said, " Call upon the saints and confess to our priests." If the Zuricher refused, he was instantly despatched as a vile heretic with oaths and curses. Among those heaps of slain was one whose eyes and hands were raised to Heaven. " Do you wish for a priest to confess yourself ? " said one of those slayers of the slain, holding the glimmering light of his torch against his expiring features. He shook his head. " If you cannot speak," said they, " invoke the mother of God, and the other saints for their intercession." He again shook his head, keeping his eyes fixed on Heaven. " This man, too, is an obstinate heretic," cried they. But a soldier, moved with curiosity, turned the head in the direction of a fire that had been lighted on the spot and exclaimed, " I think it is Zwingle ! " Whereupon, a Captain Tockinger, of Unterwalden, who came up at that moment, hearing the name, drew his sword, struck Zwingle on the throat, uttering many curses, and thus extinguished what remained of that remarkable life. And thus, too, was that Scripture fulfilled : " All they that take the sword shall perish with the sword " (Matt. 26. 52).

The night was cold ; a thick hoar-frost wrapt, as in a winding sheet, the bodies of the dead and the dying. At length the day appeared ; the body of Zwingle was recognised, and then the full hatred of his enemies—especially the foreign service men—broke out against him. After offering many indignities to the lifeless body, they held the mockery of a council, and summoned it before them. It was condemned, on the double charge of treason and heresy, to be **burnt to ashes.** The public executioner of Lucerne carried out the sentence, and the fanatical pensioners flung the ashes to the four winds of Heaven.

The condition of Zurich, when a few wounded men found their way home to tell what had happened, was beyond description terrible. But we dwell not on the agitation, confusion, sorrow. We only refer to it for the purpose of introducing one chief mourner—**Anna Zwingle.** She had heard from her own house the repeated discharges of artillery ! She feared the worst. What hours of anguish ! But at length she knows all ; her husband, son, son-in-law, brother, brother-in-law, and almost all her dear friends, lie cold on the heights of Cappel. But though a woman, a wife, and a mother, she was a true Christian, and committed herself and her young children to God's tender care, and sought to rejoice in the midst of her tears, that so many whom she loved had received the crown of martyrdom.

REFLECTIONS ON THE LIFE OF ZWINGLE.

As we have discussed pretty freely, in passing, the character and principles of **the great Swiss Reformer,** we have little to add by way of reflection. But we cannot bid farewell to this sad scene without offering our tribute of grateful respect to one whom God raised up and so wonderfully used ; and of expressing our deep sorrow that so great a light should have deviated from the narrow path, and led so many after him.

In tracing his steps from the herdsman's cottage in the Valley of the Tockenburg, we have seen much to admire and imitate, for which also posterity must be ever thankful. He pursued with constancy and fearlessness the convictions of his own mind, as to the teaching of the Word of God, so far as he understood its spiritual meaning and application. We can never forget nor undervalue the noble stand he frequently made for the absolute authority of the Word of God, and that, at a time when its existence was scarcely known, and had never been read even by the priests and monks. In those halls of public disputation, when he placed his Hebrew Bible and his Greek New Testament on the table before him, and appealed to these books as the only standard of faith and practice, God was glorified, His power was manifested, and the Catholics were utterly confounded, and driven back into the darkness of their superstitions.

Zwingle, as the representative man of his time, stood triumphant. The light of the Reformation progressed rapidly, and seemed as if it would soon shed its radiance over every mountain and valley in Switzerland. All but the Forest-cantons had received the truth, either wholly or partially ; and had he gone on in simple dependence upon the living God and the Word of His grace, even the Overland might soon have submitted to the new faith. But from the time that Zwingle counselled Zurich to punish the persecutors with the sword, he assumed the character of the politician. And though he was still the sincere Christian and the earnest Reformer, he thought it was his duty to study the cabinets of kings, the councils of the people, and the movements of armies. This was the rock on which the vessel of the Reformation struck, and struck with all sail set, and Zwingle at the helm. We have seen the wreck ; and surely it ought to be as a beacon-light to all Christians in all ages. But instead of that, there are many of the Reformed ministers so-called, even in the present day, who command the zeal of Zwingle as a patriot and a politician ; and argue that he suffered from the rashness of others.

True, he strongly objected to the blockade which led to the war ; but he advocated a direct appeal to arms, which is as far from the spirit of Christ as a commercial interdict. And the two things for which the Reformer urged the government of Zurich to take up arms were the *slanders* and the *persecutions* of the Papists. But what does the blessed Lord say ? " Blessed are ye when men shall *revile* you and *persecute* you, and shall say all manner of evil against you falsely, for My sake. Rejoice, and be exceeding glad ; for so persecuted they the prophets which were before them." And again : "Bless them which persecute you, bless and curse not." And knowing the state of irritation which slander and persecution would naturally produce, the gracious Lord condescends to approach the oppressed in terms of the greatest endearment. "Dearly beloved, avenge not yourselves, but rather give place unto wrath ; for it is written, Vengeance is Mine ; I will repay, saith the Lord. Therefore, if thine enemy hunger, feed him ; if he thirst, give him drink ; for in so doing thou shalt heap coals of fire on his head." Surely both the blockade and the appeal to arms meet their utter condemnation in these Divine precepts of our Lord and Master (Matt. 5. 11, 12 ; Rom. 12. 14, 19, 20).

The Christian is *saved* by grace, he *stands* by grace, and he ought to be the *witness* of grace, and that, under all circumstances. The last of these the great Reformer never understood. He never saw the truth of the Christian's separation from the world by the death and resurrection of Christ, or the heavenly relations of the Church as the Bride, the Lamb's wife. Still, the Word of God is plain enough, and we can find no shelter for our ignorance. At the same time, more allowance must be made for Zwingle than for many ministers of the Gospel in our own day, who take a leading part in the political affairs of the world. Emerging from the darkness of Popery, which has no argument but the sword, and nurtured in the midst of Swiss liberty, and in the histories of the ancient republics, he honestly believed from his earliest days that tyrants should be opposed, and that Christians should unite with the government in resisting them. From not seeing, after his conversion, the heavenly calling and character of the Christian, he acted on these principles as the leader of the Reformed party.

D'Aubigné, we are glad to find, so far agrees with the views we have expressed ; thus he writes : "Zwingle, observing how all the powers were rising against the Reformation, had conceived the plan of a **co-burghery**, or Christian state, which should unite all the friends of the Word of God in one holy and powerful league. This political phase of his character is in the eyes of some persons his highest claim to glory ; we do not hesitate to acknowledge it as his greatest fault. The Reformer, deserting the paths of the apostles, allowed himself to be led astray by the perverse example of Popery. The primitive Church never opposed their persecutors but by the disposition of the Gospel of peace. Faith was the only sword by which it vanquished the mighty ones of the earth." But Zwingle himself appears to have had some conflict in his mind on this subject, as he says : "No doubt, it is not by human strength, it is by the strength of God alone that the Word of the Lord should be upheld. But God often makes use of men as instruments to succour men. Let us therefore unite, and from the sources of the Rhine to Strasburg let us form but one people and one alliance."

As to his great intellectual powers, his literary and his theological works, we will allow a competent witness to bear his testimony. Dean Waddington, speaking of Zwingle, says: " When we regard the many ingenius and elaborate compositions, polemical, exegetical, hermeneutical, which he produced in little more than twelve years—years, too, distracted by a thousand other cares and occupations—and which will remain an everlasting memorial of an extensive erudition, a sound judgment, a temper, upon the whole candid and charitable, a calm, considerate, earnest faith ; it is a matter of serious sorrow, even now, that he was cut off thus unseasonably . . .

" Together with several just and profound views of Scriptural interpretation, his works contain many noble sentiments, flowing from an enlarged and elevated spirit. Gifted with much penetration, incited by an honest zeal, regulated by consummate prudence, firm and forbearing, he did not stain these great qualities by a single fault. He showed great sagacity in accomplishing his purposes ; he was never guided, either in his acts or in his writings, by any factious spirit ; and he was never suspected of any unworthy motive."*

Zwingle was not forty-eight years old when he died. He was in the full vigour of life and the maturity of his understanding. With gifts so rich and varied, what might he not have done for the Reformation of Switzerland, and even in Europe, had he restricted himself to the ministry of the Word of God ? But if we fail to do the Lord's work in His way, it may be taken from us and given to another. "No man that warreth entangleth himself with the affairs of this life ; that he may please Him who hath chosen him to be a soldier. And if a man strive for masteries, yet is he not crowned, except he strive lawfully " (2 Tim. 2. 4, 5).

TREATIES OF PEACE.

The news of the disgraceful treatment of the remains of Zwingle aroused the indignation and anger of Zurich. She rallied her forces, and the Bernese gathered from all quarters for the support of their ally. The combined army was very formidable ; they assumed the offensive, and **invaded the canton of Zug** ; but the Lord was not with them. With no combined plan of operation, they commenced in rashness and disunion, and insubordination prevailed ; while the Catholics were orderly, united, and resolute. The victory was easy and complete.

These successes, which far surpassed the expectation of the five cantons, inspired them with religious confidence as to the holiness of their cause ; and the Reformers, from their reverses,

* " History of the Reformation," vol. iii., p. 242.

became dispirited and disposed to treat for peace. Negotiations were renewed ; two treaties were drawn up and signed by the Zurichers and the Bernese, on the 16th and 23rd of November, which annulled the treaty of 1529, and gave decided advantages to the enemies of the Reformation. These treaties are of great historical importance, as they affixed a permanent boundary to the Reformation of German-Switzerland ; and no important change has been wrought among the cantons from that day even until now.

It is said that Zwingle, on his departure for Cappel, in the mournful conviction that he would never return, designated as his successor, the younger **Bullinger of Bremgarten,** who, after a short interval, was appointed chief pastor and professor of divinity, and filled the double charge for forty years, with undisputed distinction, and rendered extensive service to the Church of Christ. The same calamitous autumn witnessed the extinction of another of the brightest lights of the Reformation. The meek and gentle, the learned and devoted Œcolampadius, on hearing of the death of his friend, and the indignities which were cast upon his memory, died shortly after of a broken heart, at the age of forty-nine. When he perceived that his own departure was at hand, he assembled his friends and colleagues around him, and exhorted them in the most pathetic and affectionate manner to be steadfast, unmovable, always abounding in the work of the Lord, that God might be glorified, and the blessed cause of Christ become more resplendent through the light of their purity. Thus fell asleep the pacific Œcolampadius. His death was like his life, full of light and peace. He was succeeded at Basle by the learned and pious Oswald Myconius.*

The history of the Reformation in *French Switzerland*, which was somewhat later, and in which the names of William Farel and John Calvin bear a prominent part, we must pass over for the present, and return to Germany, that we may examine the last years and the closing scenes of the life of the great German Reformer.

* D'Aubigné, vol. iv., pp. 465-621 ; John Scott, vol. iii., pp. 104-120, with quotations from Ruckat ; " Life of Zwingle," by J. G. Hess ; Waddington, vol. iii., pp. 236-252 ; Wylie, vol. ii., pp. 77-95.

CHAPTER XLV

The Reformation in Germany

WE have already traced the history of the Reformation in Germany from the year 1517, when Luther nailed his theses to the Church door in Wittemberg, down to the year 1532, when the Emperor signed the **treaty of peace at Ratisbon.** The history of these fifteen years is certainly the most important in the annals of mankind, if we except the early part of the first Christian century. We pass through a succession of events, characterised by the grace and energy of the Holy Spirit, combined with the hand of God in government, and emerge from the darkness and superstition of Rome into the light and liberty of the truth of God. We know of no page in history which so commands not only our interest, but our adoration.

And how, it may be asked, was this mighty revolution so speedily accomplished ? Not by philosophy, not by the schoolmen, not by the Humanists, but simply by the truth of God acting on the conscience of man, through the power of the Holy Spirit. On what ground did Luther stand and triumph at the Diet of Worms ? The Word of God, sustained by His grace. On what principle did the princes prevail at Augsburg ? Precisely the same. And by what means did Zwingle put to flight the enemies of the truth at Zurich ? By appealing to the Word of God, and to that alone ; but when he shifted his position, giving up Divine ground for human, he became weak as other men. So long as conscience ruled in that noble mind, and raised that powerful voice, the mightiest of Rome's champions were confounded, and fled, ashamed, from his dignified presence. But alas ! when he connected the civil sword with the sword of the Spirit, the truth of God was dishonoured ; he had left the place of strength, and became the weakest of the weak. He had a bad conscience, his breastplate was gone ; and that always robs a man of courage, peace, and happiness. It is only by means of *conscience* that truth establishes its dominion over the minds and ways of mankind.

This fact, historically viewed, is wonderful, and demands our devout consideration. Luther was as free from fanaticism as he was far from hypocrisy ; he was perfectly simple ; but his conscience was honestly bound by the Word of God, and his affections were kindled by it, and thus, holding by that Word, all Europe was shaken by a power which faith can only understand. " To him that worketh *not*, but believeth, on Him that

justifieth the ungodly, his faith is counted for righteousness."
The two exquisite properties of faith are, to exclude human
power, and to bring in Divine. As the apostle says : " I can do
all things through Christ which strengtheneth me " (Rom. 4.
5 ; Phil. 4. 13).

We will now glance for a moment at the effects of this power
in the short period of fifteen years.

A BRIEF SURVEY.

The great truth which the early **Reformers preached**—salvation by faith without works of human merit—spread with a
rapidity resembling the light of Heaven. In a short time it had
travelled over the greater part of Europe. In the year 1530,
Luther, writing to the Elector, speaks of his dominions as if
they were a Millennial scene. " It gives me great pleasure,"
says the Reformer, " when I see the boys and girls can now
understand, and speak better concerning God and Christ than
formerly could have been done by the colleges, monasteries, and
schools of the Papacy, or than they can do even yet. There is
thus planted in your highness's dominions a very pleasant
paradise, to which there is nothing similar in the whole world."
The ground had been cleared of monasteries and convents, and
covered with Churches and schools.

Hesse, as well as Saxony, we have seen evangelised, and
planted with Churches and schools, and all regulated by the
government. In Franconia, Silesia, East Friesland, Prussia,
Brunswick, Luneburg, and Anhalt, the light of the Gospel was
spreading. Many of the free cities had opened their gates to
the preachers of the new doctrines, and were now rejoicing in the
truth, and boldly witnessing for it. The rapid conquests of the
Reformation in Switzerland, which we have examined with some
care, fall within the limits of our period. Along the chain of
Jura, by the shores of Leman, to the gates of Geneva, the light
of the Gospel had travelled. In Denmark and Sweden the
Gospel had gained a firm footing, and Bohemia, Moravia, and
Hungary had been revived. Even in the court of Francis I and
in the Sorbonne, renowned for its orthodoxy, there were true
believers in the doctrine of justification by faith alone ; but the
state ever was and is Roman Catholic ; and dearly she has had
to pay in her terrible revolutions for her rejection of the truth,
and the persecution of its witnesses. In England, the followers
of Wycliffe were revived, and the persecuted Lollards again
lifted up their heads, and testified for the truth with fresh
courage. The King, the Parliament, and the people threw off
the yoke of Rome in 1533, and Henry was declared *supreme head
of the British Church.* The authority of the Roman Pontiff was
then abolished in England. But the details of this important

event will form a distinct theme for our "Short Papers," the Lord willing.

As early as 1528, Luther's tracts and **Tyndale's New Testament** had done their blessed work in Scotland. The noble, gentle, and accomplished Patrick Hamilton was burned at the stake in the centre of the large area before the gate of St. Salvator's College, Aberdeen, on a charge of "holding and maintaining divers heresies of Martin Luther."*

A GREAT INCREASE.

After the pacification of **Ratisbon,** many who had concealed their opinions now came boldly forward and declared for the great truths of the Reformation. Princes, nobles, various regions and towns of Germany, year after year, professed without fear to have given up the old faith, and to have embraced the new doctrines.

An event, in its origin purely political, which occurred at this period, was so overruled, as to increase greatly the strength of the Reformers. In the year 1519, Ulrich, Duke of Wurtemberg, gave offence to the league of Swabia, and was expelled from his dominions, which were afterwards placed under the sceptre of Ferdinand. The exile prince, after a long captivity of seventeen years, was restored through the assistance of his kinsman, Philip of Hesse, to the dukedom of his ancestors. It appears that he attended the conferences at Marburg in 1529, and had received impressions favourable to the Reformation. "Hence," says Scultetus, "his first object on the recovery of his dominions, was to throw them open to the glory of Christ, and to introduce the preaching of the pure Word of God, and the administration of the sacraments, according to His institution." He also engaged the assistance of several theologians to organise churches, establish schools, and arrange other details on the principles of Protestantism. This must have been like life from the dead to those extensive dominions which had been under the sway of the bigoted Catholic Ferdinand.

The Reformation of the Duchy of Wurtenberg, was followed by that of Brunswick, Calenberg, Hanover, Pomerania, Mecklenburg, and the cities of Augsburg, Bremen, and Hamburg. But there was one accession to the Protestant cause about this time which demands a special notice as illustrating the overruling providence of God in those eventful times.

On the 24th of April, 1539, George, Duke of Saxony, died. He was head of the Albertine branch of the Saxony family and possessed, as Marquis of Mesnea, and Thuringia, extensive territories comprising Dresden, Leipsic, and other cities now the most considerable in the electorate. From the dawn of the

* Cunningham, vol. i., p. 220 ; Wylie, vol. i., p. 620,

Reformation he had been the most resolute and determined enemy of what he styled **Lutheranism.** It is probable that his opposition at first was from a sincere belief in the doctrines of Romanism ; but it became embittered by personal antipathy to Luther, and by the electoral princes, the other branch of the family, being his unfailing friends. By his death without issue, the succession fell to his brother Henry, whose attachment to the doctrines of the Reformation surpassed, if possible, that of his brother George to the Papacy. Like Ulrich, he invited some Protestant divines, and among them Luther himself, to meet him at Leipsic. In the course of a few weeks the whole system of ancient rites was overturned, and the full exercise of the Reformed religion established ; and that with the universal applause of his subjects.

This was an event of great advantage to the Reformation. It removed an inveterate enemy from the very centre of the Reformed states, and converted that which had been a point of weakness into a position of strength. These providential, yet mysterious, accessions greatly strengthened the Smalcald league, extending the boundaries, and increasing the numbers of the Protestants. The territories of the princes, and cities attached to their cause now extended, in one great and almost unbroken line from the shores of the Baltic to the banks of the Rhine.*

THE GREAT ACTORS PASSING OFF THE SCENE.

Many of the names with which we have become familiar, and who have sustained a conspicuous part in the **earlier history of the Reformation,** are now passing off the stage of time. " Having discharged the offices assigned to them," says Dean Waddington, " they had proceeded on their fatal journey ; and the grave which closed over their ashes might have concealed the memories of most of them in a like oblivion, had they not been cast upon one of those periods of revolutionary convulsion which breaks in like tempests upon the ordinary progression of human events, and leave behind them such lasting traces of their operations on the destinies of mankind, as to give an interest to the petty performances of the humblest agents, even with a remote and intelligent posterity." But happy they, happy all, who act in the great drama of life with a good conscience towards God and man—repentance towards God and faith towards our Lord Jesus Christ—who care for the glory of the one and the well-being of the other.

Conscience has much more to do with man's future well-being than is generally thought. A bad conscience forbids him accrediting the grace of God in Christ towards the guilty. Man knows the difference between good and evil, and, knowing that

* Robertson's " History of Charles V," p. 244.

he has chosen the evil and refused the good, he believes God is against him. In this state of mind he endeavours to keep out of the way of all that which would bring him face to face with God. Therefore as unbelief is cherished, the mind becomes darker and the heart grows harder. The effects of *self-complacency*, through the power and subtlety of the enemy are also most ruinous. Man is so blinded by the god of this world, and so occupied with *self*, that he sees no moral beauty in Jesus, no need of Him as a Saviour, and no need of the salvation which is pressed upon his acceptance. And thus it is that so many pass off the scene, outwardly respectable, but inwardly heedless of the danger against which they are so solemnly and so frequently warned.

We judge not the dead ; but offer the result of our reflections for the benefit of the living. May he not, as many do, slumber on under the influence of an evil conscience, self-complacency, and the blinding power of Satan, until he has played out his part ; and then wake up, *too late*, to the importance of the truth he has rejected, and the Saviour he has slighted. But, alas ! the day of mercy is past, the door of mercy is closed ; and, seeing his loss to be irreparable, he sinks under the weight of hopeless despair.

John, Elector of Saxony, surnamed the Constant, died August 16th, 1532. During seven critical years, this illustrious prince, guided with great wisdom and firmness the vessel of the Reformation. At Augsburg, it will be remembered, he displayed a constancy superior to the wavering of some of his theologians ; yet so tempered by moderation as to preserve him from immediate collision with the Emperor. At one time he was cruelly menaced by Charles, at another his honesty was tempted by secret but flattering overtures ; but, nobly free from personal motives, he remained true to his convictions, and generously devoted to the great public question of the sixteenth century, the Reformation. There can be no question as to the genuineness of his piety. He was affectionately attached to Luther, and on doubtful questions usually deferred to his opinion. He took such delight in the Holy Scriptures that he would frequently have them read to him by youths of noble families, as much as six hours in the day. Happily the Reformation lost nothing by his death. His son, John Frederick, the new Elector, was in the flower of his youth, warmly attached to the cause, and not less to the person of Luther, than his father. He was characterised by piety and firmness in the trying circumstances through which he was afterwards called to pass.*

As few of the **antagonists of Luther** survived him, notwithstanding the high price that was set upon his life, we will notice some of the leading ones.

* Scott, vol. i., p. 129 ; Waddington, vol. iii., p. 164.

Pope **Clement VII** died September 27th, 1534. He died, even according to Italian history : " Detested by his court, suspected by the princes, with an offensive and hateful reputation ; for he was esteemed avaricious, faithless, and by nature indisposed to do good to mankind." In addition to the evil qualities here specified, others mention an obduracy and inclemency, which grew with the decay of his frame, and the morbid weakness of declining life. The virtues commonly ascribed to him are gravity, parsimony, self-control, circumspection, or dissimulation ; for, indeed, the last was so essential a quality at the court of Rome that he who excelled in that, in which all aspired to excel, deserved the sort of praise attached to such pre-eminence."[*]

Clement is familiarly known to our readers as professing his willingness to call a council, yet persevering to the end of his life in the artifices which he knew would delay, if not finally prevent its convocation. His dark and suspicious mind dreaded the thought of a general council. He was afraid of the light ; he knew that the circumstances of his own history, and his elevation to the chair, were not free from reproach. How different the character and the end of the chief prince of Germany to the chief pastor of Rome ! May we seek to imitate all that was of God in the former, and avoid all that was of Satan in the latter.

Cardinal Cajetan, one of Luther's earliest antagonists, died the same year as Clement. He was censured by many of the dignitaries of the Church for his unsuccessful contest with Luther at Augsburg, but not disgraced by the Vatican. It is thought by some that he turned his attention more to the study of the Scriptures after his defeat ; but he lived and died in the service of the Papacy.

Lorenzo Campeggio, the legate selected for the critical occasion of the famous Diet of Augsburg, died in 1539. He ably represented his Papal majesty and the principles of the Vatican. Secretly and unceasingly he urged Charles to violent measures against the Protestants. Fire and sword, sweeping confiscations, the Inquisition, burning heretical books, were the legate's arguments behind the scene. Still he was far from exceeding his orders.

Alexander, the great Papal champion at the Diet of Worms, died in 1542. For his great zeal in the Pontifical cause he received high ecclesiastical honours ; but his life was chiefly spent in the management of public business, the affairs of state, and the councils of princes.

Erasmus, of high literary fame, and in some respects the forerunner of Luther, died in 1536, at the age of sixty-nine. His name must ever be associated with Luther and the Reformation, though latterly Luther considered him one of its greatest enemies,

---

[*] Guicciardini and Fra Paolo, quoted by Waddington, vol. iii., p. 183.

and the enemy of all true religion. He lacked the essential principles of a Reformer. He was insincere, unstable, without courage, and trembled at the results of his own work. He was a Reformer until the Reformation became a great reality. He fled from Basle when the Reformation was established on the destruction of the images, and returned to it when tranquillity was restored. Yet, notwithstanding his inconsistencies, he commanded great respect from his literary reputation, his manners and accomplishments ; and his death was deplored as a great national affliction. He died, professedly, in the bosom of Holy Mother Church, and declaiming against the new evangelical practices.

John of Eck, professor of Ingolstadt, closed his noisy career in 1543, at the age of fifty-seven. He was the indefatigable champion of the dignity and absolute supremacy of Rome Papal. He was arrogant, vain-glorious, and eminently gifted with the qualities which form an accomplished disputant. "His unwearied zeal hurried him into every field where the Reformers were encamped. Everywhere he was foremost in the strife ; everywhere he contended with force and energy, and on more than one occasion with success . . . Thus was he confronted in a long series of combats, during a space of twenty years, with all the chieftains of the Reformation." Thus he lived and thus he died, maintaining even with his latest breath the loftiest pretensions of Rome.

THE LATTER END OF LUTHER.

The **public testimony of Luther** and his associates may be said to have closed when they delivered the confession of Augsburg. The contest, then, if not before, changed its character. It was no longer between excommunicated heretics bearing witness to the truth of God against the falsehoods of Rome ; but between the princes of Germany, united in league and arrayed in arms, and the imperial confederacy. But, although retiring from the notice of the public chronicler, they still laboured unweariedly in the duties of their special vocations, and had the gratification of seeing the result of their labours, in the peaceful progress of the Word of God. Of Luther, however, one of his biographers remarks : "That though he continued to discharge, with his accustomed zeal, his official duties as a preacher and a professor, and published commentaries on various parts of Scripture, and showed no inclination to relinquish his former habit of sending forth a popular treatise whenever circumstances in the state of religion appeared to call for it ; yet, amid those various occupations, it was remarked that his enterprising spirit appeared to undergo abatement, and that in his latter years he was found to hazard no new doctrine."*

* "History of the Church," by the Rev. John Fry, p. 324.

During these years the great Reformer, who has claimed so large a portion of our attention, was chastened by long and **painful sickness** ; and was fast descending to his resting-place, where the rude contests of life, its animosities and injuries, are all forgotten. Writing to a friend a few days before he set out on his last journey, he says, " I am old, decrepit, sluggish, weary, spiritless, and deprived of half my sight ; yet, at a time when I had hoped to have a reasonable share of rest, I continue to be overwhelmed with business, writing, speaking, acting, and doing, as if I had never yet acted, written, spoken, or done anything."

In the January of 1546, the **Counts of Mansfeld,** having some difference about boundaries and inheritance, invited Luther to Eisleben—his native place—to decide it by his arbitration. Though not caring to meddle in such matters, he consented.

He left Wittemberg on the 23rd of January, accompanied by his three sons, and his faithful friend, Justus Jonas. Though feeble and suffering, he engaged in the business on which he had come for about three weeks, and matters were arranged to the satisfaction of the lords of Mansfeld. He was received by these noblemen with great honour ; they met him with an escort of one hundred horsemen, amidst the ringing of the bells in all the Churches. He occasionally preached in the Church and partook of the Communion. Every night, as he took leave of his friends, he would say, " Pray to God that the cause of His Church may prosper, for the Council of Trent is vehemently enraged against it."

On the evening of the 17th of February, he dined with his friends, including his three sons—John, Martin, and Paul—and Justus Jonas. He was persuaded to abstain from business that evening, and to keep quiet in his study. He walked about the room, looked out at the window, looked upwards, and prayed earnestly. Deep thoughts were passing through his mind, but did not depress his spirits. There he had spent the morning, and there, he now felt, he was to spend the evening of his life. " I was born and baptised here at **Eisleben,** Jonas," he would say ; " what if I should remain or die here ! "

THE DEATH OF LUTHER.

Early in the evening he began to complain of an oppression in the chest ; but he was relieved by means of friction and warm applications. Feeling better, he left his room and joined the party at supper. " During this last meal he was sometimes playful, even jocular ; sometimes profoundly serious—such as he had ever been in the unreserved society of his friends." After supper, the oppression returned, yet he would not have medical aid called in, but asked for a warm linen cloth for his chest. He fell asleep about nine on a couch, and awoke about ten. Seeing so many friends around him, he desired that they should retire to rest. He was then led to his chamber ; when he was placed in his bed, he exclaimed, " I go to rest with God... Into Thy hands I commend my spirit." And, stretching out his hand to bid all good night, he added, " Pray for the cause of God." Having slept about three hours, he awoke, feeling very ill. " Oh God ! " he said, " how ill I am ! What an oppression I feel in my chest ! I shall certainly die at Eisleben ! " " My reverend father," replied Jonas, " God our heavenly Father will assist you by Christ, whom you have preached." He removed into his study without requiring assistance, and again repeating, " O my God ! into Thy hands I commend my spirit."

Two physicians had been sent for, who presently arrived, and likewise Count Albert, accompanied by his countess, who brought cordials and other medicines. All Luther's friends and his three sons were now collected around him, and he seemed somewhat relieved ; and having laid down on a couch he fell into a perspiration. This gave the friends some hope ; but he himself said, " It is a cold sweat, the forerunner of death : I shall yield up my spirit." He then began to pray, nearly in these words :

" O eternal and ·merciful God, my heavenly Father, Father of our Lord Jesus Christ, and God of all consolation ! I thank Thee that Thou hast revealed unto me Thy Son, Jesus Christ ; in whom I have believed, whom I have preached, whom I have confessed, whom I love and worship as my dear Saviour and Redeemer, whom the Pope and the multitude of the ungodly do persecute, revile, and blaspheme. I beseech Thee, my Lord Jesus Christ, receive my soul ! O heavenly Father, though I be snatched out of this life, though I must lay down this body, yet know I assuredly that I shall dwell with Thee for ever, and that none can pluck me out of Thy hands." He then thrice repeated the words : " Into Thy hands I commend my spirit : Thou hast redeemed me, O Lord God of truth." Also these words : " God so loved the world that He gave His only begotten Son, that whosoever believeth in Him should not perish, but have everlasting life." He then became silent, and his powers began to fail him. The countess gave him some restorative, and he gently whispered, " Yes, or No." And when Jonas raised his voice and said to him, " Beloved father, dost thou confess that Jesus Christ is the Son of God, our Saviour and Redeemer ? " he clearly and audibly rejoined, " I do ; " and spoke no more. With his hands clasped, a gentle respiration interrupted by sighs, continued for a short time ; and then, amidst the deep lamentation of his surrounding friends, between two and three in the morning, he fell asleep in Jesus.*

* From the account given by Justus Jonas to the Elector of Saxony, by the hand of Count Albert's secretary. See Scott's " History," vol. i., pp. 464-477.

THE FUNERAL OF LUTHER.

The Counts of Mansfeld would gladly have retained and interred the body of Luther in his native place, but they submitted to the wishes of the Elector, who directed it to be conveyed to **Wittemberg.** The body was then removed into the largest Church at Eisleben. Great excitement prevailed. Jonas preached a funeral sermon to an immense concourse of people ; after which the body was placed under the charge of ten citizens, who were to watch it during the night. Early the following day the procession moved towards Wittemberg. The citizens crowded along the streets, and beyond the gates. " There the countrymen, summoned by the ringing of bells, joined, together with their wives and families, the sad procession. It was met on the way by a deputation from the Elector, and reached Wittemberg on the 23rd of February. When the procession arrived at the gate of the city it was received by the senate, the rector, the professors, and the students of the University, with all the principal citizens ; after which it advanced, attended by the whole population to the Church of All Saints. Then came the widow of Luther with her daughters and three sons, and the little company of friends, Melanchthon, Pontanus, Jonas, Pomeranus, Cruciger, and others, the true yoke-fellows of the departed, the veterans of the Reformation.

Suitable hymns were sung as the funeral proceeded through the streets of the city. The body was deposited on the right of the pulpit ; whence, after some further verses had been sung, Pomeranus addressed the vast multitude. Melanchthon then pronounced a funeral oration. But it has been remarked, as creditable to both orators, that their feelings were more conspicuous than their powers of oratory, and that their pious attempts to console the sorrows of others were little more than a hearty demonstration of their own."*

REFLECTIONS ON THE LIFE OF LUTHER.

To study and estimate the different characters which pass before us in history, contrasted in everything but their common design, and to trace with the eye of faith the overruling hand of God in all their works and ways, will be found both deeply interesting and highly profitable. It is the study of what God is in Government, and of what man is in himself, however richly gifted or renewed by grace. Speaking of *those great*, we must always add, but, *fallible men.* There is only One who is infallible, and, thank God, we own no Head, no centre, but Him ; and no name but His—the Name of Jesus ; and it is only from this elevated point of view that we can rightly estimate the characters and events of history.

* For Extracts of Melanchthon's Oration, see Waddington, vol. iii., pp. 353-356.

The **life and death of Luther** are full of the deepest instruction for the thoughtful student, especially when contrasted with his great compeer, Zwingle. Their object was *one*; but their ways of attaining that object were as wide apart as the poles. It would be hard to say which had the greater heart for the maintenance and spread of the truth of God. Perhaps Luther's was the warmer and deeper, Zwingle's the clearer and broader. The one was war, the other peace; the one looked for victory only through the energy of faith and the bold confession of the truth; the other thought that the sword of the magistrate might, in some cases, be allied with the Gospel of peace; the one was destined to see his labours crowned with almost universal success; the other was doomed to witness a catastrophe which threatened to engulf his dearly loved Reformation; the one died in peace, surrounded by his friends; the other by the blows of his enemies. The principle of Luther, in this respect, is one of the essential principles of Christianity. The fury of the persecutor is to be met by truth and meekness—the martyr's noblest crown—not by political edicts and men-at-arms. These two great examples are no doubt intended by God to be two great lessons to all future generations. If we follow Christ, we must be characterised by His Spirit, and walk in His footsteps. " He that saith he abideth in him ought himself also so to walk even as He walked " (1 John 2. 6).

THE LORD'S CARE OF HIS SERVANT.

We need no voice from Heaven to assure us of the Lord's watchful care over His servant Luther. He trusted in God, and His faith was not disappointed. There is no more wonderful instance of the preserving power of Divine providence on the page of history. Its lessons are well fitted to strengthen our faith in Him who rules over all. An Augustinian monk of humble condition, without authority, without protection, rose up against the most degrading, firmly-seated despotism ever imposed on the credulity of mankind, and alone he triumphed. We cannot be too often reminded of this unseen, but invincible power. Faith is always in harmony with the mind and government of God. This was the grand secret of Luther's victory. He had scarcely an avowed supporter when he stood superior to king's, princes, Popes, and prelates, to all that was mighty in power and venerable for antiquity.

No human eye could discover any adequate motive for the strange position he had taken. It was neither vanity, ambition, nor fanaticism. He never was more, and he never cared to be more than Dr. Martin Luther. It was also a time of general peace and quiet submission to Papal authority. Why then trouble the still waters ? There is but one answer to this ques-

tion—conscience. There was a power in the enlightened conscience of the monk which the double sword of Popery was
powerless to overcome. Even the natural man without conscience can never be a man in any high and noble sense of the
word. But faith placed the Reformer on the solid ground of the
Word of God, by which he was taught the difference between
truth and falsehood, right and wrong, justice and oppression.
Now he stood for the truth of God; and God, in wisdom and
power, stood with him. He boldly maintained " that Scripture
was the only test of truth; that the interpretation of Scripture
was of private right and privilege; * that conscience had her
prerogatives, which were higher than all the powers of earth;
and that despotism, whether spiritual, ecclesiastical, or intellectual, was contrary to the will of God, and to the happiness,
prosperity, and dignity of mankind." On this foundation the
Reformation was built; and by the maintenance of these principles that system of delusion, which was deemed omnipotent,
was shaken to its centre by a single monk in his brown frock and
cowl.

To have accomplished the destruction of such a heretic,
Rome would gladly have given the half of her kingdom; but she
could not touch a hair of his head, or take a day or an hour of
his life from him. For well nigh thirty years he defied her utmost
malice, her loudest thunders, and all her powers. Yes, and
powers which, only a little time before had made the proudest
monarchs to tremble on their thrones. But now there were
bolts forged at Wittemberg as well as at the Vatican, and hurled
with as little ceremony at Popes and kings as at the Anabaptists
or the revolutionary peasants. What is to be done with the
audacious monk? Will no man rid His Infallibility of this
pestilent enemy of the Papacy? Where are the daggers and the
poisoned cups of Jezebel, which have so often come to her aid?
And yet, he is always at hand, always to be seen, always in
action, writing, speaking, uttering defiance to his adversaries,
or inspiring his friends with courage and resolution. But he
has no designs of blood; his object is life, not death. When he
is most violent, it is in word only, and that he may awaken
Christendom from the slumber of ages; or rage against the high
ones of the earth because they have sought to arrest the progress
of the truth. Every hand that was engaged on the side of
Papal tyranny was raised against him, yet not one of them could
strike the fatal blow.

Such is the perfect security of the man who reposes under the
shield of the Almighty. Diet after diet of the German Empire
may be convoked, aided by the representatives of Papal authority,
but all in vain; Luther is beyond their reach, yet always in sight.

* The truer ground would have been *personal responsibility to God who has spoken to man.*

His door stands open ; the poor may come for alms ; distinguished strangers from all parts of Europe may enter, converse freely, and sup with the far famed professor ; yet no man can be found to do him harm. And so he lived in the unwalled town of Wittemberg as safely as if he had been within the gates of Heaven.

THE DOMESTIC AND INNER LIFE OF LUTHER.

" Hitherto," says a competent critic, " the too common idea of the great Reformer's character has been, that it was a mere compound of violence and ruggedness. These features have been so prominent, that the finer lines of his portrait have been completely shaded from sight. **The lion and the lamb were united in Luther.** Nothing could exceed his submissiveness and humility when a choice was left him whether to be humble or daring ; but when conscience spoke, no other consideration was for a moment attended to, and he certainly did shake the forest in his magnificent ire . . . We dwell not upon his constant content-ment in poverty, and his contempt for riches, because this is the characteristic of almost all great men who are really worth more than gold can procure them ; but his long unbroken friendship with Melanchthon—a character so opposite to his own, and in some respects so superior, as he was the first to acknowledge himself—has always struck us as a proof that he possessed much sweetness and gentleness of disposition. Envy or jealousy never interrupted for a moment the fraternal affection that subsisted between these great men. Of these passions, indeed, Luther seems not to have been susceptible. Neither did personal ambition come near him. He gave himself no air of grandeur or importance, notwithstanding the great things he had per-formed. He seemed to consider himself as a common man among common men.

" But this great simplicity of manners exhibits not only his native greatness, but that apostolic frame of mind which all the messengers of God, from Moses downwards, have displayed. Such men are moulded at once by the hand that sends them. The accidents of this world have no power—as they have upon others—to change or modify their moral conformation. There is a oneness, a wholeness of character in these elect instruments ; they are governed by one idea, and one only. Hence was begotten the simplicity and homeliness of Luther's walk in life. Had he acted the great man, he would have proved that he was not the apostle. In his family, and among his neighbours, he was pleasant, affectionate, and pious ; but his piety was not put on ; it flowed in a mingled stream with his everyday life and conversation."*

* *Blackwood's Magazine*—slightly altered—December, 1835.

LUTHER'S MARRIAGE.

The **marriage of Luther** happening about a month after the death of his friend and patron, Frederick of Saxony, and while all Germany was bewailing the blood of her peasants, appeared to us so indiscreet, that we purposely left it out of our narrative. His usual impetuosity was strikingly manifested on this occasion.

The name of **Catherine von Bora** has long enjoyed a wide celebrity. She was of a good family, and one of nine recluses, who, after studying the Scriptures, and finding that their vow was not binding, escaped from a convent in Mesnia. Within the space of two years, eight of the nine were married; Catherine alone remained unmarried. During this time they had been supported by the bounty of friends, which was administered by Luther. In this way he must have known something of Catherine's character and disposition. He first proposed to unite her to one of his friends, a humble evangelical pastor; but not falling in with this arrangement, she remarked, with great simplicity, that had he proposed to espouse her himself, or to affiance her to Amsdorf, she should have felt less objection. Luther is represented to have been entirely overpowered by so flattering a declaration. He decided at once to be married, and without any notice of his intention, he caused the ceremony to be immediately performed.

On the 11th of June, 1525, Luther went to the house of his friend and colleague, Amsdorf. He desired Pomeranus, whom he styled *The Pastor*, to bless their union. The celebrated painter, Lucas Cranach, and Dr. John Apella, witnessed the marriage. Melanchthon, the dearest friend of all, was absent. For Luther to take such a bold step, while so many calamities were hanging over the Reformation, overwhelmed him for the moment. But when the clamour arose against his friend, he warmly defended his friend's marriage.

No sooner was this quiet marriage known, than a shout of indignation arose, and all Europe was troubled. It afforded a fair opportunity for the enemies of Luther to spread the most false and wild calumnies; and it was regarded by his friends as a serious mortification. From this union of **a monk and a nun**, the Catholics confidently predicted—according to prophecy, they said—the birth of Antichrist; while the wits and scholars assailed the nuptials with their sarcastic hymns and epigrams.

We can have no idea in our own day, of the effect of such a step on the minds of men generally in that age. It was a rude violation of vows which had been considered for centuries inviolable. Even many of the disciples of the Reformation were scandalised by their chief marrying a nun. Early prejudices are difficult to overcome. But hasty as the step was, Luther was prepared to justify and defend it. He met the storm by a counterblast of invectives and sarcasms. But we have chiefly to do with that which seems to have become a matter of conscience. Marriage, he boldly affirmed, was the ordinance of God; celibacy, the institution of man. "I do not take a wife," he said, "that I may live long with her; but seeing the nations and princes letting loose their fury against me, foreseeing that my end is near, and that after my death they will again trample my doctrine under foot, I am resolved, for the edification of the weak to bear a striking testimony to what I teach here below." The war of the peasants had brought great reproach on the principles of the Reformation at that time, and Rome appeared to be recovering here and there the ground she had lost; she even flattered herself with the hope of victory. But the marriage of the monk, who was under the anathema of the Pope, and the ban of the Emperor, spread terror and surprise through her ranks, and still more fully disclosed to her the courage of the enemy she fancied she had crushed.*

THE MARRIAGE FEAST.

On the 15th of June, Luther says, in a letter to Ruchel : "I have made the determination to cast off every shred of my former papistical life, and thus I have entered the state of matrimony, at the urgent solicitation of my father." His friend was wealthy, and while inviting him to **the marriage feast** on the 27th, he tells him, with characteristic frankness and simplicity, "that any present he might choose to bring with him would be acceptable." In a letter to Spalatin about the same time, he says : "I have silenced those who calumniated me and Catherine of Bora. If I am to give a feast in celebration of these nuptials, you must not only be present yourself, but you must send me a supply of venison. Meanwhile pray for us, and give us your benediction." To Wencelaus Link, he wrote : "Quite suddenly, and while I was thinking of anything rather than marriage, God wonderfully brought me into wedlock with the celebrated nun, Catherine of Bora." He invited him to the feast, but stipulated that he should bring no present, he being poor like Luther himself. The following was addressed to Amsdorf : "The report is true, that I married Catherine, and that in great haste, before the accustomed clamours of tumultuous tongues could reach me, for I hope I shall yet live some short time, and I could not refuse this last act of obedience to the importunity of my father." The old couple from Mansfeld—John and Margaret Luther—were to be present.

It will be seen from the above extracts, that one reason, by which Luther attempted to justify his marriage, was the urgent importunity of his father. "But when we remember the

* D'Aubigné, vol. iii., p. 309,

contempt," says one of his fairest critics, " with which he had treated the parental instances, twenty years before, when he took the most important step in his early life in direct opposition to them, we may question whether the actions of his mature age were directed by that influence, and whether, with his present imperious character and habits, even the persuasion of a father would have induced him to take any step on which he was not previously determined . . . This defence would have been sufficient for any man except Luther ; but his position was so pre-eminent before that of all his brother Reformers, his achievements had been so splendid, his pretentions were so lofty, and above all, his success had been so much advanced by the unquestionable disinterestedness of his character and designs, that his followers had a right to expect greater self-denial from him than from a Spalatin or a Carlstadt.   They had a right to expect, in return for the most implicit obedience which they yielded him, that he would sacrifice any private inclination, however consistent with evangelical principles, rather than cast a certain, though it might be unmerited, scandal upon the cause over which he presided . . . Thenceforward he ceased to stand apart fron his brethren, and came nearer to the level of their common humanity."*

But though this imprudent affair unquestionably lowered Luther in public estimation, it does not appear to have inflicted any serious blow upon the cause of the Reformation.   The work was of God, and too deeply founded to be shaken by the infirmity of His servant ; and twenty peaceful years of domestic happiness may have amply remunerated the Reformer for some loss of public reputation.

THE MARRIED LIFE OF LUTHER.

The union of **Luther and Catherine,** though without the raptures of a first affection, was no doubt a happy one.   The Lord greatly blessed them.   She seems to have been a woman of great modesty, with tender affections, and more than an ordinary share of good sense.   She consoled him in his defection by repeating passages from the Bible, saved him all anxiety about household affairs, contrived to sit near him during his leisure moments, amused him by working his portrait in embroidery, reminded him of letters he had to write ; but sometimes she indulged rather more in general conversation than suited the doctor, which called forth his most playful sallies, such as : " Did you say your Pater, Catherine, before you began that sermon ? If you had, I think you would not have been allowed to preach."   And sometimes he addressed her as *my Lord Ketha,* and the *Doctress.*   But his letters overflowed with tenderness for Catherine ; and as age advanced, his affection seems to have

---

* Waddington, vol. ii., p. 121.

increased. He styles her his dear and gracious wife, his dear and amiable Ketha.

They had **six children,** three sons and three daughters. Their daughter Magdaline died at the age of fourteen. " Such is the power of natural affection," says the father, " that I cannot endure this without tears and groans, or rather an utter deadness of heart. At the bottom of my soul are engraven her looks, her words, her gestures, as I gazed at her in her lifetime and on her death-bed. My dutiful, my gentle daugther! Even the death of Christ—and what are all deaths compared to His ?—cannot tear me from this thought as it should. She was playful, lovely, and full of love."

The Elector provided for the mother and the five children after the father's death.*

CONCLUSION.

Before parting with the great Reformer, who has claimed so large a share of our attention in tracing the history of the Church, we will bring under review the **estimate formed of him** by one of our most judicious writers—the historian of Charles V ; and also Dean Waddington's review of the extent of his work.

" As Luther was raised up by Divine providence, to be the author of one of the greatest revolutions recorded in history, there is not any person, perhaps, whose character has been drawn with such opposite colours. In his own age one party, struck with horror and inflamed with rage, when they saw with what a daring hand he overturned everything which they held to be sacred, or valued as beneficial, imputed to him not only the defects and vices of a man, but the qualities of a demon. The other, warmed with admiration and gratitude, which they thought he merited as the restorer of right and liberty to the Christian Church, ascribed to him perfections above the condition of humanity, and viewed all his actions with a veneration bordering on that, which should be paid only to those who are guided by the immediate inspiration of heaven. It is his own conduct, not the undistinguished censure, or the exaggerated praise of his contemporaries, that ought to regulate the opinions of the present age concerning him. Zeal for what he regarded as truth, undaunted intrepidity to maintain his own system, abilities, both natural and acquired, to defend his principles, and unwearied industry in propagating them, are virtues which shine so conspicuously in every part of his behaviour, that even his enemies must allow him to have possessed them in an eminent degree.

" To these may be added, with equal justice such purity and

* As our space forbids indulging in extracts from Luther's letters to his children, his wife, his friends, and his many encounters with the invisible as well as with the visible world—such as the scenes in the castle of Wartburg ; we would recommend our readers, who care to understand the personal character of Martin Luther, to study Michélet's " Life of Luther," translated by Hazlitt, which may be bought second-hand for 2s.

even austerity of manners as became one who assumed the character of a Reformer ; such sanctity of life as suited the doctrine which he delivered ; and such perfect disinterestedness as affords no slight presumption of his sincerity. Superior to all selfish considerations, a stranger to the elegancies of life, and despising its pleasures, he left the honours and emoluments of the Church to his disciples, remaining satisfied himself in his original state of professor in the University and pastor of the town of Wittemberg, with the moderate appointments annexed to these offices . . . His mind, forcible and vehement in all its operations, roused by great subjects, or agitated by violent passions, broke out, on many occasions, with an impetuosity which astonishes men of feebler spirits, or such as are placed in a more tranquil situation. By carrying some praiseworthy dispositions to excess, he bordered sometimes on what was culpable, and was often betrayed into actions which exposed him to censure. His confidence that his own opinions were well-founded approached to arrogance ; his courage, in asserting them, to rashness ; his firmness in adhering to them, to obstinacy ; and his zeal in confronting his adversaries, to rage and scurrility. Accustomed himself to consider everything as subordinate to truth, he expected the same deference for it from other men ; and, without making any allowances for their timidity or prejudices, he poured forth, against such as disappointed him in this particular, a torrent of invective mingled with contempt. Regardless of any distinction of rank or character when his doctrines were attacked, he chastised all his adversaries indiscriminately, with the same rough hand ; neither the royal dignity of Henry VIII, nor the eminent learning and ability of Erasmus, screened them from the same gross abuse with which he treated Tetzel and John of Eck.

" But these indecencies, of which Luther was guilty, must not be imputed wholly to the violence of his temper. They ought to be charged in part on the manners of his age. Some parts of Luther's behaviour which to us appear most culpable, gave no offence to his contemporaries. The account of his death filled the Roman Catholic party with excessive, as well as indecent joy, and damped the spirit of all his followers ; neither party sufficiently considering that his doctrines were now so firmly rooted as to be in a condition to flourish, independently of the hand which first had planted them."*

" But the most remarkable fact in the history of the Reformation, and, in my opinion, one of the most so in the history of the world, still remains to be mentioned—that the limits which the Reformation won while Luther lived, were very nearly those which divide the two religions at this day. Almost all that was

* Robertson's " History of Charles V," vol. vi., pp. 71-76,

accomplished before his death endured ; almost all that was afterwards achieved was wrested back again by Rome. The enthusiasm of a single generation attained, under his guidance, the prescribed boundaries. No exertions of his disciples, no reverence for his name and virtues, no wider diffusion of faith, and knowledge, and civilisation, and commercial activity, and philosophical truth, during the course of three centuries of progressive improvement, have made any lasting additions to the work which he left. Such as when it passed from the hands of its architect, or very nearly such, are its dimensions now. The form, indeed, is somewhat altered, and the part, which he considered as exclusively sacred, has been much narrowed by the change. But to the uncompromising, unrelenting enemy of Rome, it was an immortal triumph, that he extorted from her, with his own hands, all that she was ordained, so far as we yet have seen, to lose, and that he witnessed the utmost humiliation to which, even to this hour, it has pleased Providence permanently to reduce her."*

* Waddington's " History of the Reformation," vol. iii., p. 362.

CHAPTER XLVI

The Opening of the Council of Trent

FOR several years before the death of Luther, appearances were unfavourable to the peace and religious liberty of the Protestants. This led them, not so much to prayer and confidence in God as their shield and protector, but to strengthen the leade of Smalcald, and prepare for war. They were now a thoroughly political body. This was the **outward character of Protestantism** at that early period. The man who loved peace was in his grave, and his counsels were forgotten by his followers. He could not conceive a greater calamity befalling the cause of truth than that the sword should be drawn in its defence. Better far be martyrs, he thought, than warriors.

The jealous Emperor narrowly watched the increasing power of the league, and pronounced it " an empire within an empire." But his fatal expedition to Algiers, his renewed war with Francis, and the successes of the Turks in Hungary, led him to temporise, to conceal his feelings and intentions. He held several diets of the Empire for the avowed purpose of settling their religious differences, and restoring peace and harmony, but with no good results. The Protestants were deceived and thrown off their guard by fair pretences, and apparent concessions. In the Diet of Spires, in 1542, the Pontiff, Paul III, by his legate, renewed his promise of a council. He signified that it should be held at Trent, a city in the Tyrol, subject to the king of the Romans, and situated on the confines between Germany and Italy. Ferdinand and the whole Catholic party expressed their immediate satisfaction, and accepted the proposal. Not so the Protestants. They rejected both the place and the council proposed by the Pontiff ; demanding a general, or Œcumenical Council. They protested that they would pay no regard to a council held beyond the precincts of the Empire, called by the Pope's authority, and over which he assumed the right of presiding. Regardless, however, of their protestations, and fortified by the general consent of his own party, he published a bull for the convocation of the council at Trent before the 1st of November, and named three cardinals to preside as his legates.

At the appointed time, the Pope's legates, the imperial ambassadors, and a few prelates appeared. But as a fierce war was then raging between the Emperor and Francis, few ecclesiastics could travel with safety. It was manifest from these circumstances, that nothing satisfactory could be undertaken ; and to avoid the ridicule and contempt of his enemies, the Pope adjourned for an indefinite time the reopening of the council. Unhappily for the dignity and authority of the Papal See at this very time, the Emperor and his brother Ferdinand, King of the Romans, found it necessary not only to connive at the conduct of the Protestants, but to court their favour by repeated acts of indulgence. Ferdinand, who depended on their assistance for the defence of Hungary against the infidels, not only permitted their protestation to be inserted in the records of the diet, but renewed in their favour all the Emperor's concessions at Ratisbon, adding to them whatever they demanded for their further security. Thus had the Reformers rest, and the evangelical principles time to deepen and spread, though not from the good will, but from the disturbed state of their adversaries' affairs.

As late as 1544, at the diet held in the same place, the politic Charles, perceiving that the time was not yet come to offend the jealous spirit of the Protestants, or to provoke the powers of the Smalcald Confederacy, contrived to soothe the Germans by new concessions, and a more ample extension of their religious privileges. Being still engaged in foreign wars, and his hands not free, he employed all his powers of dissimulation to court and flatter the Elector, and the Landgrave, the heads of the Protestant party, and through them to deceive the members of the confederacy.

Meanwhile, his Papal majesty was becoming day by day more jealous of these negotiations and concessions. He was longing as ardently as his three predecessors had done for the rooting out by force of arms of this wide-spreading, **giant heresy**. It had been the constant object of the Vatican from the beginning of the Reformation to create a hostile breach between the Emperor and the Protestants, and a consequent appeal to arms. But, so far as we can judge, the consummation of these wicked designs was prevented for nearly thirty years, in the providence of God, and chiefly in answer to the prayers of one man. But he was now off the scene, and his brethren were trusting to their military organisation and numerical strength. Besides, the determined position which they had taken with reference to the proposed council gave the Pope and the Emperor every opportunity to ensnare them ; and so it turned out, as we shall soon see.

The *avowed* object of this famous council was, of course, the pacification of the Church, the healing of her diseases, the restoring of her unity, and the blessing of her children ; but its *real* object was the condemnation of the doctrines of the Reformers, Luther, Zwingle, and Calvin, and the immediate persecution of all who should oppose its decrees. This was the secret arrangement between the Pontiff and the Emperor, for they were well aware that the Protestants would never subject themselves to the council or yield obedience to its canons.

THE TREATY BETWEEN THE POPE AND THE EMPEROR.

In December, 1545, after so many years of intrigue, dissimulation, and dispute, the long-promised **council assembled at Trent,** and continued its sittings till 1563.*

But the council which was to fix the destiny of Christendom was only a part of a great plot for the suppression of Lutheranism. The Emperor had ended his war with Francis by the peace of Crespy, he had patched up a treaty with Solyman, and secretly gained over some of the Catholic princes in Germany. He pushed on, but with great precaution, his preparations for war. The Pope, however much he had disapproved of the Emperor's late policy, or dreaded his power, most readily agreed that all other matters should give place to that one which each accounted the most important. A treaty was concluded, the main object of which was :

1. " That the Pope and the Emperor, for the glory of God, and the public good, but especially the welfare of Germany, have entered into league together upon certain articles and conditions ; and, in the first place, that the Emperor shall provide an army, and all things necessary for war, and be in readiness by the month of June next ensuing, and by force of arms compel those who refuse the council and maintain those errors to embrace the ancient religion, and submit to the Holy See."

2. " The Pope, on his part, in addition to one hundred thousand ducats which he had already given, stipulated to deposit as much more in the Bank of Vienna toward defraying the expense of the war ; to maintain, at his own charge, during the space of six months, twelve thousand foot, five hundred horse, and to grant the Emperor for this year one-half of the Church revenues all over Spain ; to empower him to alienate as much of the Abbey-lands in that country as would amount to five hundred thousand ducats ; and that both spiritual censures and military force should be employed against any prince who might seek to hinder the execution of this treaty."

3. " That the council, on its part, was to proceed at once to draw up a confession of faith, wherein should be contained all the articles which the Church required its members to believe ; that this ought to be the first and principal business of the council : and that anathemas were to be denounced in the name,

* For details, see Landon's " Manual of Councils," Father Paul's " History of the Council of Trent ; " Scott's " Church History," vol. ii., pp. 256-324 ; Dr. Robertson's " History of Charles V," vol. vi.

and by the authority of the Holy Ghost, against all who should disclaim the truth of the Confession."*

Thus was the snare most artfully laid. It was the deep device of Satan for the destruction of the Protestants, but vigorously carried out by him who assumes the title of "most holy father," and the character of "infallibility." The enemy saw that the Reformers had shifted from moral to political ground. They were no longer merely "protestors" for the truth of God against the errors of Popery, but an armed confederacy, prepared to meet the Papal and imperial armies on their own ground. This was their fatal mistake. God could not appear for them on the world's ground ; and their own folly and weakness were soon manifested. Thus it happened.

The council commenced its deliberations—though only a few Spanish and Italian bishops had arrived—with examining the first and chief point in controversy between the Church of Rome and the Reformers, concerning the rule which should be held as supreme and decisive in matters of faith ; and, by its *infallible authority*, determined, " That the books to which the designation *Apocryphal* hath been given, are of equal authority with those which were received by the Jews and Primitive Christians into the sacred canon ; that the traditions handed down from the apostolic age, and preserved in the Church, are entitled to as much regard as the doctrines and precepts which the inspired authors have committed to writing ; that the Latin translation of the Scriptures, made or revised by Jerome, and known by the name of the *Vulgate* translation, should be read in Churches, and appealed to in schools as authentic and canonical.

This was an open attack on the first principles of Protestantism, a pre-judging of every question at issue, and rendering hopeless all discussion between the two parties. Luther and his followers, from the beginning, had affirmed that the Word of God was the only rule in judgment ; that they owned no authority in matters of faith but the one infallible standard of Holy Scripture. This was the foundation and corner-stone of Protestantism ; but the first decision of the council was intended to undermine the foundation, to adjudge and condemn the whole system.

THE SMALCALD WAR.

The Protestants, perceiving that the real object of the council was not to examine their demands, but to condemn their faith as heresy, and to draw them into collision with the Emperor, that he might decide the question with the sword, firmly rejected its decrees. At the same time they published a long manifesto, containing a renewal of their protest against the meeting of the council, together with the reasons which induced them to decline

* See F. Paul, Teckendorf, Sleidan, Abbé Millot, quoted by Dr. Robertson, and Wylie's " History of Protestantism," vol. ii., p. 113.

its jurisdiction. But Charles was not yet prepared for hostilities ; therefore he pursued his policy of dissimulation. He had no wish to increase the zeal of the council, or to quicken the operations of the league. His first object was to deceive the Protestants, that he might gain time for ripening his schemes. For this purpose he contrived to have an interview with the Landgrave of Hesse, the most active of all the confederates, and the most suspicious of the Emperor's designs. To him he made great professions of his concern for the happiness of Germany, and of his aversion to all violent measures ; he denied in express terms having formed any treaty, or having begun any military preparations which pointed to war.

Such was the consummate duplicity of Charles, that he seems to have dispelled all Philip's doubts and apprehensions, and sent him away fully satisfied of his pacific intentions. On his return to the confederates, who were assembled at Worms, he gave them such a flattering representation of the Emperor's favourable disposition towards them, that they became dilatory and undecided in their operations, thinking that the danger was distant or only imaginary. Listening thus to the wiles of Satan, the Protestant leaders were smitten with blindness and folly ; even as the men of Zurich were in 1531. They were off the ground of faith and trusting to their own wisdom and strength, which led to their disgrace and humiliation. From this time every step they take is in the wrong and downward direction.

The conduct of the Emperor was everywhere directly opposite to his professions of peace, and seen by all excepting those who ought to have suspected him. Henry VIII of England secretly informed the princes that Charles, having long resolved to exterminate their doctrines, was diligently employing the present interval of tranquillity in preparing for the execution of his designs. The merchants of Augsburg, among whom were some who favoured the Protestant cause, learning from their correspondents in Italy that the ruin of the Reformers was intended, warned them of the approaching danger. In confirmation of these reports, they heard from the Low Countries that Charles, though with every precaution which could keep the measure concealed, had issued orders for raising troops both there and in other parts of his dominions. And seeing he was not at war either with Francis or Solyman, or any other power, for what could he intend such preparations, if not for the extinction of the Smalcald League, and the heresies which had so long abounded in Germany.

THE POPE REVEALS THE DARK SECRET.

The secret was now in many hands ; the officers and the allies of Charles kept no such mysterious reserve, but spoke out plainly of his intentions. The Pope, overflowing with joy, not doubting the issue of the enterprise, began to sing the war-song, as in the days of Innocent III, exhorting the faithful to take up arms in the holy cause and gain indulgences. " Proud," says Dr. Robertson, " of having been the author of such a formidable league against the Lutheran heresy, and happy in thinking that the glory of extirpating it was reserved for his Pontificate, he published the articles of his treaty with the Emperor, in order to demonstrate the pious intention of their confederacy, as well as to display his own zeal, which prompted him to make such extraordinary efforts for maintaining the faith in its purity. Not satisfied with this, he soon after issued a bull, containing most liberal promises of indulgence to all who should engage in this holy enterprise, together with warm exhortations to such as could not bear a part in it themselves, to increase the fervour of their prayers, and the severity of their mortifications, that they might draw down the blessing of Heaven upon those who had undertaken it."*

The Pope being deeply grieved with Charles for endeavouring to make that pass for a political contest which he ought to have gloried in as a war that had no other object than the defence of the ancient faith, exposed the treachery of his policy and declared the overthrow of Lutheranism as at hand. The Emperor, though somewhat embarrassed by this disclosure, and not a little offended at the Pope's indiscretion or malice, continued boldly to pursue his own plan, and to reassert that his intentions were only that which he had originally stated. Thus were the two heads of Christendom—the fountain of truth and the fountain of honour, so called—proclaiming to the world that neither truth nor honour were to be found in either. And thus they stand before all posterity, down to the latest generation, a mere compound of craft, falsehood, hypocrisy, and cruelty.

But the artifices of Charles did not impose on all the Protestant confederates. Some of them clearly perceived that he had taken arms for the suppression of the Reformation, and the extinction of the German liberties. They determined, therefore, to prepare for their own defence, and resolved neither to renounce their religious liberties nor to abandon these civil rights which had been transmitted to them by their ancestors. A deputation from the confederates waited on the Emperor, and wished to know whether these military preparations were carried on by his command, and for what end, and against what enemy ? To a question put in such a form and at a time when facts were too notorious to be denied, he avowed the intentions which he could no longer conceal, but with such fascinating duplicity as

* For details of this interesting period see the " History of Charles V.," in vol. iv., of Dr. Robertson's Collected Writings.

to deceive the deputies. True, he admitted that it was Germany he had in view in his preparations, but his only object was to maintain the rights and prerogatives of the imperial dignity. His purpose was, not to molest any on account of religion, but to punish certain factious members, and preserve the ancient constitution of the Empire from being impaired or dissolved by their licentious conduct. Though the Emperor did not name the persons whom he had destined as the objects of his vengeance, it was well known that he had in view John Frederick, Elector of Saxony, and Philip, Landgrave of Hesse.

Transparent as this deception was, and manifest as it might have appeared to all who considered the Emperor's character, it nevertheless lulled to sleep the timid and the wavering. They were furnished with an excuse for inactivity, " seeing," as they said, " the war does not concern religion, but is a quarrel merely between the Emperor and some members of the league." And such was the dexterity with which he used this division of feeling among the confederates, that he gained time and other solid advantages.

THE ARMY OF THE CONFEDERATES.

The more energetic of the confederates, soon after this, met at **Ulm,** to give the necessary directions for their future proceedings. It was resolved that they should repel force by force, and make vigorous preparation for war. They also determined, that having neglected too long to strengthen themselves by foreign alliances, they would now apply to the Venetians, the Swiss, and the Kings of France and England. So far alas ! had the leaders of the Reformation, within the short period of thirty years from its commencement, departed from the principles which triumphed at Worms and Augsburg, to say nothing of the plain teaching of the Word of God, as to apply for help to such men as Henry and Francis ; but we shall see with what results.

Their negotiations with foreign courts were all unsuccessful ; but the chiefs had no difficulty in bringing a sufficient force into the field. The feudal institutions, which subsisted in full force at that time in Germany, enabled the nobles to call out their numerous vassals, and to put them in motion on the shortest notice. "In a few weeks," says the historian of Charles, "they were enabled to **assemble an army** composed of *seventy thousand* foot and *fifteen thousand* horse, provided with a train of *an hundred and twenty cannon, eight hundred ammunition wagons, eight thousand beasts of burden,* and *six thousand pioneers.* This army, one of the most numerous, and undoubtedly the best appointed of any which had been levied in Europe during that century, did not require the united efforts of the whole Protestant body to raise it. The Elector of Saxony, the Landgrave of Hesse, the Duke of Wurtemberg, the princes of Anhalt, and the imperial cities of Augsburg, Ulm, and Strasburg, were the only powers which contributed towards this great armament. The Electors of Cologne, of Grandeburg, the Count Palatine, and several others, overawed by the Emperor's threats, or deceived by his professions, remained neutral.

" The number of their troops, as well as the amazing rapidity wherewith they had assembled them, astonished the Emperor, and filled him with the most disquieting apprehensions. He was indeed in no condition to resist such a mighty force. Shut up in Ratisbon with an army scarcely *ten thousand* strong, he must have been overwhelmed by the approach of such a formidable army, which he could not fight, nor could he even hope to retreat from it in safety."

Fortunately for Charles the confederates did not avail themselves of the advantage which lay so plainly before them. Time was wasted in writing a letter to the Emperor, and a manifesto to all the inhabitants of Germany. But, weak and perilous though the situation of Charles was, he assumed the air of the haughty inflexible Emperor. His only reply to the letter of the Protestants was to publish the ban of the Empire against the Elector of Saxony and the Landgrave of Hesse, their leaders, and against all who should dare to assist them. By this sentence they were declared rebels and outlaws, and deprived of every privilege which they enjoyed as members of the Germanic body ; their goods were confiscated ; their subjects absolved from their oath of allegiance ; and it became not only lawful, but meritorious to invade their territories. This tremendous sentence, according to the German jurisprudence, required the authority of a diet of the Empire, but Charles overlooked that formality and assumed the power in his own person.

The confederates, now perceiving that all hopes of accommodation were at an end, solemnly declared **war against Charles**, to whom they no longer gave any other title than pretended Emperor, and renounced all allegiance to him. But, now that the moment for war had come, the league was disunited and unprepared. The supreme command of the army was committed in terms of the league to the Elector and the Langdrave, with equal power. This proved disastrous from the very commencement. The natural tempers and dispositions of the two princes were widely different. The Elector was slow, deliberate, irresolute ; the Landgrave was prompt, enterprising, and wished to bring the contest to a speedy issue. But if Philip was the better soldier, John was the greater prince ; and could a Landgrave command an Elector ? All the inconveniences arising from a divided authority were immediately felt. Much time was wasted and dissensions multiplied. Meanwhile the Emperor had moved his camp to the territories of the Duke of Bavaria, a neutral prince, leaving a small garrison in Ratisbon. A few more days were spent in deliberating whether they should follow Charles or attack Ratisbon. By this time the imperial army amounted to *thirty-six thousand* men ; and, through cowardly defections, the Protestant army was reduced to *forty-seven thousand.*

THE FIRST OPERATIONS OF THE PROTESTANTS.

As no foresight had been shown by the confederates to prevent the Spanish, Italian, and other troops from joining the imperial army, the Emperor was enabled to send such a reinforcement to the garrison at Ratisbon, that the Protestants, relinquishing all hope of reducing the town, marched towards Ingoldstadt on the Danube, near to which Charles was now encamped. " They complained loudly," says Dr. Robertson, " against the Emperor's notorious violation of the laws and constitution of the Empire, in having called in foreigners to lay waste Germany, and to oppress its liberties. It came to be universally believed among them, that the Pope, not satisfied with attacking them openly by force of arms, had dispersed his emissaries all over Germany, to set on fire their town and magazines, and to poison the wells and fountains of water. These rumours were confirmed, in some measure, by the behaviour of the Papal troops, who, thinking nothing too rigorous towards heretics anathematised by the Church, were guilty of great excesses in the Lutheran states, and aggravated the miseries of war by mingling with it all the cruelty of bigoted zeal."

With passions so aroused, by the report of cruelties so great, we might have expected to see a corresponding energy to bring such calamities to a close. It was now in their power, and the campaign might have been ended at the outset, had their leaders been united and firm. On their arrival at Ingoldstadt, they found the Emperor in a camp not remarkable for strength, with a small army, and surrounded only by a slight entrenchment. But the great object pursued by Charles from the first was to decline a battle, to weary out the patience of the confederates, and induce them to separate, when his victory over each prince in succession would be sure.

Before **Ingoldstadt** lay a plain of such extent as afforded ample space for drawing out their whole forces, and bring them to act at once. No army was ever more favourably situated ; the soldiers were full of ardour and eager to seize the opportunity of attacking the Emperor ; but alas ! through the weakness or division of their leaders the advantage was lost, and so far as their credit is concerned it was lost for ever. " The Landgrave urged that, if the sole command was vested in him, he would terminate the war on that occasion, and decide by one general action the fate of the two parties. But the Elector urged, on the other hand, the discipline of the enemies' forces, the presence of the Emperor, the experience of his officers, and thought it would be unsafe to venture upon an action." While the Protestant leaders were thus debating whether they ought to surprise the Emperor or not, the imperial reinforcements arrived and the opportunity was gone.

But notwithstanding their vacillation, it was at length agreed to advance towards the enemy's camp in battle array, with the view of drawing the imperialists out of the works. But the Emperor was too wise to be caught in this snare. He was fighting on his own ground, and with his own weapons, and as such, he was more than a match for all the Protestants in Germany, who were on false ground and fighting with carnal, not with spiritual, weapons. They commenced and continued firing for several hours on the imperialists, but Charles adhered to his own system with inflexible constancy. He drew up his soldiers behind the trenches ; restrained them from any excursions or skirmishes which might bring on a general engagement ; rode along the lines, addressed the troops of the different nations in their own language ; encouraged them not only by his words, but by the cheerfulness of his voice and countenance ; exposed himself in places of greatest danger, and amidst the warmest fire of the enemy's artillery. Night fell ; and the confederates, seeing no prospect of alluring them to fight on equal terms, retired to their own camp.

The leisure was employed with great diligence by the imperialists in strengthening their works ; by the confederates, seeing they had lost their opportunity, turned their attention— with as little success—towards preventing the arrival of a powerful reinforcement from the Low Countries. Upon the arrival of the Flemings the Emperor began to act more on the offensive, though still with the greatest sagacity avoiding a battle. He had often foretold, with confidence, that discord and the want of money would compel the confederates to disperse that unweildy body ; and for this he watched and waited with long patience. They had been on the field from midsummer to the end of autumn, and little had been done, and nothing gained on either side, when an unexpected event decided the contest, and occasioned a fatal reverse in the affairs of the Protestants, and prepared the way for the tragedy that followed.

THE TREACHERY OF MAURICE.

Maurice was the son of Henry, and succeeded his father in the government of that part of Saxony which belonged to the Albertine line. " This young prince, then only in his twentieth year, had, even at that early period, begun to discover the great talents which qualified him for acting such a distinguished part in the affairs of Germany. As soon as he entered upon the administration, he struck out into such a new and singular path as showed that he aimed from the beginning at something great and uncommon."* He professed to be a zealous Protestant, but objected to join the league of Smalcald under the pretence that its principles were not sufficiently Scriptural. He avowed his determination to maintain the purity of religion, but not to entangle himself in the political interests, or combinations to which it had given rise. Such was the consummate duplicity and the Satanic policy of this young man. At this very time, with great political sagacity, he was weighing both sides, and foreseeing that the Emperor was most likely to prevail in the end, he affected to place in him the most unbounded confidence, and to court his favour by every possible means, and also the favour of his brother, Ferdinand.

At the Diet of Ratisbon, in the month of May, 1546, Maurice concluded a treaty with the Emperor, in which he engaged to assist him as a faithful subject, and Charles, in return, stipulated to bestow on him all the spoils of the Elector, his dignities as well as his territories. But so little did the Elector suspect treachery in his young relative and neighbour, who had received many kindnesses from him, that, on leaving to join the confederates, he committed his dominions to the protection of that prince ; and he, with an artful appearance of friendship, undertook the charge. The whole plan being now completed, the Emperor sent Maurice a copy of the imperial ban denounced against the Elector and the Landgrave, requiring him, upon the allegiance and duty which he owed to the head of the Empire, instantly to seize and retain in his hands the forfeited estates of the Elector.

This artifice, which made the invasion appear to be one of necessity rather than of choice, was but a thin veil to conceal the treachery of both. After some formalities were observed, to give a specious appearance to his reluctance, Maurice marched into his kinsman's territories, and, with the assistance of Ferdinand, attacked and defeated the Elector's troops, and took all things under his own administration.

THE DISSOLUTION OF THE LEAGUE.

When the news of these rapid conquests reached the good Elector, he was filled with indignation and astonishment, and resolved at once to return home with his troops for the defence of Saxony. He was most unwilling to withdraw, as he preferred the success of the common cause to the security of his own

* Dr. Robertson, vol. vi., p. 22.

dominions ; but the sufferings and complaints of his subjects increased so much that he became most impatient to rescue them from the oppression of Maurice, and from the cruelties of the Hungarian soldiers, accustomed to the merciless modes of warfare practised against the Turks. This was the fatal blow to the league of Smalcald. This diversion, which had been contrived with so much subtlety, was successful, even to the desire of the heart of Charles.

The departure of the Elector caused a separation of the confederates ; and, once divided, they became an easy prey to the Emperor. A confederacy, lately so powerful as to shake the imperial throne, and threaten to drive Charles out of Germany, fell to pieces, and was dissolved in a few weeks. How empty everything is if God is not in it ; and how weak everything is if He is not its strength ! Charles saw his opportunity, put his army in motion, and did not allow the confederates leisure to recover from their consternation, or to form any new schemes of union. He assumed the tone of a conqueror, as if they had been already at his mercy. The union being dissolved, the princes stood exposed singly to the whole weight of his vengeance. With the exception of the Elector and the Landgrave, almost all the Protestant princes and states submitted, and implored the pardon of the Catholic Charles in the most humiliating manner. And as he was in difficulties from the want of money, he imposed heavy fines upon them, which he levied with most rapacious exactness.*

With the exception of the Landgrave and the Elector, hardly any member of the league now remained in arms. And these two the Emperor had long marked out as the victims of his signal vengeance, so that he was at no pains to propose to them any terms of reconciliation. Various circumstances, for a short time, suspended the blow ; but Charles, being relieved from his apprehensions of a fresh war with France, by the death of his great rival, Francis I, resolved to march against the Elector, who had nearly recovered all his dominions from the traitor Maurice.

In the spring of 1547 there was some hard fighting between the Emperor and the Elector at Muhlberg, on the Elbe, and at Mulhausen, but the latter was defeated, wounded, and taken prisoner, which virtually terminated the war. This decisive victory cost the imperialists only fifty men ; but twelve hundred of the Saxons were slain, and a great number were taken prisoners. Maurice, as the reward of his treachery, was immediately put in possession of the electoral dominions. The city of Gotha, and the small territory attached to it were settled on the Elector's family ; but he himself was to remain a perpetual prisoner.

The Landgrave alone now remained in arms, and was not

* Dr. Robertson's " History," book viii.

inclined to surrender. But Maurice, his son-in-law, prevailed on him to submit, assuring him that he and the Elector of Bradenburg had the Emperor's guarantee for his personal liberty. But in all this Philip was cruelly deceived. And there is every reason to believe that those two nobles, while acting as mediators, were themselves deceived by the perfidious Charles. His object was to gain possession of the person of Philip, that he might have him absolutely at his disposal. But notwithstanding the assurances and entreaties of Maurice and Bradenburg, the Landgrave suspected the intentions of the Emperor, and refused to appear at his court. His reluctance, however, was at length overcome by these two princes signing a bond, in which they pledged their own lives and liberties for his. His doubts being thus removed, he repaired to the imperial camp at Halle, in Saxony.

Charles, who had assumed the haughty and imperious tone of a conqueror, was seated on a magnificent throne, with all the ensigns of his dignity, and surrounded by a numerous train of the princes of the Empire. The Landgrave was introduced with great solemnity, and, advancing towards the throne, fell upon his knees. The eyes of all present were fixed on the unfortunate Landgrave—the most popular of the Protestant chiefs in Germany. "Few could behold a prince," says Robertson, "so powerful as well as high-spirited, suing for mercy in the posture of a supplicant, without being touched with commiseration, and perceiving serious reflections arise in their minds upon the instability and emptiness of human grandeur." But there was one heart that remained unmoved by that affecting scene : the unfeeling Spaniard, with Germany prostrate at his feet, viewed the whole transaction with cold indifference.

He insisted on unconditional submission. "Philip was required to surrender his person and territories to the Emperor ; to implore for pardon on his knees ; to pay one hundred and fifty thousand crowns towards defraying the expenses of the war ; to demolish the fortifications of all the towns in his dominions, except one ; to oblige the garrison which he placed in it to take an oath of fidelity to the Emperor," etc., etc. The Landgrave, being entirely at the Emperor's mercy, ratified these conditions ; and flattering himself that he had thereby fully expiated his guilt, rose from his knees, and advanced towards the Emperor, with the intention of kissing his hand, but Charles turned away abruptly, without deigning to give the fallen prince any sign of compassion or reconciliation.

Philip was allowed to retire, apparently at liberty, along with his friends Maurice and Bradenburg, and was entertained by the Duke of Alva with great respect and courtesy ; but after supper, when he rose to depart, the duke made known the orders he had to detain him. The unhappy prince was struck dumb ; his heart sank within him ; then he broke out into those violent expressions at the injustice and artifices of the Emperor, which the circumstances naturally provoked, but all in vain. Bradenburg and Maurice had recource to the most bitter complaints, to arguments, and to entreaties, in order to extricate the distracted prince out of the ignominious situation into which he had been betrayed. They pleaded their own honour and bond in the matter ; but the Duke of Alva was inflexible. Philip was his prisoner, and placed under the custody of a Spanish guard, and did not obtain his release till, after a lapse of five years, a total reverse in the affairs of the Emperor set him at liberty, and introcuded a **new epoch** into the history of the Reformation.

THE GERMANS TREATED AS A CONQUERED PEOPLE.

The Emperor's triumph was now complete. He was master of Germany. In taking possession of Wittemberg he visited the **tomb of Luther.** While silently gazing on the peaceful resting-place of the monk who had stirred up all Europe to mutiny, and defied both the Papal and the imperial power, the Spaniards entreated him to destroy the monument of the heretic, and to dig up his bones. But Charles nobly replied : " I have nothing more to do with Luther ; he has gone to another judge, whose province we must not invade. I wage war with the living, not with the dead." But how different were his feelings when he turned from the memory of the man of faith to those that had raised the arm of rebellion against him ! The two princes, Frederick and Philip, followed him in his train, and were thus led about in triumph from city to city, and from prison to prison, exhibiting them as a public spectacle to their former subjects, their families and friends. This was a bitter humiliation to Germany. Loud complaints arose from every quarter against this wanton abuse of power, and cruel treatment of its two most illustrious princes.

But the day of adversity brought out **the real character** of these two public men. Frederick, long a true Christian, accepted the affliction from the hand of the Lord, and bowed to it. He looked beyond second causes. He dropped the spirit of the warrior, and embraced that of the martyr. All historians agree in bestowing upon him the highest praise for his meekness, patience, and Christian conduct. Even the Roman Catholic historian, Thuanus, says of him : " In the judgment of all men, he rose superior to his adverse fortune by the constancy of his mind."

But alas ! the conduct of the Landgrave was just the opposite to that of the Elector. We have seen something of his profession of religion, and of his zeal for the union of Christians, as at the conference at Marburg ; but in " the day of adversity his strength was small." Such was his impatience under his calamity that, in order to obtain his liberty, he voluntarily offered to surrender, not his dignities merely, but his religious principles. He never judged himself or his ways in the presence of God ; therefore he could not see His overruling hand in his trial. In these two men we may see illustrated the mighty difference between a mere form of religion (even when accompanied by an active, stirring mind) and the faith of the Lord Jesus Christ which takes possession of the heart. The day of trial discovers the essential difference. The one broods over the shameful treachery by which he was deprived of his liberty, and the injustice with which he is still detained, until he is driven to the wildest excesses of passion. The other is not insensible to the unfeeling cruelty with which he is treated ; but he confesses his own failure, owns a wise and over-ruling providence in it all, waits upon God, renews his strength, and daily waxes stronger and stronger, until, through Divine grace, he can rejoice in his captivity, having the sweet sense of the presence of God with him, and that it will all result in a brighter crowd in Heaven.

But we now return to the **public transactions of the Emperor.** Many of the other princes were next made to feel the power of the oppressor, though in a different way. He ordered his troops to seize the artillery and military stores belonging to those who had been members of the Smalcald League, and, " having collected upwards of five hundred pieces of cannon, a great number in that age, he sent part of them into the low countries, part into Italy, and part into Spain, in order to spread by this means the fame of his success, and that they might serve as monuments of his having subdued a nation hitherto deemed invincible. He then levied, by his sole authority, large sums of money, as well upon those who had served him with fidelity during the war, as upon those who had been in arms against him. By these exactions he amassed about one million six hundred thousand crowns—a sum which appeared prodigious in the sixteenth century."*

The Germans, naturally jealous of their privileges, were greatly alarmed at such extraordinary stretches of power, but so great was their consternation that all implicitly obeyed the commands of the haughty Spaniard ; though at the same time, the discontent and resentment of the people had become universal, and they were ready to burst forth on the first opportunity with unmitigated violence. While Charles was thus giving laws to the Germans like a conquered people, Ferdinand was exercising the same despotism over the Bohemians, and stripped them of almost all their privileges.

* Robertson, book ix., p. 178.

CHAPTER XLVII

"The Interim"

THE Emperor, now complete master of the position, and having subdued, as he thought, the independent and stubborn spirit of the Germans, held a diet at Augsburg, when he demanded of the Protestants to submit the decision of the religious dissensions which had arisen in Germany to the council of Trent. The city and assembly were surrounded by the Emperor's victorious troops, no doubt to give effect to their master's wishes. He immediately took possession of the Cathedral and some other Churches, and, after they had been duly purified, restored the Popish worship. But scarcely had the proceedings commenced, when Charles learnt, to his deep mortification, that the council had been removed by the Pope from Trent to Bologna.

The great success and assumption of Charles in Germany, naturally awakened the fears and jealousy of the Pontiff. He foresaw that the Emperor's power in that country would greatly influence the decisions of the council, and that he might employ it to limit or overturn the Papal authority. He therefore embraced the first opportunity to withdraw the Papal troops from the imperial army, and to translate the council to Bologna, a city subject to the Pope. This removal was strenuously opposed by the Emperor and by all the bishops in the imperial interest. The latter remained at Trent, while the Spanish and Neapolitan bishops accompanied the legates to Bologna. Thus a schism commenced in that very assembly which had been called to heal the divisions of Christendom, and which issued in an indefinite adjournment of the council : nor were means found of restoring the council to Trent till Julius III succeeded Paul III in the Papal chair, A.D. 1550 ; but the season was then past for the purposes of Charles.

As the prospect of a general council was now more distant than ever, the Emperor, in his pious concern for the religious dissensions of his northern subjects, deemed it necessary, in the *interim*, to prepare a system of doctrine, to which all should conform, until a council, such as they wished for, could be assembled. This new creed was styled The Interim. It was framed by Pflug, Sidonius, and Agricola, of whom the two former were dignitaries in the Romish Church ; the last was a Protestant divine ; but considered by his brethren as an apostate.

THE NEW CREED.

This famous treatise contained a complete system of Roman theology ; though expressed for the most part in " softest words, or in Scriptural phrases, or in terms of studied ambiguity." Every doctrine peculiar to Popery was retained, or, as Mr. Wylie sums it up : " The Interim taught, among other things, the supremacy of the Pope, the dogma of transubstantiation, the sacrifice of the mass, the invocation of the saints, auricular confession, justification by works, and the sole right of the Church to interpret the Scriptures ; in short, not one concession did Rome make. In return for swallowing a creed out-and-out Popish, the Protestants were to be rewarded with two paltry boons. Clergymen already married were to be permitted to discharge their offices without putting away their wives ; and where it was the wont to dispense the sacrament in both kinds, the custom was still to be tolerated. This was called meeting the Protestants half way."*

This document, which brought the most desolating calamities and oppressions on the Protestants, was submitted by the Emperor to the Diet of Augsburg, on May 15th, 1548. Having been read in presence of the diet, in due form, the Archbishop of Mentz, without giving time for any discussion, rose up hastily, thanked the Emperor for his pious endeavours to restore the peace of the Church, and in the name of the diet signified their approbation of the system of doctrine which had just been read to them. This unexpected, unconstitutional declaration amazed the whole assembly ; but not one member had courage enough to contradict what the archbishop had said. Overawed by the Spanish troops outside, the diet was silent. The Emperor at once accepted the declaration as a full ratification of the Interim, proclaimed it as a decree of the Empire, to remain in force till a free general council could be held, and to which all were to conform under pain of his displeasure. The Interim was immediately published in the German as well as the Latin language.

THE INTERIM OPPOSED BY PROTESTANTS AND PAPISTS.

The Emperor, proud of his new scheme, and believing that he was on the high road to victory, and the consummation of his plans, proceeded to enforce the Interim. But to his great astonishment he found all parties declaiming against it with equal violence. The Protestants condemned it as a system containing the grossest errors of Popery. The Papists condemned it because some of the doctrines of the Holy Catholic Church were impiously given up. But at Rome the indignation of the ecclesiastics rose to the greatest height. They exclaimed against the Emperor's

" History of Protestantism," vol. ii., p. 118. See also Robertson's " History," vol. vi., book ix.

profane encroachment on the sacerdotal office, and compared him to that apostate, **Henry VIII** of England, who had usurped the title as well as the jurisdiction belonging to the supreme Pontiff.

Among the Protestant princes there was great diversity of feeling, into the details of which we need not enter. Some yielded a feigned submission, but there were others who made a firm stand and a faithful protest against the Interim. Charles, well knowing the great influence which the example of his prisoner, Frederick, would have with all the Protestant party, laboured with the utmost earnestness to gain his approbation of the scheme. But he was not to be moved, either by the hope of liberty, or the threats of greater harshness. He now met the Emperor with weapons mightier far than all the imperial power—conscience and the Word of God. And well would it have been for the Protestants and the cause of Protestantism, had no others ever been opposed to the threatenings of the Pope and the Emperor. Some might have been honoured with martyrdom, but the country would have been saved from the desolations of war, and the moral glory of this divine principle would have been stamped on the Reformation.

After having declared his firm belief in the doctrines of the Reformation, he added : " I cannot now in my old age abandon the principles for which I early contended ; nor, in order to procure freedom during a few declining years, will I betray that good cause on account of which I have suffered much, and am still willing to suffer. Better for me to enjoy, in this solitude, the esteem of virtuous men, together with the approbation of my own conscience, than to return into the world with the imputation and guilt of apostasy, to disgrace and embitter the remainder of my days." For this magnanimous resolution, in which he set his countrymen a noble pattern, he was rewarded by the Emperor with fresh marks of his displeasure. "The rigour of his confinement was increased : the number of his servants diminished ; the Lutheran clergymen, who had hitherto been permitted to attend him, were dismissed, and even the books of devotion, which had been his chief consolation during a tedious imprisonment, were taken from him."

MELANCHTHON'S SUBMISSION.

It is deeply to be regretted that the Wittemberg divines did not testify more firmly for the truth, and against the Popish scheme of the Interim. But the feeble **Melanchthon,** partly through fear of Charles, and partly from his excessive complaisance towards persons of high rank, endeavoured to steer a middle course, and the other theologians followed him. He then introduced the pernicious principle of *essentials, non-essentials,* and things *indifferent* in religion. He decided that the whole instrument, called the Interim, could by no means be admitted, but that there was no impediment to receiving and approving it, so far as it concerned things not *essential* in religion, or things *indifferent*. This decision gave rise to several long and bitter controversies in the Lutheran Church. The genuine followers of Luther could not account as *indifferent* the teaching and object of the Interim, and opposed with great fervour the Wittemberg and Leipsic divines. They charged them with giving up their Protestantism for the Emperor's religion. This lax principle has been doing its evil work in all the Reformed Churches from that day even until now. It is a convenient covering for those who have no conscience as to the authority of the Word of God, and wish to serve their own ends. But surely no part of Divine truth can be either *indifferent* or *non-essential*. "The words of the Lord," says the Psalmist, "are pure words : as silver tried in a furnace of earth, purified seven times " (Psa. 12. 6). How different is the estimate of the Spirit of truth and theology as to " the words of the Lord...*purified seven times.*"*

THE OPPOSITION OF THE FREE CITIES.

The reception of the Interim in the different provinces depended entirely on the nearness or distance of the Emperor's power. Where his arm had not reached, it was openly resisted ; where his power was felt, there was at least an outward compliance with it ; but it was in the free cities that Charles met with the most violent opposition to his new scheme. There the Reformation had made the greatest progress ; its most eminent divines were settled in them as pastors, and schools and other seminaries for the instruction of the young flourished within their gates. They petitioned and remonstrated, but without effect ; Charles was determined to carry into full execution the resolution he had formed—universal compliance with his odious Interim.

His first attempt was upon the city of Augsburg. " He ordered one body of his troops to seize the gates ; he posted the rest in different quarters of the city ; and assembling all the burgesses in the town-hall, he, by his sole authority, published a decree abolishing their present form of government, dissolving all their corporations and fraternities, and nominating a small number of persons in whom he vested for the future all the powers of government. Each of the persons thus chosen took an oath to observe the Interim." Persecution immediately followed ; for many sought to maintain a good conscience before God and adhered to the truth of His Word. The Protestant pastors were

* See Mosheim's " History of the Lutheran Church on the Controversies," vol. iii.; also Scott's continuation of Milner on Melanchthon's Submission, vol. ii.

forced into exile, or rendered homeless in their native land ; their Churches were purified from Protestant defilement ; the old rites were restored—masses, vestments, crosses, altars, candles, images, etc., and the inhabitants driven to mass by the soldiers of the Emperor. " In southern Germany alone, four hundred faithful preachers of the Gospel fled with their wives and families, and wandered without food or shelter ; while those who were unable to escape fell into the hands of the enemy, and were led about in chains." This state of things continued for nearly five years, during which time the sufferings and calamities of the faithful were far beyond the record of the chronicler, and have no place in the history of the Church ; but there was One who heard every sigh that was heaved, and saw every tear that was shed : " and a book of remembrance was written before Him for them that feared the Lord, and that thought upon His Name. And they shall be Mine, saith the Lord of hosts, in that day when I make up My Jewels " (Mal. 3. 16, 17).

A NEW TURN IN THE TIDE OF EVENTS.

The period of their sufferings, or rather of their *purifying* was nearly accomplished, and the day of their deliverance was nigh at hand ; though nothing was farther from the thoughts of the oppressor. He imagined that his victories were complete, his plans consummated, and that now he might rest a little from the toils of government, and taste the sweetness of retirement and repose. For this purpose he went to Innspruck in the Tyrol, with only a few of his guards. But some already saw the storm gathering in various quarters, which was so soon to darken the whole firmament in his dominion and glory, and leave the master of two worlds without honour, and shut up in the solitude of a monkish cell. It happened in this way :

There were still **four cities** of note holding out against the authority of the Emperor. These were Magdeburg, Bremen, Hamburg, and Lubeck. But as the resistance of Magdeburg stands connected with events which changed the whole face of affairs in Germany, we will speak of this city only.

In a diet held at Augsburg, in the year 1550, it was resolved to send an army against Magdeburg, and besiege it in form. By an artful dissimulations of his real intention, and by a seeming zeal to enforce the observance of the Interim, the notorious Maurice of Saxony undertook to reduce the rebellious city to obedience. This proposal received the sanction of the diet, and the full approbation of the Emperor.

Deep thoughts had been revolving in the mind of Maurice and many others, previous to this appointment. By the late successes of Charles, the fears of many were awakened. The Vatican was the first to raise the alarm. The Pope repented of having contributed so largerly to the growth of a power that might one day become his master. Already Charles had shaken the foundations of ecclesiastical authority, in presuming to define articles of faith, and to regulate modes of worship. Efforts were made to form alliances with foreign powers, that a vigorous resistance might be made at once, before his power became too formidable to be opposed.

But it was now apparent to all that Charles was bent on exacting a rigid conformity to the doctrines and rites of the Romish Church, instead of allowing liberty of conscience, as he had always promised. The nation felt that they had been grossly deceived. They had been told over and over again before the war began that it was no part of the Emperor's plans to alter the Reformed religion. But now both the religion and the liberties of Germany were at the feet of the perfidious monarch. This could not fail to alarm the princes of the Empire; and none more so than Maurice. He was addressed in satires as " Judas," and accused by his countrymen as the author of these calamities. In this painful position Maurice made his choice. Only one thing will atone for the betrayal of the Protestant Confederacy —the complete overthrow of the Emperor's power in Germany; and this he resolved to accomplish.

" He saw," says Robertson, " the yoke that was preparing for his country; and, from the rapid as well as formidable progress of the imperial power, was convinced that but a few steps more remained to be taken in order to render Charles as absolute a monarch in Germany as he had become in Spain." Maurice was a Protestant—politically—at heart, and by his Electoral dignity, the head of the party. Besides, his passions concurred with his love of liberty. He longed to avenge the cruel imprisonment of the Landgrave, his father-in-law, who, by his persuasion had put himself into the Emperor's hands.

When he divulged his bold purpose to the princes, they were slow to believe him; but at length, being satisfied of his sincerity, they readily promised to assist him. Having gained the confidence of the Protestant party, he next applied all his powers of art and duplicity to deceive the Emperor. The jealousy of Charles had been somewhat excited by hearing of Maurice's friendship with some of the Protestant princes; but now, by his apparent zeal against the citizens of Magdeburg, all his suspicions were allayed, and he was inspired with fresh confidence in Maurice. As general of the army, he had a large force under his command, but he managed to protract the siege of Magdeburg till his plans were matured. He secretly formed leagues with several German princes, and entered into an alliance with the powerful King of France, Henry II, who proved a most effective ally, though a Catholic.

THE REVOLUTION IN GERMANY.
A.D. 1552.

When Maurice's preparations were accomplished, he **published a manifesto** containing his reasons for taking arms against the Emperor, namely : That he might secure the Protestant religion, which was threatened with immediate destruction ; that he might maintain the laws and constitution of the Empire ; that he might deliver the Landgrave of Hesse from the miseries of a long and unjust imprisonment. By the first proposal he roused all the friends of the Reformation to support him, who had been rendered desperate by oppression. By the second he interested all the friends of liberty in his cause—Catholics no less than Protestants. By the third he drew to his standard all the sympathy which had been universally excited by the Landgrave's unjust imprisonment, and by the rigour of the Emperor's proceedings against him. At the same time Henry of France issued a manifesto, in which he assumed the extraordinary title of " Protector of the liberties of Germany and of its Captive Princes."

The Emperor, as we have seen, was reposing at Innspruck, within three days' journey of Trent, and narrowly watching the proceedings of the council now sitting there. Maurice, still concealing his designs under the veil of the most exquisite address, despatched a trusted messenger to assure the Emperor that he would wait upon him in a few days at Innspruck ; for which friendly visit the Emperor was in daily expectation. But the time for action was now come. The trumpet of war was sounded ; and with a well-appointed army of twenty thousand foot and five thousand horse, Maurice pushed on by secret and forced marches, determined to surprise the Emperor and seize his person. The imperial garrison, by the way, offered no resistance, but tidings reached the imperial quarters that all Germany had risen, and was in full march upon Innspruck.

THE EMPEROR'S FLIGHT.

It was now late in the evening. The night was dark, and the rain falling heavily ; but danger was near, and nothing could save the **Emperor but speedy flight.** He had been suffering for some time from a severe attack of the gout, and was unable to escape on horseback. Placed in a litter, the only motion he could bear, he travelled by the light of torches, taking his way over the Alps by roads almost impassible. His courtiers and attendants followed him with equal precipitation, and all in the utmost confusion. In this miserable plight the late conqueror of Germany arrived with his dejected train at Villach, a remote corner in Carinthia.

Maurice entered Innspruck a few hours after the Emperor and his attendants had left it ; but rather than pursue them, he abandoned all the Emperor's baggage, together with that of his ministers, to be plundered by his soldiers. There was now nothing left for the fallen Emperor but negotiations, or rather to submit to the terms proposed to him ; and this he committed to his brother Ferdinand. Maurice, backed by all Germany, was absolute.

THE PEACE OF PASSAU.

On the 2nd of August, 1552, the famous **Treaty of Passau** was concluded. By this treaty it was agreed that the Landgrave should be set at liberty, and conveyed in safety to his own dominions ; that within six months, a diet should be held of all the states, to deliberate on the best means of terminating the existing religious dissensions, and that in the meantime no molestation whatever should be offered to those who adhered to the Augsburg confession ; that, if the diet thus to be held, should fail to effect an amicable adjustment of their religious disputes, the Treaty of Passau should remain in force for ever. Thus was peace restored to the Empire, and entire freedom conceded to the Protestant faith. This was followed by the "**Recess of Augsburg,**" in 1555, which not only ratified the Peace of Passau, but enlarged the religious liberties of Germany. It was this memorable convention which gave to the Protestants, after so much slaughter and so many calamities and conflicts, that firm and stable religious peace which they still enjoy. But alas ! the youthful Maurice, who played so conspicuous a part, both in the defeat and the triumph of the Protestants, fell in battle, in less than a year after the Peace of Passau, so that he was not permitted to see the full results of his bold undertaking.[*]

All these arrangements and treaties were deeply mortifying to the disappointed ambition of Charles. Protestantism, which he had intended to crush entirely, was flourishing throughout the Empire. The mass-priests were dismissed ; the banished pastors were brought back with great joy to their beloved flocks. The esteemed Frederick, who had been carried about from place to place by the Emperor for five years, had found his way home to his affectionate family and friends ; but everything shaped itself in dark and gloomy colours before the troubled mind of Charles. He never had a heart for friendship, and, it is said, he never made a friend. Thus, faint and weary, the friendless Emperor hid himself in the fastness of Carinthia. From civil history we learn that, at this very moment, war was going on in Hungary against the still advancing Turks. Henry II, according to his agreement with Maurice, took the field early, with a numerous and well appointed army, and completely defeated the Spanish forces in Lorraine and Alsace. Italy was on the eve of outbreak

* Mosheim, vol. iii., p. 157 ; Wylie, vol. ii., p. 122 ; Scott, vol. i., p. 83.

and anarchy. But the Emperor was in exile ; his treasury empty ; his credit gone ; his armies scattered and dispirited ; and, feeling himself rapidly falling from the lofty elevation which he had so long maintained, he resolved to withdraw entirely from the affairs of this world, in order that he might spend the remainder of his days in retirement and solitude.

Accordingly, at the comparatively early age of fifty-six, he filled all Europe with astonishment by resigning the imperial crown to his brother Ferdinand, and the remainder of his vast possessions in Europe and America to his son Philip II, whom he had already, on his marriage with Mary of England, invested with Naples and Sicily. The following year, after settling his affairs, he retired to the monastery of St. Juste, near the town of Placentia, in Spain. But he was still suffering so severely from the gout, that he had to be conveyed sometimes in a chair, and sometimes in a horse-litter, suffering exquisite pain at every step, and advancing with the greatest difficulty. Like most of the religious houses in those days, the monastery of St. Juste was beautifully situated. " It lay in a little vale, watered by a small brook, and surrounded by rising grounds covered with lofty trees ; from the nature of the soil, as well as the temperature of the climate, it was esteemed the most healthful and delicious situation in Spain." Here Charles lived about two years, and died on the 21st of September, 1558, in the fifty-ninth year of his age.

REFLECTIONS OF THE FOREGOING PAGES.

On the **cloister days of the Emperor** we need not dwell. They were chiefly spent in light and mechanical amusement when relief from the gout permitted him. One of these was a kind of theatrical lamentation at his funeral before his death. He ordered his tomb to be erected in the chapel ; his body was laid in the coffin with great solemnity, the monks weeping (?) ; then marching in funeral procession with black tapers in their hands to the chapel. The service for the dead was chanted, the coffin sprinkled with holy water, the mourners retired, and the doors of the chapel were closed. Then Charles rose out of his coffin and withdrew to his apartment, full of those awful sensations which such a revolting farce was calculated to create. He died almost immediately after.

Yes ! he died—died to all his dignities and humiliation, to all his ambition and disappointments, to all his plans and his policy ! Yes ! he who had sacrificed hundreds of thousands of human lives, and spent millions of money with the ultimate view of extinguishing Protestantism, died in the narrow sphere of a monkish cell, while Protestantism was now filling the vast firmament of human thought with its light and glory. There we leave the great Emperor—the greatest perhaps, as to dominions, that ever sat upon a throne. He is before the tribunal where motives as well as actions are weighed, and where all must be tried by the Divine standard.

But, alas, we search in vain for anything like repentance in that inveterate enemy of the Reformers. Within the holy walls of St. Juste, so far from repenting of his conduct towards them, his only regret was that he had not treated them with greater severity. When informed that Lutheranism was spreading in Spain, and that a number of persons had been apprehended under suspicion of being infected with it, he wrote letters from the monastery to his daughter, Joanna, Governess of Spain, to Juan de Vega, president of the council of Castile, and to the Inquisitor-general, charging them to exert their respective powers with all possible vigour, " in seizing the whole party, and causing them all to be burnt, after using every means to make them Christians before their punishment ; for he was persuaded that none of them would become sincere Catholics, so irresistible was their propensity to dogmatise." Again, he says : " If they do not condemn them to the fire, they will commit a great fault as I did in permitting Luther to live. Though I spared him solely on the ground of the safe-conduct I had sent him . . . I confess, nevertheless, that I did wrong in this, because I was not bound to keep my promise to that heretic . . . but in consequence of my not having taken away his life, heresy continued to make progress ; whereas his death, I am persuaded, would have stifled it in its birth."*

Here we have the **real heart of Charles.** There is no longer any reason for artifice and dissimulation, or pretended toleration to the Protestants. He has done with his wars and his politics ; he has no longer a double part to play ; and the real spirit of the Papist is openly expressed. The one regret of his old age is, that he did not seize the prey of his youth. He seems to gnash his teeth with rage when he thinks of Luther, and grieves that he did not violate his promise. But there was One who was watching over the life of Luther and the infant Reformation ; and so kept the hands of Charles full for upwards of thirty years ; that he had no leisure to wage war against the Lutherans. But some think that this was ever before him as the one grand object of his life and his reign—the extermination of heresy.

But in that very contest on which he had staked everything, all was lost—his dominions, his throne, his crown, his grandeur. Never was the hand of God more strikingly displayed in the affairs of any prince. In one moment, and by one stroke, all was changed. " His power collapsed when apparently at its zenith. None of the usual signs that precede the fall of greatness gave warning of so startling a downfall in the Emperor's fortunes.

* " History of the Reformation in Spain," by Dr. M'Crie, p. 119.

His vast prestige had not been impaired. He had not been worsted on the battle-field ; his military glory had suffered no eclipse ; nor had any of his kingdoms been torn from him.''* Of all the great men who started with him in life, such as Francis I, Henry VIII, Leo X, and Martin Luther, he was the sole survivor. His rivals had passed away before him, and none seemed left to dispute his possession of the field. But the hand of the Lord in retributive justice was lifted up against the oppressor of His people, and who could shelter him ? Already a finger had written on the walls of his palace : " Mene, Mene, God hath numbered thy kingdom and finished it." And, instantly, the brazen gates of his power could no longer protect him, he was compelled to flee before a power which his insidious and fraudulent policy had created. The rod which he had thus prepared for the destruction of Germany was used of God for his own complete and ignominious overthrow. What a reality is the government as well as the grace of God in the earth ! He controls the movements of the mightiest monarchs, and cares for the smallest things in creation. This, faith well knows, and finds its rest and consolation therein. " The eyes of the Lord are over the righteous, and his ears are open to their prayers ; but the face of the Lord is against them that do evil " (1 Peter 3. 12).

THE CALAMITIES OF THE PROTESTANTS.

The other lesson so plainly written on the foregoing pages is this—that God is a jealous God, and will not give His glory to another. He will have His work done by His own means and in His own way. No greater calamity could have befallen the Reformation than that its friends should have given up the Divine position of faith, and descended to the world's platform of diplomacy and arms. Had it triumphed by these means, it would have lost its true character, or perished in the land of its birth, and the Reformers would have become a mere political power. But God would not have it so, and He suffered them to be shamefully defeated and stripped, until they were utterly defenceless and cast upon Himself. They had neither league nor sword, nor treasures, nor castles, nor any means of defence. They were brought back to their first principles—faith in the Word of God, and martyrdom. But these Divine and invincible principles seemed to have died with their great leader and to have been buried in his grave ; and it was only through great suffering and humiliation that his followers were led to see their mistake.

But no sooner were they brought to feel that they had no means of defence but the Word of God and a good conscience before Him, than deliverance came. The Lord had said : " The

* " History of Protestantism," vol. ii., p. 121.

rod of the wicked shall not rest upon the lot of the righteous "
(Psa. 125. 3). Such is the goodness and the tender mercy of our
God. He withdraweth not His eyes from the righteous. But it
is always dangerous to give up the principles of God's Word, and
to be governed in our ways by the maxims and policy of this
world ; and this holds true in all the affairs of life ; but on the
subject before us the Word of God is plain, as saith the apostle :
" For the weapons of our warfare are not carnal, but mighty
through God to the pulling down of strongholds," yes, " *mighty
through God.*" And as the blessed Lord says : " All they that
take the sword shall perish with the sword " (2 Cor. 10. 4 ;
Matt. 26. 52).

The **Reformation in Germany,** embracing the Lutheran
Churches, was now definitely established. But the Reformed
Churches, embracing the followers of Zwingle and Calvin, were
excluded from the privileges secured in the treaties of Passau
and Augsburg, nor was legal toleration extended to them till the
Peace of Westphalia, nearly a century later. By this famous
treaty the pacification of Passau was confirmed to the members
of the Reformed Churches, and the independence of Switzerland
declared for the first time. " The balance of power," by which
the weak amongst the nations might be effectually protected,
and the powerful restrained from those aggressive schemes of
ambition which had been too frequently indulged, was one of the
important results of the negotiations and discussions in Westphalia.*

THE RISE OF THE JESUITS.

Before taking our leave, finally, of the reign of Charles V, we
must just notice **two memorable events** which occurred during
that reign, because of the relation they bore to the Reformation,
and the great religious struggle which was then agitating all
classes of society. We refer to the Council of Trent, and the rise
of the Jesuits. Having said a little about the former, we will
only at present speak of the latter.

We can easily conceive that the enemies of the Reformation
were now at their wits' end. What was to be done ? That
which had been looked forward to for thirty years, as the sure
means of crushing it, had not only filled, but ceased to be an
opposing power, while the Reformation was rapidly increasing
its area and multiplying its adherents. The Pope had lost
immensely in dignity, influence, and revenues in the contest,
and the imperial power could no more be appealed to. The
friars, black, white, and grey, were dispersed and their monasteries destroyed ; what was next to be done ? was a grave question
for the evil heart of Jezebel, and those with whom she took
counsel. Men-at-arms had failed ; peace and persuasion must

* " *Universal History,*" vol. vi., p. 87 ; Wylie, vol. ii., p. 122.

be our tactics now, suggested the presiding spirit. An army must be raised whose uniform should be the priestly garb, whose vows must be poverty, chastity, the care of Christians, and the conversion of infidels ; and the character of whose mission must be persuasive and pacific. Under these appearances a counter-work to the Reformation must be immediately instituted. This plausible proposal was unanimously agreed to ; and never was suggestion more plainly from beneath—even from the depths of Satan ; and never was there one more satanically executed, as the history of the Jesuits proves. The springs of human feeling, sympathy, and pity seem to have been dried up in every member of that society, and the hell-inspired springs of bigotry and cruelty, which have no parallel in history, most surely possessed them.

IGNATIUS LOYOLA.

The **Society of the Jesuits,** a religious order of the Romish Church, was founded by Ignatius Loyola, the son of a Spanish nobleman, born in the year 1491, at Guipuzoca, in the province of Biscay. In his youth he was employed as a page at the court of Ferdinand and Isabella, but he grew weary of its gaieties, and longed to be engaged in the wars of his country. In 1521 we find him defending Pampeluna against the French ; but the young intrepid Loyola was severely wounded in both legs. Fever followed, and the future restorer of the Papacy˙ was nearly brought to a premature grave.

By nature ardent, romantic, and visionary, he devoured greedily, during his long illness, the romances of Spanish chivalry, founded on the conflicts of his nation with the Moors ; and when these were exhausted, he betook himself to a series of still more marvellous romances—the legends of the saints. With a morbid intensity he studied those books of mystical devotion, until he resolved to emulate in his own life the wondrous virtues ascribed to a Benedict, a Dominic, or a Francis. Accordingly, on his recovery, he retired to a Benedictine monastery at Mont-serrat, near Barcelona ; and there he passed the night at the celebrated shrine of the Virgin Mary. He suspended his lance and shield before an image of the Virgin, vowed constant obedience to God and His Church, thereby abandoning a tem-poral for a spiritual knighthood.

To celebrate his self-dedication to Our Lady, he withdrew to the adjacent town of Manresa. Holiness, in the view of such men, does not consist in the moral likeness of the soul to Jesus, but in the mortification of the body. Next to his skin he wore alter-nately an iron chain, a horsehair cloth, and a sash of prickly thorns. Three times a day he laid the scourge resolutely on his bare back. This was not to mortify the *deeds* of the body, but the poor unoffending body itself. Such is the blinding power of

Satan, and such the suited darkness for his purpose. After travelling barefoot to Rome, Jerusalem, and other places rendered sacred by the Saviour's history, he eventually found his way to Paris. Here he met with Francis Xavier, who afterwards became the great apostle of India. Other kindred spirits joining them, a small band of zealous associates gathered round Loyola, which gave origin to the Society of Jesus—about eight or nine in all.

COMMENCEMENT OF THE ORDER OF JESUITS.

On the 15th of August, 1534, being the festival of the assumption of the Virgin Mary, in one of the subterranean chapels of Montemartre, and after receiving the sacrament, they all took the usual vows of poverty and chastity ; and then took a solemn oath to dedicate themselves to the conversion of the Saracens at Jerusalem, and the care of the Christians, and to lay themselves and their services unreservedly at the feet of the Pontiff. " The army thus enrolled was little, and it was great. It was little when counted, it was great when weighed. To foster the growth of this infant Hercules, Loyola had prepared beforehand his book, entitled 'Spiritual Exercises.' This is a body of rules for teaching men how to conduct the work of their own *conversion*. It consists of four grand meditations, and the penitent, retiring into solitude, is to occupy absorbingly his mind on each in succession, during the space of the rising and setting of seven suns ... It professes, like the Koran, to be a revelation. 'The Book of Exercises,' says a Jesuit, ' was truly written by the finger of God, and delivered to Ignatius by the Holy Mother of God.'"*

After some delays, the Pope, Paul III, approving the plan of Loyola and his companions, granted a bull in 1540, authorising the formation of the body under the name of " the Society of Jesus," and in April of the following year, Ignatius was installed as " The General Superior," who was to be subject to the Pope only. The order had now a formal existence. Its members were to dress in black, like the secular clergy ; and not being confined to cloisters, they were able to mix themselves up with all classes, and were soon found occupying courts, confessionals, and pulpits, superintending educational establishments, and otherwise securing the affections and co-operation of the young. Crowds of enthusiastic converts flocked to the new standard in all countries, and from all gradations of society.

THE JESUITS' REAL OBJECT.

Thus far we have trodden on ground over which the real character of the Jesuits does not appear—we have only had to do with vows intended to deceive ; but were we to pursue their

* " History of Protestantism," vol. ii., p. 384.

history we should have to trace in every land the blood-stained footprints of the treacherous and cruel followers of Loyola. Spreading themselves over the world, we find them secretly executing the decrees and private wishes of the Vatican. Their one grand object was to extend the power of the Pope, and the one grand fundamental principle of the fraternity was immediate, implicit, unquestioning, unhesitating obedience to him, through their general, who resides in Rome. The organisation of their society is by far the most comprehensive of any in existence. "The Jesuit monarchy," it has been said, "covers the globe." In almost every province of the world they have Generals Provincial, who correspond with the General Superior at Rome ; so that by means of the confessional, he sees and knows almost everything that is done and said, not only in the Romish Church, but in private families, and throughout all parts of the habitable globe. No place is too distant, no difficulties or dangers too great, and no means too nefarious for the Jesuit, if there is the slightest hope of extending the power of the Papacy.

The **Gunpowder Plot,** which was planned to destroy at one blow the nobility and gentry of England, is attributed to Jesuitical influence ; and so are many other plots which were intended to accomplish the death of Queen Elizabeth. The gigantic wickedness of the Spanish Armada, and the crowning slaughter of the St. Bartholomew massacre, to say nothing of the many seditions, torturings, poisonings, assassinations, and massacres on a smaller scale, must be attributed to the policy, and to the seed sown by the Jesuits. So mighty did their power become, and so ruinous, that it was often found necessary for the government to suppress them. According to modern history, they were expelled from Portugal in 1759 ; France, 1764 ; Spain and Spanish America, 1767 ; the two Sicilies, 1768 ; and in 1773 suppressed by the Pope Ganganelli, Clement XIV. But soon after he had signed the order for their banishment, he fell a victim to their vengeance, and died by poison. In 1801 they were restored by Pius VII ; in 1860 they were dismissed from Sicily ; but we need scarcely add, that they soon found ways and means to return. The late Pope, Pius IX, confirmed the restoration of the order ; so that they now occupy a very proud position in Rome. They have the command of most of the collegiate establishments in the city, and in so many other places, that merely to name them would fill a page.*

Thus was the enfeebled power of Popery greatly revived— *its deadly wound was healed.* By means of the Reformation, many of the most opulent and powerful kingdoms of Europe had thrown

---

* For a thorough exposure of the iniquity of the moral code of the Jesuits, see the "Provincial Letters" of Pascal, a Jansenist. For details of their organisation, training, operations, see "History of Protestantism," vol. ii.; "Faiths of the World—Jesuits ; " "Universal History," Bagster, vol. vi., p. 82 ; Hardwick's "History of the Reformation," p. 329.

off their allegiance to the Pope. This was a fatal blow to his grandeur and power. It abridged his dominions, abolished his jurisdiction within their territories, and diminished his revenues. But more than this, it is well known that Charles V seriously contemplated the reduction, if not the subversion, of the Papal power. Such was the low, and almost expiring condition of the Papacy, when the army of the Jesuits came to its help, which may be viewed as an illustration of Revelation 13. 3, though far from the full accomplishment of those solemn prophecies.

We now turn to our general history, and would briefly glance at the progress of the Reformation in different lands.

CHAPTER XLVIII

The Effect of the Reformation in Germany on the Nations of Europe

THE position of the **German Empire,** which had been chosen by Divine providence as the scene of the early dawn and noon-day glory of the Reformation, was most favourable ; and more likely than any other nation, to affect by its revolutions, the general state of Europe. Germany was, we learn, at that time, the connecting link between Asia and Europe, and the highway for the commerce of the two hemispheres. It was also famous for imperial diets, which always attracted crowds of dignitaries both civil and clerical ; besides the peculiarity of its constitution, its numerous princes, and its free cities, gave to its internal contests an interest and an importance to all the surrounding countries. In all this we see the wisdom of God, even as to locality ; and how naturally and quickly the whole of Christendom would be affected by the progress of the new opinions.

But not only the place, the time and circumstances were all ordered of the Lord to give immediate effect to the proclamation of the revived Gospel. The mysterious charm which had bound mankind for ages was broken at once, and for ever. The public mind which had so long been passive, as if formed to believe whatever was taught, and meekly to bear whatever was imposed, was suddenly roused to a spirit of inquiry and mutiny, and disdainfully threw off the yoke to which it had so long and so tamely submitted. But it was not the human mind only that was agitated by the new contest about religion ; the political constitutions of the most ancient kingdoms were shaken to their foundations.*

We will now trace its path in some of the countries most interesting to us.

SWEDEN AND DENMARK.

A.D. 1520-1530.

In connection with the reign of **Louis the Pious,** King of France, we have seen that the Gospel was introduced among the Danes and Swedes as early as the ninth century. The indefatigable Ansgarius laboured about forty years in those northern regions, and died in the year 865.† Other missionaries followed, but Christianity, in all probability, maintained a questionable exis-

* " History of the Church," by the Rev. John Fry, p. 333 ; Dr. Robertson's Works, vol. vi., p. 497.
† Vol. ii., p. 4.

tence in those barbarous times, and in the midst of pagan darkness. In the twelfth century Rome succeeded in completing the work of conversion, and in adding the Swedish Churches to the chair of St. Peter. An ecclesiastical constitution, according to the mystery of iniquity, was immediately imposed upon them, and soon, a flourishing priesthood, from the archbishop to the mendicant friar, covered the land, followed, as it always was, with decaying piety and an impoverished people.

At the dawn of the Reformation, the effects of the Papal superstition seemed to be nowhere more firmly rooted, nor more deeply felt than in these countries. " The people were steeped in poverty, and ground down by the oppression of their masters. Left without instruction by their spiritual guides, with no access to the Word of God—for the Scriptures had not yet been rendered into the Swedish tongue . . . the people were returning to the superstitious beliefs and pagan practices of old times." As in all other countries, the Romish hierarchy had swallowed up the wealth of these kingdoms. The bishops possessed revenues which often exceeded these of the ancient nobility, and sometimes equalled or exceeded those of the sovereign ; and not unfrequently they dwelt in castles and fortresses, which set the power of the crown at defiance.

By an ancient law, the three kingdoms, Sweden, Denmark, and Norway, like England, Scotland, and Ireland, were united under a common sovereign. The cruel tyrant, Christiern II, brother-in-law to Charles V, filled the throne of Denmark when the opinions of Luther began to spread in those countries. Being poor, compared with the priesthood, he had been waiting for an opportunity to reduce their power, that he might take possession of their wealth. Quick-sighted enough to see that Protestantism might become popular, he professed to favour the new religion ; sent for Reinhard, a disciple of Carlstadt, and appointed him professor of theology at Stockholm. But he, dying shortly after, was succeeded by Carlstadt himself. For some reason he only remained in Denmark a short time, when Christiern invited Luther to visit his dominions, but the Reformer declined the invitation. Meanwhile the conduct of Christiern was so tyrannical, that the Swedes refused to acknowledge him as their king, and appointed an administrator. He raised an army, being assisted with vast sums of money from the Romish clergy, invaded Sweden, gained an advantage over them, and treated the conquered with the greatest barbarity. Seventy noble lords and senators he massacred in cold blood in an open square, the Archbishop of Upsala, it is said, approving of his vindictive cruelty. Among the number of these noble victims was Eric Vasa, the father of Gustavus Vasa, one of the most illustrious names in the annals of Sweden.

This noble youth, having escaped the murderous hands of Christiern, fled into Germany. During his sojourn there, he studied and embraced the principles of Luther. At length emerging from his hiding-place, he raised the standard of revolt, and roused the peasantry of the Swedish provinces to attempt the restoration of their country's independence. After a severe struggle he defeated and overthrew the tyrant, delivered his country from oppression, was elevated to the throne, and created Sweden into an independent sovereignty in 1523. The Danes, following the example, broke out in open rebellion. Christiern was deposed, and driven from the kingdom in the year 1523. He fled to the low countries, and joined the court of Charles V. Frederick, Duke of Holstein, was raised to the throne. This prince favoured the Reformation, and ruled with equity and moderation.

The truly patriotic king Gustavus, when firmly seated on his throne, exerted himself in every fair and honourable way, to establish Lutheranism in his own dominions. *Instruction*, not authority, for the conversion of his subjects, was his motto. Olaus Petri and his brother Laurentius, who had studied under Luther at Wittemberg, were the first preachers of the Reformation in Sweden. They also accomplished the all-important work of translating the Scriptures into the vulgar tongue. At an assembly of the states in 1527, Gustavus publicly declared, " that he would lay down his sceptre, and retire from his kingdom, rather than rule a people enslaved to the orders and authority of the Pope, and more controlled by the tyranny of their bishops, than by the laws of their monarchs." The king's will prevailed, the hierarchy was reduced in wealth and power, but tolerated. It would be difficult for anyone to believe in our day that the Romish clergy had gained possession, by their unhallowed influence, and were enjoying the revenues, of more than *thirteen thousand* estates in Sweden in less than a hundred years. But such was the prevailing power of the Protestant element in the assembly, that it was decreed, " that the estates, castles, farms, and lands, which had fallen into the hands of the Church, should be restored ; part to be returned to the nation, and part to those nobles from whose ancestors they had been wrested. The bishops submitted and signed the decree. Thus was the Reformation widely introduced and firmly established in Sweden.

The work in **Denmark** was very similar to that in **Sweden**. Frederick procured an edict at the assembly of the state in 1527, declaring that every subject of Denmark was free to adhere to the Church of Rome or to embrace the doctrines of the Reformation. This was enough ; the new religion prevailed, teachers flocked from Wittemberg, the Scriptures were translated into the

Danish tongue, the singing of hymns was introduced into their public and private worship, and the Reformation advanced amid the new sounds of melody and praise. " It is not easy adequately to describe the change that now passed over Denmark. A serene and blessed light arose upon the whole kingdom. Not only were the Danes enabled to read the Scriptures of the New Testament in their own tongue, and the Psalms of David, which were also often sung, both in their Churches and in their fields, and on their highways, but they had likewise numerous expounders of the Divine Word, and preachers of the Gospel, who opened to them the fountains of salvation."*

ITALY.

In no country outside of Germany did the reforming opinions find so early an entrance as in the provinces of **Italy.** In this we see the hand of the Lord, and the *silver line* of His sovereign grace. But He had a people there, and they must be brought to Jesus. Many believed and nobly witnessed for the truth of the Gospel, as the record of their martyrdoms abundantly testifies. But the light was intolerable to Jezebel, who loves darkness, and it was soon extinguished by the activity of her tribunals.

No people had so little respect for the Papal dignity as the Italians. The power of the Pope was greater, and his commands were more implicitly obeyed, in the countries most remote from the seat of his government. The personal vices of the Popes, the corruption of their administration, the ambition, luxury, licentiousness, and deceitfulness which reigned in their courts, fell immediately under the observation of the Italians. The main object of almost every succeeding Pope was to raise money by means of the sacred mysteries, that he might enrich his sons, nephews, and other relatives, with immoderate wealth, even with principalities and kingdoms. Thus all thoughtful Italians, seeing the artifices by which the Papacy was upheld, and the impostures on which it was founded, were ready to welcome something better.

" A controversy," says Dr. M'Crie,† " which had been carried on for several years with great warmth in Germany and which was at last brought before the Papal court for decision, contributed in no small degree to direct the attention of the Italians, at an early period, to the reformed doctrines." A professed convert from Judaism, leagued with an inquisitor of Cologne, obtained from the Imperial Chamber a decree ordaining all Jewish books, with the exception of the Bible, to be committed to the flames, as filled with blasphemies against Christ. John Reuchlin,

---

* For minute and lengthy details of the progress of the Reformation in Sweden, Denmark, Norway, and Iceland, see " History of Protestantism," by the Rev. J. A. Wylie—Cassell & Co.
† History of the Reformation in Italy."

the restorer of Hebrew literature among the Christians, exerted himself, both privately and from the press, to prevent the execution of the barbarous decree. But alas ! the clergy sided with the apostate, and sentence was pronounced against Reuchlin, both by the divines of Cologne and the Sorbonne of Paris. He appealed to Rome. Erasmus and other distinguished friends of learning in all parts of Europe, wrote warmly in favour of Reuchlin, and determined to make his cause a common one. The monks, who dreaded and hated Erasmus, and all men of learning, exerted themselves with the clergy, to obtain the execution of the decree ; but the court of Rome protracted the affair from time to time, until the contention that arose between Luther and the preachers of indulgences was carried to Rome for decision ; and thus the former controversy was lost sight of in the latter.

THE WRITINGS OF LUTHER.

In this remarkable, providential way, the attention of the Italians had been directed to the Germans, and even to the great Reformer, who had taken part with Reuchlin. " Within two years from the time of his first appearance against indulgences his writings had found their way into Italy, where they met with a favourable reception from the learned." **John Froben,** the celebrated printer at Basle, writing to Luther about this time, says : " Blasius Salmonius, a bookseller at Leipsic, presented me, at the last Frankfort fair, with certain treatises composed by you, which being approved of by learned men, I immediately put to press, and sent six hundred copies to France and Spain. My friends assure me that they are sold at Paris, and read and approved of, even by the Sorbonists. Calvus, a bookseller of Pavia, himself a scholar and addicted to the Muses, has carried a great part of the impression into Italy . . . In spite of the terror of Pontifical bulls, and the activity of those who watched over their execution, the writings of Luther, Melanchthon, Zwingle, and Bucer, continued to be circulated and read with avidity and delight in various parts of Italy. Some of them were translated into the Italian language, and, to elude the vigilance of the inquisitors, were published under fictitious names . . .' " Hail ! faithful in Christ," wrote a Carmelite monk of Locarno to the Christians in Switzerland, " think, O think of Lazarus in the Gospels, and of the lowly woman of Canaan, who was willing to be satisfied with the crumbs which fell from the table of the Lord. As David came to the priest in a servile dress, and unarmed, so do I fly to you for the shewbread, and the armour laid up in the sanctuary. Parched with thirst, I seek the fountain of living water : sitting like the blind man by the wayside, I cry to Him that gives sight. With tears and sighs, we, who sit here in darkness, humbly entreat you who are acquainted with the titles and authors of the book of knowledge, to send us the writings of such elect teachers as you possess, and particularly the works of the divine Zwingle, the far-famed Luther, the acute Melanchthon, the accurate Œcolampadius. The prices shall be paid to you through his excellency, Werdmyller. Do your endeavour that a city of Lombardy, enslaved by Babylon, and a stranger to the Gospel of Christ, may be set free."*

These extracts plainly show—and many more might be given—what an abundant entrance the Gospel had into Italy, and at a very early period of the Reformation. And for more than twenty years the followers of Luther and Zwingle were allowed to spread the truth, publicly preach the Gospel, and otherwise witness for Christ, almost unmolested. The wars, which we have had occasion to refer to in tracing the history of the Reformation in Germany, greatly affected Italy. Engrossed by foreign politics, and deeply involved in the struggle between Charles and Francis, the court of Rome disregarded, or thought exaggerated, the representations that were made to them of the progress of heresy. But these wars, so disastrous to the Pope and the patrimony of St. Peter, proved an inestimable blessing to thousands of precious souls. Many of the German soldiers who followed Charles V in his Italian expeditions, and the Swiss auxiliaries who followed the standard of his great rival, Francis I, were Protestants. "With the freedom of men," says Dr. M'Crie, "who have swords in their hands, these foreigners conversed on the religious controversy with the inhabitants among whom they were quartered."

The impressions made on the people's mind, in favour of the new opinions, were greatly strengthened by the bitter and never-ending contests between the Pope and the Emperor. We have seen Charles by turns an abettor of the Pope, and a restraint on his authority as the fluctuations of his contests with Francis I rendered it politic ; but with the deceitfulness of Clement VII he was maddened to fury. He accused the Pope of kindling the flames of war in Europe, that he might evade, what was universally called for, a general council for the Reformation of the Church in its head and members. It was at this time that he threatened to abolish the jurisdiction of the Pope throughout Spain ; but, not satisfied with these threatenings, he sent an army into the Papal territories under the command of his general, the Duke of Bourbon. Rome was besieged and sacked, and the Pontiff taken prisoner, in the year 1527. "The Germans in the Emperor's army behaved with great moderation towards the inhabitants of Rome after the first day's pillage, and contended themselves with testifying their detestation of idolatry ; but the Spaniards never relented in their rapacity and cruelty, torturing the prisoners to make them discover their treasures." Marching

* " History of the Reformation in Italy," p. 29.

up to the palace windows of the captive Pontiff, a whole band of Germans, raising their hands and voices, exclaimed, "**Long live Pope Luther**! Long live Pope Luther!"

Thus were the hands of the Pope and his counsellors filled with their own troubles, and the Reformers left tolerably free to pursue their happy work of conversion and instruction, by the good providence of God.

THE PERSECUTION OF THE CHRISTIANS.

It was not until the year 1542 that the court of Rome became seriously alarmed at the progress of the Reformed doctrines. By this time they were widely spread in nearly every province of Italy. Some of the most attractive and brilliant preachers in that country had embraced the simple Gospel and were preaching to large audiences a free salvation through faith in the Lord Jesus Christ. Among these, Bernardino Ochino, a Capuchin, Peter Martyr, a canon-regular of the order of St. Augustine, and the interesting **Aonio Paleario,** a pious and learned professor. Spies were set to watch their movements, listen to their sermons, and even then provoke conversation, with the view of procuring evidence against them. Ochino and Martyr saw their safety in flight, crossed the Alps, found an asylum in Switzerland, and ultimately in England ; but the career of Paleario was crowned with martyrdom in his own country.

When asked by his accusers, "What is the first means of salvation given by God to man ? " he answered, "Christ." "What is the second ? " he replied, "Christ." "And what is the third ?" he again answered, "Christ." From that moment, having rejected good works as the second means, and the Church as the third, he was a doomed man. But that which gave the greatest offence was a most influential treatise which he wrote on the *Benefit of the Death of Christ*. When the Inquisitor at length arose to crush the Lutherans and collect their heretical books, as many as *forty thousand* copies of this book fell into his hands. Paleario was at last condemned on four charges : 1, For denying Purgatory ; 2, For disapproving of the dead being buried in Churches ; 3, For ridiculing the monastic life ; 4, For ascribing justification solely to confidence in the mercy of God forgiving our sins through Jesus Christ. After an imprisonment of three years in the dungeons of the Inquisition, his body was given to the flames, in the year 1570, and in the seventieth year of his age.

His sufferings were soon over, and they would all soon be forgotten in the unmingled blessedness of his Lord's presence ; but the fruit of his faithful testimony will endure for ever. Who could estimate the effects, with God's blessing, of forty thousand copies of his book in the hands of the Italians ? But the fruit will all appear on that morning without clouds, and like Paul with his beloved Thessalonians, he will find his Italians to be his joy and crown of rejoicing, in the presence of the Lord Jesus Christ at His coming. What a mercy to be called of God, sustained by His grace, and enabled to witness for Him in any age and in every sphere of life ! Time will soon be over, the Lord will soon be here, and bright will the future be of all that have been faithful to Him. But His threatenings will be as surely executed as His promises will be fulfilled. It has ever been the policy of Rome to destroy the character, abolish the memory, and blot out the very names of those whose lives she has taken away. But their record is on high ; and all that has been of grace will be revealed in the light to the utter confounding, and eternal shame and anguish of their once haughty inquisitors. And their remembrance in Hell of the perfect happiness of their innocent but helpless victims, must give vitality to the worm that never dies and vehemence to the flames that will never be quenched.

A number of excellent men, whose only crime was their love to the Lord Jesus, and their faith in His Word, suffered about the same time as Paleario. Commissioned spies, in the pay of the Vatican, were dispersed over Italy, who insinuated themselves into private families, and the confidence of individuals, conveying the information which they obtained to the inquisitors. Assuming a variety of characters, they were to be found in the company of the rich and the poor, the learned and illiterate. Many excellent private persons were thus caught in the toils spread by these pests of society. In a short time the prisons of the Inquisition were filled with victims, including persons of noble birth, male and female, industrious mechanics, and many of good reputation for learning and piety. Multitudes were condemned to penance, the galleys, and the flames. To give even an outline of the imprisonments, tortures, and deaths among the Italian Protestants would be to write a martyrology.

" Englishmen," Dr. M'Crie observes, " were peculiarly obnoxious to the inquisitors. Dr. Thomas Wilson, afterwards secretary to **Queen Elizabeth,** was accused of heresy, and thrown into the prisons of the Inquisition at Rome, on account of some things which were contained in his books on logic and rhetoric. He made his escape in consequence of his prison doors being broken open during the tumult which took place at the death of Pope Paul IV. Among those who escaped by this occurrence was also John Craig, one of our Reformers, who lived to draw up the National Covenant, in which Scotland solemnly abjured the Popish religion. Dr. Thomas Reynolds was less fortunate. In consequence of being subjected to the torture, he died in prison. In the year 1595, two persons were burnt alive in Rome, the one an Englishman, the other a native of Silesia." But enough for the present of these details of misery. A brief notice of those who fled for their lives and liberties, will give the reader some idea of the great and blessed work of God's Holy Spirit in Italy during the sixteenth century. Perhaps in no country in Europe did the Word of God so prevail from 1520 to 1550 as in that land of blind superstition, luxury, and licentiousness. Such is the mercy of our God ; where sin abounds grace much more abounds, to His praise and glory. " All that the Father giveth Me shall come to Me : and him that cometh to Me I will in no wise cast out " (John 6. 37).

ITALIAN EXILES.

Surely no truer testimony can be given to the reality and power of our religious convictions than a readiness to leave our homes and all that is dear to us, in obedience to the Word of God and the dictates of conscience. The very sight of a number of foreigners, male and female, reaching our shores as exiles, would produce an impression highly favourable to the refugees, and deeply interesting to those among whom they had sought an asylum. Such were the Italian exiles, and such the impression produced, not only on their fellow Protestants, but on their adversaries the Roman Catholics. They could not understand how men of illustrious birth, rank, learning, position, civil and ecclesiastical, could voluntarily renounce their wealth and honours, leave their dearest friends, encounter poverty with all the hardships and dangers of a speedy flight, rather than do violence to the voice of conscience.

The **Republic of the Grisons,** owing to its proximity to Italy, was the country they first visited. " It was calculated that, in the year 1550, the exiles amounted to two hundred, of whom a fourth or fifth part were men of letters, and those not of the meanest name. Before the year 1559 the number had increased to eight hundred. From that time to the year 1568 we have ground to believe that the increase was fully as great in propor- tion ; and down to the close of the century, individuals were to be seen, after short intervals, flying to the north, and throwing themselves on glaciers of the Alps to escape the fires of the Inquisition." Happily for the exiles, and for the Grisons them- selves, the Reformation had made such progress there, that a statute law was passed, as early as 1526, securing religious liberty to all classes in the republic. In a national diet it was moved and agreed to : " That it shall be free to all persons of both sexes, and of whatever condition or rank, within the ter- ritories of the Grison confederation, to choose, embrace, and profess either the Roman Catholic or the Evangelical religion ; and that no one shall, publicly or privately, harass another with reproaches or odious speeches on account of his religion, under an arbitrary penalty. That the ministers of religion shall teach nothing to the people but what is contained in the Scriptures of the Old and New Testament, and what they can prove by them ; and that parish priests shall be enjoined to give themselves assiduously to the study of the Scriptures as the only rule of faith and manners." This noble statute, notwithstanding, some attempts that have been made to overthrow it, remains to this day the charter of religious liberty in the canton of the Grisons.

Many of the inhabitants in that part of Switzerland, who had come originally from Italy, and had preserved their ancient language and manners, were like a people ready for the ministrations of the exiles. And these, finding themselves perfectly free and safe, grudged no labour in communicating instruction privately and publicly, and were blessed of God to the winning of many souls for Christ. Congregations were formed, pastors appointed, the Lord's Supper celebrated, and worship conducted on the principle of the Reformed Churches. Others of the exiles made themselves masters of the different languages of the canton that they might be able to preach the Gospel to the inhabitants. Their preaching was of the most attractive and thrilling style. They detailed the cruelties of the Inquisition ; they laid bare the artifices, the superstitions, ignorance, vices, and corruption of the court of Rome and its priesthood, contrasting with great enthusiasm the liberty of conscience and the pure preaching of the Gospel enjoyed in the Grisons.

Thus did Rome, by her short-sighted and cruel policy, reduce her own strength at home, and send forth a band of her choicest subjects to expose her wickedness, weaken her influence abroad, and instruct many in the way of salvation. After a time many of these exiles spread themselves over the other cantons, and passed into other countries, carrying the light of the Gospel with them ; but alas, alas, their native and sunny Italy was doomed to be the abode of darkness, for few of the disciples of the Reformed doctrines were able to survive the barbarous and fiendish malice of the Inquisition.*

SPAIN.

The term **heresy,** about the time of the Reformation, was held in the highest detestation by the Spanish nation. The loudest boast of the proud Spaniard was purity of blood. The poorest peasant looked upon it as a degradation to have a drop of Jewish or Moorish blood in his veins. Yet in no country in Europe had there been such an intermixture of races. But this pride of a pure old Christian, or holy Catholic, ancestry made them peculiarly jealous of all forms of worship except their own. Besides, they had succeeded in cleansing the land by expelling the Jews, the inveterate enemies of Christ, from their courts ;

*For full details see Dr. M'Crie's " History ; " Miss Young's " Life and Times of Palearo, " 2 vols.; D'Aubigné's " History of the Reformation in Europe," vol. iv.; Hardwick's " Church History," p. 105.

and they had overthrown the Mohammedan Empire which had been established for ages in the fairest provinces of their land ; and would they now be traitors to the Cross under which they had conquered, and renounce their ancient faith for some new opinions of an obscure German monk ? Their successes at home, with their wonderful discoveries abroad, so increased the wealth and raised the reputation of Spain, that they began to think themselves the favourites of Heaven, and destined to propagate and defend the true faith throughout their vast dominions.

To the **discovery of America** by Columbus, and other magnificent territories by navigators of lesser name, must be added the vast increase of strength which the Spanish monarchy received by the succession of their youthful sovereign, Charles V, to his paternal dominions in the Low Countries, Austria, Bohemia, and Hungary, and his elevation to the imperial throne of Germany.

THE INTRODUCTION OF THE REFORMED DOCTRINES INTO SPAIN.

Such was the greatness and glory of the Spanish nation when the new faith knocked at her gates for admission. But notwithstanding the national antipathy to the German Reformation, there were many serious and thoughtful men predisposed in its favour. The scandalous corruptions of the clergy and the cruel energies of the Inquisition had alienated the hearts of many from the old religion. Accordingly, we find the writings of Luther translated and distributed in the Peninsula as early as the year 1519. The Reformer's commentary on the Galatians, a work which exhibits his doctrinal sentiments on the most important points, was translated into Spanish in 1520. This was followed by translations of his treatise on Christian Liberty and his reply to Erasmus on free will. These books were read and approved of by many who were illustrious for their rank, learning, and influence ; and had not the throne and the Inquisition combined to suppress both the books and their readers, Spain, we believe, would have produced a noble band of thorough Reformers. For the first ten years at least, the Papal briefs and the state authorities seemed ineffectual in arresting its progress.

" Headed by two brothers," says Hardwick, " Juan and Alfonso de Valdés, the reforming school increased from day to day in numbers and importance. It had representatives among the retinue of Charles V himself ; and both in Seville and Valladolid the crowd of earnest Lutherans was so great that cells could hardly be at last procured for their incarceration." Many noble witnesses for the Gospel follow these two leading brothers, down to the year 1530, when Charles, and a great body of Spanish nobles and clergy, had an opportunity of hearing for themselves the true doctrines of the Protestants, from the confession of faith which was read to the imperial diet of Augsburg. The public reading and examination of this confession had the effect of dissipating the false ideas of the opinions of Luther which had been industriously propagated by the monks. Alfonso de Valdés, the Emperor's secretary, of whom we have already spoken, had several friendly interviews with Melanchthon, and read the confession before it was presented to the diet. A. de Virves, chaplain to Charles, was also convinced of the truth of the protest, and became what was called a Lutheran. Valdés, Virves, and others on their return to Spain, being suspected of Lutheranism, were seized by the Inquisitors, and thrown into prison. A long list of nobles, priests, burgesses, monks, and nuns follow, but for details of their imprisonment, tortures, and death, we have no space.*

THE SUPPRESSION OF THE REFORMATION IN SPAIN.

For a number of years the Lord in mercy sheltered the **infant Church in Spain.** The Christians were in the habit of coming together with great secrecy, and breaking bread in private houses. On no other principle could we account for the truth spreading, the disciples multiplying, and the Church being edified, and all in the very place where the King, the Pope, and the Inquisition had sworn to keep Spain Roman Catholic. True, there were many individual cases of persecution and imprisonment, but nothing very definite, or on a large scale, was attempted till the year 1557.

The first thing which seems to have aroused the Inquisitors from their security, was the sudden disappearance of a number of persons, who were known to have settled in Geneva and different parts of Germany, where they were at liberty to worship God according to His Holy Word. This led to searching inquiries as to the cause of their departure ; and, finding it was the question of religion, the inquisitors naturally suspected that those who had left were not the only persons who were disaffected, and immediately set their whole police in motion to discover their brethren who remained behind. Besides their vigilance at home, spies were sent to Geneva and Germany, that they might, through feigning themselves to be friends, obtain information as to those who had embraced Lutheranism.

This information, it is painful to relate, was obtained by the treachery of one of the preachers' wives through the wicked arts of the confessional. At Valladolid, **Juan Garcia,** a goldsmith, being aware of the influence of the priest over the superstitious mind of his wife, concealed from her both the time and place of

* See Brief Account of the Inquisition, " Short Papers," vol. ii., pp. 486-489 ; Llorente's " History of the Inquisition ; " M'Crie's " History of the Reformation in Spain."

their assembling. But this poor deluded woman, in obedience to her harlot-mother Jezebel, dogged her husband one night, and having ascertained the place of meeting, communicated the fact to the priest. Having made this important discovery, messengers were despatched to the several tribunals throughout the kingdom ; the ramifications of heresy were to be diligently traced, guards were to be placed at convenient places to seize such persons as might attempt to escape ; and by a simultaneous movement the Protestants were seized in all parts of the country. In Seville and its neighbourhood, two hundred persons were apprehended in one day ; and, in a short time the number increased to eight hundred. In Valladolid eighty persons were committed to prison, and similar numbers by other tribunals. The common prisons, the convents, and even private houses were crowded with the victims. The storm of persecution burst with equal fury on the monasteries and nunneries that were known to favour the Lutheran doctrines.

The cruel and heartless king, Philip II, and his Inquisitors, were now determined to strike terror into the minds of the whole nation, and consequently, the unoffending prisoners were treated with the view of accomplishing this fiendish end. Many suffered in body and mind from a long imprisonment ; others from the severity of the tortures ended their days by a lingering and secret martyrdom ; while some of the most distinguished, either for rank, or of the clerical order, were reserved for a public execution, or the Spanish Auto de Fé.* But there was one family amongst the Protestants of Seville whose tragical history is so touching that we cannot withhold it from our readers.

" The widow of **Fernando Nugnez,** a native of the town of Lepe, with three of her daughters and a married sister, were seized and thrown into prison. As there was no evidence against them, they were put to the torture, but refused to inform against one another. Upon this the presiding Inquisitor called one of the young women into the audience chamber, and after conversing with her for some time, professed an attachment to her person. Having repeated this at another interview, he told her that he could be of no service to her unless she imparted to him the whole facts of her case ; but if she entrusted him with these, he would manage the affairs in such a way as that she and all her friends would be set at liberty. Falling into the snare, the unsuspecting girl confessed to him, that she had at different times conversed with her mother, sisters, and aunt, on the Lutheran doctrines. The wretch immediately brought her into court, and obliged her to declare judicially what she had owned to him in private. Nor was this all : under the pretence that her confession was not sufficiently ample and ingenuous, she was put

* See an account of the Auto de Fé, vol. ii., p. 490.

to the torture by the most excruciating engines—the pulley and the wooden horse ; by which means evidence was extorted from her, which led, not only to the condemnation of herself and her relatives, but also to the seizure and conviction of others who afterwards perished in the flames."*

No language could describe the meanness, perfidiousness, fiendishness, of one in human form that could do such a thing, and the reader may easily imagine from the treatment of the widow, the fatherless children, and the aunt, what the victims of the Inquisition (which could be counted by thousands) had to endure, and all for the crime of believing the truth of God, and rejecting the lies of Satan.

REFLECTIONS ON THE POLICY OF SPAIN.

It is difficult to conceive in our day, and in our land of civil and religious liberty, what could have induced the Church, aided by the government, to persecute thousands of the choicest of her members, for a difference of opinion on some points of religion. By far the greater part of those who were apprehended, and thrown into a dungeon, or were burnt at the stake, had not left the communion of the Romish Church. They might have accepted a New Testament in the Spanish language, or might have been drawn into conversation on the subject of the new opinions, either of which was sufficient to awaken the suspicion of the Familiars, and secure them imprisonment. We must look deeper down than the blind and infatuated policy of the government, or the tyranny of the Papal tribunals. The source is purely Satanic. The main object of this suicidal policy was to perpetuate the reign of darkness. Popery could not live in the light ; therefore the true Gospel—which ameliorates the condition of society, generates a spirit of liberty among the people, discerns and corrects abuses by its sure and Divine light— must be suppressed, no matter what it may cost.

The arch-enemy of God and man rules in the darkness and superstition of Popery, though at the same time God overrules. He saw from the beginning that society, in all countries where the Reformation had been received, was greatly improved and enlightened. It gave a higher tone to morals, and imparted to the human mind a strong impulse of inquiry and improvement. The progress of useful knowledge, the cultivation of literature, and the extension of commerce, which exalt a nation, would be the downfall of the Papal power. Therefore every movement, intellectual, civil, or religious, that would tend to raise the condition or enlighten the minds of the people, must be put down. The ruling clergy and the Inquisitors exercise the most rigid and vigilant inspection of the press and the seminaries of education,

* M'Crie, p. 130.

that they may arrest the progress of general or useful knowledge. This is abundantly proved by the list of prohibited books which they publish from time to time.

As the persecution grew hotter, the number of exiles increased. While the Italians were crossing the Alps, the Spaniards were crossing the Pyrenees, and not unfrequently met in the country of their adoption, and even united in the same Church. Thousands of the **Spanish exiles** found a happy home in England, which the Lord has not forgotten. But the kindness which they received here gave great offence to the blood-thirsty Philip and the Pope, and formed one of the charges against Elizabeth in the bull of her excommunication. Philip wanted them to be sent back, not for their capital or labour as useful citizens, but for their blood, that he might celebrate another victory in a grand Auto de Fé. But England on this occasion proved worthy of her well-known character for hospitality to the oppressed.

"The queen," nobly writes Bishop Jewell, "of her gracious pity, granted them harbour. Is it become a heinous thing to show mercy ? God willed the children of Israel to love the stranger, because they were strangers in the land of Egypt. He that showeth mercy shall find mercy. But what was the number of such who came in unto us ? *Three or four thousand.* Thanks be to God ; this realm is able to receive them, if the numbers were greater. And why may not Queen Elizabeth receive a few afflicted members of Christ, which are compelled to carry His Cross ? Whom when He thought good to bring safely by the dangers of the sea, and to set in at our havens, should we cruelly have driven them back again ? . . . Would the Vicar of Christ give this counsel ? Or, if a king receive such, and give them succour, must he therefore be deprived ? They are our brethren ; they live not idly. If they take houses of us, they pay rent for them ; they hold not our grounds but by making due recompense. They beg not in our streets, nor crave anything at our hands, but to breathe our air and see our sun. They labour truly, they live sparefully ; they are good examples of virtue, travail, faith, and patience. The towns in which they abide are happy, for God doth follow them with His blessing."

The reader will now see, what has so greatly interested us, that the work of God's Spirit in Catholic Spain must indeed have been a great and a blessed work. If we think of the thousands who became the victims of the Inquisition, and the thousands who found a refuge in England, besides those who settled in Switzerland, Germany, the Low Countries, and France, how great indeed must the work of the Spirit, by means of the scanty truth which they possessed, have been ; and that, too, in a very short time ! Towards the close of the century Spain boasted that she had extirpated the German heresy from her territories.

But she saw not in her blindness that she had inflicted a deeper and more fatal wound on herself than on the unoffending victims of her tyranny, and had sown the seeds of a national misery and despotism which she has been reaping ever since.

During the early part of the sixteenth century her sceptre extended over nearly half the world ; but what is her condition now ? Prostrate, sunk, and degraded, compared with the other nations of Europe. **Holland,** with no land but what she rescued from the ocean, became rich and independent, while **Spain,** with all her vast possessions, has become poor and helpless.*

How true it is, not only with individuals but with nations, that, " whatsoever a man soweth, that shall he also reap." This is the principle of the government of God, however much grace may overrule the failure of the Christian for his blessing ; as in the case of David. Nevertheless the sword was not to depart from his house. " Be not deceived," says the apostle, " God is not mocked ; for whatsoever a man soweth, that shall he also reap." This is a hard saying, many will say, yet it is most true and righteous. If a man sow tares in the spring, can he expect to reap wheat in the autumn ? And if he sow wheat, he will not have to reap tares. But, thank God, grace reigns, not on the ruins of law and justice, but " through righteousness unto eternal life by Jesus Christ our Lord." No thanks be to us when our failures turn to our deeper blessing, but to the grace of God which freely meets us on the ground of the finished work of Christ. When self is judged, the will broken, the eye of faith fixed on the blessed Lord, there is not only peace, but joy, through the power of the Holy Ghost (Gal. 6. 7 ; Rom. 5. 21).

THE NETHERLANDS.

For some time before the days of Luther, there had existed in the **Netherlands** a spirit of religious inquiry ; and a calm but firm resistance to the domination of the Romish Church. In the fifteenth century, a school of pious mystics, represented by such men as Thomas à Kempis, had revived a spirit of devotion in many countries of the west, especially in Flanders and some parts of Germany.† It was also the land of John Wessel, who, in many things, anticipated Luther ; and of Erasmus, at a later period. Most of the Reformers' books, both Swiss and Saxon, were translated, printed, and sent out from Antwerp in large quantities. The provinces were wealthy and prosperous from their extensive manufactures and commerce. Antwerp was, in that age, the emporium of the world. Hence their great facility in sending books into all parts, by concealing them in their bales of goods. It was from Antwerp chiefly that both

* See Dr. M'Crie's " History "---Blackwood, Edinburgh.
† Hardwick's " Middle Ages," p. 372.

Italy and Spain received the new books. The writings of Erasmus against the monks may also have helped to prepare the way for the deeper doctrines of Luther and Zwingle. It was only natural, we may say, under these circumstances, that the light of the Reformation should have penetrated the Low Countries at an early period.

THE POLICY OF CHARLES.

Such was the state of things in the hereditary dominions of Charles when he ascended the throne of Spain, in 1519. Indeed, the movement which convulsed the whole of Germany, was early transmitted to all the other territories of the Emperor. Being a Catholic king, this fact was no doubt the cause of his double policy towards the Reformers from the Diet of Worms in 1521. With Francis I, the Pope, and the Turks watching his movements on every side, and he theirs, he had no leisure to chastise the heretics. Besides, the ample revenues, which flowed into the imperial treasury from those wealthy provinces, made him unwilling to resort to severe measures, with a view to check the progress of the new opinions. At the same time, he did not fail to exhort those in power to use their authority in suppressing heresy. This is evident from a placard which was published in the name of that monarch, by Margaret of Austria, his father's sister, Governess of the Netherlands, in the year 1521. Luther is there described as a " devil in the shape of a man and the habit of a monk, that he may more easily occasion the eternal death and destruction of mankind." The placard is very long, giving strict orders for the prohibition of all books which contained any allusion to the Scripture or its doctrines, and that no book was to be circulated without the approbation of the faculty of divinity in the University."*

THE TRUTH PREVAILS IN SPITE OF THE FLAMES.

The history of **the Low Countries** from this time is so full of martyrdoms, that it is like a gradual extermination of the population. Nevertheless the Spirit of God wrought wonderfully ; and the holy courage which was shown by many, proved the Lord's presence with them in sustaining grace and power. It was discovered that the Austin friars in the city of Antwerp had read and approved the books of Luther. Many of them were thrown into prison. Three of the monks were degraded and condemned to the flames in 1523. While the fire was being lighted, they repeated the creed, and then sang together the Te Deum in alternate verses, until the force of the flames silenced their heavenly praise. Erasmus is made to witness on this

* See the noble work of Gerard Brandt, on the Reformation in the Netherlands, in four vols. folio. There the reader has almost the daily occurrences of these most interesting and tragical times. See also " The Rise of the Dutch Republic," by Mr. Motley, three vols. 8vo.; also his book on " The United Netherlands." Both embrace the political as well as the ecclesiastical history of these times

occasion, that these martyrdoms had the very opposite effect which the persecutors intended. " The city of Brussels," where they were executed, he says, " had been perfectly free from heresy till this event. But many of the inhabitants immediately after began to favour Lutheranism."

Persons of eminence, among both the clergy and the laity, ventured to espouse the cause of truth, though the martyrdoms were constantly occurring. This has always been the case. If persecution keep some at a cold selfish distance, it brings the accession of a greater number, through that instinct—in connection with the truth—which impels the human conscience to rise against injustice, and incline to the side of the oppressed. The fires were now kindled all over the country, and edict followed edict, with increasing severity, kept them burning. It was death to read a page of the Scriptures ; death to discuss any article of the faith ; death to have in one's possession any of the writings of Luther, Zwingle, or Œcolampadius ; death to express a doubt respecting the efficacy of the sacraments, or the authority of the Pope. In the year 1536, that good and faithful servant of the Lord, William Tyndale, was strangled and burnt at Vilvordi, near Brussels, for translating the New Testament into English, and printing it in 1555.*

In the year 1555, Charles, though only fifty-five years of age, feeling himself growing old, passed the sceptre to his son. The sceptre and the faggot, it has been said, were closely united during the reign of the father, but they were to be still more so under the reign of the son. And there was this difference : Charles persecuted from policy, for he was burning heretics at the very time he sacked Rome, and imprisoned the Pope and his cardinals. Philip persecuted from the convictions of his bigotry, and the cool vindictiveness of his nature. It was under the reign of the latter that more violent exterminating measures were devised, and carried into execution by the Duke of Alva, and the persecution became so intolerable, and so exasperated the people, that they ultimately rebelled, threw off the Spanish yoke, and asserted their ancient laws and liberties. But this was not done in haste ; the people were slow to move, notwithstanding their unparalleled sufferings.

THE ASSOCIATION OF THE NOBLES.

In 1566 most of the nobles, though generally Catholic, entered into an association to protect and defend the liberties of the country. The Protestants, trusting to a promise of toleration from Margaret, began to meet in great numbers in open day ; and, being without places of worship they assembled in the fields, where the preachers proclaimed the truths of the Gospel

* For particulars, see " Annals of the English Bible," by Christopher Anderson ; also the biographical notice prefixed to his writings, published by the Parker Society.

in the midst of overwhelming numbers. One of these field preachers, named Dathen, is said to have gathered as many as fifteen thousand at a time to listen to his discourses. But in the existing state of things such assemblies were not likely to be continued without some disturbances. A magistrate, on one occasion, furious in his bigotry, attempted to disperse them, brandishing his sword, and making as if he would apprehend the minister, but was saluted with such a plentiful shower of stones that he barely escaped with his life. The Psalms of David were usually sung on such occasions ; which, from the multitude of voices, were heard at a great distance, and attracted great attention. The enthusiasm of the Calvinists and the hostility of the Catholics were thereby increased, and the danger of an outbreak became every day more imminent. In order to avoid this, and prevent the need of field-preaching, those who really knew and valued the truth had, in a short time, a number of wooden Churches erected. " Men of all classes engaged in the labour, while the females sold their jewels and ornaments to provide the necessary funds ; and, had they been left to themselves, the power of the religion they professed would soon have quieted the storm of passion, and healed the evils of the land."*

The Protestants, now **one hundred thousand in number,** respectfully petitioned the king for toleration, having been led by the Governess, Margaret, to expect it. By taking advantage of the brief period of repose from the conciliatory spirit of the Governess, they had formed nearly sixty congregations in Flanders, which were attended by nearly as many thousand persons. Similar meetings were opened in Artois, Brabant, Holland, Utrecht, Iceland, Friesland, and other places. But in place of listening to the reasonable demands of so large and so respectable a body of his subjects, the poor narrow-minded bigot utterly rejected the plea for " freedom to worship God, and personal liberty by settled law." Margaret had recommended moderate measures, and, when the question came before his own ministers, the Spanish council did the same ; but all was in vain. Violence, duplicity, and bloodshed were the only features of his policy, especially in the Netherlands. Rejecting Margaret's advice as to moderation, he directed her to raise an army of *three thousand horse*, and *ten thousand foot soldiers*, to enforce the execution of his decrees.

Attempts were now made by the government to disperse the congregations of the Protestants by force, so that the people went armed to their places of worship. Such was the melancholy state of things through the superstition and obstinacy of a single man. Many from amongst the lowest classes of the people in different parts of the country, excited by all that was going on,

* " Universal History," vol. vi., pp. 197,

began to rise. They broke into Churches, tore down pictures and everything in the way of ornament ; images, altars, crosses, and stained windows were broken to pieces ; and the organ in the cathedral at Antwerp, said to be the finest in the world, was subjected to the same destructive enthusiasm. About four hundred Churches were thus plundered and defaced in a few days. The Christians in both the reformed and Lutheran Churches were deeply grieved because of this outbreak, and drew up remonstrances to Philip ; and while they condemned those violent proceedings, they again petitioned for the public exercise of their religion, " in which they were resolved to live and die." The Prince of Orange, the Counts Egmont and Horn, endeavoured to move Philip to some consideration of the state of religious feeling in the Low Countries ; but it was all to no purpose. The troops were ordered to be distributed over the distracted country, that his persecuting edicts might be enforced. The Protestants were reduced to great straits ; many were put to death, and many fled the country ; the association of the nobles melted away, and the Netherlands had all the appearance of a conquered land.

THE DUKE OF ALVA.

But the cold-hearted bigot was not yet satisfied. A second invasion was arranged for exterminating the Reformed, tens of thousands though they were. In the year 1567 the cruel **Duke of Alva** was sent into the Netherlands with an army of fifteen thousand Spaniards and Italians ; and the Inquisition was to put forth all its energies. This added greatly to the general consternation. The reign of terror began. The very name of Alva, and the mention of the Inquisition, made the whole land shudder. The Counts of Egmont and Horn, and other persons of eminence, suspected of holding liberal opinions, were immediately arrested, and executed. The Prince of Orange escaped to Germany, and crowds of Protestants forsook their homes and fled to other countries. The foreign merchants, manufacturers, and artisans fled from Antwerp, and other once thriving cities, as if the plague were raging within their gates. The wooden Churches were pulled down, and, in some places the beams were formed into a great gallows on which to hang the minister and his flock.

As the Inquisitors, by the authority of Charles, before his abdication were doing their dreadful work, we will give particulars of a few cases, to show the reader what was to be witnessed almost daily in the country for nearly forty years ; yet the Word of God prevailed mightily, and thousands were converted.

One of the Inquisitors of the name of **Titelmann,** notorious for the number of his victims, boasted that he only " seized the virtuous and the innocent, because they made no resistance."

Thomas Calberg, tapestry weaver, of Tournay, being convicted of having copied some hymns from a book printed in Geneva, was instantly burned alive. About the same time, 1561, Walter Kapell, a man of property, and benevolence, and greatly beloved by the poor people, was burned at the stake for heretical opinions. A most touching scene occurred as Titelmann's officers were binding him to the stake : a poor idiot, who had often been fed by his kindness, called out, " Ye are bloody murderers ; that man has done no wrong, but has given me bread to eat." With these words he cast himself headlong into the flames to perish with his beloved benefactor, and was with difficulty rescued by the officers. A day or two afterwards he visited the scene of the execution, where the half-burnt skeleton of Walter Kapell still remained. The poor idiot laid it upon his shoulders, and carried it to the place where the magistrates were sitting in session. Forcing his way into their presence, he laid his burden at their feet, crying, " There, murderers ! Ye have eaten his flesh, now eat his bones." The fate of the poor man is not recorded ; but the testimony of so daring a witness would most likely be effectually silenced.

The year following, Titelmann caused one Robert Ogier, of Ryssel, in Flanders, to be arrested, together with his wife and two sons. Their crime consisted in not going to mass, and in practising private worship at home. They confessed the offence, for they protested that they could not endure to see the profanation of their Saviour's Name in the idolatrous sacraments. They were asked what rites they practised in their own house. One of the sons, a mere boy, answered : " We fall on our knees, and pray to God that He may enlighten our hearts and forgive our sins. We pray for our sovereign, that his reign may be prosperous, and his life peaceful. We also pray for the magistrates and others in authority, that God may protect and preserve them all." The boy's simple eloquence drew tears even from the eyes of some of his judges. The father and eldest son were, however, condemned to the flames. " O God," prayed the youth at the stake, " eternal Father, accept the sacrifice of our lives, in the Name of Thy beloved Son." " Thou liest, scoundrel ! " furiously interrupted a monk who was lighting the fire ; " God is not your father ; ye are the devil's children." As the flames rose about them, the boy cried out once more : " Look, my father, all Heaven is opening, and I see an hundred thousand angels rejoicing over us. Let us be glad, for we are dying for the truth." " Thou liest ! thou liest ! " again screamed the priest, " all Hell is opening ; and ye see ten thousand devils thrusting you into eternal fire." Eight days afterwards, the wife of Ogier and his other son were burned ; so that they were soon privileged to meet in the bright and happy regions above—in the perfect repose of the paradise of God. Little did these ignorant and hardened Inquisitors think that they were sending so many of the children of God home to their Father's house on high, "to be with Christ, which is far better."

THE ADMINISTRATION OF ALVA.

In the year 1567, "**the council of blood,**" as it was called, held its first sitting. There are few readers who have not heard something of the infamous character of Alva. "Such an amount of ferocity," says Motley, "of patient vindictiveness and universal bloodthirstiness was never found in a savage beast of the forest, and but rarely in a human bosom." It was no longer the trial of ones and twos that occupied the council, as it was thought more expeditious to send the accused at once in large numbers to the flames. But no crime at that moment was so great as being rich. No belief, no virtues, could expiate such guilt. Bloodshed and confiscations were the daily amusements of the tyrant who thus gratified his avarice and his cruelty. He boasted that a golden river, a yard deep, should flow through the Netherlands, from confiscations, to replenish the treasury of his master. In the town of Tournay alone, the estates of above a hundred rich merchants were confiscated.

Blood now flowed in torrents. "Thus, for example, on the 4th of January, eighty-four inhabitants of Valenciennes were condemned ; on another day, ninety-five from different places in Flanders ; on another, forty-six inhabitants of Malines ; on another, thirty-five persons from different localities. Yet, notwithstanding this wholesale slaughter, Philip, Alva, and the Holy Office were not satisfied with the progress of events. A new edict was issued, affixing a heavy penalty upon all waggoners, carriers, and ship-masters, who should aid in the emigration of heretics. They had resolved that none should escape.

Early in the second year of *the council of blood*, "the most sublime sentence of death," says Motley, "was promulgated, which has ever been pronounced since the creation of the world. The Roman tyrant wished that his enemies' heads were all upon a single neck, that he might strike them off at one blow. The Inquisition assisted Philip to place the heads of all his Netherland subjects upon a single neck for the same fell purpose. Upon the 19th of February, 1568, a sentence of the Holy Office condemned *all the inhabitants* of the Netherlands to death as heretics. From this universal doom *only a few persons, especially names,* were excepted. A proclamation of the king, dated ten days later, confirmed this decree of the Inquisition, and ordered it to be carried into instant execution, without regard to age, sex, condition. This is probably the most concise death-warrant that was ever framed. Three millions of people—men, women, and children, were sentenced to the scaffold in three lines."*

"This horrible decree," says Brandt, "against a whole nation, drove many with their wives and children to seek a place of safety in the *West-woods* of Flanders, from whence, turning savages through the solitude of the place, and the extinction of their hopes, they made excursions on the priests and friars, serving themselves of the darkest nights for revenge and robbery."

THE REAL CHARACTER OF POPERY.

Under this universal condemnation the reader will see the real spirit of Popery, and what all had to expect who did not yield an absolute, though blind submission, to all her idolatries and superstitions. Men in the highest and humblest positions were daily and hourly dragged to the stake. Alva, in writing to Philip about this time, seeks to satisfy his master by assuring him that the executions, which were to take place immediately after the expiration of holy week, would not be less than *eight hundred heads*. To prevent the victims on their way to the scaffold from addressing their friends or the bystanders, the tongue of each prisoner was screwed into an iron ring, and then seared with a hot iron.

The tendency of **this monster's policy** was evidently to effect the utter depopulation of the country. History informs us, that the "death-bell tolled hourly in every village; not a family that was not called to mourn for its dearest relatives; the blood of its best and bravest citizens had already stained the scaffold; the men to whom the nation had been accustomed to look for guidance and protection were dead, in prison, or in exile. Submission had ceased to be of any avail, flight was impossible, and the spirit of vengeance had alighted at every fireside. The mourners went daily about the streets, for there was hardly a house that had not been made desolate... The door-posts of private houses, the fences in the fields, were laden with human carcases, strangled, beheaded, and burned. The orchards in the country bore on many a tree the hideous fruit of human bodies." It was about this time that Don Carlos, the king's son died in prison, or, as it was believed by some, was put to death by his father's orders. "This conduct of his in not sparing his only son, as being a favourer of heretics, was highly extolled by Pope Pius V."†

Such was the character of the reign of Alva for nearly six years. The heart sickens in attempting to detail the atrocities of this furious tyrant. The extent of the appalling massacres may be imagined from the boast of Alva himself, who gloried in having caused *eighteen thousand* of the inhabitants to perish, without

* Motley, vol. ii., p. 155; Brandt, vol. i., p. 266.
† Brandt, vol. i., p. 270; Motley, vol. ii., p. 142; "Universal History," vol. vi., p. 199

reckoning those who fell in war. And it is thought that more than a *hundred thousand* effected their escape, and fled into other countries. Crowds flocked to the English ports, bringing with them that industrial skill which amply repaid this country for the hospitality they received.

We wonder that the Church was not consumed in the flames or drowned in blood. But God had mercy on the Netherlands in preserving many of His faithful witnesses through their fiery trial that they might testify for Him in a future day. When the grass began to grow in the streets of those cities which had recently employed so many artisans, a national synod of the **Dutch Reformed Church** was held at Dort in 1578 ; at Middleburg in 1581 ; and at the Hague in 1586. The very means which the royal bigot, with his Inquisitors and Jesuits, employed to preserve the old religion, instead of securing it from the dangers to which it was exposed, occasioned its total overthrow. The civil war, which broke out both by sea and land, resulted in the formation of a new Protestant state in Europe, under the title of THE SEVEN UNITED PROVINCES.

THE TRIUMPH OF TRUTH AND RIGHTEOUSNESS.

The history of this long and deeply interesting struggle for liberty of conscience belongs to the civil historian. We will only add, that William of Nassau, Prince of Orange, or, as he was usually called, **William " the Silent,"** felt impelled to adopt more decisive measures to prevent the utter ruin of his country. In this enterprise he was assisted by Elizabeth, Queen of England ; the King of France ; and the Protestants in Germany. He also sold his jewels, plate, and even the furniture of his house to raise the necessary funds. But it was difficult to contend with the experience and power of Alva, and for a length of time William was unsuccessful. His brother Louis was defeated, and his brother Adolphus was killed ; but many of the towns were thrown into revolt, and Philip at length felt that some change of policy should be tried. Alva was recalled, and even Philip is said to have reproved him for his inhumanity. The war was renewed and continued to rage, with brief intervals of peace, until the year 1580, when the States-general, assembled at Antwerp, issued their declaration of national independence, and threw off the Spanish yoke for ever. Thus the infant republic, under the guidance of the Prince of Orange, secured that freedom of person and liberty of conscience which are the inalienable right of all ; and took its place among the nations of the continent.*

Philip now eyed the great patriot with the most deadly hatred. He saw in him the animating soul of these struggles for liberty,

* For the civil history of the new state, see Motley's " History of the United Netherlands," and for the ecclesiastical, see " Faiths of the World ; " also Mosheim, vol. iii.

and hence he sought his life. " Five unsuccessful attempts had been made to assassinate William ; but Philip would not give up hope. In 1580 he published a ban of proscription, in which he denounced the prince as guilty of the foulest crimes, and declared that it was permitted to all persons to assail him in his fortunes, person, and life ; and promised *twenty-five thousand golden crowns, a pardon for all offences whatsoever, and a patent of nobility*, to anyone who should deliver up to him this implacable monarch. William of Nassau, dead or alive." This infamous document soon did its work. On the 10th of July, 1584, a Jesuit, named Gerard, who had passed himself off to the unsuspecting prince as one of the Reformed faith, shot him through the heart, in the hall of his own house, with a pistol which he had bought with money obtained from the prince himself a short time before. " God have mercy on my soul, and on this unfortunate nation," exclaimed the wounded patriot and instantly expired. He had married the widow of Teligny, the daughter of the brave Coligny, who both fell in the St. Bartholomew massacre. Thus had she seen her first and second husband, and her noble father, assassinated by her side.

Thus died one of the most unselfish, wise, courageous, and memorable characters in history. " He had headed the armies of his oppressed countrymen, and led them on to victory ; he had regulated their treaties ; and though for twenty years he had spent his fortune, his ease, and his health, for the common good, calumny has failed to show that he had in any instance used his power for any selfish purpose ; so that he well deserved the title of ' Father of his country.' " The news of the atrocious deed filled the land and all the surrounding countries with grief and consternation. Vengeance was speedily executed on the assassin; but in the midst of a deep and universal sorrow, Philip rejoiced. Transported with joy, he exclaimed : " Had it only been done two years earlier, much trouble would have been spared me ; but better late than never ! better late than never ! "*

REFLECTIONS ON BIGOTRY AND CHRISTIANITY.

It is difficult to close this paper without drawing the reader's attention to **the effect of bigotry,** and a bigotry dignified by the name of religion, or zeal for the glory of God. We have seen what this Satanic delusion has done in the Netherlands, and also in many other places. But what has Christianity suffered from bigotry these thirteen hundred years and more ! The one is the religion of the New Testament, the other that of the dogmas of Rome. The former is peace on earth, and good will to men ; for as Christ in Spirit says, " My delights were with the sons of men." What could be sweeter than this—more gracious, more

* " Universal History," vol. vi., p. 202 : Wylie's vol. iii., which we have just seen, gives a long and detailed account of the struggles and triumphs in the Netherlands.

softening, more likely to fill us with love to all men, especially to them that believe ? The latter is unfeeling obstinacy, and inexorable cruelty ; and this, be it observed, to those whom they deem in error, or unsaved ; so that they become the murderers, not only of the body, but of the soul. In place of trying to convert the soul, they hurry it out of this world, proclaiming it unsaved, and only fit for the flames of Hell.

Philip stands before us as the personification of the religion of bigotry—the religion of the Papacy. Never was there a man more suited for the enemy's purpose than this wretched king— a cold heart, a stern and morose temperament, sullen and gloomy, with an incredibly small mind, and millions of human beings at his mercy. He died in 1598, at the age of seventy-two, after protracted and excruciating sufferings, under a complication of dreadful maladies, said to be Herod's disease.

Our only safety is to have Christ ever before us as our all-governing object ; and the more steadfastly we look on Him, the more will His character be mirrored on our souls, and the more distinctly shall we reflect it to others. In looking to Him, we are enlightened ; to have any other object before us is to be in darkness ; and there are many shades of darkness between the blindness of popish bigotry and the clouds that arise in the Christian's heart from self-occupation. To be true witnesses of a heavenly Christ, we must be heavenly minded, and heavenly in our ways. And heavenly-mindedness is the result, not of trying to be so, but of occupation with a heavenly Christ, according to the revelation which we have of Him, through the power of the Holy Spirit. In what direction is the eye ? is always the important question, for the heart is sure to follow the eye, and the feet the heart.

The following passage may be accepted as a practical view of Christianity, both negatively and positively. "For the grace of God that bringeth salvation hath appeared to all men, teaching us, that denying ungodliness and worldly lusts, we should live soberly, righteously, and godly in this present world ; looking for that blessed hope, and the glorious appearing of the great God and Saviour Jesus Christ ; who gave Himself for us, that He might redeem us from all iniquity, and purify unto Himself a peculiar people, zealous of good works " (Titus 2. 11-14).

CHAPTER XLIX

The Reformation in French Switzerland

IN tracing the *silver line* of God's grace, in the operations of His Spirit, we are arrested by the different forms it takes in different countries. We have just left a land where the sky was reddened with the flames of martyrdom, and the earth soaked with the blood of God's saints. Such is the history of every land where the Inquisition was established. In Germany—and where it never gained a footing—the struggle was with the princes and the imperial power ; but in Switzerland the question of retaining the Romish, or adopting the Reformed faith, was not unfrequently decided by vote. This mode of determining the religion of a state strikingly illustrates the popular, or republican character of the Swiss government.

In German Switzerland, the principal Reformers—Zwingle, Œcolampadius, Bullinger, Haller, Wittenbach, and others, were natives ; while the agents used of God for the conversion of French Switzerland, with a single exception, were foreigners. William Farel, a Frenchman, and almost single-handed, had accomplished the overthrow of Popery in several French districts, before he reached Geneva or saw John Calvin. D'Aubigné speaks of Farel as the Luther of French Switzerland, and of Calvin as the Melanchthon.

This remarkable man—**William Farel**—was born of a wealthy and noble family at Gap, in Dauphiny, in the year 1489, and diligently instructed by his pious parents in the faithful observance of the devout practices of the Romish Church. Naturally sincere, upright, full of ardour, and true to his convictions, he invoked the Virgin and the saints night and day, as he has himself related. He scrupulously conformed to the fasts prescribed by the Church, held the Pontiff of Rome to be a god upon earth, saw in the priests the sole channel of all celestial blessings, and treated as infidels whoever did not exhibit an ardour similar to his own.*

THE EARLY HISTORY OF WILLIAM FAREL.

After attending school for some time in Dauphiny, he obtained the permission of his parents to finish his education at the University of Paris—said to be the mother of all learning, the true light of the Church which never knew eclipse. **James**

* Félice, p. 18.

Lefevre, a doctor of Etaples, then the most renowned doctor of the Sorbonne, was professor of divinity. His genius, piety, and learning greatly attracted the young Dauphinese. From the centre of the Sorbonne he fearlessly proclaimed, "That true religion has but one foundation, one object, one head—Jesus Christ, blessed for evermore. Let us not," he continued, "call ourselves by St. Paul, Apollos, or St. Peter. The Cross of Christ alone openeth the gates of Heaven, and shutteth the gates of Hell." Thus, as early as 1512, the leading doctrines of the Reformation were proclaimed in the presence of the most learned of the Sorbonnists. The University was in a ferment ; some applauded, some condemned ; and daily, groups of men met, most anxious to discuss the new doctrines.

But there was one amongst the listening crowds in the lecture room whose heart the Lord had prepared for the Word of life. This was William Farel. His soul was deeply agitated when he heard that salvation comes through faith of Jesus Christ alone, and that works without faith are futile. He thought of the lessons and the habits of his home ; his early associations, his tender recollections, his prayers, his hopes. But the declarations of Scripture had produced convictions, both deeper and firmer. In his search after truth he studied the Word of God in the original tongues ; light broke in upon his mind ; he saw that it was Jesus only ; Jesus only. "Now," he exclaimed, "everything appears to me in a new aspect ; Scripture is cleared up ; prophecy is opened ; the apostles shed a strong light upon my soul. A voice, till now unknown, the voice of Jesus, my Shepherd, my Master, my Teacher, speaks to me with power. Instead of the murderous heart of a ravening wolf, He has given me one of meekness and quietness, so great is the change that has come over me. Now my heart is entirely withdrawn from the Pope, and given to Jesus Christ."

William Farel, so far as we know, was the first person who professed the Reformed religion in France, and was converted in the University at Paris, so renowned for its Romish orthodoxy. Farel and Lefevre conceived for each other the closest friendship, which lasted through life ; but we shall meet with them again, when speaking of the Reformation in France. When persecuted in Paris because of their doctrines, William Brissonnet, Bishop of Meaux, a pious and pure-minded man, invited them to visit him, and preach the Gospel to his people. Numbers came to hear, and when they heard the preachers pressing them to give, not their money to the Church, but their hearts to Christ, the surprise and excitement of the inhabitants became extreme. The priests and monks of the diocese, seeing their credit weakening, and their revenues diminishing, aroused the demon of persecution, and the preachers had to preserve their lives by a speedy flight. Farel, on quitting Meaux, went to preach in Dauphiny. "Three of his brothers," says Félice, "shared his faith. Encouraged by this success, he went preaching from town to town, and place to place. His appeals agitating the whole country, the priests sought to excite the people against him ; but he was neither of an age nor of a character to be stopped by persecution ; his ardour increased with the danger. Wherever there was a place to plant his foot—on the border of the rivers, on the points of the rocks, in the bed of the torrents—he found one to preach the Gospel. If he was threatened, he stood firm ; if surrounded, he escaped ; if thrust from one spot, he reappeared in another. At last, when he saw himself environed on all sides, he retreated by mountain paths into Switzerland, and arrived at Basle in the commencement of the year 1524."

FAREL'S PREACHING IN SWITZERLAND.

Having formed an intimate friendship with Bucer, Capito, Œcolampadius, and others, which death only interrupted, he was obliged to leave Basle on account of the hostility of the Roman Catholic clergy. He proceeded to **Montbeliard,** where he laboured with so much zeal and success under the protection of the Duke of Ulric, that within two years the whole principality professed the new opinions ; and to this day the inhabitants in general are Protestants. At Neuchatel the opposition was so violent that he remained only a short time. **Aigle** was the next scene of his labours. The town at that time was under the jurisdiction of Berne, and the Bernese Government, being favourable to the Reformation, sent him a patent constituting him pastor of Aigle. Thus sanctioned by the powerful Government of Berne, he instantly commenced preaching, to the great consternation of the monks, and the delight of many of the people who heard him. "Though he had dropped from the clouds," says history, "the priests could not have been more affrighted, nor the people more surprised. His bold look, his burning eye, his voice of thunder, his words, rapid, eloquent, and stamped with the majesty of truth, reached the conscience, and increased the number of those in the valley of Aigle, who were already prepared to take the Word of God for their guide."*

The priests, and the lower classes, who followed them, raised a great tumult, being secretly supported by the Syndic. Farel was insulted in every way in their power ; they refused to obey the Bernese in these matters, and were determined to maintain their ancient religion. Many, by this time, however, had received the Gospel, professed themselves one with Farel, and were ready to defend him. But to prevent the effusion of blood, to which matters were fast tending, Farel quietly withdrew, and preached

* "History of Protestantism," vol. ii., p. 248.

the Gospel in other places which were under the Government of Berne. The question, however, as usual, came to the vote, and Aigle had a majority in favour of Reform.

In the spring of 1531 Farel returned to **Neuchatel,** determined to complete his conquests there. Since his first visit the Reformed doctrines had made great progress among the people. The priests clamoured as usual and did all in their power to raise a tumult. They sounded the tocsin to rouse the magistrates and the people, as if an invading army had reached their gates. But many gathered round Farel, and forced him to ascend the pulpit of the Cathedral in spite of all opposition. His sermon was so powerful, that all the people cried out at its close : " We will follow the Protestant religion, both we and our children ; and in it we will live and die." The priests and monks were furious, and sought the life of Farel. But the people determined to have the matter lawfully settled, presented themselves before the governor and deputies of Berne, to vote on the question, whether Romanism or Protestantism should be the religion of Neuchatel. A majority of eighteen votes gave the victory to the Reformation. No one was compelled to abandon Popery, but the Reformation was legally established.

Such was the character of Farel's work in the French-speaking parts of Switzerland, at the foot of the Jura, and on the shores of its lakes. But this was no easy work in those days. Everywhere he met with violent opposition from the Catholics ; and the mob, instigated by the priests, frequently raised tumults. This was an excuse for sounding the tocsin and ringing the alarm-bells, causing the inhabitants to rush from their houses to the scene of the uproar. On such occasions it fared hard with Farel, and with those who helped him in his work. At Vallengin he was seized, beaten, struck with stones, forced into a chapel, and asked to kneel before the images of the saints. On his refusing, he was again beaten with such violence that the stains of his blood were long to be traced on the walls of the chapel. He was then thrown into a dungeon, but afterwards released through the intercession of his friends at Neuchatel. At St. Blaise he met with similar treatment. He was so disfigured with bruises as scarcely to be recognised by his friends ; but after some care and nursing at Morat, he set out for Orbe to evangelise.

On the other hand, those who had embraced the new opinions, were often in too great haste to destroy the symbols of the old religion. This practice generally assumed the character of popular vengeance. Churches were entered, altars dismantled, images broken, pictures torn down, priceless statues, precious relics, all fell before the fury of the multitudes. But there was no Inquisition in that primitive country, no Familiars amongst the simple people who were occupied in feeding their cattle on the mountains, or in cultivating corn and the vine within their fertile valleys ; and no Alva, with his ruthless Spaniards, to slay, burn, and ravage.   Their tumults generally ended without bloodshed, the Reformed generally being the stronger party.*

FAREL REACHES GENEVA.

But Farel had **Geneva** before him ; he was working his way to what he considered the centre of his operations.   The Genevese had been contending for some time with the Duke of Savoy, and their unprincipled bishop for political freedom.   And in the struggle, Berthelier, Bonevard, and Lévrier, names of famous memory, suffered as martyrs of liberty.   Now they were to be drawn into a fresh contest, but for a higher and holier liberty.

Farel arrived in Geneva in the autumn of 1532, accompanied by Anthony Saunier, like himself a native of Dauphiny, and recommended by letters from the Government of Berne.   As Geneva becomes, from this time, the second centre in Reformed Christendom, we will favour the reader with an extract from the copious pen of the historian of Protestantism as to its situation and ecclesiastical condition.   "There is no grander valley in Switzerland than the basin of the Rhone, whose collected floods, confined within shining shores, form the Leman.   As one looks towards sunrise, he sees on his right the majestic line of the white Alps ; and on his left, the picturesque and verdant Jura.   The vast space which these magnificent chains enclose is variously filled in.   Its grandest feature is the lake.   It is blue as the sky, and motionless as a mirror.   Nestling on its shores, or dotting its remoter banks, is many a beautiful villa, many a picturesque town, almost drowned in the affluent foliage of gardens and rich vines . . . Above the forests of chestnuts and pine-trees soar the great peaks as finely roved as the plains, though after a different manner—not with flowers and verdure, but with glaciers and snows.

"But this fertile and lovely land, at the time we write of, was one of the strongholds of the Papacy.   Cathedrals, abbacies, rich convents, and famous shrines, which attracted yearly troops of pilgrims, were thickly planted throughout the valley of the Leman.   These were so many fortresses, by which Rome kept the country in subjection.   In each of these fortresses was placed a numerous garrison.   Priests and monks swarmed like the locust . . . In Geneva alone there were nine hundred priests.   In the other towns and villages around the lake, and at the foot of the Jura, they were not less numerous in proportion.   Cowls and shaven crowns, frocks and veils were seen everywhere.   This generation of tonsored men and veiled women formed the *Church*.   And the dues they exacted of the lay population, and the processions,

* D'Aubigné, vol. iii., p. 496 ; Scott, vol. iii., p. 70 ; Wylie, vol. ii., p. 247.

chants, exorcisms, and blows which they gave them in return, were styled *religion*."*

Such was the moral and ecclesiastical condition of Geneva when Farel and Saunier entered it. And if we add to this account of its ecclesiastical swarms, that the population at that time numbered only about twelve thousand, we may well wonder how such a ravenous host could be sustained. But a still greater wonder is, how could an evangelist, almost single-handed, venture to assail such a host, and that on their own ground—the region of darkness and wickedness ? Only through faith in the living God, we answer. Doubtless Farel was a great preacher, one of the greatest in the sixteenth century. Still he required faith in the presence of God, and in the power of His Holy Spirit through the Word preached.

FAREL'S FIRST PREACHING IN GENEVA.

The subject of Farel's first sermon was the Holy Scriptures. He maintained that they were the only source of Divine knowledge, and the only authority on earth to which the conscience of man was subject. He denounced the traditions of the Fathers and the decrees of Councils as having no authority over the conscience in the sight of God. His second subject was the full and free forgiveness of all sin, on the ground of the work of Christ on the Cross. This pardon was free to the chief of sinners, through faith in Christ ; Papal pardons had to be bought with money or with penance. We can imagine the burning zeal of the preacher, placing the absolute truth of God in striking contrast with the mere superstitions of the Papacy, and many through grace believing.

When the canons and priests gained information of his proceedings, they were in a state of great dismay. They had heard of his desolating work in the Pays de Vaud. He was instantly arrested and carried before the Council. As usual on all such occasions, it was alleged that he was an enemy to the civil government, a trumpet of sedition. Farel replied : " That he was no instrument of sedition, but only a preacher of the truth ; that he was prepared to lay down his life for the Divine doctrine ; that the patronage of Berne was a sufficient guarantee for his honesty ; that he had a right to a public and impartial trial ; and that this could not be refused him without offence to God, and to the Gospel, and to the lords of Berne." This last consideration had weight with the council, as Geneva was in alliance with Berne ; so Farel was dismissed with an admonition to refrain from further preaching.

But the clergy were not so easily satisfied as the town council. Farel and Saunier were summoned to appear before the epis-

* Wylie, vol. ii., p. 256.

copal tribunal, under the pretext of discussing the question in dispute. And then, indeed, William Farel at least might have perished from private violence, had not two magistrates accompanied them as deputies from the council. Some of the clergy had arms concealed under their sacerdotal robes. But Farel was undaunted, notwithstanding the unbridled fury of the clergy. He demanded that his doctrines should be heard, assailed, and defended in public disputation. This was, of course, refused. Farel, then, with great boldness defended his doctrine, concluding with these words : " I have no authority but that of God, whose messenger I am." " He hath spoken blasphemy," exclaimed one of the judges, " What further need have we of witnesses ? He is guilty of death. Away with him ! To the Rhone ! to the Rhone ! Better that the wicked Lutheran die, than live and trouble the people." " Speak the words of God," Farel quickly replied, " not the words of Caiaphas ! " On which all the assembly cried aloud with one voice : " Kill the Lutheran, kill him ! " They closed round the two evangelists, the priests were pulling out their arms, and both must have perished, but for the interposition of the two magistrates. They were ordered forthwith to leave the city.

But it was now too late. The Reform movement was really begun ; God was working and the priests were impatient to arrest the progress of His grace. Nevertheless they were allowed to manifest the spirit of their leader. When the evangelists left the episcopal tribunal they were with difficulty preserved from the fury of a mob of women, instigated by the priests, who would have consigned the preachers, without trial or mercy, " to the Rhone ; " but as the Lord would have it, at the critical moment, a military band came up which rescued the Reformers, and escorted them to their lodgings.

It was now thought by the friends of Reform that the preaching of Farel was too powerful and his name too formidable, to begin the work in Geneva ; that he should retire for a time and that some unknown name should carry on the work, now manifestly begun, in a quieter way. Farel agreed, left the place, feeling he had done so little ; but he had accomplished more than he at that moment knew. Meanwhile several other preachers had arrived ; but we hear only of one **Froment,** or Fromentius, who turned schoolmaster, seeking to introduce his doctrines to the parents through the children and by means of classes, New Testaments, and books, which he distributed. Still the Lord was working, and a number of influential people were brought to the knowledge of the truth.

FAREL RETURNS TO GENEVA.

In the December of 1533, Farel re-entered the gates of Geneva, determined not again to leave it till the Reformation had been consummated there. **Peter Viret,** of Orbe, arrived about the same time. Thus there were three of the most powerful preachers of that period in Geneva—Farel, Viret, and Froment. The internal struggle had been excited afresh by the Reformers observing the Lord's Supper, according to its original institution. Some of the rich and honourable of Geneva had united with them, which caused great sensation. A fierce sedition was the consequence.

But the Catholics, still the stronger party, would listen to nothing but the complete suppression of the new movement. They assembled with the deliberate purpose of perpetrating a general massacre of the Reformers. "It is affirmed," says Waddington, "that they were conducted by no fewer than five hundred armed priests ; and that they were fortified by a *carte blanche* from the bishop, expressing his approbation of every act that, under any circumstances, they might be led to perform against the enemies of the Catholic faith." A number of women, with their aprons filled with stones, helped to swell the Roman Catholic host. The tumult was allayed, however, before much mischief was done. It happened that several merchants from Friburg were in Geneva at that moment, and seeing the Catholics brandishing swords and other weapons, they boldly interfered and prevented them from carrying out their purpose. Two days afterwards an edict of peace was issued by the Council of Sixty, which rather favoured liberty of conscience. Among other things they said : "It is forbidden to preach anything that cannot be proved from Holy Writ."

But these terms of pacification lasted but a short time. In less than six weeks the Catholics broke forth again into a still ruder commotion, attended by more serious consequences. Its instigator appears to have been Canon Werali, a man of great strength, and a great warrior. It is said that he could wield his battle-axe as he could fling about his breviary. He headed the tumult, clothed in complete armour, and brandishing a two-edged sword. After nightfall rumours of war were heard in the street, the tocsin was sounded, and according to the habits of those times, most of the inhabitants rushed into the street armed ; but the darkness made it difficult to distinguish between friend and foe. In the confusion, however, the great Papal champion was slain, and the Catholics dispersed. Werali being a member of a noble and powerful family of the Popish canton of Friburg, that state had now a plausible pretext for interfering in the troubles of Geneva by demanding the prosecution of the murderers of her citizen, and for a general intervention in favour of the established religion. Thus were the enemies of the Reformation greatly multiplied, and fresh troubles arose through the violence of the Duke of Savoy, and the treachery of the bishop.*

* For lengthy details, see D'Aubigné's " History of the Reformation in Europe," vols. i. and ii.

A PUBLIC DISPUTATION.

Many eyes, from all quarters, were now turned to the small town of Geneva. Clement VII and Charles V were anxiously watching the struggle ; but God's purpose was to bless, and He overruled all these commotions for the accomplishment of His gracious object. After a great deal of menacing and remonstrance between Berne and Friburg, the grand question came to a public disputation.

On the 30th May, 1535, the disputants met in the grand hall of the Convent de Rive. Caroli, a doctor of the Sorbonne, and Chapius, a Dominican of Geneva, appeared as the champions of the Church ; while one Bernard, a newly converted Franciscan, took the lead in defence of the Reformed doctrines, supported by Farel, Viret, and Froment. Eight members of council were appointed to preside, and four secretaries were to take down all that was said on both sides. The disputation lasted four weeks. Victory, as usual on such occasions, rested with the Reformers. Indeed, it was so complete, that both Caroli and Chapius acknowledged themselves vanquished, and declared, in presence of the vast assembly, their conversion to the Reformed faith. Multitudes professed their faith in the truth as brought forward by the Reformers ; and many ecclesiastics and monks followed the stream.

But Rome's resources were not yet exhausted ; she had not given up hope. The anathemas of the Pope, the armed priests, the furious women, had all failed ; but to uphold the Catholic faith a darker deed was yet to be perpetrated. It so happened that the three ministers, Farel, Viret, and Froment, lodged in the house of Bernard, which gave a favourable opportunity to cut off the three at once **by poison.** A woman was induced to leave Lyons, on pretence of religion, and come to Geneva. She was received into the house of Bernard as a servant. Shortly after she mixed her poison with the dinner prepared for the ministers. Happily, however, Froment dined elsewhere that day, and Farel, being indisposed, did not dine ; but Viret tasted the drugged dish, and was brought to the point of death. He recovered, but the effects of the poison remained with him till the end of his days. The wretched woman confessed the crime, but accused a canon and a priest of having bribed her to commit the offence. They denied the accusation by oath and were released, but the poor woman was executed.

The miscarriage of this and several other cruel plots of the Catholics opened the eyes of many, and tended greatly to hasten the downfall of the Romish superstition in Geneva. The feeling of the public was now in favour of Reform ; but the council was disposed to check, rather than to encourage the popular zeal. At length, however, after the sense of the great majority of the citizens had been ascertained, the council of Two Hundred was assembled, and the celebration of the mass was officially suspended. This decree was followed by a general edict to the effect : " That the services of God were thenceforward to be performed according to the statutes of the Gospel ; and that all acts of Papal idolatry were to cease altogether." Ever after that day the evangelical ministers preached with perfect freedom. The monasteries were next invaded ; and there were some startling revelations of the frauds by which the people had been so long and so grossly deluded, and the vast superstition upheld.

HOW THE MONKS DECEIVED THE PEOPLE.

Many of these secret machinations and **impostures** are too vile to be transferred to our pages ; but one, which is more amusing than revolting, we may quote. A number of strange lights, or small flames of fire, would sometimes be seen moving about the churchyard at night, to the utter amazement of the people. What could they be ? was the question. " These," answered the priests, gravely, " are souls from Purgatory. They have come to excite on their behalf the compassion of their living relatives. Will fathers and mothers, husbands and wives, not freely give of their money for prayers and masses that we may not have to return to the place of torment ? was their pitiful cry." The effect of this imposture was another golden harvest to the priests. But what were these livid lights and blue flames really ? They were simply a number of crabs with little bits of candle stuck on their backs, the heat of which may have propelled their movements. The enlightened public, indignant at having been so long deceived, relieved the crabs of their fiery burdens, and threw them back into the cool waters of the lake.*

Thus far the triumph of the Reformation was confined to the city of Geneva. The next step was to extend it to the rural clergy. Ministers were commissioned to instruct them, and to preach the new doctrines to their congregations ; and so effectual was this reasonable plan, that all the dependent villagers speedily adopted the creed of the metropolis.

THE REFORMATION ESTABLISHED AT LAUSANNE.

Lausanne and its territory are also to be included among the places in which the Reformation was now established. In Popish times this was a city of great importance. It was the resort of pilgrims who flocked thither to pray before the image of Our Lady, and to purchase indulgences ; a traffic which added greatly to the riches of the Church. This city could boast, besides its bishop, a chapter of thirty-two canons, a convent of Dominicans, and another of Franciscans, and a numerous staff of priests ; but, with all the provision thus made for its religious

* Waddington, vol. iii., p. 275 ; Wylie, vol. ii., p. 273.

instruction and improvement, it was sunk even below the habitual ignorance, superstition, and vice of the times. Farel's first visit to Lausanne, in 1529, was unsuccessful; but the current of ecclesiastical affairs had been running strongly since then in favour of Reform; and when Viret visited the place in the spring of 1536, the effect of his preaching was so great, that some images were broken by the popular indignation, amidst the clamour of priests and canons. After various negotiations between Berne and Lausanne, a public disputation was called for by the Reformers. It lasted eight successive days, and ended much the same as the one at Geneva had done. Thus the triumph of the Reformation was also complete in Lausanne.

The two chief results which generally followed these great religious changes, and which were especially pursued by the Swiss Reformers, were the purification of morality, and the advancement of education. Being much in the spirit of Old Testament saints, the most rigid laws were enacted against gambling, against blasphemous oaths, against farces, lewd songs, dances, masquerades, and against every form of intemperance. We find the enactment of such laws immediately following the triumphs of Reform in all important places. It was particularly so at Geneva. There, the citizens, struck a new coin to commemorate the foundations of their Protestantism, and adopted a new civic motto—"After darkness, light."

THE ARRIVAL OF CALVIN IN GENEVA.

During the August of 1536, amongst the crowds of exiles who were daily arriving at the gates of Geneva, one presented himself a Frenchman, a native of Picardy, young, being only in his twenty-eighth year, of slender figure, and pale face; he had come to rest for the night and depart on the morrow. This man was **John Calvin.** But though young, and of a modest bearing, he was not without celebrity, both as a scholar and a divine, nor untried as a friend of the Reformation. He was on his way from Rome, with the intention of fixing his permanent residence at Basle or Strasburg; but the war, which was then raging between France and the Empire, compelled him to take a circuitous route by Geneva. But the energetic Farel thought that the author of the *Christian Institutes* was just the man for Geneva, and urged him to remain. The God of all goodness, he thought, had sent him at that critical moment.

Calvin replied that his education was yet incomplete; that he required still further instruction and application before he should be qualified for so difficult a position as the state of Geneva presented, and begged to be allowed to proceed to Basle or Strasburg. On this, Farel raised his voice as with the authority of a direct messenger from God, and said, " But I declare to you on the part of God, that if you refuse to labour here along with us at the Lord's work, His curse will be upon you ; since, under the pretence of your studies, it is yourself that you are seeking, rather than Him." Calvin had hitherto thought that his proper sphere was his library, and the main instrument of work his pen ; but feeling overwhelmed by so authoritative a declaration of the will of God, proceeding from so illustrious an apostle of the Reformation, he did not dare to decline the yoke of the ministry evidently imposed on him by the Lord. He gave his hand to Farel, and his heart to the work of the Lord in Geneva. " He was immediately appointed professor of theology, and soon afterwards minister of one of the principal parishes. This double occupation afforded space enough for the display of his great qualities, and opened the path to that singular influence, which he afterwards acquired, both in Church and state."* Here he laboured for twenty-eight years—with the exception of a brief banishment—and became the great leader in the cause of Protestantism, and the most illustrious chief of the Reformation.

THE EARLY HISTORY OF CALVIN.

As the celebrated French Reformer is now established at Geneva, and will be henceforth the central figure in the great Reform movement, it will be interesting to the reader to know something of his early history. He was born at **Noyon,** in Picardy, July 10th, 1509. His parents were of moderate fortune, and much respected by the people among whom they lived. His father, Gerard, was secretary to the bishop, and was so esteemed by the neighbouring gentry, that his son John received his early education with the children of a family of rank—the Momors.

At the age of fourteen Calvin went to Paris, and had there for his Latin tutor, in the College de la Marche, the celebrated Mathurin Cordier. One of his books is still well known in some of our schools as *Cordier's Colloquies.* But he was more than an eminent teacher ; he was a man of true piety. Having embraced the Reformed faith, he ultimately removed to Geneva, where he continued to labour as a teacher in the public college to the end of his days. He died in 1564, about six months after his distinguished pupil, at the advanced age of eighty-five.

Calvin, having fulfilled his course under Cordier, passed in 1526 to the College of Montaigu, a seminary for the training of priests. As it was the manner of those times for very young persons to hold even high ecclesiastical offices, his father solicited, and obtained for him at the age of twelve years, the chaplaincy of la Gesine, a small Church in the neighbourhood. He had his crown shaven by the bishop, and, although not yet admitted into priest's orders, he became a member of the clergy.

* Waddington, vol. iii., p. 278.

CALVIN'S CONVERSION.

It is with no small interest that we trace an intimate connection between the conversion of Calvin and the Sorbonne of Paris. Lefevre, as we have already seen, was the means of Farel's conversion. It now appears that another young man was listening to the lectures about the same time, and brought to the knowledge of the truth as it is in Jesus. This was Peter Robert Olivetan, born at Noyon, cousin to Calvin, and a few years older. It was this same Olivetan who afterwards translated the Bible into French from Lefevre's version. When his cousin arrived in Paris, he made known to him the Gospel he had embraced. The young Calvin at that time was a firm Romanist, and fortified himself against his cousin's arguments by the rigid observance of all the rites of his Church.

" True religion," said Olivetan, " is not that mass of ceremonies and observances which the Church imposes upon its followers, and which separates souls from Christ. O my dear cousin, leave off shouting with the Papists, The fathers ! The doctors ! The Church ! and listen to the prophets and apostles. Study the Scriptures." " I will have none of your new doctrines," answered Calvin, " their novelty offends me. I cannot listen to you. Do you imgaine that I have been trained all my life in error ? No ! I will strenuously resist your attacks." Olivetan put the Bible into his hands, entreating him to study the Word of God.

The Reformation at that time was agitating all the schools of learning. Masters and students occupied themselves with nothing else—some, no doubt, from mere curiosity, or to throw discredit upon the Reformers and their new doctrines ; but there was a general awakening of conscience, and a readiness to believe the true Gospel of the grace of God. Happily for Calvin he was among the latter class. The Holy Scriptures, by the blessing of God, separated him from Roman Catholicism, as they had done his cousin Olivetan.

It is supposed that Calvin was under deep exercise of soul for more than three years—from 1523 to 1527. D'Aubigné, who is the best authority on this point, says : " Yet Calvin, whose mind was essentially one of observation, could not be present in the midst of the great movement going on in the world, without reflecting on truth, on error, and on himself. Oftentimes, when alone, and when the voices of men had ceased to be heard, a more powerful voice spoke to his soul, and his chamber became the theatre of struggles, as fierce as those in the cell at Erfurt. Through the same tempests, both these great Reformers reached the haven of rest." But the **conversion of Calvin** lacks the thrilling interest which all have found in the conversion of Luther, and chiefly from the absence of details. The letters which he wrote to his father at this time, and also those of

Olivetan to his friends, have not been found. Theodore Beza, his most intimate friend, says : " Calvin having been taught the true religion by one of his relations named Peter Olivetan, and having carefully read the holy books, began to hold the teaching of the Roman Church in horror, and had the intention of renouncing its communion." Here, it is only the *intention* of leaving Rome ; but his own words in after life are positive : " When I was the obstinate slave of the superstitions of Popery," he says, " and it seemed impossible to drag me out of the deep mire, God by a sudden conversion subdued me, and made my heart more obedient to His Word."

Thus we see the various spiritual links between the Sorbonne and the first and greatest Reformers. " Farel," says D'Aubigné, " is the pioneer of the Reformation in France and Switzerland. He rushes into the wood, hews down the giants of the forest with his axe. Calvin came after, like Malanchthon, from whom he differs indeed in character, but whom he resembles in his part as theologian and organiser. These two men built up, settled, and gave laws to the territory conquered by the first two Reformers." And Beza speaks of Lefevre as the man who " boldly began the revival of the pure religion of Jesus Christ ; and that from his lecture room issued many of the best men of the age and of the Church."*

CALVIN A STUDENT OF LAW.

The Divine light which now filled the soul of Calvin showed him the midnight darkness of the Church of Rome. That which once possessed to his mind the most dazzling splendour, the weight of antiquity, and which he believed to be the habitation of God and the very gate of Heaven, was now to his newly opened eyes the temple of idols and the very gate of perdition. This we gather from the fact that he could no longer minister at her altars, and he resigned his sacred office. Happily this was with the consent of his father ; and he immediately turned his attention to the study of civil law at Orleans and at Bourges. But the lessons of the law, to which he had now to listen, must have ill-suited the taste of one who had just fled from the flames of martyrdom in Paris. " It is the magistrate's duty," said his teacher, " to punish offences against religion as well as crimes against the state." " What ! " he would exclaim, " shall we hang a thief who robs us of our purse, and not burn a heretic who robs us of Heaven ? " The effect of such a maxim on the minds of the people, when taught and amplified by the priests, would certainly destroy their sympathies, and lead them to approve of the death of heretics. Such was the teaching of Calvin and of Frenchmen at that time, and as it had an appearance of justice, and professed to be applied for the protection of the true religion,

* D'Aubigné's " Calvin," vol i., chaps. vii., viii.; D'Aubigné's " Luther," vol. iii., p. 501.

it took a firm hold of the superstitious mind, and may have left deeper traces on Calvin's own mind than he was aware of.

CALVIN GIVES UP THE STUDY OF CIVIL LAW.

When at Bourges Calvin seems to have abandoned the study of the law, and turned again to the Church as he now saw it in the Holy Scriptures. He applied himself to the study of the Greek language, and also to Hebrew and Syriac, in order to the better understanding of the Old Testament, for theology was still the favourite object of his attention. He was also most willing to make known the truth to others in which he now believed and delighted. Listeners flocked around him, and the solitude he loved became impossible to him. " As for me," he says, " inasmuch as being naturally diffident and retiring, I have always preferred repose and tranquillity ; I began to seek for some hiding-place and means of withdrawing myself from the world, but, so far from obtaining my wish, every retreat and every secluded spot were to me so many public schools." But he was not of those who were silent on what they believe. He preached in the secret meetings at Bourges and at Paris. Theodore Beza says : " He advanced wonderfully the cause of God in many families, teaching the truth not with an affected language, to which he was always opposed, but with a depth of knowledge and so much gravity of speech, that no man heard him without being filled with admiration."

Calvin once more ventured to **Paris.** He had fondly hoped that France might be the sphere, and Paris the centre of his work ; but the violence of the persecution compelled him to conceal both himself and his intentions. He was now about twenty-four years of age, and full of zeal and activity. One of his friends, Nicolas Cop, son of a citizen of Basle, who was first physician to the king, and rector of the University of Paris, had to deliver an oration according to the custom on All Saints' Day. What an opportunity, suggested Calvin to his friend Cop, of having the Gospel preached in the most public of all the pulpits of Christendom ! But, Cop feeling unequal to the task of composing such an address it was agreed that Calvin should write and that Cop should read the oration. On the 1st of November, 1533, in the midst of the learned men of Paris, the rector delivered his address to a silent and surprised audience. Calvin had forgotten to say anything about the saints, though it was " All Saints' Day," but extolled the grace of God as man's only hope of pardon and salvation through the precious sacrifice of Christ.

When the assembly rose the storm burst forth. It was denounced as treason against the saints, and a blow struck at the very foundation of Rome. But Cop was the king's first physician and a great favourite ; what was to be done ? He was denounced by the Sorbonne to the Parliament, and to the executioner of heretics. Cop saw his danger in time, fled to Basle, and so escaped the flames of martyrdom. Cop was gone, but his friend Calvin was suspected of being the real author of the oration. The lieutenant-criminal, the notorious John Morin, had orders to apprehend him. While sitting safely, as he thought, in his obscurity, a fellow-student rushed into his chamber, begging him to flee that instant ; the serjeants were at the outer gate. Dropping from the window by means of a sheet, he escaped ; and under the name of Charles Heppeville, clothed in a peasant's dress, with a garden hoe on his shoulder, he reached Angoulême, and was received into the house of the Canon Louis du Tillet, where he stayed for some time, and had a rich library at his service.

THE INSTITUTES PUBLISHED.

Calvin was already occupied with his great work on the Christian religion, and may have collected some of his materials from Du Tillet's library. But being in peril of his life, he removed to Basle, the city of refuge for the French exiles at that time. Here he completed and published the most celebrated of all his writings, the **Institutes of the Christian Religion.** The work appeared in the month of August, 1535.

" This was the first theological and literary monument of the French Reformation," says Félice. " Spreading abroad in the schools, the castles of the gentry, and the houses of the burghers, even the workshops of the people, the *Institutes* became the most powerful of preachers. Round this book the Reformers arrayed themselves as round a standard. They found in it everything— doctrine, discipline, ecclesiastical organisation ; and the apologist of the masters became the legislator of their children." In his dedicatory epistle to Francis I, he supplicated the king to examine the confession of faith of the Reformers, so that, beholding them to be in accordance with the Bible, he might treat them no longer as heretics. " It is your duty, sire," he says to the king, " to close neither your understanding nor your heart against so just a defence, especially when the question is of such high import, namely, how the glory of God shall be maintained on earth . . . a matter worthy of your ears, worthy of your jurisdiction, worthy of your royal throne." But there is too good reason to believe that the king never deigned to read the preface to the *Institutes.*

Calvin was now the acknowledged leader of the French Reformation. Luther was too distant ; Farel was too ardent ; but Calvin had the solid character and the lively sympathies suited to the French. He paid a visit about this time to the justly celebrated Renée of France, daughter of Louis XII, and Duchess of Ferrara, one of the first provinces of Italy that received the

Reformation. Like her cousin, Margaret of Valois, she had embraced the true Gospel, and become the patroness of the persecuted Reformers in Italy, for which she afterwards suffered severe persecution though she was the daughter of a king. This visit established a friendship which was never interrupted ; we find Calvin addressing a letter to her when on his death-bed.*

In 1536 Calvin was appointed pastor and professor at Geneva. The religious, moral, intellectual, and even political revolution he brought into that city with him, is beyond the limits of our " Short Papers." His life and labours have been often written. We will notice that which enters into the plan of this history.

Calvin soon found that it was no easy post that he was called to occupy. The people were just emerging from a state of ignorance, superstition, and immorality, in which the city had been sunk for ages, and the corruption of her " nine hundred " priests, had no doubt produced its own likeness in the manner of the citizens. But all laxity of morals, and all amusements which had that tendency, were sharply and sternly rebuked by Calvin and Farel both publicly and privately. They were not only the avowed enemies of the least vestige of Popery, but they were strict disciplinarians. The majority of the people were not yet prepared for such self-denial. They had fought hard to cast off the yoke of Rome and the yoke of the Duke of Savoy, and they were determined to resist what they thought the hardest yoke of all—to give up all their pleasures and live according to a rigid ecclesiastical discipline. Even many of those who had outwardly embraced the Reformation doctrines were not in heart prepared for Calvin's system. His idea was to treat the state as a theocracy and compel the citizens to conform to the law of God, under the threatened judgments of the Old Testament.

CALVIN AND FAREL BANISHED FROM GENEVA.

The Reformed ministers, as might have been expected, were soon involved in stormy contests with their congregations. They were evidently mistaken in seeking to bind the people, who had been accustomed to live according to their own pleasure, to so rigid a system, without sufficient moral training and preparation of heart by the grace of God. Immediately after his settlement at Geneva, Calvin drew up a " Formulary of Christian Doctrine and Discipline," and set himself with the other ministers to induce the citizens at large, in their popular assembly, to abjure Popery, and *swear* to observe the scheme of doctrine and order thus prepared for them. Many objecting to do this, troubles arose, party spirit began to run high ; but as the ministers were unyielding, it resulted in their refusing to celebrate the

* Dr. M'Crie gives many interesting details of this amiable and accomplished princess in his " History of the Reformation in Italy."

Lord's Supper among the people ; and the citizens, on their part, resolved to banish the ministers, and forbade them the use of their pulpits.

In the year 1538, the two banished ministers, with sad hearts, left the city on which they had bestowed much labour ; but, as they have not informed us, we will not conjecture their feelings as they turned their backs upon Geneva. Farel went to **Neufchatel,** where he had formerly laboured, and where he remained till the end of his days. He there succeeded in establishing the system of discipline which was opposed in Geneva ; and sought to serve the Lord and His Church with all diligence till the year 1565, when he fell asleep in Jesus at the advanced age of seventy-six.

CALVIN AT STRASBURG—HIS WORK AND MARRIAGE.

Calvin proceeded to Basle and thence to **Strasburg,** to which he had been earnestly invited by the pastors of that city, Bucer and Capito. He was immediately appointed a professor of divinity, and pastor of a congregation composed of French refugees. Nothing could speak more solemnly of the fierceness of the persecution which was at that time raging in France than the fact that about *fifteen thousand* French exiles gathered around Calvin to hear the Gospel in their native tongue. And if fifteen thousand were found in Strasburg alone, what numbers besides must have fled to England, Germany, and other places ! Here Calvin laboured in preaching and writing for three years. The advanced state of society, a more polished congregation than the one he had left in Geneva, suited his taste, and was as balm to his wounded heart. He republished his *Institutes,* much enlarged, wrote his commentary on the Epistle to the Romans, and a treatise on the Lord's Supper.

So happy was the stern, severe disciplinarian in Strasburg, that he consented to marry if his friends could find for him a suitable wife. The first lady that was named was of noble birth and richly dowered ; but Calvin objected to marry one above his own degree ; still, if the lady would consent to learn the French language, he would give his final answer. But this the lady refused to do, and that was the end of the first nomination. Another lady was proposed, and Calvin, in this case, made certain advances himself, but, happily, he discovered in time sufficient reasons for not going farther. At last, by the advice of his friend Bucer, he married Idolette de Bure, a widow of deep piety and Christian courage. The reader will readily recall and contrast the impulsive, hasty, and unseasonable marriage of Luther with the matrimonial negotiations of Calvin, so characteristic of the two great Reformers.*

* " History of Protestantism," vol. ii., p. 303.

CALVIN'S RETURN TO GENEVA.

But while Calvin was thus happily employed at Strasburg, everything was falling into great disorder, both political and religious on the banks of the Leman. The libertines, Anabaptists, and Papists, now that the stern Reformers were gone, became riotous and ungovernable, while some of the magistrates, who had made themselves leaders in the violent proceeding against the ministers, came to a most tragic end. These troubles and these judgments, led the people to believe that they had sinned against God in banishing His faithful ministers, and to cry aloud for their return. The council of two hundred resolved in 1540, "in order that the honour and glory of God may be promoted, to seek all possible means to have Master Calvin back as preacher." And it was ordered in the general council, or assembly of the people, "to send to Strasburg to fetch Master Jean Calvinus, who is very learned, to be minister in this city."

Besides these assurances of a warm welcome, an honourable deputation was sent to him from the council to solicit his return. But the very thought of going back to Geneva greatly troubled him. He dreaded the course rough abuse which he had received from his rude opponents—especially the libertines. And was he again to leave his peaceful and happy situation in Strasburg, and plunge into that sea of troubles ? Yet he wished to do the will of the Lord and to follow His guidance. Besides his official invitations, he had letters from private Christian friends urging him to return. One of them, pressing his return, assures him "that he will find the Genevese a new people—become such by the grace of God, and through the instrumentality of Viret." The pastors of Zurich also pressed his return, urging the vast importance of the situation of Geneva, as situated on the confines of Germany, Italy, and France.

At length he consented to return, but in real subjection of heart to what he believed to be the will of his Lord and master. "There is no place under Heaven," he said, "that I more dread than Geneva, yet I would decline nothing that might be for the welfare of that Church." And writing to Farel, informing him of his decision, he says : "Since I remember that I am not my own, nor at my own disposal, I give myself up, tied bound, as a sacrifice to God." His departure took place on the 13th of September, 1541. A mounted herald from Geneva rode before him ; and the proceedings which accompanied his reception were highly honourable to all parties concerned.*

* Scott's " History," vol. iii., p. 200 ; D'Aubigné's " Calvin," vol. vi., chaps. xv.-xvii.; Wylie's " Protestantism," vol. ii., chap. xiv.

CALVIN AND SERVETUS.

The condemnation and death of **Michael Servetus,** the arch-heretic, at Geneva, have always been spoken of, both by Romish and Protestant writers, as a deep stain on the otherwise unsullied reputation of the great Reformer. But, in judging of Calvin's connection with this melancholy affair, we must bear in mind the mighty difference between the sixteenth and the nineteenth centuries. Many of the leading Reformers, both in Germany and Switzerland, believed it a duty to punish heresy with death. Yet notwithstanding these considerations, Calvin's conduct in the matter must be utterly condemned by every enlightened Christian. And we are apt to wonder, in the nineteenth century, why such a student of Scripture did not see the grace which shines throughout the New Testament. The Christian is saved by grace, stands in grace, and ought, surely, to be the witness of grace in an evil world. Besides, we have the example and teaching of our Lord, " who, when He was reviled, reviled not again ; when He suffered He threatened not ; but committed Himself to Him that judgeth righteously." And in His sermon on the Mount, he thus teaches His disciples : " Love your enemies, bless them that curse you, do good to them that hate you, and pray for them which despitefully use you, and persecute you ; that ye may be the children of your Father which is in Heaven ; for He maketh His sun to rise on the evil and on the good, and sendeth rain on the just and on the unjust . . . Be ye, therefore, perfect, even as your Father which is in Heaven is perfect." Which simply means, Be ye perfect according to the perfect pattern of grace which is here shown by your heavenly Father.

But, strange to say, Calvin not only overlooked all such Scriptures, but considered " Nebuchadnezzar as highly honoured in Scripture for denouncing capital punishment against any who should blaspheme the God of Shadrach, Meshach, and Abednego ; and doubts not that, had a pious and zealous Christian magistrate been at hand, St. Paul would willingly have delivered over Hymenaeus and Alexander to him, to receive the chastisement they deserved." But while charity is ready to grant that these were more the errors of the age than of the man, we must bear in mind, that unless we have Christ before us as our example and rule of life, we shall not be effectually delivered from such legal thoughts in any age. Moses and Elias must disappear, and Jesus be found alone. " If we say that we abide in Him, we ought also to walk even as He walked."

THE CHARACTER AND EXECUTION OF SERVETUS.

Michael Servetus was a Spaniard, born in the same year with Calvin ; of an active, vigorous mind ; capable of applying himself to various pursuits ; but, unfortunately, too speculative in

Divine things. He had studied medicine, law, and theology. In the latter, he was led away by a daring, self-confident spirit, into the wildest extravagances of pantheism, materialism, and a virulent opposition to the doctrine of the Trinity. But under all this heresy, like the Anabaptists—the celestial prophets—he was seditious and revolutionary. Such men generally aim at the overthrow of existing governments, as well as Christianity. This was the great sin, and the real cause of the persecution of the Anabaptists in those days. They followed the Reformers into every country, and sought to upset their work by affirming that they only went half way, and that Christians—like themselves, should rule the state as well as the Church—that the time was come for the saints to take the kingdoms of this world.

Just before Servetus came to Geneva, he had escaped from the prison at Vienna, where he had been confined for the publication of an offensive and blasphemous work, and where he was afterwards burned in effigy, with five bales of his books. Calvin, who knew him well, and had exposed his heresies years before this affair at Vienna, is represented as saying : "If Servetus came to Geneva, and his influence could prevent it, he should not go away alive." Servetus did come, and Calvin informed the council of his arrival, and drew up the articles of indictment from his writings, which led to his condemnation and death. These charges he was required by the council to retract, deny, explain, or defend, as he should see good. For this preparation he was allowed all the time he demanded. But in place of conciliating enemies, or making friends by a spirit of sobriety and moderation when he made his defence, he conducted himself in the most insolent manner. He gave to Calvin the lie direct over and over again, and called him by such names as "Simon the sorcerer." Particulars of this case were sent to several other states for an opinion, and it was said : "With one consent they all pronounced that he has revived the impious errors with which Satan of old disturbed the Church ; and is a monster not to be endured." With these concurring opinions, and the council of Geneva being unanimous, he was condemned to be led to Champel and there burned alive.

The wretched man, up to the last, showed no signs of repentance, but the most dreadful fear of death. When Calvin heard the sentence he was greatly affected, and interceded with the council, not that Servetus might be spared, but that his sentence might be mitigated. He prayed that the sword might be substituted for the fire—decapitation for burning. But this was refused ; and on 27th of October, 1553, he was led to the summit of Champel, where the stake had been fixed. At the first glare of the flames, it is said, Servetus gave a shriek so terrible that it made the crowd fall back, and was heard at a great distance.

His books were burned with him, but the fire burned slowly, and he lived half-an-hour at the stake.*

CALVIN'S WORK.

In the midst of the many conflicts in which Calvin was engaged, he was unwearied in his pastoral labours, and in his endeavours to expose and to counteract errors both in Church and State, and to diffuse light and truth in all the churches. "Through the fame and the influence of this distinguished theologian, the Geneva Church rapidly increased in numbers, and was looked upon as the centre of the Reformed cause. At his suggestion a college was established by the senate in 1558, in which he and Theodore Beza, along with others of great erudition and high talents, were the teachers. This seat of learning soon acquired so great fame that students resorted to it from England, Scotland, France, Italy, and Germany, in pursuit of sacred as well as secular learning." By this means the principles of the Reformation spread widely over the various countries of Europe. "To John Calvin the Protestant Churches must ever owe a deep debt of gratitude, and, among Presbyterians in particular, his memory will be embalmed, as having given to their system of Church polity the weight of his influence and name." Along with this beautiful notice from " Faiths of the World," we are bound to add a line from the very solid Mr. Fry, an Episcopalian historian : " Geneva soon sunk in estimation with the Church of England, because of the countenance she gave to the Presbyterian form of Church government, and of the violent attack by some of her divines upon the ancient Episcopal government, which was still retained with considerable splendour in England and in Ireland " (page 487).

The published works of Calvin are most voluminous. The Geneva edition amounted to twelve volumes, folio. The Amsterdam edition—said to be the best—by using larger paper, and printing closer, was reduced to nine volumes. A translation has also been published by the " **Calvin Society**," in fifty-four volumes octavo. These contain his commentaries, expository lectures, miscellaneous pieces, the " Institutes," and the author's correspondence. The commentaries, no doubt, have formed the foundation on which the young divines of the Calvin school, from that day until now, have built up their studies ; and in this respect, who can speak of the greatness or the effect of his work ? But besides these works that have come down to us, we must bear in mind that a considerable amount of time is spent with such public men in seeing visitors from all parts of the world.

* See the original records of the trial of Servetus before the " Little Council of Geneva," discovered by M. Albert Rilliet, and published in 1844, with a short treatise on the subject, translated from the French, by Dr. Tweedie. The production of these records, though at this late hour, will go far to soften public opinion as to Calvin's share in the death of Servetus.

Then there is the daily public ministration of the Word, and public business of every kind. His advice or counsel by letter, for the help of other Churches is also expected. " When we think of his letters," says one of his admirers, " written on the affairs of greatest weight, addressed to the first men of position and intellect in Europe ; so numerous are they, that it might have been supposed he wrote letters and did nothing besides. When we turn to his commentaries, so voluminous, so solid, and so impregnated with the spirituality, and fire, and fragrance of the Divine Word, again, it would seem as if we had before us the labours of a lifetime."*

CALVIN AND CALVINISM.

Whether we agree with the doctrinal teaching of Calvin, and the style in which he treated some of his subjects, we must give him full credit for zeal, devotedness, and industry. In a feeble and sickly body, and in a comparatively short lifetime, he accomplished a great work. It is to be feared, however, that some of his extreme statements, and his harsh language as to " **reprobation** " and " the reprobate," unsanctioned, we believe, by Scripture, have done much harm to many precious souls. "But the fact, I believe is," says Scott, " that there was a coldness and hardness about Calvin's mind, which led him sometimes to regard as objects of mere intellect, those things which could not but deeply move the feelings of minds differently constituted ; and hence, I cannot but concur, he did not duly appreciate the effect of the language he was using upon other persons. And to these extreme statements and this obnoxious language, I must think, is to be traced a considerable portion of that storm of obloquy and odium which has not ceased to beat upon the head of Calvin and Calvinism to this day."†

THE CLOSING DAYS OF CALVIN.

But, though we may not be able to follow the learned theologian in his vast researches, or to receive the doctrines which he taught, we shall feel that he is of one heart and one mind with us, as we gather around **his death-bed.** His old and faithful friend, Farel, hearing of the serious illness of Calvin, wrote to say he must come and see him. He was then seventy-five, and in feeble health. Calvin, wishing to save him the fatiguing journey immediately dictated the following brief and affectionate reply : " Farewell, my best and most faithful brother ; and, since it is God's pleasure that you should survive me in this world, live in the constant remembrance of our union, which, in so far as it was useful to the Church of God, will still bear for us abiding fruit in Heaven. Do not expose yourself to fatigue

* " History of Protestantism," vol. ii., p. 346. † Vol. iii., chap. xxvi.

for my sake. I respire with difficulty, and continually expect my breath to fail me ; but it is enough for me that I live and die in Christ, who to His people in life and death is *gain*. Once more, farewell to thee, and to all the brethren, thy colleagues.— Geneva, May 2nd, 1564."

The good old man, however, a few days afterwards, came to Geneva, and spent a little time with his friend in his sick-chamber ; but history has not recorded what passed between them. Unlike Luther, who was always surrounded with admiring friends, who immediately chronicled all he said or did, and thereby gave a dramatic character to every incident of his life, we know nothing of the homely, familiar social life of Calvin, which greatly detracts from the interest of one who is made a central figure.

Having seen the members of the senate, and the ministers under the jurisdiction of Geneva, and having faithfully and affection-ately addressed them, he felt that his work was done. The remainder of his days he passed in almost perpetual prayer. As he was repeating the words of the apostle : " The sufferings of this present time are not worthy to be compared with the glory to be . . . ," without being able to finish, he breathed his last, May 27th, 1564.

"He lived," says Beza, " fifty-four years, ten months, and seventeen days ; half of which time he passed in the sacred ministry. His stature was of a middle size, his complexion dark and pale, his eyes brilliant even unto death, expressing the acuteness of his understanding. He lived nearly without sleep. His power of memory was almost incredible ; and his judgment so sound that his decisions often seemed oracular. In his words he was sparing, and he despised an artificial eloquence ; yet was he an accomplished writer, and, by the accuracy of his mind, and his practice in dictating to an amanuensis, he attained to speak little differently from what he would have written . . . Having given with good faith the history of his life and of his death, after sixteen years' observation of him, I feel myself warranted to declare that in him was proposed to all men an illustrious example of the life and death of a Christian, so that it will be found as difficult to emulate as it is easy to calumniate him."*

* Beza's Narrative, quoted by Scott, vol. iii., p. 485.

CHAPTER L

The Reformation in France

THE history of the Reformation in France awakens, as we approach it, the most mingled feelings. The wonderful progress of the truth in that gay, frivolous, and dissolute kingdom, creates the deepest interest, gratitude, and admiration, while the enemies' opposition and triumph fill the heart with deepest sorrow. It was then a great nation, and early blessed with the doctrines of the Reformation. Four years before the voice of Luther or Zwingle was heard, the University of Paris had been convulsed by the proclamation of a free salvation to the chief of sinners, through faith in Christ, without works of human merit. The **doctrine of the Reformation** was not, therefore, imported from Germany or Switzerland, but was the native fruit of French soil. We cannot but lament that a kingdom so great, so central, so intelligent, did not throw off the Papal yoke like England, Scotland, Denmark, Sweden, and the half of Germany. But dearly she has had to pay in her periodical revolutions for the rejection of the light. The two elements, the Gospel of the grace of God, and the superstitions of Rome, strove mightily with each other, and produced the most violent struggles and the most tragic scenes that history has recorded.

The awakening of souls by Divine grace, to the importance of the truth, evidently commenced, as we have already seen, by means of James Lefevre, then nearly seventy years of age, and his youthful convert, William Farel. Then came Olivetan ; and he, in his turn, was the means of leading Calvin to the knowledge of Jesus. In the commentary published by Lefevre, as early as 1512, he says : " It is God who gives us, by faith, that righteousness, which by grace alone justifies to eternal life." These few words—as in the case of Luther when he discovered the great truth—"The just shall live by faith "—show us plainly that the doctor of the Sorbonne, as well as the monk of Erfurt, was taught of God, that Divine light had filled his own soul, and that this heavenly ray was sufficient to illumine the souls of others. And thus we find it. While Lefevre was sowing the seed of eternal life in his lecture room, Farel, now fully emancipated from the superstitions of Rome, and well instructed in the Gospel of Christ, was preaching outside with great boldness. " Young and resolute," says Félice, " he caused the public places to resound with his voice of thunder ; " and being now master of arts, he had the privilege of lecturing in the celebrated college of the Cardinal Lemoine, one of the four principal colleges of the theological faculty in Paris, equal in rank to the Sorbonne. Other young evangelists were also engaged in preaching the Gospel and circulating the truth.

The priests and the doctors of the Sorbonne became greatly alarmed for the interests of Holy Mother Church; and the University issued a formal declaration condemnatory of the new opinions. But before going farther in the order of events, it may be well to notice the entrance upon the scene of **three persons,** on whose will the destinies of France henceforth depended, namely, Francis I, Margaret, his sister, and their mother, Louisa of Savoy, Countess of Angoulême.

The good King Louis XII, styled the father of his people, died on the 1st of January, 1515. No sovereign of France had before been so honoured and loved; his death struck consternation into all hearts. When his funeral passed along the streets to the Cathedral of Notre Dame, the public criers headed the procession, ringing their bells, and proclaiming in a voice almost inaudible through tears : " *Le bon roi Louis, père du peuple, est mort* " (" The good king Louis, the father of his people, is dead "). Judging from circumstances, had the Reformation taken place during his reign, the whole of France might have become Protestant; but his successor was a prince of a widely different character.

On the 25th of January, 1515, **Francis of Angouleme,** Duke of Valois and cousin to the king, was crowned at Rheims with great display. He was of tall stature, handsome in person, possessed of every accomplishment as a cavalier and a soldier, but of dissolute character, and following rashly wherever his passions led him. His education, however, under de Boisy, his tutor, had not been neglected, so that he was considered the most learned prince in France, and greatly honoured literature and learned men. His queen, Claude, is little spoken of, but his sister Margaret, afterwards Queen of Navarre, always occupies a prominent place. She was his senior by two years, had great influence over her brother, and being early converted, and amongst the first to embrace the Reformed doctrines, she often sheltered the persecuted, and succeeded in moving the king's heart to clemency. But state policy, his pretended zeal for the Church, and the influence of the Parliament and the Sorbonne, frequently proved stronger than his sister's love. Like her brother, she was tall, extremely beautiful, fascinating in her manners, and possessed of a great mind and ability, both natural and acquired. But after her conversion, all her powers, due allowance being made for the times and her position, were consecrated to the Lord and His people.

In the history of these remarkable persons we have an instructive and an important illustration of the effect of grace and truth on the heart and in the life. They were the only children of Louisa, who was only twenty years old when she became a widow. Her daughter Margaret had not attained her fourth year; while the infant Francis had just completed his fifteenth month. Brave of heart, highly gifted, and strong in the consciousness of duty, Louisa applied herself in every possible way to the responsibilities of her position. Her two cherished children became the objects of her affection and of her unceasing care, for which she was fully repaid in after life by the devotion of her children; though, morally, they pursued such widely different paths. But we must now return to the more direct line of our history.

FIRSTFRUITS OF THE REFORMATION.

Meaux was the first city in France that heard the doctrines of the Reformation publicly expounded, and where the first fruits of the Gospel were gathered. About twenty-five miles east of Paris, and not far distant from the then Flemish frontier, it was a place full of working people—mechanics, wool-carders, fullers, cloth-makers, and artisans. The bishop of the place, **William Brissonnet,** a man of high rank, also Count of Montbrun, became a convert to the new doctrines. Being a man of noble family, and of imposing address, he had been twice sent ambassador of Francis I to the Holy See; but he returned to Paris less a son of the Church than he had been before going. He may, like Luther, have had his eyes opened to the dazzling wickedness of Rome, and to the utter hollowness of her gorgeous ceremonies.

On his return from his diplomatic missions he was astonished to find the interest which had been awakened and the change which had been wrought by the preaching of the new doctrines. The Universities were full of debate and tumult on the subject, and the hearts of the artisans in his own diocese were greatly moved by the tidings of the Gospel which had reached them. This was in 1521, four years after Luther had affixed his thesis to the door of his Cathedral, and the very year in which he appeared before the Diet of Worms. The proximity of Meaux to Flanders, and the similarity of its trade to that of the larger Flemish towns occasioned a degree of intercourse between them, which doubtless contributed to the spread of the new opinions.

The bishop, evidently a pious, humble, but timid man, sought an interview with Lefevre, that he might be better instructed in the new doctrines. The aged doctor placed the Bible in the prelate's hands, assuring him that it was the Bible, and the Bible only, which ever leads the soul back to the truth as it was in the beginning of the Gospel of Christ. Before there were schools, sects, ceremonies, or traditions, the truth was the means, and the Holy Spirit the power, of salvation. He searched the Scriptures with great diligence ; and, with the Lord's blessing, they became a source of great happiness to him. Writing to Margaret, over whom he exercised a wholesome influence, he says : " The savour of Divine food is so sweet, that it renders the mind insatiable ; the more one tastes, the more one desires it. What vessel is able to receive the exceeding fulness of this inexhaustible sweetness ? "*

THE CONVERSION OF MARGARET.

Many of the eminent men who composed the court of Francis at this time, and who enjoyed the confidence of the king, were favourable disposed towards the doctrines of Lefevre and the bishop. They were literary men whom Francis and Margaret had already encouraged and protected from the attacks of the Sorbonne, who regarded the study of Hebrew and Greek as the most pernicious of heresies. Francis, who loved learning, invited into his states learned men, " thinking," says Erasmus, " in this manner to adorn and illustrate his age in a more magnificent manner than he could have done by trophies, pyramids, or by the most pompous structures." For a time he was carried away by the influence of his sister, by Brissonnet, and the learned men of his court. He would often be present at the conversations of the learned, listening with delight to their discussions. It was then that he prepared the way for the Word of God by founding Hebrew and Greek professorships.

But there is one thing to be borne in mind respecting the favour shown by many learned men to the idea of Reform at that time. They, no doubt, felt the power and truth of the doctrines set forth by the Reformers, but were not prepared to separate from the communion of the Church of Rome. They felt and owned the need of Reform, and hoped that Rome and her priesthood would take the lead in the needed Reformation, and in this way have their hopes realised. But there was one in that brilliant circle whose convictions were deeper, whose conscience was at work, and who was diligently reading the New Testament in the Greek tongue. Such was the gifted **Margaret of Angouleme.** But she was unhappy ; she was sad at heart amidst the gaieties of the court. Francis was passionately fond of his sister, whom he always called his " darling," and Margaret was not less devoted in affection to her brother. They had grown up together, wandered in the fields and gardens together as children, and for a time their lives and tastes were one. But the time was come when they must be parted—parted morally at least.

* Freer's " History of Margaret," vol. i., p. 98 ; D'Aubigné, vol. iii., p. 509 ; Smiles' " History of the Huguenots," p. 18.

The time, too, when this moral divergence took place made it the more trying. Her grace and beauty made her the ornament of her brother's court, and he wished her to be always at his side. "Francis," says Wylie, "after wavering some time between the Gospel and Rome, between the pleasures of the world and the joys that are eternal, made at last his choice, but, alas! on the opposite side to that of his lovely and accomplished sister. Casting in his lot with Rome, and staking crown and kingdom and salvation upon the issue, he gave battle to the Reformation." The mother, alas! followed her son in all the intrigues and dissimulation of state policy. She exercised the most unbounded influence over the king, and some of the calamities of France are attributed to her unjustifiable policy. He constituted her regent of France, during his absence on his Italian campaign, to the great mortification of his Parliament.

Margaret, through Divine grace, was led, chiefly by means of Brissonnet, to clearer and fuller views of the Gospel, and to a saving knowledge of the Lord Jesus. This took place about the year 1521, just as the persecution was beginning to burst forth, and many of the persecuted found within her gates a shelter which a merciful providence had provided against the evil days that were at hand.

The influence of Margaret's conversion was felt. among the high personages of the court, and the literary circles of the capital. The surprise was great, and all talked of the king's sister embracing the new opinions. Those who sought to arrest the work of the Lord sought the ruin of Margaret. She was denounced to the king, but he pretended to think it was untrue. "Meanwhile," says Brantôme, "she was very kind, mild, gracious, charitable, affable, a great almsgiver, despising nobody, and winning all hearts by her excellent qualities." The heart loves to dwell on such an instance of the rich sovereign grace of God, in the midst of the corruption and frivolities of the court of Francis. But God would have His witnesses and light-bearers even in the palace in the morning of the Reformation. The dear young Christian, however, was severely tried. Her struggles between conscience and what was expected of her were great and frequent. "The timid heart of the princess," says D'Aubigné, "trembled before the anger of the king. She was constantly wavering between her brother and her Saviour, and could not resolve to sacrifice either . . . However, such as she is, she is a pleasing character on the page of history. Neither Germany nor England present her parallel." Her light, we have no doubt, was often clouded and her testimony silenced by the angry looks of the king, as he manifested his hatred of the Reformation, and of the friends whom Margaret loved. But the Lord was with her though her feminine character may have sometimes drawn her into the shade.

THE REFORMATION OF BRISSONNET.

The courtly bishop was a constant and welcome guest at the palace. It was there he put the Bible into the hands of Margaret; and the friendship he enjoyed with Francis gave him many opportunities of spreading the new doctrines among the philosophers and scholars whom that monarch loved to assemble around him. And being a bishop, and in such favour at court, he had many listeners, and it may be at this period, and to such conversions as Brissonnet and Margaret, that we should trace the inclination of so many French nobles to embrace Protestantism. But the king and a large majority of the people remained faithful to Rome, and many of the nobility, intimidated by her threatenings and martyrdoms, hesitated, drew back, until at length their convictions waned in their minds, and left them captives to the darkness from which they lacked the moral courage to extricate themselves.*

Brissonnet, now full of zeal for the Reformation of the Church, determined to set the example by reforming his own diocese. On his return from Paris to Meaux, he inquired into the lives and doctrines of the preachers, and discovered that nearly all the pulpits were filled with Franciscan monks, while the deans, the incumbents, vicars, and curates, spent their time in idleness and their revenues in Paris. He ascertained that throughout his diocese there were scarcely ten rèsident priests, and out of one hundred and twenty-seven curates, there were only fourteen whom the bishop could approve of or permit to officiate in his diocese. Then the bishop, turning towards men, who did not belong to his clergy, called around him, not only his old friend Lefevre, but Farel, D'Arvande, Roussel, and Francis Vatable. Thus the light of the Gospel was gradually withdrawn from Paris, where God in His sovereign grace had kindled its earliest sparks ; and thither the persecutors were determined to follow, but as yet the tempest is forbidden to burst. The Reformers must be protected by the hand of a Divine providence until their work is more complete.†

THE BIBLE IN FRENCH AT MEAUX.

Like our English Wycliffe, the aged Lefevre greatly desired that every man in France should have the privilege of reading the Holy Scriptures in his mother tongue. For this he laboured, and with the assistance of Brissonnet, the four Gospels in French were published in October, 1522 ; the remaining books of the New Testament soon followed ; and in October, 1524, a complete edition of the New Testament was published at Meaux. There the great fountain of light was first introduced which placed the

* Freer's " History of Margaret," vol. i., p. 97.
† D'Aubigné, vol. iii., p. 532 ; Freer, vol. i., p. 98.

work on a solid basis, and there the first Protestant congregation publicly assembled.

The pious bishop greatly furthered this good work by his wealth and his zeal. The Word of God was speedily and widely circulated, the poor were supplied gratis. Never did prelate devote his income to nobler purposes, and never did a seed-time promise to bear a more glorious harvest. The preachers, transferred from Paris to **Meaux,** and finding themselves unfettered, were acting with great liberty, while the Word of God was diligently read in the homes and workshops of the people. The effect was sudden and great. Divine light had taken the place of Papal darkness. The new book became the theme of their constant conversation, for while they handled their spindles and their combs, they could talk to each other of some fresh discovery they had made in the Gospels or the Epistles ; and so the villagers in the vineyards, when the meal-hour came, one read aloud, while the others gathered round him. "There was engendered in many," says a chronicler of that day, "an ardent desire for knowing the way of salvation, so that artisans, fullers, and woolcombers took no other recreation, as they worked with their hands, than to talk with each other of the Word of God, and to comfort themselves with the same. Sundays and holidays especially were devoted to the reading of Scripture, and inquiring into the good pleasure of the Lord."

The following quotation from a Catholic historian, though hostile, bears witness to the positive influence of the Word of God on the people. "Lefevre, aided by the renown of his great learning, contrived so to cajole and circumvent Messire Brissonnet with his plausible talk, that he caused him to turn aside grievously, so that it has been impossible to this day to free the city and diocese of Meaux from that pestilent doctrine, where it has so marvellously increased. The misleading that good bishop was a great injury, as until then he had been so devoted to God and to the Virgin Mary."*

THE BLESSED EFFECTS OF THE WORD OF GOD.

These simple people soon became better instructed than their former teachers, the Franciscan monks. Christianity had taken the place of superstition, and the Word of God had revealed Christ to their souls as the sun and centre of Divine light. They now saw that praying to the saints is idolatry ; that Christ is the only Mediator between God and man ; and that the throne of grace is open to all. Meaux had thus become a focus of light ; tidings of the great work spread through France, so that it became a proverb with reference to anyone noted for the new opinions that " he had drunk at the well of Meaux."

* Quoted by D'Aubigné, vol. iii., p. 544.

The preaching of the new ministers was for a time confined to private assemblies ; but as the number of their hearers increased, they gained courage and ascended the public pulpits. The bishop preached in his turn ; he entreated his flock to lend no ear to those who would turn them aside from the Word of God ; even if an angel from Heaven were to preach another gospel, be sure you do not listen to him. Lefevre, energetically expounding the Word on one occasion, exclaimed : " Kings, princes, nobles, peoples, all nations should think and aspire after Christ alone ! . . . Come near, ye Pontiffs, come ye kings, come ye generous hearts ! . . . Nations awake to the light of the Gospel, and inhale the heavenly life. The Word of God is all-sufficient ! " And this, henceforth became the motto of that school : **The Word of God is all-sufficient.**

Thus the ray of light which we have seen shining through the darkness of prejudice about the year 1512, when Lefevre proclaimed from the tribune of the Popish Sorbonne the futility of works without faith, declared the one Mediator between God and man ; and boldly denounced the idolatry of those who invocated, and offered prayers to the Virgin and the saints. That Divine ray was not suffered to become extinct. For nearly twelve years it has been expanding until, like a beacon in the surrounding gloom, it is showing thousands and tens of thousands the way of life and peace, and how to avoid the ways of death and Hell.*

COMMENCEMENT OF PERSECUTION IN FRANCE.

We must now look at the other side of the picture. If the young flock of Meaux was peacefully feeding on the green pastures under the bishop's care, the monks, who cared little for the green pastures of the Gospel, were losing their influence and their revenues, and the begging friars were returning home from their rounds with empty wallets. " These new teachers are heretics," said they ; " and they attack the holiest of observances, and deny the most sacred mysteries." Then, growing bolder, the most incensed among them proceeded to the palace. On being admitted, they said to the prelate : " Crush this heresy, or else the pestilence, which is already desolating the city of Meaux, will spread over the whole kingdom." Brissonnet was moved, and for a moment disturbed by the audacious monks, but did not give way. Yet admirable as were the piety and zeal of the bishop, he was of a timid and temporising nature when danger assailed him. He lacked the firmness and constancy of spirit which enables some men, in days of persecution, to yield life rather than conscience and truth ; and so he fell, yielding truth and conscience, and saving his life and liberty.

* Freer, vol. i., p. 70.

The monks, enraged at their unfavourable reception by the bishop, determined to lay their complaints before a higher tribunal. They hastened to Paris, and denounced the bishop before the Sorbonne and the Parliament. "The city of Meaux," said they, "and all the neighbourhood, are infected with heresy, and its polluted waters flow from the Episcopal palace." Thus was the cry of heresy raised, and France soon heard the cry raised of persecution against the Gospel. The notorious Syndic, **Noel Beda,** eagerly listened. War was his native element. Shortly before the accession of Francis to the throne, he had been elected the head of the Sorbonne ; so that he felt bound to wage war against any assertion or dogma at variance with the philosophy of the schools, or the articles of the Romish faith. "He eagerly dissected the writings of the Reformers," says Miss Freer, "to drag forth their errors, and exhibit them in triumph to the hostile Sorbonnist. His fiery oratory raged against the study of the Greek and Hebrew languages ; and Paris and the University rang again with the angry protests of the irascible Syndic. His expressions of fanatical joy at the prospect of the war he was about to wage caused a thrill of horror to pervade the University. No one dare pronounce himself when the cruel scrutiny of Beda might detect heresy where none but himself even dreamed that it existed." Such was the man that the timid Brissonnet had to face, along with others of a like spirit. "In a single Beda," Erasmus used to say, "there are three thousand monks."

The defeat of Pavia, where the flower of the French nobility fell, and where the knightly monarch was made the prisoner of Charles V, and carried to Madrid, made Louisa, the king's mother, Regent of France.* This augured badly for the Reformers ; for she inherited the Savoy enmity to the Gospel, and had become the leader of a licentious gallantry, which not only polluted the court of her son, but proved a great hindrance to the spread of the pure Gospel.

BRISSONNET ACCUSED OF HERESY.

As regent, she proposed the following question to the Sorbonne: "By what means can the damnable doctrines of Luther be chased and extirpated from this most Christian kingdom ?" The answer was brief, but emphatic : "**By the stake.**" And it was added, that if the remedy was not soon put in force there would result great damage to the honour of the king, and of Madame Louisa of Savoy. Thus it was, according to a usual hollow pretence to uphold the throne, maintain the laws and order, that the authorities were compelled to unsheath the sword of persecution. The Parliament was convoked. Brissonnet was

* For a brief but graphic description of this memorable engagement, which Wylie truly calls the " Flodden of France," see Freer's " History of Margaret," vol. i., p. 153.

summoned to appear. Beda and the monks of Meaux carried on the prosecution against the bishop and his friends, the Reformers, with unflagging vindictiveness. He was accused of holding Lutheran doctrines. The French edition of the New Testament, the joint labour of Brissonnet and Lefevre, was vehemently denounced; especially Lefevre's preface, addressed "to all Christian readers." Beda had extracted from this address, and other works published at Meaux, forty-eight propositions which were declared by the faculty of theology to be heretical.

Brissonnet now saw what was before him; he must abandon the new doctrines or go to prison, perhaps to the stake. He had not the courage necessary for resistance. Naturally timid, the menaces of Beda terrified him. Besides, he was persuaded by his friends to concede as much as would satisfy Rome, and then carry on the work of the Reformation in a less open way. He had also the powerful protection of Margaret to count upon, who was at this moment at St. Germain. But alas! he was not prepared to bear the scorn of the world, leave the Church of Rome, and give up his riches and his station for the truth's sake. At last the power of present things prevailed, and he yielded to the terms of the Sorbonne. He accordingly issued, in October, 1523, his episcopal mandates: 1, To restore public prayers to the Virgin and the saints. 2, To forbid anyone to buy, borrow, read, possess, or carry about with him, Luther's works. 3, Not only to interdict the pulpits to Lefevre, Farel, and their companions, but to expel them from the diocese of Meaux. In addition to these stipulations, he had to pay a fine of two hundred livres.

What a blow this first fall of their kind and munificent friend must have been to both ministers and people! The flocks scattered, and the shepherds, with heavy hearts, turning their backs upon Meaux. Lefevre found his way to **Nerac,** where he terminated his career, under the protection of Margaret, at the advanced age of ninety-two. Farel escaped to Switzerland, where we have seen him happily engaged in the Lord's work. Gerald Roussel contributed to the progress of the Reformation in the kingdom of Navarre. The members of the Church were, by persecution, dispersed throughout France; the rest of the flock, too poor to flee, had to abide the brunt of the tempest.*

THE FIRST MARTYRS OF FRANCE.

Brissonnet fallen, Lefevre and his friends compelled to flee, the Reformed Church at Meaux dispersed, the monks again in the pulpits; this was the beginning of victory! But Rome was not satisfied, and never was, without the blood of the saints. "The sacerdotal and the civil power, the Sorbonne and the

* Wylie's "Protestantism," vol. ii., p. 141; D'Aubigné, vol. iii., chap. vii.; Freer's "History of Margaret," vol. i., p. 134; Fry's "History," p. 356.

Parliament, had grasped their arms—arms that were soon to be stained with blood. They set to work again ; and blood, since it must be so, was ere long to gratify the fanaticism of Rome." The Christians at Meaux, though left without a shepherd, continued to meet in some private place for the reading of the Word and prayer. One of their number, **John Leclerc,** a wool-comber, was so well instructed in the Word that he was soon regarded as one whom the Lord had raised up to strengthen and encourage them. True, he had neither received a college education, nor the imposition of hands, but he had the credentials of Heaven, and took the oversight of the flock which the learned bishop had deserted.

Leclerc began well. He visited from house to house instructing and confirming the disciples ; but his spirit was stirred within him as he witnessed the monks so jubilant over their victory. Could he have overthrown the whole edifice of Popery and filled France with the truth of the Gospel the desire of his heart would have been answered. But like many others of a similar spirit in those times, his zeal carried him beyond the limits of prudence. He wrote a proclamation, styling the Pope the Antichrist, predicting the downfall of his kingdom, and that the Lord was about to destroy it by the breath of His mouth. He then boldly posted his " placards " on the gates of the Cathedral. Presently all was in confusion. Priests, monks, and citizens gathered before the placards. Leclerc was suspected, seized, and thrown into prison. His trial was finished in a few days. The woolcomber was condemned to be whipped three days successively through the city, and branded on the forehead. He was led through the streets with his hands tied, and his neck bare, and the executioners willingly fulfilling their office. A great crowd followed, the Papists yelled with rage ; his friends showed him every mark of their tender compassion. When the brand of infamy was imprinted on his forehead with a hot iron, one woman drew near the martyr, with his bleeding back and burning brow, and sought to encourage him—she was **his mother.** Faith and maternal love struggled in her heart. At length, faith triumphed and she exclaimed with a loud voice, " Glory to Jesus Christ and His witnesses." The crowd, so thrilled with her emotional voice, made way for her to return home unmolested, while her son was banished from Meaux.

Leclerc found his way to Metz, where the Reformation had made some progress. Though with the brand of heretic on his brow, his zeal was unabated, his courage unabashed, and his prudence as greatly at fault. One of the great festivals of the place was approaching. A little way outside the gates of the city stood a chapel, containing images of the Virgin, and of the most celebrated saints of the province, and whither all the inhabitants of Metz were in the habit of making a pilgrimage on a certain day in the year, to worship these gods of stone, and to obtain the pardon of their sins. The pious and courageous soul of Leclerc was violently agitated. To-morrow, he thought, the whole city, that should worship the one living and only true God, will be bowing down before these blocks of wood and stone. Without consulting the leading brethren there, he stole out of the city before the gates were closed, and sat down before the images in great conflict of mind. The passage in Exodus 33 : " Thou shalt not bow down to their gods, nor serve them, nor do after their works ; but thou shalt overthrow them, and quite break down their images," he believed, was now brought home to his conscience by the Spirit of the Lord ; and, as Beza says, " Impelled by a Divine afflatus," he broke down the images, and indignantly scattered their fragments before the altar. At daybreak he re-entered Metz.

In a few hours all were in motion in the ancient city of Metz. Bells were ringing, the population assembling, banners flying, and all, headed by canons, priests, and monks, moved on amidst burning tapers and smoking incense, to the Chapel of Our Lady. But, suddenly, all the instruments of music were silent, and the whole multitude filled with indescribable agitation, as they saw the heads, arms, and legs of their deities strewn over the area where they had expected to worship them.

THE MARTYRDOM OF LECLERC.

The branded heretic was suspected. Death, death to the impious wretch, was the cry ; and all returned in haste and disorder to Metz. Leclerc was seized. He admitted his crime, and prayed the deluded people to worship God only. When led before his judges, he boldly confessed his faith in Christ, God manifest in the flesh, and declared that He alone should be adored. He was sentenced to be burnt alive, and immediately dragged to the place of execution. His persecutors contrived to render his **punishment most fearful** and appalling. He beheld the terrible preparation of his torture ; but he was calm, firm, and unmoved as he heard the wild yells of monks and the people ; and through the marvellous grace and power of God, no sign of weakness marred the glory of his sacrifice. They began by cutting off his right hand ; then tearing his flesh with red-hot pincers, they concluded by burning his breasts. While his enemies were in this way wearying themselves by their new inventions of torture, Leclerc's mind was at rest. He recited solemnly and in a loud voice the words of the Psalmist : " Their idols are silver and gold, the work of men's hands. They have mouths, but they speak not ; eyes have they, but they see not ; they have ears, but they hear not ; noses have they, but they smell not ; they have hands, but they handle not ; feet have they, but they walk not ; neither speak they through their throats. They that make them are like unto them ; so is every one that trusteth in them. O Israel, trust thou in the Lord ; He is their help and their shield " (Psa. 115. 4-9). After these tortures, Leclerc was burnt by a slow fire. Such was the death of the first martyr of the Gospel in France.*

But the priests of Metz were not satisfied with the blood of the poor wool-comber. **Dean Chatelain** had embraced the Reformed doctrines, and could not be shaken from the faith. He was denounced before the cardinal of Lorraine, stripped of his priestly vestments, and in a layman's dress, handed over to the secular power, which condemned him to be burnt alive ; and soon the minister of Christ was consumed in the flames. But the effect of these tragedies as might have been expected, was to cause Lutheranism to spread through the whole district of Metz. " The beholders," says a chronicler, " were astonished ; nor were they untouched by compassion ; and not a few retired from the sad scenes to confess the Gospel for which they had seen the martyrs, with so serene and noble a fortitude, lay down their lives."

REFLECTIONS ON THE FALL OF BRISSONNET.

It is difficult to leave the ashes of Leclerc without a mournful thought of the poor bishop. If Leclerc is to be condemned for his indiscretion, he must be admired for his courage. But what of Brissonnet ? Having many friends at court, he saved his mitre, his palace, and his riches ; but at the cost of conscience, truth, and a crown of life. " What Brissonnet's reflections may have been," says Wylie, " as he saw one after another of his former flock go to the stake, and from the stake to Heaven, we shall not venture to guess. May there not have been moments when he felt as if the mitre which he had saved at so great a cost, was burning his brow, and that even yet he must needs arise and leave his palace with all its honours, and by the way of the dungeon and the stake, rejoin the members of his former flock who had preceded him, by this same road, and inherit with them honours and joys, higher far than any the Pope or the King of France had to bestow. But whatever he felt, and whatever at times may have been his secret resolutions, we know that his thoughts and purposes never ripened into acts."

Humanly speaking, we are disposed to attribute the fall of Brissonnet to a natural weakness of character, the deceitfulness of riches, and the influence of plausible friends. His case was conducted with closed doors before a commission, so that it is unknown to what extent he renounced the faith he had preached,

* D'Aubigné, vol. iii., p. 582.

and laboured to diffuse with a zeal apparently so ardent and so sincere. He remained in communion with Rome till his death—which happened a few years after his recantation—and contrived so to live that there should be no more question about his orthodoxy.

But judging of such cases in the present day, there are many things to consider. They were just emerging from the darkness, superstitions, and indescribable wickedness of Popery. Men of pure and pious minds such as Brissonnet really was, saw the great need of reform, and honestly wished to promote it, although they may not have contemplated a complete secession from her communion. The idea of separation as taught by our Lord in John 17, where He gives the disciples His own place of rejection on earth, and His own place of acceptance in Heaven, formed no part in the teaching of those early times. Luther, a man of deep convictions and strong faith, was never really separated in spirit from the *idolatry* of Rome. He was no image-breaker, and his doctrine of the sacraments contradicted the truth he preached.

The heavenly relations of the Christian and the Church not being seen, there was very little separating truth in the teaching of the early Reformers. It was chiefly doctrinal; comparatively little for the heart. The dwelling of the Holy Spirit in the saints individually and in the Assembly as the house of God, and the hope of the Lord's return, were overlooked by the Reformers in the sixteenth century. So that we must make great allowance, and not think too hardly of some who hesitated, or even drew back for a time, when they saw the stake ; and, on the other hand, we must admire the grace of God which triumphed in many who knew very little truth. The Holy Spirit was their teacher, and they knew what was necessary to their own salvation and the glory of God.

THE CONVERSION AND FAITH OF LOUIS BERQUIN.

One of the most illustrious victims of those early times was **Louis Berquin,** a gentleman of Artois, and an officer of the king's body-guard. "He would have been another Luther for France," says Beza, "if he had found in Francis another Elector of Saxony." Unlike the knights of his time, acquainted only with the helmet and the sword, he was learned, contemplative, frank, open-hearted, and generous to the poor. He had acquired a great reputation at the court of Francis ; and, being sheltered by the powerful patronage of his royal master, he studied diligently the works of the Reformers, and soon became one of the most zealous of their converts. His conversion, through the grace of God, proved to be genuine. His learning, his eloquence, his influence, were from that hour all consecrated to the service of the Gospel. Many looked to him as the Reformer of his native land. His leisure hours were spent in translating the works of Luther, Malanchthon, and Erasmus into French, and writing tracts on the leading doctrines of the Christian faith, which he privately printed himself.

This heretic, thought Beda, is worse than Luther; but so unobtrusive was this Christian knight that it was difficult to find a charge on which to found an indictment of heresy. Spies were now employed. A rigorous watch was kept over every word uttered by Berquin. At length witnesses were found to prove that he had asserted it was heretical to invoke the Virgin Mary instead of the Holy Spirit before the sermon in the mass. This was enough; the Syndic, obtaining authority from the Parliament to search the dwelling of Berquin, made a forcible seizure of his books, and papers, which he laid before the faculty of theology. These were condemned as having an heretical tendency, and Berquin was thrown into prison. "This one," said the sanguinary Beda, "shall not escape us, like Brissonnet and Lefevre." He was kept in solitary confinement, preparatory to his formal trial and certain condemnation to the stake.

Margaret, who had ever professed admiration of Berquin's talents, and had distinguished him by marks of her regard, was immediately informed of his fate, and asked to interest herself in his favour. With the unhappy case of her friend Brissonnet before her, and dreading to see Berquin dragged to the stake, she wrote to her brother. She represented to the king the insolence of the Sorbonne in daring to arrest one of his officers upon so frivolous a pretence, without having first ascertained his royal pleasure. The suggestion touched the pride of Francis, who broke out into violent transports of passion, menaced the Parliament, and sent an order for the instant liberation of his officer.

A second time he was imprisoned, and again the king came to his rescue, advising him to be more prudent. But his strong convictions of duty, as a witness for Christ, could not be suppressed. He laboured to spread the truth among the poor in the country, and among his friends in the city and at the court. But the burning desire of his heart was to communicate his convictions to all France. A third time he was imprisoned, and the Sorbonne thought that this time they had made sure of their prey. The king was a prisoner at Madrid; Louisa was all-powerful at Paris, and along with Duprat, the unprincipled chancellor, supported the persecutors. But no; Margaret's word again prevailed with her impulsive brother, and a royal order, dated April 1st, 1526, commanded the suspension of the matter until the king's return.

When again at liberty, his lukewarm friends entreated him to avoid giving offence to the doctors who had evidently marked him for destruction. Erasmus, in particular, who, having learned that he was about to publish a translation of one of his Latin works with the addition of notes, wrote to him letter upon letter to persuade him to desist. " Leave these hornets alone," he said, " above all, do not mix me up in these things ; my burden is already heavy enough. If it is your displeasure to dispute, be it so ; as for me, I have no desire of the kind." Again he wrote : " Ask for an embassy to some foreign country ; travel in Germany. You know Beda and his familiars ; a thousand-headed hydra is shooting out its venom on all sides. The name of your enemies is legion. Were your cause better than that of Jesus Christ, they will not let you go until they have brought you to a cruel end. Do not trust in the protection of the king. But in any case do not commit me with the faculty of theology." This letter, so characteristic of the timid philosopher, who always steered a middle course between the Gospel and Popery, only redoubled the courage of Berquin. He determined to stand no longer on the defensive, but to attack. He set to work, and extracted from the writings of Beda and his brethren, twelve propositions which he accused before Francis as being false, contrary to the Bible, and heretical.

The Sorbonnists were confounded. The outcry was tremendous. What ! even the defenders of the faith, the pillars of the Church, taxed with heresy by a Lutheran, who had deserved death a thousand times.* The king, however, not sorry to have an opportunity of humbling these turbulent doctors, commanded them to condemn or to establish the twelve propositions from Scripture. This might have been a difficult task for the doctors ; the matter was assuming a grave turn, when an accident occurred which turned everything in favour of the Sorbonne. An image of the Virgin happened to be mutilated just at that moment in one of the quarters of Paris. " It is a vast plot," cried the priests ; " it is a great conspiracy against religion, against the prince, against the order and tranquillity of the country ! All laws will be overthrown ; all dignities abolished. This is the fruit of the doctrines preached by Berquin ! " At the cries of the Sorbonne, the priests, the Parliament, and of the people, the king himself was greatly excited. Death to the image-breakers ! No quarter to the heretics ! And Berquin is in prison a fourth time.

THE SENTENCE OF THE SORBONNE, AND THE MARTYRDOM OF BERQUIN.

A commission of twelve, delegated by the Parliament, condemned him to make a public abjuration, then remain in prison without books, pen, or paper for the rest of his life, after having had his tongue pierced with a hot iron. "I appeal to the king,"

* Félice, p. 26.

exclaimed Berquin. "If you do not submit to our sentence," replied one of the judges, "we will find means to stop your appeals for ever." "I would rather die," said Berquin, "than only approve by my silence that the truth is thus condemned." "Let him then be strangled and burned upon the Place de Gréve!" said the judges with one voice. But it was deemed advisable to delay the execution till Francis was absent; for it was feared lest his lingering affection for his favourite and loyal servant might be awakened, and that he might order Berquin's release a fourth time.

A week's delay was craved in the execution of the sentence. "Not a day," said Beda; "let him be put to death at once." That same day, April 22nd, 1529, Berquin was led forth to die. Six hundred soldiers and a vast stream of spectators escorted him to the place of execution. Erasmus, on the testimony of an eyewitness, thus describes his appearance. "He showed no sign of depression. You would have said that he was in his library pursuing his studies, or in a temple meditating on things Divine. When the executioner, with husky voice, read to him his sentence, he never changed countenance. He alighted from the cart with a firm step. But his was not the stoical indifference of the hardened criminal; it was the serenity, the peace of a good conscience." As a peer of France, he was dressed according to his dignity. "He wore a cloak of velvet, a doublet of satin and damask, and golden hose;" there was no sign of mourning, but rather as if he were to appear at court; though not the court of Francis, but the court of Heaven.

Wishing to make known the Saviour to the poor people around him, Berquin tried to speak to them, but he could not be heard. The monks gave the signal, and instantly the clamour of voices and the clash of arms prevented the sacred words of the dying martyr being heard. But his death spoke to all France, and that, in a voice which no clamours could silence. The fire had done its work, and where had stood the noble of France and the humble Christian, there was now a heap of ashes. "**Berquin's stake** was to be, in some good measure, to France, what Ridley's was to England—' a candle which by God's grace, would not be put out, but would shine through all that realm.' "*

THE RAPID SPREAD OF THE REFORM DOCTRINES.

The two examples of martyrdom which we have given—one from the humbler and one from the higher ranks of life—may be considered as types of a vast crowd of others. Our limited space prevents us from recording the patient sufferings and the triumphant death of many noble witnesses for Christ. But notwithstanding the violence of the persecution the converts

* Wylie, vol. ii., p. 162 ; D'Aubigné's "Calvin," vol. ii., p. 56 ; Félice, p. 27.

were more numerous than ever. The fame of Francis I, as showing favour to men of learning, and having, through the influence of his sister, invited Melanchthon to take up his residence in Paris, led many of the Reformers in Germany and Switzerland to visit France and help on the good work of the Lord. In this way the writings of Luther, Zwingle, and others, found an entrance into that country, were extensively read, and the new opinions made rapid progress among all classes of the people. Here and there missionaries of the Reformation arose, congregations were formed, and from time to time one and another, torn from the prayer-meeting or the Scripture reading, went to seal his faith with his blood.

But in 1533 better days seemed to dawn on the Reformation. The queen-mother, Louisa of Savoy, one of its bitterest persecutors, had just died. Francis had made an alliance with the Protestants of the Smalcald League, and the influence of Margaret had thence increased. Taking advantage of this favourable moment, she opened the pulpits of Paris to Roussel, Courault, and Bertault, who leaned towards the Reformed doctrines. The bishop, John du Bellay, offered no opposition. The Churches were crowded. Beda and the doctors of the Sorbonne tried to raise the people, but were prevented. Meanwhile Francis returned to Paris from Marseilles, where he had an interview with Clement VII for the marriage of his son Henry with **Catherine de Medici.** His renewed friendship with the Pope, Catherine's uncle, strongly bent his mind against the heretics. Many of them were cast into prison, and the three suspected ministers interdicted from preaching.

Such was Francis I, on whose humour so much depended. On the important subject of religion he had never come to a decision. He neither knew what he was nor what he wished. Still, from his natural hatred of the monks, and the powerful influence of his sister, he had hitherto favoured the Reformers. But an incident for which the latter were much to blame, took place about this time, which ended the many struggles between Margaret and her brother, as to the conduct to be pursued towards the Reformers, and also put an end to the king's vacillation.

Many of the Reformers were led, or rather misled, to depend upon the favour of the court for the furtherance of the Gospel, and proposed to proceed moderately, desiring to do nothing that might offend. These were called **Temporisers.** The other party, called the *Scripturalists*, thought that they should place no dependence on the favour of princes, but boldly preach the Gospel and resist everything that might bring back the superstitions of Rome. The young Church of France being thus divided, they agreed to consult their old teacher, Farel, and the other exiles. A young Christian, by name Feret, accepted the mission and proceeded to Switzerland. Scarcely had he crossed the Jura when a spectacle, so different from Paris, met his eye. In the towns and villages the altars were being demolished, the idols cast down, and all idolatry removed from public worship. This, as we have already seen, was the work of Farel, Viret, Saunier, Olivetan, Froment, and others. But France was altogether different. A powerful prince and a haughty priesthood were there to contend with a mere handful of Reformers.

"These médleys of the Gospel and Popery," said the Swiss evangelists, "can never exist together, any more than fire and water." They recommended bold measures. A vigorous blow must be struck at that which is the citadel of the Papal empire. The mass must be abolished. "If the Papal hierarchy was the tree whose deadly shade killed the living seed of the Word, the mass was its root." The writing and posting of placards all over France was proposed.

THE YEAR OF THE PLACARDS.

At length the **evangelical protest** was written. Farel has been commonly credited with the authorship. Historians vie with each other in describing the violence of its style. "Indignation guided his daring pen," says one. "It was a torrent of scathing fire," says another. "It was a thunderbolt, fierce, terrific, and grand, resembling one of those tempests that gather in awful darkness on the summits of those mountains amid which the document was written, and finally explode in flashes which irradiate the whole Heavens, and in volleys of sound which shake the plains over which the awful reverberations are rolled."*

When the placards reached Paris, many of the Christians thought the style too bitter and violent, but the majority were in favour of their publication. A night was fixed, October 18th, 1534, for the work to be done all over France. The eventful night came, and the venerable walls of the University of Paris, the public buildings of the capital, the Church doors, and the Sorbonne itself were covered with placards. The movement was simultaneous throughout France. The placard was headed in large letters : " True articles of the horrible, great, and intolerable abuses of the Popish mass ; invented in direct opposition to the Holy Supper of our Lord and only Mediator and Saviour Jesus Christ." Popes, cardinals, bishops, monks, and every distinguishing tenet of the Romish faith were attacked with sharpest invectives. The long placard—which occupies over five pages in D'Aubigné's history—thus concludes : " In fine, truth has deserted them, truth threatens them, truth chases

* Wylie, vol. ii.; D'Aubigné's " Calvin," vol. iii.; Félice, p. 35 ; Freer, vol. ii., p. 138.

them, truth fills them with fear ; by all which shall their reign be shortly destroyed for ever."

No language can describe the one universal cry of rage and consternation which resounded throughout France on the morning of the 19th. The people gathered in groups around the placards. The priests and monks kindled the rage. The Lutherans, it was said, had laid a frightful plot for burning the Churches, firing the town, and massacring every one ; and the whole multitude shouted, "**Death, death to the heretics !** " The king at the time was living at the Chateau de Blois. A placard was posted—no doubt by the hand of an enemy—on the very door of the king's apartment. Montmorency and the Cardinal de Tournon drew the king's attention to the paper. The prince was greatly agitated, he grew pale and speechless. He saw therein an insult, not only against his authority, but against his person, and these enemies of the Reformation— Montmorency and Tournon—so fixed this notion in his mind, that in his wrath he exclaimed : " Let all be seized, and let Lutheranism be totally exterminated." The members of the faculties also demanded that by a general Auto de Fé the daring blasphemy might be avenged.

Now it was that the storm, long held back by a good providence, burst forth in awful fury. The king was fully committed to the system of persecution. But, making every allowance for the times, the Reformers were not free from blame. Would the apostles have written and posted such placards ? We have no standard of action, no guide but the Word of God. Yet there can be only one feeling towards the sufferers—that of tenderest compassion. Orders were immediately issued by the king to seize the Sacramentarians, dead or alive. By the help of a traitor, their houses were pointed out, and all were in a short time seized and thrown into prison. The criminal officer having entered the house of one, named **Bartholomew Millon,** a cripple, wholly helpless in body, said to him, " Come, get thee up." " Alas ! sir," said the poor paralytic, " it must be a greater master than thee to raise me up." The sergeants carried him out, but so full of peace and holy courage was Bartholomew, that his companions in captivity grew firm through his exhortations. Formerly, when lifted by his friends, he felt pain in every limb, but the Lord in great mercy took that sensitiveness away, so that in prison he used to say, " The roughest handling seemed tender."

THE EXECUTIONS.

The trial of the Lutherans was soon over, and the **executions began.** An expiation was required for the purification of France, and the heretics must be offered in sacrifice. The burning piles were distributed over all the quarters of Paris, and the executions followed on successive days. **Millon** was the first. The turnkey entered his cell, lifted him in his arms, and placed him on a tumbril—a cart. The procession then took its course towards the Place de Gréve. Passing his father's house, he smiled, bidding adieu to his old home, as one in sight of that house not made with hands, eternal in the Heavens. "Lower the flames," said the officer in command, "the sentence says he is to be burnt at a slow fire." He had to be lifted and flung into the flames, but he bore his lingering tortures as if miraculously sustained. Only words of peace, with great sweetness of spirit, dropped from his lips, while his soul, ransomed by the precious blood of Jesus, ascended on angels' wings to the paradise of God.

A long list of names follows. **Du Bourg,** of the Rue St. Denis, Calvin's friend, was the next ; and many persons of distinction suffered at that time, and many, having warning, made their escape.

While these tumultuous scenes were convulsing the capital, Margaret was residing at her castle at Nérac. The news filled her with dismay. Her enemies, now that they had the ear of the king, laboured to inflame his mind against her. In times past, the slightest reflection on the reputation of his beloved sister would have been instantly and vehemently silenced by Francis. But now, in his gloomy state of mind, he listened to the representations of his ministers. It was insinuated to the king that "if he had a mind to extirpate the heretics out of his kingdom, he must begin by his court and his nearest relations." **Margaret** was summoned to Paris. She immediately obeyed, confident in the integrity of her intentions, the love of her brother, and fearless of the hostile theologians, whom she neither dreaded nor respected. For the first time, perhaps, in his life, Francis received Margaret at the Louvre with cold severity, and reproached her for the evils which her support of heresy had brought on his kingdom. Margaret wept, but she concealed her tears from her angry brother. She gently expostulated with him, and soon found that bigotry had not quite extinguished his love for her. She became bolder, and ventured to suggest that it was the intolerance of the fanatical party that had filled the kingdom with discord. She was as grieved about the placards as he was, but felt sure that none of the ministers whom she knew had any hand in their publication.

Without entering into particulars, we need only further add, that her entreaties obtained the liberation of the three preachers— Roussel, Berthault, and Couralt ; and that the king's countenance was changed towards those who had maligned the motives of his sister. Her presence in Paris for a time hindered the designs of the persecutors ; but as Francis was determined to command a public procession through the streets of Paris to cleanse away the pollution of the placards, she petitioned the king to permit her departure into Béarn, which he reluctantly granted.

THE PROCESSION AND MARTYRDOMS.

On the 21st of January, 1535, the " **Peace Offering** " **Procession** marched through the most public streets of Paris in gloomy majesty, and striking awe into the hearts of all beholders. The houses along the line of procession were hung with mourning drapery. All the religious orders of Paris took part in the procession, bearing aloft the sacred relics possessed by their respective converts—the head of St. Louis, the patron saint of France, a piece of the true cross, the real crown of thorns, a holy nail, and also the spear-head which had pierced the side of our Lord. On no former occasion had so many relics been paraded in the streets of Paris. The cardinals, archbishops, and bishops followed, wearing their robes and mitres. They immediately preceded the host, which was borne by the Bishop of Paris, under a canopy of crimson velvet, supported by the Dauphin, the Dukes of Orleans, of Angoulême, and of Vendôme. Around the holy sacrament marched two hundred gentlemen of the king's household, each bearing a torch. The king followed on foot with his head bare, carrying a burning torch of white virgin-wax, surrounded by his children and the princes of the blood royal. Afterwards came a countless throng of all the noblemen of the court, princes, ambassadors, and foreigners, each carrying a flaming torch. In front of their houses stood the burgesses with lighted tapers, who sank on their knees as the holy sacrament passed them. But the end of the procession was not yet; it still moved on in mournful silence; the guilds of the capital, the municipality, the officers of the court, the Swiss guards, the choristers of the royal chapels—amounting to several thousand persons, and every individual carrying a lighted taper. This was the comedy of the fanatical frenzy of the king; the tragedy was to follow, "to implore the mercy of the Redeemer for the insult offered to the sacrifice of the mass."

Having marched from the Church of the Louvre to Notre Dame, the king seated himself on a throne, and then pronounced a harangue against the new opinions, as violent as thought could suggest, or words express. " If my arm were infected with this pestilence," he said, " I would cut it off. If one of my children were so wretched as to favour this new Reform, and to wish to make profession of it, I would sacrifice him myself to the justice of God, and to my own justice." From declamation he proceeded to action. The same day **six Lutherans were burned alive.** The most courageous had their tongues cut out, lest they should offer a word of exhortation to the people, or be heard praying to God. They were suspended on a movable gibbet, which, rising and falling by turns, plunged them into the fire, where they were left a few moments, then raised into the air, and again plunged into the flames ; and this continued until the ropes that fastened them to the beam were consumed ; then, for the last time, they fell amid the burning faggots, and in a few moments their souls ascended, as in a chariot of fire, to the bright realms of unmingled and eternal blessedness.

RETRIBUTIVE JUSTICE.

The epoch of persecution and martyrdom was now solemnly inaugurated in France. The **21st of January** must be a date of evil omen in that land of revolutions. Two hundred and fifty-eight years after Francis had devoted to death the humble followers of Christ, one of the simplest and most generous of the Bourbons was condemned to death by misguided and furious men, and received his death-blow on the **21st of January, 1793.** The sight must have been beyond all conception pitiful. The poor king, Louis XVI, unlike the martyrs of his predecessors, who laid down their lives willingly for Jesus' sake, was dragged by his jailers to the block, and held down by force till the axe gleamed in the air, and his head rolled on the scaffold. But there is a third 21st of January, and the most humiliating of the three to the pride of France. It is said that Paris resolved to capitulate to the victorious Germans on the **21st of January, 1871.** The coincidence of these dates is most striking and suggestive, but we offer no comments ; those who have studied history aright will surely believe in a just and retributive providence. But God gives none account of His ways ; or, as the Psalmist says : " Thy way is in the sea, and thy path in the deep waters, and Thy footsteps are not known " (Psa. 77. 19).

Félice, the historian of the Protestants of France, observes with reference to this dismal day, " that it marks an important date in our history ; for it was from this moment that the Parisian populace took part in the contest against the heretics ; and once mounted on the stage they never quitted it until the end of the league. In the chain of events, this procession, inter-mingled with executions, was the first of the bloody days of the sixteenth century ; the massacre of St. Bartholomew, the Barricades, the murder of Henry III, and the assassination of Henry IV, could but follow " (p. 36).

The Protestant princes of Germany, justly indignant when they heard of the cruelties of Francis, threatened to ally them-selves against him with the house of Austria. Fearing a breach, he sent in the following spring an ambassador to Smalcald. His excuse was that of all persecutors in every age—" seditious tendency." Those whom he had put to death were men of a rebellious spirit, sacramentarians, and not Lutherans. He even professed a strong desire for better information respecting their doctrines, in order, no doubt, to effect a reconciliation with the League of Smalcald, and requested that one of their most eminent divines might be sent to his court. He attempted to induce Melanchthon to take up his abode in Paris ; but his double dealings and hypocrisies availed little. Melanchthon refused, and the Smalcald League objected to an alliance with the persecutor of their brethren.

The gloomy determination which had now taken possession of Francis to crush heresy, decided Margaret to leave Paris. She retired to her own little **Kingdom of Bearn,** an ancient province of France. Her court became the asylum of the celebrated men who escaped from persecution. "Many refugee families brought their industry and their fortunes. Everything assumed a new face. The laws were corrected, the arts cultivated, agriculture was improved, schools were established, and the people were prepared to receive the teaching of the Reformation. In a short time the foundations were laid of that remarkable prosperity which made the little kingdom in the Pyrenees resemble an oasis amid the desert which France and Spain were now beginning to become."*

Margaret, the pious Queen of Navarre, died 1549, and was deeply lamented by the Béarnais, who loved to repeat her generous saying : "Kings and princes are not the lords and masters of their inferiors, but only ministers whom God has set up to serve and to keep them." She was the mother of **Jeanne d'Albret,** one of the most illustrious women in history, and grandmother of Henry IV.

* "History of Protestantism," vol. ii., p. 212.

CHAPTER LI

The Great Progress of the Reformation

TOWARDS the end of the reign of Francis, and under that of his son, Henry II, the Reform movement made such rapid progress, that it becomes utterly impossible to follow it in all its details. We can do little more than give a mere outline of the principal events from the death of Francis I till the massacre on the eve of St. Bartholomew.

FRANCIS I

Francis lived and died as kings generally do. He commenced his reign with great splendour, but closed it in darkness and dismal forebodings. When he ascended the throne, all was brilliant and loyal ; he was surrounded by a vast assemblage of gallant knights, and with few exceptions, chieftians of the princely aristocracy of France ; and the noblest ladies of the realm were in attendance on their gentle mistress, Queen Claude, or, rather, as the female ornaments of his court. But how different when he descended from the throne to the grave ! The luxury of his court, its chivalry, its festivals, its pageants, which were once the admiration of Europe, afford him no comfort now. In excruciating agonies of body from the life he had led, and in deep anguish of soul from what had been done by his orders : " He groans deeply ; his starts are sudden and violent. There flits at times across his face a dark shadow, as if some horrible sight afflicting him with unutterable woe were disclosed to him ; and a quick tremor at these moments runs through all his frame." He is heard to mutter, as if suffering from an accusing conscience : " I am not to blame ; my orders were exceeded "—referring no doubt to the merciless slaughter of the unoffending Waldenses. He was surrounded by a crowd of priests, courtiers, and courtesans, but they cared nothing for the dying monarch ; they only increased the weight of his agony by their cold, selfish indifference.

The scene closes, the last groan is uttered, the line is crossed, and the soul, under a responsibility entirely its own, appears before God. Solemn thought ! all is reality now. The judgment-seat cannot bend to royal prerogative. There is no respect of persons with God ; every man must be judged according to the deeds done in the body. But what must be the judgment of those who stand there with hands red, and garments stained with the blood of God's saints ? Nothing but a timely repentance and the efficacy of the precious blood of Jesus could cleanse such guilt away. May all those who are willing to pause a few moments over the melancholy scene of these closing hours believe this, and turn to the Lord Jesus, God's Son, whose blood cleanses from *all* sin. " Him that cometh to Me, I will in no wise cast out," are His own words of gracious assurance. Three hundred years have rolled away since Louisa, Francis, and Margaret died. We cannot help lingering a moment over this solemn thought, that our reader may be prepared for that change which admits of no succeeding change for ever. Every tree is known by its fruits ; and as the tree falls so it lies. Who would not say that Margaret's was the happiest course of the three ? True, she had in her lifetime to suffer reproach and shame for the Name of Christ, and be branded as a heretic, but she willingly identified herself with the suffering saints of God, and great is her reward in Heaven. Better suffer for a few years, and even die at the stake, than be three hundred years in hell, " where their worm dieth not, and the fire is not quenched " (Mark 9. 44.50 ; Matt. 5. 10-12).

O reader, beware ! God is not mocked ; as a man sows in time, so shall he reap in eternity !

HENRY II.

Francis I died in 1547, and was succeeded by his son, **Henry II,** the husband of the notorious **Catherine de Medici,** who, like Jezebel of old, was well fitted and inclined to stir him up to persecute the Naboths, and take possession of their vineyards. And this was actually done to a great extent, and the confiscations applied in many instances to the most shameful purposes. Surrounded by hostile and designing councillors, besides the example of his father and the influence of his wife, he was indeed *stirred up* to pursue a persecuting policy, and a great multitude of martyrs fell during his reign. When the great battle of St. Quentin was lost, and the Spaniards expected daily at the gates of Paris, the old pagan cry against the primitive Christians was raised : " We have not sufficiently avenged the honour of God, and God takes vengeance upon us." The disaster was ascribed to the mildness with which the heretics had been treated. So it was when Rome was attacked by the barbarians ; the Pagans accused themselves of having been too lenient towards the Christians.

The clergy, becoming alarmed at the unaccountable progress of the Reformation, used every artifice to alarm the king. They assured him that the **Huguenots**—as they were now called, from one *Hugues,* the name of a Genevese Calvinist—were the great enemies of monarchs and of all ecclesiastical and regal power ;

that, should they prevail, they would trample his throne in the dust, and lay France at the feet of atheists and revolutionists. The effect of these misrepresentations, which were chiefly made by the Cardinal de Lorraine, was to multiply the executions ; and as they were viewed as appeasing the wrath of Heaven, the more the king himself sinned, the more he burned to atone for his sins.   But so great was the energy of God's Spirit in connection with the spread of Bibles and religious books, that all the means used to exterminate the Huguenots proved utterly fruitless.   Exceeding great armies seemed to arise from the ashes of the martyrs.   " Men of letters," says Félice, " of the law, of the sword, of the Church itself, hastened to the banner of the Reformation.   Several great provinces—Languedoc, Dauphiny, the Lyonnese, Guienne, Saintonge, Poitou, the Orleanese, Normandy, Picardy, Flanders (the most considerable towns in the kingdom), Bourges, Orleans, Rouen, Lyons, Bordeaux, Toulouse, Montpellier, La Rochelle—were peopled with Reformers.   It is calculated that they comprised in a few years nearly a sixth of the population, of whom they were the *elite*."

And still the funeral piles blazed in all quarters of Paris, and in all towns of France ; and persons of all ages and both sexes fed the flames, suffering the most fearful barbarities and tortures. But as the rigour of the persecutions increased, the number of the disciples multiplied.   Among these were now enrolled princes of the blood, the King of Navarre, the Duke of Vendôme, the Bourbons, Prince of Condé, Coligny, Châtillon, and a great number of the nobility and gentry of France.   " Besides these," says a Catholic historian, " painters, watchmakers, sculptors, goldsmiths, booksellers, printers, and others, who, from their callings have some nobility of mind, were among the first easily impressed."*

Meanwhile **Wm. Farel** and his fellow exiles were inundating France with religious books and Bibles from the printing presses of Geneva, Lausanne, and Neuchâtel, by means of pedlars, who hazarded their lives to introduce the precious wares into the mansions of the noble and the hut of the peasant.

The king's alarm grew great.   A little longer, and all France would be Lutheran.   The first and most sacred duty of a prince, said his councillors, was to uphold the true religion, and cut off its enemies.   The irritated prince proceeded to the House of Parliament to consult his senators as to the best means of appeasing the religious differences in the realm.   This event happened on the 10th of August, 1559.   Though the presence of the king may have been intended to overawe the members, it did not prevent them from speaking freely on the subject.   The chief president, Gilles Lemaitre, spoke in favour of burning, and

* Félice, p. 52; Wylie, vol. ii., 522.

recommended the example of Philip Augustus to be followed, who had in one day caused six hundred of the Albigenses to be burned. The men of middle course confined themselves to vague generalities. The secret Calvinists, especially Annas du Bourg, demanded religious reforms by means of a national council. "Every day," he said, "we see crimes committed that go unpunished, while new tortures are invented against men who have committed no crime. Should those be guilty of high treason who mentioned the name of the prince only to pray for him ? and should the rack and the stake be reserved, not for those who raised tumults in the cities, and seditions in the provinces, but for those who were the brightest patterns of obedience to the laws, and the firmest defenders of order ? It was a very grave matter to condemn to the flames men who died calling on the Name of the Lord Jesus."

The angry king, stung to fury by the honest speech of **Du Bourg,** ordered him to be arrested in full Parliament by the captain of his guards, and said aloud that he would see him burned with his own eyes. He was thrown into the Bastile, and other members were arrested the following day. Fourteen days after this memorable visit to his Parliament, Henry was displaying his strength and skill as a cavalier in a tournament, to the admiration of many. He had resisted the attacks of the Duke of Savoy and the Duke of Guise, the two best generals in the service of France, and might have left the gay scene amidst the praise and acclamations of the ladies and nobles of Paris ; but he insisted on having a tilt with Count Montgomery, the captain of his guard. He meant, no doubt, to give the king the best of the shock, like his other assailants, but by some mismanagement, the lance of Montgomery broke in the king's visor, and a splinter passed through his eye to the brain. The king lay forward on his horse ; a thrill of horror ran through the spectators. He died soon after, but never saw with his eyes the burning of Du Bourg, and, as the Lord would have it, the same hand that arrested the senator dealt the death-blow to the monarch.

THE MARTYRDOM OF DU BOURG.

The death of the king did not release the prisoners. Du Bourg heard his sentence read without a change of countenance. As a criminal of the deepest dye, his execution was reserved for the Christmas holidays, December, 1559. He prayed to God for the pardon of his judges. "I am a Christian ; yes, I am a Christian," he said, " and I will shout still louder for the glory of my Lord Jesus Christ." When suspended on the gibbet, he proclaimed the truth to the vast crowds around him, and cried aloud : "My God, my God, forsake me not, that I may not forsake Thee."

Thus died this pious and illustrious magistrate at the age of thirty-eight. He belonged to a good family ; his uncle had been Chancellor of France. He was a man of great learning, integrity, and devotion to his duties. His only fault was, that he had spoken in favour of the new religion. Florimond de Ramond, then a student, avows, " that every one in the colleges was moved to tears ; that they pleaded his cause after his death, and that his martyrdom did more harm to the Catholic religion than a hundred ministers could have done by their preaching "

THE FIRST PLANTING OF THE REFORMED CHURCH IN FRANCE.

It was in the year 1555, that the **first avowed French Church on Reformed principles** was established at Paris. Forty years had passed away since Lefevre first preached the Gospel in the University ; during which time we have met with many noble disciples, confessors, and martyrs, but no public congregations. There had always been secret gatherings of the faithful, but without fixed pastors or regular administration of the sacraments Calvin was their acknowledged leader, and he recommended them not to observe the Lord's Supper until they had duly recognised ministers. In consequence of this, though they were a large body in the aggregate, they were as isolated individuals, acting apart from each other, without the knowledge of the grand uniting principle—the presence and indwelling of the Holy Ghost. "For where two or three are gathered together in My Name, there am I in the midst, of them " ought to have been warrant enough for remembering His love, and showing forth His death in the breaking of bread.

A Church was now formed in Paris on the Genevan or Presbyterian model, with a minister, elders, and deacons. Poitiers, Angers, Bourges, and other places soon followed the example. From this time, the work of organisation went on vigorously, and in the short period of five years, over **a thousand Calvinistic Congregations** existed in France. The next step to be taken was the uniting of these isolated Churches into one General Church ; and for this purpose a General Synod was convoked to meet at Paris, which took place on the 25th of May, 1559. But the difficulties that attended the ministers travelling from all parts of France was so great, that only thirteen Churches sent their deputies to the Synod, and these braved an almost certain death. "There was in the deliberations of this assembly," says Félice, " a simplicity and moral grandeur that fills us with respect. Nothing of declamation or violence, but a calm dignity, a tranquil and serene force prevailed, as if the members of the Synod debated in a profound peace, under the guardianship of the laws."

The ecclesiastical foundations of the French Reformation

61

were then laid. The basis consisted of four grades of power, or **Church Courts.** 1, The consistory, or Kirk Session—composed of the elders and deacons, the minister being their president—the affairs of the congregation were the objects of their care. 2, the Colloquy, or the congregations of a district consulting each other by their deputies on their mutual interests. 3, The Provincial Synod, or court of appeal from the Kirk Session, in a meeting of the Churches of the province. If possible, the minister and an elder from each were expected to be present. 4, The National Assembly. Two ministers and two elders were expected from each of the Provincial Synods. It was the highest court. It heard all appeals, determined all great causes, and to its authority in the last resort all were subject.*

FRANCIS II—THE BOY KING.

The new king, **Francis II,** was about sixteen years old when he ascended the throne. He is represented as a sickly boy, feeble in body, and mind, and his wife, Mary Stuart of Scotland, a thoughtless beauty, spending her time in pleasure, was about the same age. Thus was monarchy represented in France in 1559, when a strong hand and a powerful will were required to protect the royal authority. The profligacy and extravagance of the last reign had borne their natural fruits. There was anger and discontent all over the land; the court was a hot-bed of intrigue, and the nation, broken into factions, was on the brink of civil war. Catherine de Medici, the Guises, Châtillons, Bourbons, the constable Montmorency, all worked to their own advantage these feeble children of royalty, and mingled with the religious discussions the quarrels of their political ambition.

The two **Guises**, the cardinal and the general, became managers of the court. Uncles of the fair young queen, the guardians of the feeble sovereign, they had the ear of both, which gave them immense advantages over their rivals. But there was one at the foot of the throne who was a match both for the general and the cardinal. The queen-mother, Catherine de Medici, hated the Huguenots as much as the Guises—who were the heads of the Roman Catholic party—but she also hated all who would supplant her in power. Artful and vindictive, unscrupulous and ambitious, without religious faith or moral feeling, the crafty Italian dissembled that she might ruin the authority of the Guises, in order to consolidate her own. This threw Catherine for a moment on the side of the Huguenot party, which was overruled by a merciful providence to weaken the power of the Guises, divide the strength of the Popish party, and save the

---

* For minute details of this ecclesiastical constitution, see Félice, Wylie, or " Faiths of the World."

Reformers. Affecting to hold the balance between the two parties, she was only biding her time in all changes of circumstances, by turns embracing and deserting all parties alike.

We now come to the **wars of religion.** Parties began to be formed from political motives, which threw the whole of France into the most ruinous, desolating, civil war, which lasted, with brief intervals, for many years—we might say, centuries. All the liberalism of France became Huguenot, which then simply meant *antipapist.* And thus, to their great injury and final destruction, the French Protestants became a great political party in the State. Meanwhile Francis II, after a reign of seventeen months, died ; and Catherine, emerging from the obscurity in which she had restrained her ambition, claimed the custody of her next son, Charles IX, who was only nine years of age ; and before the court could assemble, assumed the guardianship of the king, and in fact, if not in name, the regency of the kingdom.

THE SAINT BARTHOLOMEW MASSACRE.

The Italian mother, having thus become supreme in the kingdom, began to mature her plans for stamping out heresy in the dominions of her son. Possessed in an eminent degree of the family arts of dissimulation and concealment, she pursued, with steadiness of purpose and recklessness of means, the object before her. She has justly been compared to the shark which follows the vessel through storm and calm in expectation of its prey. The country was divided into two, apparently equally matched and irreconcilable camps. Several campaigns had been fought, and there was no immediate prospect of the Catholics overcoming the Huguenots in the field ; therefore Jezebel has recourse to her old policy—which she thoroughly understood—treachery and secret assassination. At the same time, it is affirmed by Félice, that no state reason can be advanced in justification of the massacre. Rome had no longer anything to fear for her supremacy, or the crown for the maintenance of its political power. It was fanaticism, resentment, Jezebel's unquenchable thirst for the blood of God's saints, which led to the crushing of the minority in 1572.

The first and real **authors of the massacre** were Catherine, Pope Pius V, and Philip II of Spain—none of them French. Others were drawn into the plot, but nothing could be done without the sanction of the king. The mother, with the assistance of the Pope, accomplished this. By a gross perversion of Scripture the crafty Pontiff pointed out to the young king that he was now in the position of Saul, King of Israel, who had received the orders of God, by the mouth of Samuel the prophet, to exterminate the infidel Amalekites, and not to spare one in any case. But as he did not obey the voice of God, he was deprived of his throne and his life. Charles saw the application of the allusion, and ultimately consented to kill all the Huguenots, that not one might be left to reproach him with the deed.

THE KING'S SNARE TO ENTRAP THE HUGUENOTS.

The next question was : How is it to be accomplished ? The chiefs of the Reformed were in the provinces. It was necessary to draw them out and concentrate them, in order to get them into their power. The perfidious Charles, who was now committed to the plot, pretended an earnest desire for the establishment of a lasting peace, and proposed a marriage between the young King of Navarre, afterwards Henry IV, and his sister, Margaret of Valois. This was a grand alliance for the poor house of Navarre, but the mother, Jeanne d'Albret, was not dazzled by it. She preferred the fear of the Lord to great riches. " I would rather," she said, " descend to be the most humble maiden of France, than sacrifice my soul and that of my son to grandeur." But the greatest Reformer in France must be brought within the toils of Catherine.

Jean d'Albret was the daughter of the accomplished and pious Margaret of Angoulême ; but the daughter in some respects was greater than her mother ; at least she was more decided as to the Reformation. But it is due to Margaret to bear in mind that she was greatly hindered by her dissolute brother and mother. In 1560 Jeanne d'Albret made open profession of the Protestant faith, abolished the Popish service throughout her kingdom, and introduced the Protestant worship. When we remember that her little kingdom lay on the slope of the Pyrenees, touching France on the one side and Spain on the other, we shall not consider her wanting in courage. The Popes thundered their anathemas against her, the powerful kings of France and Spain threatened to invade her territory and raze it from the map of Europe ; but for twelve years the Lord protected this pious queen, during which time she had the Bible translated into the dialect of the country ; established colleges and schools, studied laws like a senator, and mightily improved the conditions of her subjects.

The next person of great note was **Admiral Coligny.** He was a true Christian, a really good man, and the most skilful leader of the Huguenot armies. The envoys of the court set before Jeanne, Coligny, and the chiefs of the Huguenots, that this marriage would be the best guarantee of a solid peace between the two religions. Charles declared that he married his sister, not only to the Prince of Navarre, but to the whole Huguenot party. Coligny allowed himself to be deceived ; the prospect was indeed bright ; the entire kingdom would be united ; and he thought they should trust the sincerity and oath of his majesty.

THE KING'S CONSUMMATE DUPLICITY.

At last Jeanne d'Albret gave her consent to the marriage, and visited the Court of Blois in March, 1572 ; but leaving her son behind her from a lingering feeling of distrust. The king and the queen-mother caressed her with much apparent tenderness, especially the king, who called her his great aunt, his all, his best-beloved, and entertained her with so much honour and respect that every one was astonished. She reached Paris in May ; on the 4th of June she fell ill, on the 9th she died. It was said that a Florentine perfumer, Master René, known by the name of the " **queen's poisoner,**" had sold her some poisoned gloves. Her end was peace, she was happy to go home, she uttered no complaints against her murderers, and seemed only anxious for the spiritual welfare of her son Henry and her daughter Catherine. Committing them to the Lord's tender care, she fell asleep in Jesus at the age of forty-four.

Admiral Coligny had also gone to court. In his first interview he knelt before the king. Charles raised him up, called him his father, and embraced the illustrious old man thrice. "We have got you now," said the king, " and you must remain with us. This is the happiest day of my life." The other chiefs of the Huguenots being assembled in Paris, the marriage was celebrated with great splendour in the Cathedral Church of Notre Dame, on the 18th of August, 1572, the principal members of the nobility, Protestant as well as Catholic, being present on the occasion. It was followed by a succession of feasts and gaieties, in which the leaders of both parties alike participated ; and the fears of the Huguenots were thus completely disarmed. Charles by his dissimulation, and Catherine by her treacherous smiles, had succeeded in deceiving all parties. Indeed all seemed to hope that the age of bloodshed was closed, and that this marriage was the harbinger of a peaceful and prosperous future for a country so long afflicted with civil wars. But at that very moment, when all classes were rejoicing and full of hope, a secret council was held, at which it was determined to arrange a general massacre of the Huguenots.

Fifty thousand crowns were offered by the king for the head of Coligny, whom Charles was embracing so warmly only a day before. To earn the reward, one Maurevert lay in wait for the admiral on the 22nd of August, in a house near the Church of St. Germain. He was struck by three balls shot from an arquebuse, which shattered the forefinger of his left hand, and wounded his left arm. The assassin escaped. He is styled by historians of that day, " *The slayer on the king's wages, the common assassin.*" Coligny succeeded in reaching his hotel, where he was attended by the celebrated surgeon, Ambrose Paré. The king and his mother, like two innocents, visited the admiral, professed the greatest horror at the dastardly act, swore that they would take such terrible revenge that it should never be forgotten. "*You* bear the wound," said the king, " and *I* the perpetual pain "— unparalleled deceitfulness !

SAINT BARTHOLOMEW'S EVE.

Meanwhile the day fixed for the general massacre drew near. Between two and three o'clock in the morning of the 24th of August—the **Feast of St. Bartholomew**—as the king sat in his chamber with his mother and the Duke of Anjou, the great bell of St. Germain rang to early prayers. This was the preconcerted signal. Scarcely had its first peal disturbed the silent hour of midnight, when the firing commenced. Charles was greatly agitated ; a cold sweat stood upon his forehead ; he started, and sent word to the Duke of Guise to precipitate nothing. It was too late. The queen-mother, distrusting the constancy of her son, had commanded that the hour for the signal should be anticipated. In a few moments every steeple in Paris was sending forth its peals, and with the clamour of a hundred bells, there mingled the shoutings, cursings, and howlings of the assassins ; and the shrieks, groans, and cries for mercy of the surprised Huguenots. To distinguish the assailants in the dark, they wore a white sash on their left arm, and a white cross on their hats. At the sound of the tocsin armed men rushed out from every door, shouting, " For God and the king." The streets of Paris flowed with human blood, and the savage ferocity of the Catholics knew no bounds.

The **Duke of Guise,** accompanied by three hundred soldiers, hastened to the dwelling of Coligny. He had been awakened by the noise of firing, and, dreading the worst, was engaged in prayer with his minister Merlin. His servants came rushing into his room, exclaiming : " Sire ! the house is broken into, and there is no means of escape ! " " I have been long prepared to die," answered the admiral calmly ; " as for you, save yourselves if you can ; you cannot save my life." Behem, a servant of the Duke of Guise, was the first to enter the room. " Are you not the admiral ? " he demanded. " Yes, I am," replied Coligny, looking with great composure on the naked sword of the assassin ; and began to say a few serious words to the young man, who instantly plunged his sword into the veteran's breast, and gave him a second blow on the head. Guise, who was waiting impatiently in the courtyard, called aloud, " Behem, hast thou done it ? " " It is done, my lord," was the reply. " But we must see it to believe it. Throw him out at the window." In lifting up the body of the admiral, who was still breathing, he clutched the window-frame, but was instantly flung into the courtyard. The Duke of Guise, wiping off the blood from his face, said : " I know him, it is he," and kicking the dead body with his foot, he hastened into the streets, exclaiming, " Courage, comrades ; we have begun well—now for the rest. Sixteen years afterwards, in the castle of Blois, this same Henry of Guise was assassinated by order of Henry III, who, when the dead body lay before him, kicked it in the face. Oh ! the sovereign retributive justice of God !

In that awful night, Teligny, son-in-law of the admiral, and five hundred of the Protestant nobility and gentry, were sacrificed to the Moloch of bigotry, and that in the sacred name of religion. " Thick grass is more easily mown than thin," was the proverb acted upon, and the leading Protestants were lodged in the same quarter of Paris. This field was kept as the special preserve for the grim, cruel, Duke of Guise. The retinue of the young King of Navarre were lodged in the Louvre, as the special guests of the monarch, but with the Satanic intention of having them all conveniently murdered. They had come in the train of their royal chief to be present at the celebration of his marriage with the sister of the king. One by one they were called by name from their rooms, marched down unarmed into the quadrangle, where they were hewn down before the very eyes of their royal host, and piled in heaps at the gates of the Louvre. A more perfidious cold-blooded butchery is not to be found in the annals of mankind.

Over all Paris the **work of massacre** by this time extended. Ruffians by thousands—armed with the poignard, the pike, the knife, the sword, the arquebuse, every weapon of the soldier and the brigand—rushed through the streets murdering all they met who had not the white cross on their hats. They forced their way into the houses of the Protestants, slaughtered the inmates in their night-clothes, men, women, and children, and threw their mangled bodies into the streets. No pitiful wail for mercy was heard ; the obscurest haunts were searched, and nobody was spared. By and by the sun rose upon Paris. The wretched Charles, who had shuddered for some moments at the commencement of the massacre, had tasted the blood of the saints, and became as ravenous for slaughter as the lowest of the mob. He and his blood-stained Italian mother, at the break of day went out on the palace balcony to feast their eyes on the slaughtered heaps. Rivers of blood flowed in the streets ; corpses of men, women, and children blocked up the doorways ; on all sides the groans and death-cries of the dying were heard, and the blasphemies and imprecations of the maddened populace.

Some, however, who had managed to escape were seen struggling in the river, in their efforts to swim across ; and Charles, seizing an arquebuse, fired on his subjects, shouting, " Kill ! Kill ! " " Two hundred and twenty-seven years after-

wards," says Félice, " Mirabeau picked the arquebuse of Charles
IX out of the dust of ages to turn it against the throne of Louis
XVI." Satan may rule for a time, but God overrules ! On the
same Sunday morning, Charles sent for Henry of Navarre, his
new brother-in-law, and Henry of Condé, and in the most furious
tone said to them : " *The mass, death, or the Bastile ?* " After
some resistance, the princes consented to attend mass, but no
one believed in their sincerity. On the fourth day, when the
fury of the assassins had become satiated, and the Huguenots
were for the most part slain, there fell a dead silence on the streets
of Paris. The priests now followed the tragic scene with a play.
On the Thursday, ankle-deep in blood, the clergy celebrated an
extraordinary jubilee, and made a general procession to keep up
the excitement. The pulpits also re-echoed with thanksgiving,
and a medal was struck with this legend : " *Piety has awakened
justice.*"

MASSACRE IN THE PROVINCES.

But the thirst of Jezebel for blood was far from being satisfied.
Orders were sent from the court to all the provinces and principal
cities to pursue the same course. About a dozen of the provincial governors refused, and one priest whose name deserves
to be mentioned with thankfulness to the Lord. When the
king's lieutenant called on **John Hennuyer,** Bishop of Lisieux, and
gave him the order for the massacre of the Huguenots, he
answered, " No, no, sir ; I oppose, and will always oppose the
execution of such an order. I am the pastor of Lisieux, and these
people whom you command me to slaughter are my flock.
Although they have at present strayed, having quitted the
pasture which Jesus Christ, the sovereign Shepherd, has confided
to my care, they may still come back. I do not see in the Gospel
that the shepherd can permit the blood of his sheep to be shed.
On the contrary, I find there that he is bound to give his blood
and his life for them." The lieutenant asked him for his refusal
in writing, which the bishop readily gave him.

At Rouen, Toulouse, Orleans, Lyons, and in nearly all the
great towns of the kingdom, the work of blood was renewed with
undiminished fury ; the carnage went on without pity and without
remorse for about six weeks. Thousands of dead bodies were
thrown into the rivers, which were either washed on shore at
different bends of the rivers, or borne to the sea. The faithful
of Meaux—our early friends—were slaughtered in the prisons ;
and, the sword being too slow, iron hammers were employed.
Four hundred houses in the most handsome quarter of the town
were pillaged and devastated. But we grow weary, weary of
this recital ; and were it not that the St. Bartholomew massacre
is **the greatest and darkest crime of the Christian era**—and gives
us, as nothing else does, a true picture of the essential principles

of Popery—we should willingly have ended our notice of the Reformation in France before coming to it. If ever the depths and wiles of Satan were seen in human wickedness, it is here. The premeditation, the solemn oaths of the king—which drew the Calvinists to Paris—the royal marriage, and the dagger put into the hands of the mob by the chiefs of the State, at a time of universal peace, represent a plot which has no parallel in history. And then, from the Pope downwards, the Catholic community lifting up their hands to Heaven and thanking God for the glorious triumph !

At Rome the news was received with transports of joy. The bearer of the glad tidings was rewarded with a present of a thousand pieces of gold. The Pope caused the guns of the castle of St. Angelo to be fired, declared a jubilee, and struck a medal in honour of the event. Philip II of Spain, the Duke of Alva, and the Cardinal of Lorraine, shared in these transports of joy. But the impression produced by the massacre in Protestant countries was altogether different. In England, Germany, and Switzerland, numbers of exiles arrived, horror-struck and half dead, to tell the sad tale, and the petrified nations cursed the name of France. Geneva, tenderly related to the **seventy thousand victims** whose bodies covered the plains of France or lay stranded on the banks of its rivers, instituted a day of fasting and prayer, which is still observed. In Scotland, the aged **John Knox,** in prophetic strains, pronounced the Divine vengeance against the house of Valois in the following terms : " The sentence is gone forth against this murderer, the King of France, and the vengeance of God will not be withdrawn from his house. His name shall be held in execration by posterity ; and no one who shall spring from his loins shall possess the kingdom in peace, unless repentance come to prevent the judgment of God." In England, **Elizabeth** put her court into mourning, and when the French ambassador sought an audience to offer his hypocritical explanation, he was received with profound silence. The lords and ladies of the court, in long mourning apparel, suffered the ambassador to pass between them without saluting him, or deigning to give him so much as a look.

THE NUMBER OF VICTIMS.

The whole number that perished in the massacre cannot be accurately ascertained. The victims in Paris were probably from three to four thousand. Brantôme says that Charles IX might have seen four thousand bodies floating down the Seine. " There is to be found," says Wylie, " in the account-books of the city of Paris, a payment to the grave-diggers of the cemetery of the Innocents, for having interred one thousand one hundred dead bodies, stranded at the turns of the Seine, near Chaillot,

Auteuil, and St. Cloud. It is probable that many corpses were carried still further, and the bodies were not all thrown into the river." The number of victims throughout the whole of France was probably about seventy thousand. Perefixe, Archbishop of Paris, in the seventeenth century, raises it to one hundred thousand. "This last figure," says Félice, "is probably exaggerated, if we reckon those only who met with a violent death. But if there be added those who died of misery, hunger, grief, the aged, who were helpless and abandoned, women without shelter, children without bread, the many wretched beings whose lives were shortened by this great catastrophe, it will be confessed that the number given by Perefixe is still below the truth."*

THE END OF THE LEADING ACTORS IN THE MASSACRE.

So wonderfully had the Spirit of God wrought in France by means of the truth, that when men expected to see only the ruins of the crushed Huguenots after the massacre, they were surprised to find them resolved in many parts of the country to offer a determined resistance to the royal troops. There can be no doubt that **French Protestantism** had become a great political association ; but not wholly so. There must have been many thousands of real Christians amongst them, though led to believe that it was right to oppose their oppressors, and fight for their lives, their families, and their religion. In the siege of Sancerre, when nearly all the young children died from hunger, we give one instance of perfect grace. A boy of ten years old, drawing nigh unto death, seeing his parents weeping near him, and handling his arms and legs, which were as dry as wood, said to them : " Why do you weep to see me die of hunger ? I do not ask you for bread, mother. I know you have none. But since God wills that I must thus die, we must be content. The holy Lazarus, did he not suffer hunger ? Have I not read that in the Bible ? " Thus passed away that precious lamb, with many others, to be folded in the everlasting embrace of the Good Shepherd who died for them ; of them may not it be truly said, " They shall hunger no more, neither thirst any more ; neither shall the sun (of persecution) light on them, nor any heat. For the Lamb which is in the midst of the throne shall feed them, and shall lead them unto living fountains of waters, and God shall wipe away all tears from their eyes " (Rev. 7. 16, 17).

But not so died the perfidious and cruel king. The terrible crime in which he had taken so prominent a part, weighed heavily on his mind to the last moment of his life. Night and day **the king was haunted** by the scenes he had witnessed on St.

---

* The above account of the massacre is chiefly drawn from the French historian, Félice, who is more inclined to abridge than to exaggerate the details of his nation's dishonour. See also, Wylie's " History of Protestantism ; " Smiles' " History of the Huguenots ; " White's " History of France."

Bartholomew's eve. He imagined he saw his murdered guests sitting at his bedside and at his table. Sleeping or waking, the murdered Huguenots seemed ever present to his eyes with ghastly faces, and weltering in blood. But, as the Lord would have it, he—who had stipulated when giving his orders for the St. Bartholomew massacre, that not a Huguenot should be left alive to reproach him with the deed—was attended on his death-bed by a Huguenot physician, and waited upon by a Huguenot nurse. He evidently had not the slightest confidence in any of his former associates. He was even haunted by the terrible feeling that his own mother was causing his death by slow poisoning. He died of a strange and frightful malady, which caused his blood to ooze from the pores of his body, in less than two years after the St. Bartholomew massacre, having lived twenty-five years, and reigned fourteen.

It is said that all the actors in the St. Bartholomew massacre, with one exception, **died by violence.** But we need not trace their tragic history. These bloody men were overtaken by Divine vengeance, and brought down to the grave in blood. Catherine de Medici lived to see the utter failure of all her schemes, the death of all her partners in guilt, and the extinction of her dynasty. The cardinal of Lorraine was assassinated in prison, and Henry III, the last of the Valois, fell by the dagger of the assassin in his own tent, and thus was the prophecy of John Knox fulfilled.

The vast materials furnished by the Reformation in France have detained us a little longer, and occupied more of our space than we can well afford ; but the greatness of the Lord's work there, the mighty struggle between light and darkness, and the melancholy interest which all must feel in the results of that work give it a peculiar place in the great revolutions of the sixteenth century.

THE COUNCIL OF TRENT.

At the famous **Council of Trent,** which met in 1545, and continued its sittings till 1563, during which the events we have rapidly described were in progress, the laws of the Roman Catholic Church were more accurately defined, and measures were devised for the more effectual suppression of heresy. Their deliberations and decisions must have been greatly affected by the general state of Europe at that particular moment. But as the original object and character of this council have been already noticed,* we need only add what has not been previously mentioned.

What particularly distinguished this council was not the framing of new laws, but undertaking to define and fix the doctrines of the Romish Church in a more accurate manner than

* See page 842.

had ever before been attempted, and to confirm them by the sanction of its authority.

"The Trentine fathers," says Mosheim, "authorised nothing new ; but it is equally true, that they authorised much hitherto thought, from its want of any sufficient authority, open to individual acceptance or rejection. To these divines, therefore, forming a body chiefly Italian and Spanish, sitting in the sixteenth century . . . is the Church of Rome indebted for the formal authentification of her peculiar creed." By the servility of the indigent Italian bishops, the Popes acquired such influence in the council that they dictated all its decrees, and framed them, not with any intention of healing the divisions, reforming the ancient abuses, restoring unity and concord to the Church, but to establish their own dominion. "Doctrines," says Scott, " which had hitherto been considered as mere private opinions, open to discussion, were now absurdly made articles of faith, and required to be received on pain of excommunication. Rites— which had formerly been observed only in deference to custom— supposed to be ancient, were established by the decrees of the Church, and declared to be essential parts of its worship."*

POPE PIUS'S CREED.

Pope Pius IV issued a brief summary of the doctrinal decisions of the council, which is called by his name, and has ever since been regarded as an authoritative summary of the Catholic faith.

"I profess, also, that there are truly and properly seven sacraments of the new law, instituted by Jesus Christ our Lord, and for the salvation of mankind, though all are not necessary for every one ; namely, baptism, confirmation, eucharist, penance, extreme unction, orders, and matrimony, and that, they confer grace ; and of these, baptism, confirmation, and orders cannot be reiterated without sacrilege.

"I also receive and admit the ceremonies of the Catholic Church, received and approved in the solemn administration of all the above said sacraments.

"I receive and embrace all and every one of the things which have been defined and declared in the holy Council of Trent, concerning original sin and justification.

"I profess, likewise, that in the mass is offered to God a true, proper, and propitiatory sacrifice for the living and the dead ; and that, in the most holy sacrifice of the Eucharist, there is truly, really, and substantially, the body and blood, together with the soul and divinity of our Lord Jesus Christ ; and that there is made a conversion of the whole substance of the bread

---

* Mosheim, vol. iii., p. 894 ; Scott, vol. iii., p. 256. The great authority as to our knowledge of the proceedings of this assembly is Father Paul's history. " He has described its deliberations," says Dr. Robertson, " and explained its decrees, with such perspicuity and depth of thought, with such various erudition, and such force of reason, as have justly entitled his work to be placed among the most admired historical compositions.

into the body, and of the whole substance of the wine into the blood, which conversion the Catholic Church calls transubstantiation.

" I confess also, that under either kind alone, whole and entire, Christ and a true sacrament is received.

" I constantly hold that there is a Purgatory, and that the souls detained therein are helped by the suffrages of the faithful.

" Likewise, that the saints reigning together with Christ, are to be honoured and invocated ; that they offer prayers to God for us ; and that their relics are to be venerated.

" I most firmly assert, that the images of Christ, and of the mother of God, ever virgin, and also of the other saints, are to be had and retained ; and that one honour and veneration are to be given to them.

" I also affirm that the power of indulgences was left by Christ in the Church, and that the use of them is most wholesome to Christian people.

" I acknowledge the Holy Catholic and Apostolic Roman Church, the mother and mistress of all Churches. And I promise to swear true obedience to the Roman Bishop, the successor of St. Peter, the prince of the apostles, and vicar of Jesus Christ.

" I also profess, and undoubtedly receive all other things delivered, defined, and declared by the sacred canons and general councils, and particularly by the holy Council of Trent. And likewise, I also condemn, reject, and anathematise, all things contrary thereto, and all heresies whatsoever condemned, rejected and anathematised by the Church.

" This true Catholic faith, out of which none can be saved, which I now freely profess, and truly hold, I, N., promise, vow, and swear most constantly to hold and profess the same whole and entire, with God's assistance, to the end of my life ; and to procure, as far as lies in my power, that the same shall be held, taught, and preached by all who are under me, or are entrusted to my care, by virtue of my office. So help me God, and these holy Gospels of God."

CHAPTER LII

The Waldenses

HAVING brought down the history of this interesting people to the year 1560,* when they suffered so severely in their own valleys, and on **the plains of Calabria,** we shall now briefly notice their history from that period. Yet we must not expect to find in this remarkable people the grace that should characterise the followers of the blessed Lord and His apostles. Not that they did not believe in the Lord Jesus as their Saviour, and in His precious blood as the only and all-sufficient remedy for sin. And had they been left unmolested in their beautiful valleys they would have been as harmless as their flocks and herds ; but when assailed and persecuted by the Catholics they looked upon Joshua, Gideon, and David as their models, not the Lord and His apostles. And being sincere and honest, and believing that their God was the God of battles, they fought under His banner, and believed that nothing was impossible to Him. It is no doubt from this principle that their persecutions form one of the most heroic pages in the Church's history.

Like many in our own day, they did not see the difference between law and grace ; but being a God-fearing people, He graciously heard and answered their prayers. Allegiance to Christ ruled in their hearts, which, after all, is the chief thing. The Scotch Covenanters who fought for the crown and kingdom of Emmanuel resemble them in this.

Such were "the poor men of the valleys." They believed the Bible to be a revelation from God, and were governed by it, so far as they understood it. Their neighbours, the Catholics, on the other hand, believed that God had given to the Church of Rome and its head, dominion over the whole Christian world, and that all who refuse subjection to her authority are not only heretics, but rebellious subjects, whom the sovereign has a right to punish according to his pleasure. This was and is the established belief of Rome ; and, seeing it remains so, there could be no security for life or liberty to any who dared to question her claims, had she the power to execute her arrogant assumption. Sometimes the magistrate refused to obey the priest, and the people were thereby spared ; but the reader will see how easily Rome could find a plausible pretext for persecution when it suited her purpose, and how constantly the mitre prevailed over the crown.

* See vol. ii., p. 542.

For some time after the **desolating wars of 1560** the remnant of the Waldenses were allowed to re-enter their native valleys, rebuild their houses, and replant their vineyards. Their fruit trees had been cut down, their hamlets and villages made a heap of ruins, and their fields left uncultivated and unsown. Starvation stared them in the face ; but a deeper grief weighed on the hearts of many. Where are our parents, husbands, sons, pastors, and many whom the enemy hath trodden down ? They were now with the Lord, and the Lord in His unfailing mercy was with them ; and from the nature of the country it was not difficult to exist for a time.

"Chestnut trees of luxuriant growth," says Dr. Beattie, speaking of the **valley of Rora**, "shade the inferior acclivities, and from these, in seasons of scarcity, a wholesome bread is prepared, which, with the luxury of new milk, furnishes a repast which the daintiest appetite might partake of with relish. Over the higher grounds nature has spread a rich carpet of vegetation ; and thither, as the pastoral season arrives, the inhabitants repair with their families and cattle. After spending their summer on the hills, in a life of patriarchal simplicity, they again descend to the valley as symptoms of winter set in, and there prosecute those branches of industry by which they may best satisfy the state, and minister to their own mutual necessities." Speaking of the **valley of Angrogna,** the same poetical writer says : "When we describe it as a picture in miniature of Switzerland, the reader will form a just conception of its general features. All the ingredients of Alpine landscape, torrents, rocks, precipices, gloomy ravines, and gushing fountains, forests that at once afford shelter and sustenance, verdant meadows to which the meandering streams carry freshness and fertility, fields and gardens containing the produce of different climates clinging to the very precipices, and evincing that unwearied industry on the part of the inhabitants which has purchased the means of life under the most unfavourable circumstances."*

Reflecting on the primitive simplicity of the natives of these valleys, their peaceful lives, their industrious habits, their rigid morality, their strict observance of the *Sabbath Day*, their exactness in paying their rents and all claims, and the absence of drinking, swearing, and all such vices, we may well inquire : Why should their prince and landlord seek to exterminate the race ? The answer will be found in what follows.

THE WARS OF EXTERMINATION.

The brief periods of apparent peace which the Waldenses sometimes enjoyed were by no means intervals of security and repose ; but rather, of painful reflection and fearful anticipation.

* "History of the Waldenses, and Graphic Descriptions of the Protestant Valleys of Piedmont," by Wm. Beattie, M.D.

True peace, with security as to their persons, their property, and liberty of conscience—the inalienable rights of man—they knew not for hundreds of years.

In the year 1650 two events occurred which are sufficient to account for the exterminating wars which followed that period. 1, The **throne of Savoy** was then filled by Charles Emmanuel II, a youth of fifteen. He was a prince of a mild and humane disposition, but like Charles IX of France, he was counselled by his mother, and she was of the house of Medici, and grand-daughter to that Catherine whose deeds of blood have justly merited the execrations of mankind. The boy-sovereign was ruled by his mother, who was regent during his minority, and she was ruled by the Vatican. 2, The Society for the " **Propagation of the Faith** " was established in the same year at Turin. Noble lords, ladies, laymen, priests, and people, pressed to join the society, the inducement being a plenary indulgence to all who should take part in the good work ; the watchword reveals its character : " The conversion or the extermination of heretics."

The propagandists commenced their ruinous work under the fair pretext of conversion. Ladies of the court, and others of inferior rank, with swarms of monks, became zealous supporters of the society, visiting from house to house. About this time convents were established in the valleys, and the schools and colleges of the Vaudois were suppressed. The abduction of males under twelve and of females under fourteen years of age for the purpose of conversion, was sanctioned by law. But these nefarious means were soon followed by a violent persecution similar to that of 1560.

" The bloody **edict of Gastaldo** "—so named from its consequences—appeared in January, 1655. In vain did the threatened inhabitants, by every means of appeal and supplication to the different members of the Government, seek to avert the impending storm. More than a thousand families in the depth of winter, were driven from their homes and properties to the shelterless heights of their ice-covered mountains. And this they were commanded to do within three days on pain of death. Anything more inhuman, more barbarous, under the circumstances, cannot be imagined. A whole population, including little children, old men, the sick, the feeble, and the bed-ridden, must leave their homes amidst the terrors of an Alpine winter. Their journey lay through valleys buried deep in snow, across rivers swollen with the flood, and over mountains covered with ice. True, an alternative was offered them—they might go to mass. The historian Leger informs us that he had a congregation of well-nigh two thousand persons, and that not a man of them all accepted the alternative. " I can well bear them this testimony," he observes, " seeing I was their pastor for eleven years, and I knew every one of them by name. Judge, reader, whether I had not cause to weep for joy, as well as for sorrow, when I saw that all the fury of these wolves was not able to influence one of these lambs, and that no earthly advantage could shake their constancy. And when I marked the traces of their blood on the snow and ice over which they had dragged their lacerated limbs, had I not cause to bless God that I had seen accomplished in their poor bodies what remained of the measure of the sufferings of Christ, and especially when I beheld this heavy cross borne by them with a fortitude so noble ? "*

THE TREACHERY OF PIANESSA.

" Had the persecution ended here," says Mr. Hugh Acland, " humanity would yet have been saved from an indelible stain. The **Marquess of Pianessa** entered the valleys at the head of fifteen thousand men ; the consequent massacre is too horrible for detailed narration." Only a part of the Waldenses had suffered from the decree of Gastaldo, but the fixed object of the propaganda was the extirpation of the entire race. The marquess being well aware of the desperate resistance he must encounter if the Vaudois should flee and unite in the mountains, betook himself to the old weapon of Jezebel—treachery. He feigned a wish for conciliation, and invited deputies to confer on the necessary terms. The wiles of the enemy, alas ! were successful. Well skilled in craftiness, he thoroughly deceived the simple honest-hearted Vaudois, after treating them with great kindness, and assuring them that all would be amicably settled if they would receive, as a token of fidelity on their part, a small company of soldiers in the different villages. Some of the more sagacious, especially the pastor Leger, suspected treachery ; but the people in general, willing to hope for a time of peace, opened the doors of their houses to the soldiers of Pianessa. Two days were spent in great friendliness ; the soldiers and the villagers eating at the same table, sleeping under the same roof, and conversing freely together. These two days were employed by the enemy in making preparations for the general massacre. The villages and roads throughout the valleys were occupied by the soldiers.

At four o'clock on the morning of the third day, April 24th, a signal was given from the castle, and the assassins began **their work of death.** But with the exception of Pastor Leger, no historian attempts to give details ; and he did it as a matter of duty, being an eye-witness, and had his narrative verified by others. A priest and a monk accompanied each party of soldiers, to set fire to the houses as soon as the inmates had been despatched. " Our valley of Lucerne," exclaims Leger, " which was like a Goshen, was now converted into a Mount Etna, darting forth cinders, and fire, and flames. The earth resembled a furnace, and the air was filled with a darkness like that of Egypt, which might be felt, from the smoke of towns, villages, temples, mansions, granges, and buildings, all burning in the flames of the Vatican." But here it was not, as in the St. Bartholomew massacre, the instant despatch of their victims, but the deliberate invention of barbarities and cruelties hitherto unknown. As many of the strongest escaped by their knowledge of the hills, tiny children, their mothers, the sick, and the aged were the chief victims of the soldiers of the propaganda. But we would not subject our readers to the heart-sickening details of Leger's awful narrative.

THE FAITH AND HEROISM OF GIANAVELLO.

During this terrible persecution which carried fire and sword into so many of the valleys, Rora had its full proportion of calamities ; but it called forth one of those ardent spirits which from time to time God raises up to exhibit those virtues which are seldom brought into action but in moments of great emergency. We allude to **Joshua Gianavello,** a native of the valley of Rora, but truly a mighty man of valour, whose genius and intrepidity are the subject of unqualified admiration. On the morning of the 24th, which witnessed the merciless slaughter in the valleys of Lucerne, Angrogna, La Torre, Villar, St. John, and others, a similar doom was intended for Rora, and Count Christovel, with four hundred soldiers, was charged with its execution.

Gianavello had narrowly watched their movements, and, seconded by a small determined band, seven in all, he threw himself into the defile by which the enemy was advancing upon Rora. There was not a moment to lose. The soldiers—naturally thinking that the ruthless proceedings on the other side of the Pelice had paralysed all further resistance, and ensured them an easy entrance into Rora—advanced with little attention to order. Under cover of the rocks and trees, Gianavello and his band could hear the conversation, and as one of the soldiers, counting on their work being easy, observed that the people of Rora would only be waiting to bid us welcome. " We do ! ' exclaimed a voice of thunder, when a volley of musketry from right and left carried death into the advancing column. Seven of the troop were killed. Then, reloading their pieces, and quickly changing their ground, they fired again with a like effect. No enemy was visible ; but the volume of curling smoke that rolled down the rocks, convinced them that they were caught between two fires. Thrown into utter confusion by this unexpected salutation, they began to retreat in terror and precipitation. But Gianavello and his men bounded from cover to cover kept up a deadly fire, until the superstitious soldiers began to feel as if every tree discharged a bullet. Fifty-four of their number were left dead behind them, and Rora was saved from the meditated destruction.

The disgrace which attached to this enterprise Pianessa resolved to retrieve by a fresh attempt. He organised a battalion of nearly a thousand men to cross the mountain. Fully aware that such would be the case, Gianavello was on the watch, and saw the enemy enter. His band was now increased to seventeen men—eleven good marksmen, and six expert slingers. When the invaders had advanced to a certain point, this invisible army opened so galling a fire upon them that they were again driven back to their quarters with great loss.

The news of this second defeat was the signal for vengeance. To increase his host, Pianessa ordered detachments from the neighbouring stations, and having completed his muster, sent them once more on the pass to Rora. The numbers were so overwhelming on this occasion that the patriot and his band waited for a favourable moment. Meanwhile they knelt down in prayer and gave thanks to God who had twice by their hands saved the people, and prayed that their hearts and arms might be strengthened to work yet another deliverance. A company of soldiers, laden with booty, were immediately attacked ; and, as if possessed by a superstitious terror, endeavoured to make their escape, throwing away their plunder. Their flight became most disastrous ; great pieces of rock were rolled down upon them, mingled with deadly bullets ; and many in their haste fell over the precipices, so that only a few survived.

But in place of the blinded bigot, Pianessa, seeing in these events the finger of God, he was only the more inflamed with rage, and jealous for his own military character. He assembled all the royal troops—to the number of eight or ten thousand men—and calling his officers together, he held a council of war. What was to be done ? A mere handful of peasants had foiled the tactics of a disciplined army ; and the troops were charged with cowardice and incapacity. It was resolved that the whole army should be divided into three separate companies, and, by a simultaneous movement from every accessible avenue, secure the destruction of Rora. To meet this overwhelming force, Gianavello was compelled to take up his position on the summit of the pass, and while bravely combating with the first troop of three thousand, the other divisions forced a passage in the opposite direction.

THE MASSACRE OF RORA.

The village of Rora is now in the hands of the Pope's soldiers, who, meeting with little resistance, abandoned themselves to the work of destruction. The inhabitants consisted of old men,

women, and children ; the effective members of the community
were now expanding their patriotic efforts on the frontier. A
general massacre followed. Nearly ten thousand assassins fell
upon the helpless and unoffending peasants with all the impetuosity of wolves rushing upon a fold. No distinction was
made of age or sex. Happy they who were slain at once, and
thus escaped indignities and barbarities, to which we cannot
give utterance.

"Every soldier," says Dr. Beattie, "took upon himself the
office of an executioner, till the devoted hamlet presented the
spectacle of a vast scaffold strewn with victims, and streaming
with blood. When the morning sun rose upon the village, not
a voice was heard, nor a hearth left standing ; but a mass of
smouldering ashes, through which protruded at intervals the
ghastly features of the slain, carried its appeal to the gates of
Heaven " (p. 56).

The wife and three daughters of Gianavello, Pianessa spared
from the sword, that he might work on the feelings of the father
and husband. He threatened to burn them alive unless he
surrendered himself a prisoner and abjured his religion. **Gianavello nobly replied** : "As for the first condition, my wife and
children are in thy hands, and if such be God's will, thou mayest
accomplish thy threat ; but this barbarous act can only affect
their bodies, for which their religion teaches them not to be over-
solicitous. If brought to the stake, they will be supported in
the hour of trial. Their faith is proof against terror, and enables
the innocent to look with complacent eye upon what is terrible
only to the guilty. What was once said to Pilate, I now say to
Pianessa : ' Thou couldest have no power at all against me except
it were given thee from above.' As to the question of *apostasy*,
shall I abjure these principles I have so long defended with my
blood—principles unchangeable as the Word of God ? Shall I
desert His cause for the hopes of a renegade ? No ! in that cause
which I have thus feebly espoused, I am ready to perish. The
terrors of the Inquisition are mild compared with the upbraidings
of conscience ; and I shall never incur the one by shrinking from
the other." He escaped to Geneva.

What could Pianessa do ? What could the Papal armies do ?
What could the legions of hell do against a religion that produced
such faith in God, and such champions for His truth ? They
might crush for a time the feeble few, " the poor of the flock,"
and seem to triumph ; but God is in the midst of them, and in the
most wonderful manner preserves a remnant for Himself, a seed
to serve Him, the *silver link* in the unbroken chain of witnesses ;
and the happy day will come when He will vindicate their cause
in the presence of an assembled universe, and lifting up their
heads on high, He will honour them with the martyr's crown,

while their enemies, covered with shame and branded with eternal infamy, will seek the darkest regions of the lost that they may conceal the enormity of their guilt, and the undying agonies of hopeless despair. Those shrieks and groans of the dying which echoed and re-echoed among the Alpine hills shall be heard again ; and those quivering limbs of frightened children for whom there was no pity, shall be seen again, but in awful frightful vision. Haunted by such sights and sounds, with a load of guilt which now oppresses the imagination, what must that place of torment be ? What vitality to the worm that never dies, what vehemence to the flame that shall never be quenched, must that recollection of such deeds for ever give ! Still the grand truth remains, that, by a timely repentance and a genuine faith in the Lord Jesus, our sins, however many, are all washed away ; but the soul that dies impenitent is lost for ever !

THE SYMPATHY OF ENGLAND.

The **Protestant States** of Europe were horror-struck when they heard of these massacres. But nowhere did the cry from the valleys awaken a deeper sympathy, or draw forth a stronger expression of indignation, than in England. " **Cromwell,** who was then at the head of the State, proclaimed a fast, ordered a collection for the sufferers, and wrote to all the Protestant princes, and to the King of France, with the intent of enlisting their sympathy, and aid on behalf of the Vaudois. **Milton,** the Protector's Latin secretary, wrote the letters ; and in token of the deep interest Cromwell took in this affair, he sent Sir Samuel Morland with a letter to the Duke of Savoy."*

The ambassador wisely visited the valleys on his way to Turin, and saw with his own eyes the frightful desolations which they still presented. After a partial allusion to the cruelties he was sent by the Protector to complain of, he, with great plainness and fervour of speech proceeded : " Why should I mention more ? Though I could enumerate infinitely more, did not my mind altogether revolt from them. If all the tyrants of all times and ages were alive again—I speak without offence to your royal highness, as convinced that none of these things are to be attributed to your highness—they would doubtless be ashamed to find that nothing barbarous, nor inhuman, in comparison of these deeds, had ever been invented by them. In the meantime the angels are stricken with horror ! Men are dizzy with amazement ! Heaven itself appears astonished by the cries of the dying, and the very earth to blush with the gore of so many innocent persons ! Avenge not Thyself, O God, for this mighty wickedness, this parricidal slaughter. Let Thy blood, O Christ, wash out this blood ! "

* " History of Protestantism," vol. ii., p. 486.

Ambassadors from the cantons of Switzerland, Geneva, Holland, and the Protestants of France, all denounced the late cruelties in the strongest terms. "So deep an interest was perhaps never displayed on any other occasion, neither as to the number of potentates partaking in it, nor as to the vast sums contributed to relieve the greatly afflicted Waldenses."*

The **Duke of Savoy,** pretending to listen to such remonstrances, was induced to propose peace to the "men of the valleys." The youthful prince found himself completely deceived by his mother and her advisers. He had lost thousands of his best subjects, the best tillers of the ground, the best rent-payers, the most faithful to his throne ; but more—he had lost the best of his army, and spent his treasure. He declared that "to kill one Vaudois cost him fifteen soldiers." But what was his advantage ? It was all lost in this life, but the priests assured him that he had secured the favour of Heaven.

When the "**Grand Monarch,**" Louis XIV of France, was dying, he asked his confessor, Father La Chaise : "By what good deed as a king he might atone for his many sins as a man." "Extirpate Protestantism from France," was the Jesuit's ready reply. He speedily complied, and revoked the edict of Nantes, which led to the slaughter and banishment of tens—we may say, of hundreds—of thousands of God's witnesses in France. In this way was the humane Duke of Savoy influenced to send an armed force into the valleys, in order to reduce the inhabitants to the Romish obedience, or to exterminate them. But he saw his mistake, and we have no doubt was willing enough to conclude peace, such as it was. The death of Cromwell, which took place in 1658, deprived the Waldenses of their sincerest friend and most powerful intercessor. He had sanctioned a collection for them, and contributed from his own purse two thousand pounds. The whole amount collected at that time was thirty-eight thousand pounds.

THE PEACE OF 1655.

The peace which followed the great massacre of 1655 lasted about **thirty years** ; but history speaks of this period as rest only, when contrasted with the storms that preceded it. The Catholics still found many ways in which to annoy and oppress those whom they could neither conquer nor convert. The condition of the Vaudois, after the treaty of peace was signed, is thus described by Sir Samuel Morland, the English ambassador : "To this very day, they labour under most heavy burdens, which are laid on their shoulders by those rigid task-masters of the Church of Rome . . . Those very valleys which they inhabit are no other than a prison or dungeon, to which the fort of La Torre serves as a

* "History of the Vaudois," by Hugh Dyke Ackland, p. 69.

door. To all this I must add, that, notwithstanding those large supplies which have been sent them from England or foreign states, yet so great is the number of hungry creatures, and so grievous the oppression of their Popish enemies, who lie in wait to bereave them of whatsoever is given them, and snatch at every morsel of meat that goes into their mouths, that verily ever and anon they are ready to eat their own flesh for want of bread. The tongue of the suckling cleaves to the roof of its mouth, and the young children ask bread and no man gives it to them. The young and the old lie on the ground in the streets. Their miseries are more sore and grievous than words can express—they are in a manner dying while they yet live. No grapes in the vineyard, no cattle in their fields, no herds in their stalls, in corn in their garners, no meal in their barrels, no oil in their cruse.''*

THE PERSECUTION AND EXPULSION OF THE WALDENSES.

Thus the inhabitants of the valleys struggled on until the year 1686, when a fresh war broke out under the sovereignty of **Victor Amadeus II,** but chiefly through the influence of Louis XIV of France. When joined by the French auxiliaries, the united force amounted to between fifteen and twenty thousand men. Though vast numbers of the invaders were killed, the peasants were overpowered, and those who escaped the exterminating vengeance of the sword were dragged to prison, and the valleys were quite depopulated. We have no space for details, but would just add, that treachery and atrocity, as usual, on the one side, and heroic devotedness on the other, marked the progress of the war; but treachery accomplished its end, and atrocities followed. "Fourteen thousand healthy mountaineers," says Henri Arnaud, "were thrust into the dungeons of Piedmont. But when, at the intercession of the Swiss deputies, their prisons were opened, three thousand skeletons only crawled out." Such were the tender mercies of Holy Mother Church; and such would be her tender mercies to-day, were her opportunities the same. At a distance of nearly two hundred years, the heart sickens, the imagination is oppressed recoiling from the contemplation of such cold-blooded heartless cruelties. Eleven thousand perished in a few months from fetid air, cold, hunger, disease, inhumanity, and utter neglect. What must have been the state of the atmosphere with such fearful mortality! But we cannot proceed further.

The prisons were thrown open in the beginning of October; but only on condition that the prisoners should immediately leave the country and embrace perpetual exile. Winter was already advancing in all its terrors, but no mercy could be shown

* Ackland, p. 71.

to such heretics, and the famished band, the same evening, was driven forth to the Alps. They commenced their dreary **march towards Mount Cenis** ; darkness soon overtook them, and before sunrise more than one hundred and fifty had perished on the road. But the most afflicting spectacle in this harrowing procession was that of the poor mothers and their infants. They turned their backs to the storm, so as to protect the child in arms, but many of them dropped with fatigue, and were wrapped in the stern winding-sheet of the Alps. The distressed exiles earnestly entreated the officer in command to let them rest for a day, especially as the weather showed signs of an approaching hurricane. The officer, however, had no authority to grant their prayer, and the dreary march was resumed.

" During the hurricane," says Dr. Beattie, " the snow, resembling pounded ice, is tossed furiously around—like waves of sea-foam carried into the air—and deposited in overwhelming masses along the travellers' path. In its effect the snow-storm of the Alps is like the sandstorm in the Great Desert, saturating the air with its particles, and when blowing in the face, produces blindness and blistering of the skin. Under such circumstances, every hour must have been marked by some distressing incident— some new disaster that rapidly diminished their number, and sickened their hearts."*

THE ARRIVAL OF THE EXILES AT GENEVA.

About the middle of December the survivors of this way-worn band arrived at **the gates of Geneva** ; but so exhausted, that several of them died between the outer and the inner gates of the city, " finding," as one has said, " the end of their life at the beginning of their liberty." Some could not speak from their tongues being swollen, and others could not hold out their hands to receive the kindness of their new friends, from their arms being frost-bitten. All, however, that humanity could suggest, all that Christian brotherhood could supply, was brought to their relief. But Geneva could not contain them all, and arrangements were made for distributing the exiles among the Reformed cantons. And the inhabitants of these cantons—to their praise be it recorded—vied with one another in offering them the most cordial sympathy, united with the most friendly ministries of brotherly love. But neither present comforts nor future prospects could make them forget their ancestral homes. As they wandering by the banks of the Rhine, they were like the Jews of old by the rivers of Babylon—they hung their harps upon the willows, and sat down and wept as they remembered their much loved valleys with all their tender recollections and cherished associations.

* For details and illustrations, see Dr. Beattie's " Waldenses ;" Wylie's " History of Protestantism—Waldenses."

For the attainment of this grand object they made several attempts which proved unsuccessful. The enterprise being discovered, the senates of the different cantons in which the exiles resided, forseeing that their departure might compromise them with the Papal powers, took measures to prevent their embarkation. This was a great disappointment to the yearning heart of the Vaudois, and though they returned to their different communes, and resumed their industrious occupations, they were secretly engaged in devising measures for renewing the enterprise under more favourable circumstances. In the meantime the Duke of Savoy, being made acquainted with the intention of the exiles, caught the alarm, and kindling his signals along the frontier, placed everything in a war-like attitude. He also ordered two regiments of one thousand strong, commanded by officers of high birth and merit, to take possession of the roads, bridges, and passes. While yet deliberating on the best measures to be adopted in this painful dilemma, their pastor and captain, **Henri Arnaud,** addressed them from the words of Luke 11 : " Fear not, little flock," etc., which greatly revived their spirits and their patriotism.

THE EMBARKATION OF THE EXILES.

At length, however, many circumstances combined to lead the Vaudois to believe that the hand of the Lord was opening the way for their return. Their place of appointed rendezvous was a large forest, in the Pays du Vaud, near the town of Néon, on the northern shore of the Leman. When all was ready, their chief offered up prayer to God in the midst of his devoted followers, and committed the expedition to Him. They embarked between ten and eleven o'clock, August 16th, 1689, and crossed the lake by starlight. When all had arrived on the southern shore of the lake, they numbered between eight and nine hundred. M. Arnaud—a man spoken of in the highest terms for his piety, patriotism, courage, and skill in military tactics—divided the whole into three bodies—advance-guard, rear guard, and centre, according to the system of regular troops, which the Vaudois always pursued. Thus they commenced their march back to their native valleys, supposed by some historians to be one of the most wonderful exploits ever performed by any people. Besides the natural difficulties of the way, such as the height of the mountains, the depth of the snow, the treachery of the glaciers, and the heavy rain, the roads were covered, and the passes guarded by the duke's soldiers, aided by the French ; so that every inch of the way was disputed, and they had to fight their way right through to the valleys.

The feelings which sprung up in their hearts when their native mountains first burst upon their sight, will be more easily imagined than described. Some could, no doubt, individualise the very peaks under whose shadow they had spent their infancy and youth, with a thousand other tender recollections, and for the recovery of which they had exposed themselves these thirty-one days to every danger, hardship, and privation, which could afflict the body or depress the mind.

> " But now with that blest landscape in their view
> No fear could daunt them, and no foe subdue.
> A voice still whispered in their ear—Advance !
> So Heaven restores you your inheritance !
> Beneath your mountains, where the sun goes down,
> Your sires have bled, and martyrs won their crown ;
> But henceforth, at their hearths, and on their tombs,
> Peace shall preside—the olive branch shall bloom ;
> And they who now lay watch to shed their blood,
> Shall own at last one cause—one brotherhood ! ''*

The **march of the Vaudois** from the borders of the Lake of Geneva to their native valleys, not only was signalised by incidents unsurpassed in the history of events, but was crowned with success. As the Lord would have it, a quarrel arose about this time between the King of France and Victor Amadeus, which induced the latter to take this heroic band into favour. " Hitherto," said he, to the scattered remnant of his Piedmontese subjects, " we have been enemies ; but from henceforth we must be friends ; others are to blame more than myself for the evils you have suffered." This happy turn in their affairs was followed by treaties between the English and the Piedmontese Governments, in the reigns of **William III** and **Queen Anne**. From that period to the present Great Britain has been empowered, by virtue of these solemn compacts, to interpose for their protection, and their Churches ought to have had rest. But again and again, under false pretences, these oppressed people have had to contend against petty injuries and harassing grievances.†

During the French Empire of **Napoleon,** when the iron crown of Italy was placed upon the head of " the Corsican," the Waldenses enjoyed equal rights and privileges in common with the rest of their countrymen. But at the restoration of the House of Savoy to the kingdom of Sardinia, they were replaced under their former disabilities. This was the effect of evil counsel, for the restored prince acknowledged, on more occasions than one, " the constant and distinguished proof which the Waldenses had ever given to his predecessors of attachment and fidelity. I know," he added, " that I have faithful subjects in the Waldenses ; and that they will never dishonour their character."

---

* Dr. Beattie, p. 211.

† See a most interesting book, entitled " The Glorious Recovery by the Vaudois of their Native Valleys, by Henry Arnaud, their Commander and Pastor, with a Compendious History of that People," by Hugh Dyke Ackland. The march lasted thirty-one days, and there the reader will find the particulars o each day. Our space forbids even a sketch of these interesting days.

But evil counsellors prevailed, and the yoke was again placed upon their necks.

The chief difficulty with which the Waldenses have now to contend is poverty, which need excite no surprise. But the Protestants of England have not been inattentive to the condition of their brethren in the valleys of Piedmont. Public collections have on several occasions been made throughout the kingdom ; and the Society for the Propagation of the Gospel in Foreign Parts is the trustee of considerable funds raised on their behalf.

Thus the Lord has watched over, preserved, and maintained a witness and a testimony for Himself in these valleys from time immemorial. And still the oil of His grace flows, and the lamp of His truth burns, while the thrones of their oppressors have been cast to the ground, and their dynasties extinguished for ever. Even the gates of Rome have been thrown open, so that we leave the Waldensian Church, through the wonderful providence of God, in a wide and open field, for the exercise of their Christian zeal and missionary labours.*

* " Encyclopædia Britannica," vol. xxi., p. 543 ; " History of Protestantism," vol. ii., p. 511. For details of the creeds, confessions, catechisms, etc., of the Waldenses, see Gilly's " First and Second Visits to the Valleys of Piedmont."

CHAPTER LIII

The Reformation in the British Isles

IRELAND

ALTHOUGH we can scarcely speak of a **Reformation in Ireland,** we may briefly notice the changes in her ecclesiastical history. The connection of Ireland with the crown of England originated, as we have already seen, in a compact with Henry II, Pope Adrian IV, and the Irish prelates of the day. " This treaty," says Dr. Phelan, " would be memorable, if it had no other claim to the consideration of posterity than the hypocrisy, the injustice, and the mutual treachery of the parties ; but their views and pretensions, descending regularly to their successors, and exerting a constant influence on Irish affairs, make it an object of nearer interest. Without attention to these, it is impossible either to unravel the history of Ireland, or to judge correctly of its state at the present crisis." " The acquisition of a superiority by Henry over Ireland was greatly aided," says Mosheim, " by a desire of the national hierarchy to attain that independent and prosperous condition which was then common to all clerical communities closely connected with Rome." Thus was the position of the bishops greatly improved, and their revenues increased, though at the high price of the independence of their nation.

In 1172 Henry completed his conquest of the country ; the clergy submitted to the Papal dictation, agreed to pay Peter's pence to Rome, proclaimed Henry's title to the sovereign dominion of Ireland, and took the oath of fidelity to himself and his successors. " Adrian's sentence," says a friend of Romanism, " violated the rights of nations, and the most sacred laws of men, under the special pretext of religion and Reformation. Ireland was blotted out from the map of nations, and consigned to the loss of freedom without a tribunal and without a crime." The hierarchs, however, did not regret the change. Hitherto, the native chieftains had exercised a power over the Church, which tended to keep its clergy poor and subservient ; so that they welcomed the sovereignty of England and the power of Rome as protection against the ravages of their lay-lords.

" Under the ancient system, an Irish prince was as absolute master of the priesthood as of any other class among his followers. But a new order of things was introduced by Henry II, and thenceforward kept regular pace with the advance of British

* See vol. ii., p. 510.

and Papal power. All the privileges of the English Church, and all those vexatious pretensions, which had just attained a temporary triumph in the canonisation of **Thomas a Becket**, were communicated to the Irish clergy, and maintained by them with more pertinacity, in proportion to the weakness of the civil power."

From this period the Irish Church came to be essentially Romish, the Papal encroachments were tamely submitted to, and both the civil and spiritual rights of the Irish prelates were at the entire disposal of the Roman Pontiff. Henry, in order to maintain his sovereignty over the Irish clergy, filled up the vacant sees mostly with Englishmen, and the consequence was, that a spirit of jealousy and bitter hostility began to be manifested between the English and the Irish ecclesiastics. Disputes arose ; the English sovereign asserted his privilege in nominating whom he would ; the Irish clergy, meanwhile, appealed to Rome to decide the question, or rather, to confirm their nomination. The mitre usually prevailed over the crown, and the Pope's authority steadily increased.*

Thus the contest between the English sovereign and the Irish clergy commenced ; the latter sought to transfer their allegiance as churchmen from the sovereign of England to the Pope of Rome, so that the struggle for supremacy lasted for centuries, even until the era of the Reformation.

HENRY VIII AND THE IRISH CHURCH.

When Henry had secured the cordial compliance of his English subjects with the principles of the Reformation, he resolved to obtain, if possible, a like reception for the new doctrines in Ireland also ; but to his deep mortification, his proposal was treated with the greatest indifference and neglect. The advocates of the Pope's supremacy in opposition to the king's were zealous and determined. **George Cromer,** a prelate of ability and learning—who, being primate of all Ireland, filled also, at one time, the high office of chancellor—headed the opposition to Henry's proposed assumption of Papal privileges, defeated his purpose for a time, and retarded the progress of what might be called the Reformation in Ireland.

The chief agent in forwarding the royal designs was **George Brown,** the first Protestant Prelate that held a See in Ireland, having been appointed by Henry, Archbishop of Dublin. His zeal for the doctrines of the Reformation in opposition to the dogmas of the Romish Church, met with the most violent opposition from the bigoted Catholics, and his life was frequently in imminent danger from the zealots of that party. At the suggestion of Brown an Irish Parliament was convened at Dublin, in

* For minute and most reliable details, see Dr. Phelan's " History of the Policy of the Church of Rome in Ireland."

1536, by which all opposition was silenced, and the national religion was formally changed, the Reformed faith, being established as the recognised religion of the country. "Various statutes were enacted with the view of carrying out this great object. The king was declared supreme earthly head of the Church in Ireland; he was invested with the firstfruits of bishoprics, and other secular promotions in the Irish Church, as well as the firstfruits of abbeys, priories, colleges, and hospitals; all appeals to Rome in spiritual causes were forbidden; the authority of the Pope was solemnly renounced, and all who should dare to acknowledge it in Ireland were made subject to praemunire—a heavy penalty. All officers of every kind and degree were required to take the oath of supremacy, and the refusal to take it was pronounced, as in England, to be high treason. Thus was Protestantism declared to be the religion of Ireland by law established. The religious houses were suppressed, and their lands vested for ever in the crown."[*]

The Popish party in Ireland was very indignant at the assumption of such spiritual authority by the King of England. Numbers of the Irish chieftains avowed their readiness to take up arms in defence of the old religion. Special emissaries were secretly despatched to Rome to express the devotion of Cromer and his party to the Holy Father, and to implore his interposition on behalf of his spiritual authority in Ireland. Papal commissioners were immediately despatched to encourage those who were opposing the recent enactments, to rouse the chieftains of the north, and more particularly **O'Neill,** to rally round the sacred standard of their forefathers, and draw the sword in defence of Papal supremacy. O'Neill joyfully accepted the part assigned him by his Papal majesty. A confederacy was formed for the suppression of heresy; an army was raised; O'Neill had himself proclaimed head of the northern Irish on the ancient hill of royalty, according to the custom of the native monarchs of Ireland. But this idle display and pomp was soon brought to an end. The deputy suspected a rising, and was prepared to meet it. The victory of Bellahoe, on the borders of Meath, broke the power of the northern chiefs. Struck with an unaccountable panic, they all gave way and fled.

Several attempts were afterwards made to do battle in defence of the Pope's authority, but the prompt measures of the Government frustrated every new scheme at insurrection, and the chieftains with their tumultuous bands were dispersed in all directions. These repeated defeats weakened the influence of the Ulster nobles, rendered the cause of the Pope more hopeless, and led some of the most turbulent of the chiefs to profess reconciliation to the king's Government.

* "Faiths of the World," vol. ii., p. 153; Mosheim, vol. iii., p. 491.

HENRY, KING OF IRELAND.

The act of supremacy, which was passed in 1537, was followed in 1542 by another to recognise the sovereign as **King of Ireland,** instead of *lord.* Hitherto the only title which the Pope had allowed the sovereigns of England to assume was the subordinate one of lord. But this term was now changed by act of Parliament into that of king. The alteration was commemorated by conferring peerages on several of the heads of the great families, thereby sinking the chieftain in the peer ; and some of inferior note were created barons. Thus was peace restored to Ireland in so far as the great laymen were concerned, but the priesthood was not so easily won over to the cause of Reform.

After the death of Henry, and the accession of **Edward VI** to the throne, the Lord-Deputy of Ireland received a royal order to see that the Romish ritual was superseded by the new English liturgy. This fresh innovation roused the clergy to a bold and determined opposition. An assembly of the prelacy and inferior clergy was immediately convened. The new liturgy was treated with the utmost scorn ; Dowdale, the primate was as violent in his opposition to Edward's liturgy as Cromer had been to Henry's supremacy. This opposition, however, was not allowed to prevail. By order of the Government the English service was used in the Cathedral of Christ Church, Dublin, on Easter Day, 1551.

A new revolution, occasioned by the early death of Edward, and the accession of **Mary,** added to this state of distraction and confusion. The religion of the country was again changed. Dowdale, who had withdrawn to the continent during the reign of Edward, was recalled to the primacy ; the most violent of his opponents fled the country, and many of the clergy returned to their former faith. Liberty was given for the celebration of mass without penalty or compulsion ; and the Roman Catholic faith was once more established in Ireland. The profession of Protestantism was made penal by an Irish Parliament in 1556, and the sanguinary spirit of intolerance spoke of trampling down all opposition to the Papacy by fire and sword ; but happily the slow pace of colonial business long delayed the transmission of authority for commencing an active persecution. "At length, however," says Mosheim, "a commission for that purpose was prepared, and Dr. Cole, one of the commissioners, left London with it for Dublin. Exulting over the prospect of thus crushing Irish Protestantism, he indiscreetly boasted of his charge before a woman at Chester, who was a staunch adherent of the Reformation and had a brother in the Irish metropolis. She managed to steal the commission, and to place in its room a pack of cards with the knave of clubs uppermost. Unsuspicious of his loss, the talkative messenger went on to Dublin, where he landed

October the 7th, 1558, and there, looking for his credentials, was confounded by finding them so ridiculously supplanted . . . A new commission was, after some delay, obtained, but before it reached Dublin, Queen Mary was dead."*

On the accession of **Elizabeth** at her sister's death, the queen's well-known adherence to the cause of the Reformation revived the hearts of Protestants throughout her dominions, gave a new impulse to Irish affairs, and set the whole country, lay and clerical, once more in motion. The whole ecclesiastical system of Mary was reversed ; Protestantism was restored, and proclaimed to be henceforth the established religion of Ireland.

IRISH PRESBYTERIAN CHURCH.

Having said thus much about the establishment of Episcopacy in Ireland, we must briefly notice the origin of **Presbyterianism** in that country.

When Elizabeth ascended the throne she found the whole island, from the restless ambition and jealousy of the chieftains, in a state of petty warfare. During the latter part of her reign, as well as the early part of the reign of her successor James I, the northern provinces had been the scene of incessant conspiracies and insurrections. One rebellion after another kept the country in a state of commotion, fomented always by the Popes of Rome, sometimes aided by Philip II of Spain, and Cardinal Richelieu of France. Bull after bull was issued, calling upon the princes, prelates, nobles, and people of Ireland to contend for the recovery of their liberty, and the defence of the Holy Church ; and rather to lose their lives than take that wicked and pestilent oath of supremacy, whereby the sceptre of the Catholic Church was wrested from the hand of the Vicar of God. Such appeals, coming from the Pope himself, could not fail to exert a powerful influence upon an ignorant and superstitious people.

Details of these long continued civil wars, the extinction of titles, and the confiscation of property, fall not within the limits of our " Short Papers," but we may just add, that by the death of some of the leaders of the rebellion, and by the flight of others, nearly the whole of **Ulster** was forfeited to the crown, and fell into the hands of King James. This vast tract of land comprehended six northern counties, and spread over five hundred thousand acres. The king resolved to remodel the province by removing the ancient possessors, and introducing a colony of Scotch and English settlers in their stead. This led to the plantation of Ulster, the benefits of which are felt to this day. Industry, in a short time, changed the face of the country. The lands were cultivated and improved, a number of flourishing towns were established, and the province of Ulster became the

* Mosheim, vol. iii., p. 496.

most prosperous district in Ireland. But that evil spirit of Popish hatred towards every aspect of Protestantism and England never ceased to plot, until it burst forth in the great rebellion and the revolting massacre of 1641. On the 23rd of October the carnage began ; on the 30th, the order for a general massacre was issued from the camp of Sir Phelim O'Neill, and, shortly after, the manifesto of the Bishop MacMahon proclaimed the commencement of a WAR OF REBELLION.*

William, Prince of Orange, after the battle of the Boyne, commenced his reign by assuring the Irish Protestants that he had come to Ireland to free them from Popish tyranny, and he doubted not, by the Divine assistance that he would complete his design. The war was brought to a close, peace was restored, and the Presbyterian Church being reinstated in all its privileges, addressed itself to the great work of preaching the Gospel and spreading the truth to the blessing of many precious souls.

RELIGION IN SCOTLAND.

Having already noticed the religious condition of Scotland from the earliest times down to the **dawn of the Reformation,**† we may commence our present sketch with the *effects* of that great revolution on the people of that country ; but we must retrace our steps for a moment, and renew our acquaintance with the existing state of things.

Before the Reformation, which commenced in Germany, had found its way to the distant shores of Scotland, a spirit of religious Reform had begun to display itself in several districts, especially in the Lowlands. Many of the Lollards, or disciples of Wycliffe, who had fled from the persecution in England, found a refuge in Scotland and there remained. These, meeting with the descendants of the ancient Culdees, may have quietly formed a little missionary band, maintained unbroken the chain of God's witnesses, and kept the lamp of His testimony burning in that benighted land. They denied the dogma of transubstantiation and the power of the priesthood ; affirming, " That there is a universal priesthood, of which every man and woman who believes in the Saviour is a member ; that the Pope, who exalts himself above God, is against God ; that it is not permissible to take up arms for the things of faith ; and that priests may marry."

Among the protectors of these enlightened Christians—compared with many of the Reformers, especially as to universal priesthood and arms—was **John Campbell,** Laird of Cessnock, a man well versed in the Scriptures, but not equal to his wife, who could " set the dogmas of the priests face to face with the Holy Scriptures, and show their falsehood." " On the testimony of

* Dr. Phelan's " History," p. 332 ; " Faiths of the World," vol. ii., p. 158. For lengthy and minute details, see Froude's " History of Ireland."
† Vol. i., p. 267 ; Vol. ii., p. 511.

63

both friend and foe," says another historian, "there were few counties in the Lowlands of Scotland where these Lollards were not to be found. They were numerous in Fife; they were still more numerous in the districts of Cunningham and Kyle, hence their name, *The Lollards of Kyle*. In the reign of James IV, about 1494, some thirty Lollards were summoned before the archiepiscopal tribunal of Glasgow on a charge of heresy. They were almost all gentlemen of landed property in the districts already named, and were charged with denying the mass, Purgatory, the worshipping of images, the praying to saints, the Pope's vicarship, his power to pardon sin—in short, all the peculiar doctrines of Romanism. Their defence appears to have been so spirited that the king, before whom they argued their cause, shielded them from the doom that the archbishop, Blackadder, would undoubtedly have pronounced upon them."*

The flames of martyrdom had not yet been kindled, we may say, and the spirit of burning had not yet taken full hold of the priesthood, or such heretics would not have escaped. But such witnesses plainly prove, what we have found in different countries, that the Spirit of God was working and preparing a people in all parts of Europe for the great revolution in the sixteenth century.

THE PROGRESS OF THE REFORMATION.

As early as the year 1526, the doctrines of the Reformation had made considerable progress in Scotland. Vessels from the continent were arriving at Aberdeen, Montrose, Dundee, and Leith, bringing fresh tidings of the progress of Protestantism, and secretly discharging packages of pamphlets and sermons of the Reformers. In this way the shores of the Firth of Forth were broadcast with the seeds of **Lutheranism**. When Tyndale had translated the New Testament into English, large numbers were imported from Flanders, and industriously circulated among the people. The Reformation on a Divine basis now began. The darkness that had so long brooded over that country was being rolled away by the light of Heaven. Almost every person had a New Testament in his hand, and God was using it in much blessing.

This was God's great mercy to Scotland, for the clergy had become so violent, that the living voice would have been instantly suppressed, though this, too, was needed for the great work, but the people must first be prepared by the teaching of the Word of God. The Bible was Scotland's only missionary and Reformer at that moment. "With silent foot," says one, "it began to traverse the land; it came to the castle gates of the primate, yet he heard not its steps; it preached in cities, but its voice fell

* D'Aubigné's "Calvin," vol. vi., p. 7; Wylie, vol. iii., p. 468.

not on the ear of bishops ; it passed along the highways and byways unobserved by the spy. To the churchman's eye all seemed calm, . . . but in the stillness of the midnight hour men welcomed this new instructor, and opened their hearts to its comforting and beneficent teaching. The Bible was emphatically the nation's one great teacher. It was stamping its own ineffaceable character upon the Scottish Reformation ; and the place the Bible thus early made for itself in the people's affections, and the authority it acquired over their judgments, it was destined never to lose."* But however sacredly and firmly we believe this noble testimony of a most reliable witness, the living voice, the confessor and martyr, were all needed to arouse the nation from the deadly sleep of Popery in which it had been so long and so fatally sunk.

FIRST MARTYRS OF THE SCOTTISH REFORMATION.

Few martyrdoms have had such a place in the human mind as **Patrick Hamilton's.** His youth, his accomplishments, his refinement, his learning, his blameless life, his noble and gentle spirit, all united to make him an object of universal pity. But he was guilty of Rome's unpardonable sin. On him was the honour conferred by his Divine Lord and Master, to be the first preacher of the glad tidings of salvation to his countrymen, and the first to seal his testimony with his blood. But more, the cruel death of this royal youth was made a great blessing to many, among both the learned and the common people.

He was the son of Sir Patrick Hamilton, of Kincavil, and the great-grandson, by both the father's and the mother's side, of James II. He was born in the year 1504, and being designed for the Church, the abbacy of Ferne was conferred upon him in his childhood, according to a custom which prevailed at that time He received his early education at St. Andrews ; and about the year 1517 he left Scotland to pursue a course of study in the University of Paris, where he acquired his degree of Master of Arts. He may also have learnt something of the truth in the school of Lefevre and Farel. In 1523 he returned to his native country, and entered himself at St. Andrews University. From the character of his conversation, and the free language which he used in speaking of the corruptions of the Church, he drew down upon himself the suspicions of the clergy, and inquisition was made into his opinions. Under these circumstances he again left Scotland, and, attracted by the fame of Luther, repaired to Wittemberg. Having spent some time with Luther and Melanchthon, he went to pursue his studies at the University of Marburg, then newly opened by the Landgrave of Hesse. There he had the advantage of the friendship and instructions

* " History of Protestantism," vol. iii., p. 169.

of the learned and pious Francis Lambert of Avignon.   The ex-Franciscan—whom we have met with before at Marburg— conceived a strong attachment to the young Scotsman, and had a powerful influence in moulding his character.   But while he was daily advancing in the knowledge of the Scriptures, he became increasingly desirous of imparting to his countrymen the knowledge of Christ and salvation, which he found to be so precious to himself.   " This young man," said Lambert to Philip, " has come from the end of the world to your academy, in order to be fully established in God's truth.   I have hardly ever met a man who expresses himself with so much spirituality and truth on the Word of the Lord."

In 1527 he was in Scotland once more, and not ashamed of the Gospel of Christ.   He proceeded to the family mansion of **Kincavil,** near Linlithgow, and preached the Gospel to his kinsfolk and neighbours.   Many of the nobility and the common people seem to have embraced the new religion.   He next resolved to carry the Gospel to the Church of St. Michael's, Linlithgow, termed by historians, " the Versailles of Scotland." The palace was also a fortress and a prison ; it was the pleasure house to which the court used to retire for relaxation, and within its walls the unfortunate Mary Stuart was born.   Here the young evangelist brought the Gospel within the hearing of the priests of St. Michael's and the members of the royal family.   The simplicity and elegance of his style were fitted to win the hearts of his hearers, but the Gospel he preached did not suit the priests. He maintained that there was no salvation for the guilty but through the death of the Lord Jesus Christ, who died for the chief of sinners ; and that it is the anointing of the Holy Spirit that replenishes the soul with grace, not the chrism of the Church. He was denounced as a pestilent Lutheran to **Archbishop Beaton** of St. Andrews ; and Beaton was too zealous a churchman to let Lutheranism escape with impunity.

Still there were difficulties in the way.   He was not a heretic of low degree, but of royal lineage ; and would no doubt be protected by the Hamilton family and other nobility, and perhaps by the king himself.   What was to be done ?   Pretending to wish a free conference with him on some points of Church Reform, the cruel and crafty archbishop decoyed him to St. Andrews.   Both Hamilton and his friends suspected treachery but he thought it his duty to go.   He had only been married to a lady of noble birth a few weeks, who, with others besought him with tears to keep out of Beaton's way ; but he seemed to feel that the Lord might make his death of more service to his country than his life and labours, and so set out for St. Andrews.

On his arrival he was received with every mark of consideration and respect, the archbishop smiling on the youth he had resolved to sacrifice. Knowing the difficulties which surrounded this case, Beaton required time to prepare the way for success, and so allowed Patrick something like liberty in the castle. Questions were freely discussed by the young Reformer with the doctors, students, and priests, as if he had been on equal terms with them. But Beaton was only biding his time, for the opposition was great and powerful. The court in which he was tried and condemned was surrounded by some thousands of armed men, which showed the fears of the priesthood. He was found infected with divers heresies of Martin Luther, condemned as a heretic, deprived of all dignities, orders, and benefices, and delivered over to the secular arm to be burnt alive. The priests decided that the sentence should be executed the same day, as his brother, Sir James, was not far distant with a military force, determined to rescue him. The condemnation had hardly been pronounced when the executioners' servants were seen before the gates of St. Salvator's College, raising the pile on which the royal youth was to be burnt.

THE MARTYRDOM OF PATRICK HAMILTON.

At noon, on the last day of February, 1528, the noble confessor stood before the pile. He uncovered his head, and, lifting up his eyes to Heaven, remained motionless for some time in prayer. He then turned to his friends, and handed to one of them his copy of the Gospels—the volume he so much loved. Next, calling his servant, he took off his gown and gave it to him, with his coat and cap : " Take these garments ; they can do me no service in the fire, and they may still be of use to thee. It is the last gift thou wilt receive from me, except the example of my death, the remembrance of which I pray thee to bear in mind. For albeit it be bitter to the flesh, and fearful before man, yet it is the entrance to eternal life, which none shall possess that deny Christ Jesus before this wicked generation." As the executioners passed the iron chain round his body, and fastened him to the stake, he again exclaimed : " In the Name of Jesus I give up my body to the fire, and commit my soul into the hands of the Father." By the ignorance and awkwardness of his executioners, his sufferings were protracted for nearly six hours. The details are too harrowing to be transferred to our pages. Three times the pile was kindled, and three times the fire went out because the wood was green. Gunpowder was then placed among the faggots, which, when it exploded, shot up a faggot in the martyr's face, which wounded him severely. Turning to the deathsman, he said mildly : " Have you no dry wood ? " Dry wood was brought from the castle, but it was six o'clock in the evening before his body was reduced to ashes ; " but during these six hours," says an eyewitness, " the martyr never gave one sign of impatience or anger, never called to Heaven for vengeance on his persecutors : so great was his faith, so strong his confidence in God." His last words that were heard were : " How long, O Lord, shall darkness cover this realm ? How long wilt Thou suffer this tyranny of man ? Lord Jesus receive my spirit ! "

So died the **proto-martyr** of the Lutheran Reformation. The rumour of his death ran speedily over the whole land, and all heard it with a shudder. People everywhere wanted to know the cause for which the young man had suffered such a cruel death. All turned to the side of the victim. It was, no doubt, around his funeral pile that the first decided movement of the Scottish Reformation took place. His gracious manners, and the mildness, patience, and fortitude which he displayed at the stake, combined to give unusual interest to his martyrdom, and were well fitted to touch the heart of the nation. " The murder of Hamilton," says a modern historian, " was afterwards avenged in the death of the nephew and successor of his persecutor ; and the flames in which he expired were, in the course of one generation, to enlighten all Scotland, and to consume with avenging fury, the Catholic superstition, the Papal power, and the prelacy itself."*

The overruling hand of the Lord is most distinctly seen in the whole history of Patrick Hamilton. So far as we are able to judge, a life, long and laborious, would not have served the cause of the Reformation so much as his trial, condemnation, and death, all accomplished in one day. Nothing less than the fiery stake of the confessor would have aroused the nation from that sleep of death into which Popery had lulled it. It began to bear fruit immediately. **Henry Forrest,** a Benedictine in the monastery of Linlithgow, was brought to a knowledge of the truth by the preaching of Hamilton, and he is the first to come forward and repeat his martyrdom. It was told the archbishop that Forrest had said that " Hamilton was a martyr, and no heretic," and that he had a New Testament. " He is as bad as Master Patrick," said Beaton ; " we must burn him." James Lindsay, a wit, standing by, ventured to say : " My lord, let him be burned in a hollow ; for the reek of Patrick Hamilton's fire has infected every one it blew upon." The archbishop, not heeding the satire, had the stake of Forrest planted on the highest ground in the neighbourhood, that the population of Angus and Forfar might see the flames, and thus learn the danger of falling into Protestantism. Henry Forrest was Scotland's second martyr.

MANY OF THE CLERGY AND NOBLES EMBRACE THE REFORMATION.

It is a remarkable feature of the **Scottish Reformation** that it

* See Dr. M'Crie's " Life of Knox," p. 14 ; D'Aubigné's " Calvin," vol. vi.; " History of Protestantism," vol. iii.

began among the clergy, and was early embraced by the nobility and landed gentry. Almost all her first martyrs and confessors were monks or parish priests. **Alesius,** Canon of St. Augustine at St. Andrews, was brought to the knowledge of the truth, and confirmed in the faith of the Gospel by the testimony which Hamilton had borne to the truth during his trial, and by the simple and heroic beauty of his death, which he had witnessed. The death of Hamilton being the subject of much conversation among the canons at that time, Alesius could not refrain from expressing what he now felt and believed. He spoke of the wretched state of the Church, her destitution of men competent to teach her, and that she was kept from the knowledge of the Holy Scriptures. This was enough ; the canons could not endure it. He was denounced to Prior Hepburn, a base, immoral man ; he was treated with the most brutal violence, and thrown into a foul and unwholesome dungeon. When this was noised abroad, it exicited great interest both among citizens and nobles. The king was appealed to ; but the archbishop and the prior succeeded in detaining him in prison for about a year, when the canons, who were friendly to him, opened his prison door, and urged him to leave the country immediately, without saying a word to anybody. This he did, though most reluctantly, and found a refuge on the continent.

Alexander Seaton, a monk of the Dominican order, and confessor to the king, was also brought to see that salvation is through faith in the Lord Jesus Christ, without deeds of law. In 1532, having been appointed to preach in the Cathedral of St. Andrews in Lent, he resolved courageously to avow the heavenly doctrine which was making exiles and martyrs. " A living faith," he said, " which lays hold on the mercy of God in Christ, can alone obtain for the sinner the remission of sins. Christ is the end of the law for righteousness, and no one is able by his works to satisfy Divine justice. But for how many years has God's law, instead of being faithfully taught, been darkened by the tradition of men ! " The people wondered at his doctrine, and why he did not speak about pilgrimages and meritorious works ; and the priests were afraid to say much, as he was the king's confessor, and a great favourite. But Beaton was not the man to hesitate. " This bold preacher is evidently putting to his mouth the trumpet of Hamilton and Alesius. Proceedings must be taken against him." The archbishop succeeded in turning the king's mind against Seaton, so that he saved his life by taking flight, went to London, where he became chaplain to the Duke of Suffolk, and had the opportunity of preaching a full Gospel to large congregations.

Many of the students of the college and noviciates of the abbey, under the teaching of **Gawin Logie,** principal of St.

Leonard's College, and John Winram, sub-prior of the abbey were convinced of the truth for which Hamilton suffered, and embraced the doctrines of the Reformation. But the blessed results of Patrick's martyrdom were not confined to St. Andrews. Everywhere persons were to be found who held that the young Abbot of Ferne had died a martyr, being no heretic, and that they believed as he did. Alarmed at the progress of the new opinions, the clergy adopted the most rigorous measures for their extirpation. David Straiton, a Forfarshire gentleman, and Norman Gourlay, who had been a student at St. Andrews, and was in priest's orders, were tried at Edinburgh in Holyrood House, condemned, and taken to the rood of Greenside, and burned alive as heretics. About this time a change took place in the See of St. Andrews, but not for the better. James Beaton died, and was succeeded by his nephew, David Beaton—a more cruel and bloodthirsty tyrant than his uncle—whom the Pope made a cardinal for his zeal, and to increase his power.

THE FIERY ZEAL OF CARDINAL BEATON.

Strict inquisition was now made after heretics. The flames of persecution were kindled in all quarters of the country. From the year 1534, when Straiton and Gourlay were burned, till the year 1538, the spirit of persecution had greatly subsided, and the number of those who confessed Christ as their only Saviour and Lord had greatly increased. This prosperity of the Gospel was most irritating to the new cardinal, who resolved to suppress it by fire and sword. Dean Thomas Forrest, Vicar of Dollar, Sir Duncan Simpson, a priest; Keillor and Beveridge, black friars; and Forrester, a notary, in Stirling, were immediately apprehended and tried for heresy before a council held by **Cardinal Beaton,** and were condemned to the flames. A huge blazing pile was raised the same day on the Castle hill of Edinburgh, and these five faithful men were seen in the midst of it— serenely suffering, and rejoicing. To faith the fire had no terror, because death had no sting. Other names might be given, who soon followed the five martyrs on the Castle hill, and whose faith, confession, and sufferings deserve a more prominent place than can be given in our limited space; but their names are in the Lamb's book of life, their record is on high, and duly enrolled in the noble army of martyrs, and they will receive, on the morning of the first resurrection, that crown of life promised to all who are faithful unto death, with their Lord's eternal approving smile. In that day of His glory and theirs, all these sufferings will be completely forgotten, save as the remembrance of His grace which sustained them and gave them the distinguished honour of suffering for His sake. Already they have been " with Christ," in the calm repose of paradise for three hundred years, but then, in their bodies of glory, fashioned like unto His own body of glory, what praise can they offer for the grace that honoured them with the crown of martyrdom ? Heaven's estimate of Rome's heretics and their persecutions will then be manifest ; for all murderers shall have their part in the lake which burneth with fire and brimstone : which is the second death (Rev. 21. 8).

The fury of the clergy, now presided over by the tyrant David Beaton, daily waxed greater and greater ; and numbers, to escape the stake, fled to England and the continent. Some of these were men illustrious for their genius and learning, of whom were John Macbee, John Fife, John Macdowal, John Macbray, James Harrison, Robert Richardson, and the celebrated George Buchanan, who was surely helped by the Lord to escape from prison, and saved his life by a speedy flight. He is well known as the author of the metrical version of the Psalms, as used in Scotland, and bound with the Bible. A few, whose constancy was overcome by the terrors of the stake, professedly returned to the old religion, but the confessors of the truth rapidly increased. By the year 1540 many eminent men had received the evangelical doctrines. The Earls of Errol and of Glencairn, Lord Ruthven, Lord Kelmains, **Sir David Lindsay,** Sir James Sandilands, Melville of Raith, and a large number of other influential persons, appeared to be attached to the Gospel by genuine conviction.

CARDINAL BEATON'S PROSCRIPTION-ROLL.

The circumstances of the Scottish king, **James V,** about this period were peculiar and embarrassing. He was overwhelmed with sorrow at the loss of his only children, Arthur and James ; he was in debt, and much in need of money. He had offended his uncle, Henry VIII of England, by refusing to make Scotland independent of Rome, as he had made England. He also urged him to confiscate the property of the Church, and in this way fill his empty exchequer. But the influence of the hierarchy— Henry's deadly enemies—under whose power James had fallen, succeeded in producing a rupture between the uncle and the nephew, which led to war and the death of James.

Cardinal Beaton, on the other hand, proposed that the property of the heretic nobles should be confiscated for the king's benefit, and not the sacred revenues of the Holy Church. "He drew out a list," says Cunningham, "of three hundred and sixty persons of property who were suspected of heresy, and whose possessions, if confiscated, would amply supply all the requirements of royalty." Dr. M'Crie, in his "Life of Knox," referring to the same period, says : "Twice did the clergy attempt to cut off the Reformed party by a desperate blow. They presented to the king a list containing the names of some hundreds, possessed of property and wealth, whom they denounced as heretics ; and endeavoured to procure his consent to their condemnation by flattering him with the immense riches which would accrue to him from the forfeiture of their estates." D'Aubigné and Wylie speak of a list, " compiled by Beaton, containing over a hundred names, and among those marked for slaughter were Lord Hamilton, the first peer in the realm, the Earls of Cassillis and Glencairn, and the Earl Marischall."*

This last list may be one of the two spoken of by Dr. M'Crie, and may have been revised and reduced to those who were intended for immediate slaughter as well as plunder. As the statements of the different historians vary, we have given all, but we have no doubt they are substantially correct. Here the reader may pause for a moment : can he take in the appalling thought ? The alleged head of the Church in Scotland, the chief shepherd of the flock of Christ—who should be ready to lay down his life for the brethren—a priest, in holy orders, coolly writes out a list containing the names of some hundreds of the nobles and gentry of the land, and endeavours to tempt the king to sanction their condemnation by flattering him with the wealth of their possessions. Was ever plot more deeply laid in Hell, or more diabolical in its character ? But it was not to supply the king with money that Hell moved in this matter ; but to cut off by violence all who were known to favour the Reformed opinions, quench the light of truth for ever in Scotland, maintain the authority of the clergy, and preserve inviolate those debasing corruptions from which they derived their wealth.

When this proposal was first made to the king, he is said to have driven the messengers from his presence with marks of strong displeasure. But so violent was the dislike which he at last conceived against his nobility, especially after their meeting on Fala Muir, and so much had he fallen under the influence of the clergy, that but for the watchful hand of an overruling providence, it is highly probable he would have yielded to the latter, and executed the deed of blood. Instead, however, of the nobility and gentry, it was the poor king himself whom the clergy brought to an early grave.

THE PERPLEXITY AND DEATH OF THE KING.

Henry VIII had been at great pains to bring about a personal interview with James ; and had obtained a promise that he should meet him at York. Henry arrived according to appointment, and remained there during six days, but no James appeared. The priests, dreading Henry's influence with James on the subject of the Reformation, prevailed upon him to remain at home ; which he did, and sent a courteous apology. But the

* Cunningham's " Church History of Scotland," vol. i., p. 237 ; M'Crie's " Life of Knox," p. 17 ; D'Aubigné's " Calvin," vol. vi., p. 168 ; Wylie's " Protestantism," vol. iii., p. 479.

haughty revengeful English king was not to be so easily pacified. He conceived himself slighted and insulted, and vented threatenings and curses against the Scotch. **A border war** was the result. The priests instigated James to go to war without summoning to his banner the proscribed nobles. Bishops, priests, and their partisans were to form the army ; and when the king returned in triumph from the defeat of Henry, all those suspected of heresy should be seized and executed as a thank-offering for victory. But alas ! when James was waiting in Lochmaben Castle for the news of triumph, some of the fugitives arriving made known the total rout of his army on Solway Moss. His distress was unbounded. So great was his agony of mind he could hardly breathe, and only muttered some vague cries. The high-spirited monarch could bear no more. He had been deceived by that despicable man in whom he trusted, which disturbed him as much as the victory of the English.

In this state of despair he shut himself up in Falkland Palace, and the violence of his grief soon induced a slow fever. While rapidly sinking, intelligence was brought that his queen, who was at Linlithgow, had been delivered of a girl, afterwards Queen Mary. This was a fresh wound, as he had no son ; and feeling as if his family was extinct and his crown lost, he muttered an old saying : "It cam wi' a lass, and it will gang wi' a lass." Seven days afterwards the king died, on December 14th, 1542. When disrobing him, the dreadful proscription roll was found in his pocket. The nation then saw what a merciful providence had saved them from, and how narrow its escape had been from so fearful a catastrophe. The discovery helped not a little to increase the number of the Reformed, and to prepare the way for the downfall of a religion which was capable of conceiving such plans of cruelty and avarice.

The throne was now vacant, and "Cardinal Beaton lost no time in producing a document purporting to be the will of the deceased monarch, appointing him regent of the kingdom during the minority of the infant queen ; " but it was generally believed to be forged, and the **Earl of Arran** was peaceably established in the regency by the nobles. Thus it was, by the gracious overruling hand of God, the man whose name was first on the list of nobles marked for slaughter, was now at the head of the Government, and used by the same providence to place the Bible in every Scotchman's hand. The change produced in the political state of the kingdom by the death of James and the regency of Arran, was favourable to the Reformation.

The earl having formerly professed faith in the Reformed doctrines, was now surrounded with counsellors of the same opinions. It is deeply interesting to observe that, at this early stage of the Scottish Reformation, the very flower of the nobility and gentry were on its side. Not that we think of them all as true Christians ; but at that time the prospect of overturning the ancient religion was distant and uncertain, and they were taking a step which exposed their lives and fortunes to the most imminent hazard, so that we cannot attribute to them a lower motive than their personal convictions.

THE BIBLE RESTORED TO THE NATION.

In the month of March, 1543, an important step was taken by the Parliament toward the Reformation of the Church, by making it lawful for every subject in the realm to read the Holy Scriptures in his mother tongue. **Lord Maxwell,** who brought the matter before the lords of the articles, proposed that " It should be statute and ordained that it shall be lawful for all our sovereign lady's lieges to have the Holy Writ, to wit, the New Testament and Old, in the vulgar tongue, English or Scotch, of a good and true translation, and that they shall incur no crime for having and reading the same." The bishops, as we may suppose, protested loudly against this measure, but it was passed notwithstanding, and instructions given to the Clerk of Register to have it duly proclaimed at the market-cross ; and sent into all parts of the kingdom by order of the regent. This public act in favour of religious liberty was a signal triumph of truth over error. The priests began to cry out with one voice : " Heresy, heresy ! " and that the regent was the promoter of heresy.

"The victory," says Knox, " which Jesus Christ then won over the enemies of the truth was of no little importance. The trumpet of the Gospel gave at once a certain sound, from Wigtown to Inverness, from south to north. No small comfort was given to the souls, to the families, who till then durst not read the Lord's prayer or the ten commandments in English, through fear of being accused of heresy. The Bible, which had long lain hidden in some out of the way corner, was now openly placed on the tables of pious and well-informed men. The New Testament was indeed already widely circulated, but many of those who possessed it had shown themselves unworthy of it, never having read ten sentences in it through fear of man. Now they brought it, and would chop their familiars on the cheek with it. The knowledge of God was wonderfully increased by the reading of the sacred writings, and the Holy Spirit was given in great abundance to simple men." This important act of the Scottish Parliament was never repealed.*

Hitherto the Reformation had been advanced in Scotland by books imported from England and the continent ; but now the truth was disseminated, and the errors of Popery were exposed by books which issued from the Scottish press. The poets and

* D'Aubigné's " Calvin," vol. vi., p. 194 ; Cunningham, vol. i., p. 242 ; M'Crie, p. 20.

satirists were also busy. With the poet's usual license, they employed themselves in writing ballads, plays, and satires, on the ignorance and immoralities of the clergy, and the absurdities and superstitions of the Popish religion. Such compositions in the Scottish language were read with great avidity by the people, and operated powerfully in alienating the public mind from the Catholic religion.

GEORGE WISHART.

In the summer of 1544, shortly after Scotland had received the inestimable blessing of a free Bible, one of the most remarkable characters we meet with in ecclesiastical history appeared on the troubled scene. We refer to **George Wishart.** He was the son of Sir James Wishart of Pitarrow, an ancient and honourable family of the Mearns. He had fled from the persecuting spirit of the Bishop of Brechin in 1538, and spent about six years on the continent and at Cambridge, as a learner and a teacher. When he returned, he is said to have excelled all his countrymen in learning, especially in his knowledge of the Greek tongue. As a preacher, his eloquence was most persuasive ; his life irreproachable ; he was courteous and affable in manners ; his piety fervent ; his zeal and courage in the cause of truth were tempered with uncommon meekness, modesty, patience, and charity.

He immediately commenced preaching the doctrines of the Reformation in Montrose and Dundee. But his reputation had gone before him, and great crowds gathered to hear him. Following the Swiss method, he expounded in a connected series of discourses the doctrine of salvation, according to the Epistle to the Romans ; and his knowledge of Scripture, his eloquence, and his invectives against the falsehoods of Popery, moved the populace so mightily that in Dundee they attacked and destroyed the convents of the Franciscan and Dominican friars. So great was the excitement with the clamour of the priests and monks and the tumultuous state of the people, that the magistrates had to interfere, and Wishart prudently retired to the western counties, where his friends were all-powerful. Lennox, Cassillis, and Glencairn, were able to protect him, and secure him an entrance into every Parish Church. But Wishart, being essentially a man of peace, when any opposition was made to his preaching in the Church, he refused to allow force to be used, and retired to the market cross or the fields. But it was a needless precaution to shut the Church doors against Wishart, for no Church could have contained the thousands that flocked to hear him. He preached at Barr, Galston, Mauchline, and Ayr ; but as the hired assassins of Beaton were constantly on the watch for his life, he was generally surrounded with armed men.

THE PLAGUE IN DUNDEE.

Not long after Wishart had been driven from Dundee, **the plague** entered the town. Hearing of this, with great devotedness, he hurried thither, was unwearied in preaching the Gospel, visiting the sick, and seeking to prepare the dying for death. Those who were plague-stricken were kept outside the east gate, while the healthy were inside. To reach his audience on both sides, he mounted the gate, called the *Cowgate*, and, opening his Bible, read from Psalm 107 : " He sent His Word and healed them." The mercy of God in Christ, he assured them, was free to all, and whosoever turned to him truly would receive the blessing—a blessing which the malice of men could neither eik nor pair, add to nor diminish. Some of his hearers assured him—they were so comforted by his sermon—that they were ready to depart, and counted it more happy to go to Jesus than to remain behind. The people were greatly troubled lest " the mouth from which such sweetness flowed should be closed." They seemed to have a presentiment that danger was near, and so it was.

A priest named Wigton, hired by Cardinal Beaton to assassinate him, stood waiting at the foot of the steps by which Wishart must come down. A cloak thrown over him concealed the naked dagger which he held in his hand. But the keen eye of the evangelist, as he came down the steps, noticed the priest with his hand kept carefully under his gown, and read murder in his face. " My friend," said Wishart, " what would you do ? " at the same moment grasping the priest's hand, and snatching the weapon from him. The assassin fell at his feet and confessed his intention. " Deliver the traitor to us," cried the people, and they rushed on him ; but Wishart put his arms round the assassin, and said, " Whosoever troubles him troubles me ; for he has hurt me in nothing ; " and thus saved the life of him who sought his.*

Through the Lord's mercy the plague began to abate ; a new life was soon felt in the stricken city ; and Wishart exerted himself for the afflicted in organising measures for the distribution of food and medicine. While thus employed, he received a message from the Earl of Cassillis to meet him and some other friends from the west at Edinburgh for the purpose of having a public disputation with the bishop. He obeyed the summons, although he knew that Cardinal Beaton was bent upon his destruction, and that a cruel death awaited him. He arrived at Leith, but as that town is near Edinburgh, his friends entreated him to conceal himself for a day or two. This he could not endure. " What differ I from a dead man," he said, " except that I eat and drink ? To this time God has used my labours to the disclosing of darkness ; and now I lurk as a man that was ashamed,

---

* See Knox's " History of the Reformation," folio ed. p. 49.

and durst not show himself before men." "You know," said his friends, "the danger wherein you stand." "Let my God," he replied, "provide for me as best pleases Him."

Wishart began at once to preach in Leith; and afterwards proceeded to **East Lothian,** where he was entertained by the Lairds of Brunston, Longniddry, and Ormiston. While here, he preached at Musselburgh, Inveresk, Tranent, and Haddington. On these occasions he was surrounded by the armed retainers of his friends, and a sword was borne before him. It was here that **John Knox**—who was then a tutor in the family of Douglas of Longniddry—joined him. Previously to this, he had openly professed the evangelical doctrine; now he attached himself to Wishart, waited constantly on his person, and bore the sword before him. Wishart was highly pleased with the spirit and zeal of Knox, and seems to have presaged his future usefulness. After preaching at Haddington, he proceeded to Ormiston house, where he was to lodge. Knox insisted for liberty to accompany him, but the martyr dismissed him with this reply: "Nay, nay; return to your bairns"—meaning his pupils—"and God bless you. One is sufficient for a sacrifice."*

THE APPREHENSION AND MARTYRDOM OF WISHART.

Meantime Beaton had come to Edinburgh; and, hearing that Wishart was in the neighbourhood, resolved upon his instant apprehension. At midnight Ormiston House was surrounded by a troop of cavalry under the command of the Earl of Bothwell, who demanded Wishart. But neither promises not threatenings could induce the laird to deliver up his guest. Bothwell assured him on his honour that he would be perfectly safe with him, and that no power of the cardinal would be allowed to harm him. Ormiston was disposed to confide in this solemn promise, and told Wishart what had occurred. "Open the gates," he replied, "the blessed will of my God be done." But alas! Bothwell violated his pledge, and the victim of a faithless earl and a bloodthirsty priest was hurried from Edinburgh to St. Andrews, and thrown into prison.

The zeal of Arran in the cause of the Reformation by this time had greatly declined; and the cardinal, who had great influence over the mind of the weak and timid earl, was dominant in the nation. As it was contrary to the canon law for clergymen to meddle in matters of blood, Beaton asked the governor to appoint a lay judge, who might pronounce sentence of death upon Wishart, if found guilty of heresy. But Arran, irresolute as he was, refused to do this, and strongly urged delay. But Beaton was a man not to be hindered by canon law, or by the expostulations of the regent. Wishart was arraigned before a

* M'Crie, p. 21; Cunningham, vol. i., p. 248.

clerical tribunal, was found guilty of heresy, and condemned to the flames.

On the 1st of March, 1546, a scaffold was erected before the **Castle of St. Andrews,** and faggots of dried wood were piled around it. As the civil power refused to take part in the proceedings, the cardinal acted instead. His men were equipped with lances, swords, axes, and other warlike array ; and the guns of the castle were brought to bare upon the spot, lest Wishart's many friends should attempt to rescue him. Meanwhile the balcony of the castle was adorned with silken draperies and velvet cushions, that Beaton and other prelates might enjoy at their ease the spectacle of the pile, and the tortures of the holy sufferer. When all was ready, two deathsmen brought Wishart from his prison. He was dressed in black ; small bags of gunpowder were tied to various parts of his body ; his hands were firmly tied behind him ; a rope round his neck, and an iron chain round his waist to fasten him to the stake. He knelt down and prayed before the pile ; then he exhorted the people to love the Word of God, and suffer patiently and with a comfortable heart for the Word's sake, which was their undoubted salvation and everlasting comfort. " For the true Gospel," he added, " which was given to me by the grace of God, I suffer this day by men, not sorrowfully, but with a glad heart and mind. For this cause I was sent, that I should suffer this fire for Christ's sake. This grim fire I fear not ; I know surely that I shall sup with my Saviour Christ this night, for whom I suffer." And many other beautiful words did he say—according to Knox, Buchanan, and others.

When bound to the stake, he said : " Saviour of the world, have mercy on me ! Father of Heaven, into Thy hands I commit my spirit." The fire was lighted. The cardinal, **Dunbar,** and other prelates were on the balcony watching the progress of the fire, and the sufferings of the martyr. Wishart, catching sight of the cardinal and his courtiers, fixed his eyes on the cardinal, and said : " He who in such state, from that high place, feedeth his eyes with my torments, within a few days shall be hanged out at the same window, to be seen with as much ignominy as he now leaneth there with pride." The rope round his neck was now tightened, so that he spoke no more, and the fire reduced his body to ashes.

THE DEATH OF CARDINAL BEATON.

The death of Wishart produced a powerful impression all over Scotland, and excited feelings of the most diverse character. Churchmen extolled Beaton as the great champion of Rome, and the defender of the priesthood. Piety wept over the ashes of the martyr without a thought of revenge. But there were men of birth, without sharing Wishart's views, who declared openly there must be life for life : the liberties of the subject were in danger when the tyrant could set aside the authority of the regent and suppress the voice of the people. A conspiracy was formed against his life ; and a small but determined band—some of whom were instigated by resentment for private injuries ; others were animated by a desire to revenge his cruelties, and deliver their country from his oppression—**broke into the cardinal's apartments** in the Castle of St. Andrews, beat down the barricades with which he had attempted to defend his bedroom door, and putting him instantly to death, hung out his naked and mangled body over the window, as Wishart had predicted. They then seized the castle, dismissed the household servants unharmed, and sent off a messenger to the English court to inform Henry of their success. It is well known that there was nothing for which the English monarch was more anxious than the death of Beaton. He had been the great obstacle to the accomplishment of Henry's favourite project—the uniting of the two crowns by a marriage between the infant queen and his son, Prince Edward. Some say the conspirators were in the pay of England.*

THE RESULTS OF CARDINAL BEATON'S DEATH.

The murder of the cardinal-primate was followed by results the most important. It removed from the head of affairs the most powerful and unscrupulous enemy of the Reformation, and the **greatest defender of Romanism** in Scotland. Like Wolsey, he was all but a king. His government was characterised by political intrigue, energy, and resolution ; but his one main object was the persecution of the saints, the extinguishing of the Reformation, and the definite triumph of Rome. But the work of God's Spirit needed not the assistance of the assassin. The Christian life and martyrdom of Patrick Hamilton and George Wishart contributed far more powerfully to the advancement of the work of God in Scotland than the violent death of its enemy. The faith, the constancy, and the serenity of the martyrs, rose far above the ferocity of their persecutors, and through that instinct, which impels the human conscience to rise against injustice, and incline to the side of the oppressed, numbers were added to the ranks of the Reformed. One of the mistakes of the early Reformers, to which we have repeatedly referred, was their trusting to the protection of princes ; but the Scotch Reformers had to learn through a long period of suffering that their strength lay in an arm mightier far than the kings of the earth, which alone could give victory to the weak and defenceless. Hence their great idea was *Christ as King* ; and the motto on the banners of the Covenanters was, " **Christ's Crown and Covenant.**"

* See " Encyclopaedia Britannica," vol. xix., p. 731 ; Cunningham, vol. i., p. 251 ; Tytler's " History of Scotland," vol. iv., p 372.

"The new life," says D'Aubigné, "which sprang up in the sixteenth century was everywhere the same, but nevertheless it bore a certain special character in each of the countries in which it appeared. At Wittemberg it was to man that Christian thought especially attached itself—to man fallen, but regenerated and justified by faith. At Geneva it was to God, to His sovereignty and His grace. In Scotland it was to Christ—Christ as Saviour through death, but above all as King, who governs and keeps His people, independent of human power." While we think the Genevese historian very correct in his estimate of the character of the new life in the different countries, we must also add, that Christ is nowhere spoken of in Scripture as the King of the Church, but everywhere as the King of the Jews. He is spoken of as the head of the Church—of His body the Church, and as Head over all things to the Church. A king gives the idea of subjects, but as the Church is One with Christ—His body and His bride, He is never spoken of as her King. He is a King, of course, and as such He will reign when "the kingdoms of this world shall become the kingdoms of our Lord and of His Christ." There are three ways in which the glory of God will be revealed by Christ : 1, In grace, as when on earth and since then. 2, In government. This will be in the Millennium, when the saints will reign with Christ a thousand years. 3, In glory—also connected with government. This will be for ever. "For all the promises of God in Him are yea, and in Him, amen, unto the glory of God by us" (2 Cor. 1. 20 ; John 1. 17 ; Rev. 20. 6 ; 21. 1-8).

JOHN KNOX.

The vacant See of St. Andrews was soon filled by John Hamilton, Abbot of Paisley, and brother to the regent. But although he did not equal his predecessor in vigour of mind, he equalled him in the unrelenting zeal with which he pursued all who favoured the Reformation ; so that the persecution did not abate in the absence of Beaton. The conspirators who had seized and held the castle, welcomed within its walls all who were in danger of their lives from having embraced the new doctrines. They were soon joined by many adherents, both political and religious ; and the place was garrisoned by a band of determined men, who bade defiance to the regent and his brother the archbishop. Among those to whom they opened their gates, the most noted was **John Knox,** the great advocate and supporter of the Reformation.

This remarkable man, whose name has long been a household word in Scotland, and whose future career was connected with so many great events, was now forty years old. He was born, according to the prevailing opinion, at the village of Giffard, near Haddington, in 1505. It seems his parents were in the middle rank of rural life, and wealthy enough to give him a learned education ; and had probably destined their son for the Church. From the grammar school of his native town, he passed at the age of sixteen to the University of Glasgow, where the celebrated John Mair was then principal. It is said that he distinguished himself in philosophy and scholastic theology, and took priest's orders previous to his having attained the regular canonical age. After leaving college, he passes out of view, and little is known of his history till we find him in the company of Wishart, immediately before his martyrdom.*

KNOX'S CALL TO THE MINISTRY.

The Reformer was no doubt warmly welcomed by the party inside the castle, and earnestly entreated to become one of their preachers. These solicitations he steadfastly resisted, " alleging that he could not run where God had not sent him." When he received a unanimous invitation from the whole congregation, and was solemnly pressed by Mr. Rough, a preacher, not to refuse God's call as he would avoid His heavy displeasure, Knox burst into tears, and withdrew himself to his chamber. He had now very different thoughts as to the importance of the ministerial office, from those he had entertained when invested with priest's orders. The charge of declaring " the whole counsel of God, keeping nothing back," however ungrateful it might be to his hearers, with all the consequences to which the **preachers of the Protestant doctrines** were then exposed, filled his mind with anxiety and fear. He evidently passed through much conflict of mind on this occasion ; for though he possessed great strength of character, being naturally bold, upright, and independent, he was thoroughly honest, conscientious, and modest. But when he felt satisfied that he had the call of God to engage in His work, he resolved to undertake it with all its responsibilities, and say, with the apostle : " But none of these things move me, neither count I my life dear unto myself, so that I might finish my course with joy, and the ministry, which I have received of the Lord Jesus, to testify the Gospel of the grace of God " (Acts 20. 24).

He commenced his labours as a preacher with his characteristic boldness, and was greatly blessed both to the garrison and to the inhabitants of the town. In his **first sermon** in the Parish Church of St. Andrews, he undertook to prove that the Pope of Rome was the man of sin, the Antichrist, the Babylonish harlot spoken of in Scripture. He struck at the root of Popery that they might destroy the whole system. During the few months that he preached at St. Andrews, a great number of the inhabitants, besides the garrison in the castle, renounced Popery, and made

* M'Crie's " Life of Knox ; " Tytler's " History of Scotland," vol. iv., p. 374.

profession of the Protestant faith, by partaking of the Lord's Supper after the Reformed mode in Scotland. But his useful labours were soon interrupted.

MARY OF GUISE AND THE FRENCH FLEET.

After the death of Beaton, the queen-dowager, Mary of Guise, sister to Henry, the cruel duke who fought against the Huguenots and directed the massacre of St. Bartholomew's Eve, was openly opposed to the Reformation; and, like her family, was entirely devoted to France and Rome. Soon after the regent had completely failed to reduce the Castle of St. Andrews, a French fleet of sixteen armed galleys, commanded by Leo Strozzi, appeared in the bay. The vessels took up their line, so as at full tide completely to command the outworks towards the sea, while the forces of Arran besieged it by land. A breach was soon effected, and within less than a week a flag of truce was seen approaching. Thus fell the Castle of St. Andrews; and all in it, including **Knox,** were put **on board the galleys** and conveyed to France. The terms of capitulation, it is said, were violated; and at the solicitations of the Pope, the Scottish queen, and clergy, the principal gentlemen were incarcerated in Rouen, Cherbourg, Brest, and Mont St. Michel. Knox, with a few others, was confined on board the galleys, loaded with chains, and exposed to all the indignities with which Papists were accustomed to treat those whom they regarded as heretics.

During their captivity, threatenings and violence were employed to induce the prisoners to change their religion, or at least to countenance the Popish worship. But so great was their abhorrence of that system, that not a single person of the whole company, on land or water, could be induced in the smallest degree to join them. Mass was frequently said within their hearing, and on such occasions they were threatened with torture if they did not give the usual signs of reverence; but instead of complying, they covered their heads as soon as the service began. One day a fine painted image of the Virgin was brought into one of the galleys, and a Scottish prisoner—probably Knox—was desired to give it the kiss of adoration. He refused, saying that such idols were accursed, and he would not touch it. "But you shall," replied one of the officers, at the same time forcing it towards his mouth. Upon this the prisoner seized the image, and throwing it into the water, said, "Let oor Ledie noo save hersel; sche is licht eneuch, let hir leirne to swyme." The officers with some difficulty saved their goddess from the waves; and the prisoners were not again troubled with such importunities.*

The Lord had no doubt important lessons to teach His beloved

---

* Knox's "History," folio, p. 83; M'Crie, p. 34.

servant and his associates by their rigorous confinement. To escape the persecution of Hamilton, he was obliged to conceal himself, and to remove from place to place, to provide for his safety. Under these circumstances we need not be surprised that he took refuge in the castle. Nevertheless, it was like casting in his lot with the assassins of the cardinal, and with them he reaped the consequences. He was detained nineteen months a galley-slave in French waters. Not one of his associates suffered death !

By what means the prisoners obtained their liberty, historians are not agreed. Dr. M'Crie very reasonably concludes, " That the French court having procured the consent of the Parliament of Scotland to the marriage of Queen Mary to the Dauphin, and obtained possession of her person, felt no longer any inclination to avenge the quarrels of the Scottish clergy."

JOHN KNOX REGAINS HIS LIBERTY.

Upon regaining his liberty, **Knox repaired to England,** emaciated in body, but vigorous and unshaken in mind. The reputation which he had gained by his preaching, and his late sufferings, recommended him to the English court, and he was chosen one of the chaplains to Edward VI. He was offered the living of All-hallows in London, which he refused as he did not agree with the English liturgy. The early death of Edward, and the accession of Mary, compelled him to flee for his life. He travelled through France to Switzerland, and after visiting the most noted divines of the Helvetic Church, he settled in Geneva.

The celebrated **John Calvin** was then in the zenith of his reputation and usefulness. Knox was affectionately received by him as a refugee from Scotland, and an intimate friendship was soon formed between them. The two great Reformers of that day were now together, nearly of the same age, very similar in their sentiments as to doctrine and the government of the Church, and not unlike as to the more prominent features of their character. " Knox was a rough, unbending, impassioned, impetuous man, but full of humour. Calvin was calm, severe, often irritable, but never impassioned ; rising in pure intellect above all his compeers, like Mont Blanc among the mountains, touching the very heavens, yet shrouded in eternal snows. There is no doubt but that Calvin exercised a great influence upon the mind of his fellow-Reformer. Knox was but beginning his work ; Calvin's work was done. Knox was but rising into fame ; Calvin was giving laws to a large section of Christendom."*

But no friendships, no prospect of personal safety, no sphere of usefulness, could banish from his mind the thoughts of his persecuted countrymen. He was constantly writing letters to

* Cunningham, vol. i., p. 308.

encourage, and papers to strengthen them, in the truth of God ; and he was no doubt well supplied with information as to all that was going on.

KNOX RETURNS TO SCOTLAND.

In the year 1555, after an absence of eight years, Knox again visited his native land. He was entertained by James Syme, a respectable burgess of Edinburgh, in whose house the friends of the Reformation assembled to talk over their prospect and plans. Up till this time many of the warm friends of Reform had attended mass, and were not outwardly separate from the communion of the Romish Church ; but the earnest uncompromising discourses of Knox convinced them of their error, and decided them to participate no longer in the Romish worship. Soon after this the Lord's Supper was celebrated according to the Protestant form ; and in this united act the foundations were laid of the coming Reformed Church of Scotland.

Among the nobles who now gathered round the Protestant standard were Lord Lorne, Lord Erskine, Lord James Stewart, the Earl of Marischall, the Earl of Glencairn, John Erskine of Dun, and William Maitland of Lithington. These were diligent in attending the sermons of Knox, and helping him in his work. With such a body-guard the Reformer became free and indefatigable in preaching, not only in the capital, but in the provinces. In the winter of 1555-6 he preached in Kyle, Cunningham, Angusshire, and other places, imparting with God's blessing, new life to the Reform movement, and powerfully consolidating the good work in many souls. Rumours of all this work flew through the country, the clergy were alarmed, his apprehension was determined upon, and Knox perceiving that his continued presence in the country would draw down a fresh storm of persecution on the infant community, prudently withdrew to Geneva.

THE FIRST COVENANT.

From this period the **progress of the Reformation** in many parts of Scotland was rapid and decisive. The brief visit of the Reformer proved to be of immense service to the cause of Reform. Nobles, barons, burgesses, and peasants, separated from the communion of Rome, and assembled for the reading of the Word and prayer. According to the Presbyterian form, they could not have the sacraments administered without a duly ordained minister ; but these small meetings paved the way for the more complete organisation. The next step of the nobles was the framing of what is known in Church history as the **First Covenant,** and the framers are called the " lords of the congregation." In this covenant they promised before " the majesty of God and His congregation, to apply their whole power, substance, and their very lives, to maintain, set forward, and establish the most blessed Word of God and His congregation," etc., etc. This third day of December, 1557. God called to witness : Earls of Argyle, Glencairn, Morton, Lord of Lorne, Erskine of Dun.

These measures alarmed the clergy. They saw that their downfall was near, unless strong and decided means were taken to prevent it. But they had only one weapon—the flames of martyrdom ; and these were speedily kindled. **Walter Mill,** a godly old man, was accused of heresy, and burnt alive at St. Andrews, August 28th, 1558. As he stood at the stake, he addressed the people in these words : " As for me, I am four-score and two years old, and could not live long by course of nature ; but a hundred better shall rise out of the ashes of my bones. I trust in God that I shall be the last that shall suffer death in Scotland for this cause." He had been a parish priest near Montrose, but suffered as a true believer in the Lord Jesus Christ.

The clergy were at their wits' end. Martyrdoms only increased the number of Protestants. The people were rapidly leaving the mass, and openly uniting with the Reformers. It was now perfectly clear that unless the Papists could strike a decisive blow, they must surrender. The friars appealed to the bishops, and the bishops to the civil power. The queen dowager, the bigoted Catholic of the House of Lorraine, now openly avowed herself on the side of Romanism. Hitherto she had been playing a part between the bishops and the lords of the congregation. Now she issued a proclamation prohibiting all persons from preaching or dispensing the sacraments without authority from the bishops. The Reformed preachers disobeyed the proclamation. They were summoned to appear before her at Stirling, and answer to a charge of heresy and rebellion. The lords of the congregation interfered, and the queen, amazed at their firmness, agreed to delay the prosecution until she had examined the affair more seriously.

KNOX'S FINAL RETURN TO SCOTLAND.

In the midst of these stirring and threatening times a powerful leader was wanted. A deputation was sent to Geneva, to entreat **Knox to return** ; and on May 2nd, 1559, he arrived at Leith. The news of his arrival fell like a thunderbolt on the Papal party. A royal proclamation was immediately issued, declaring Knox a rebel and an outlaw. But these proclamations were now little heeded. Chancing to pass through Perth soon after, he preached one of his vehement sermons against the idolatry of the mass, and the worship of images. The people were ripe for such a discourse, and greatly moved by it, but quietly dispersed when it was over. A priest, remaining behind, to show his contempt for the doctrine which had just been delivered, uncovered a rich altar-piece, decorated with images, began to say mass.   A boy standing near shouted, " Idolatry ! " The priest in anger struck the boy ; and he retaliated by throwing a stone, which, missing the priest, broke one of the images.   A few idle persons who were loitering in the Church, sympathised with the boy, and in the course of a few moments the altar, images, crucifixes, and all the Church ornaments were torn down and trampled under foot.   The noise soon collected a mob ; the excitement became great, and some one shouted, " To the monasteries," and in a short time the monasteries of the Black and Grey Friars were in ruins.   The excited mob next bent their way to the Abbey of the Charterhouse ; and soon nothing was left of that magnificent structure but the bare walls.   The magistrates of the town and the preachers hastened to the scene of the riot as soon as they heard of it, but neither the persuasion of the one nor the authority of the other could calm the tempest.*

POPULAR TUMULTS.

The **work of demolition**, which was begun in a frenzy of popular rage at Perth, rapidly extended to St. Andrews, Cupar, and other places in Fife ; and to Scone, Cambaskenneth, Linlithgow, Stirling, Edinburgh, etc., etc.   It was upon the monasteries, chiefly, that the violence of the popular hatred expended itself.   They were in evil repute among the people, as nests of idleness, gluttony, and wickedness.   Tradition has ascribed to Knox the party-cry : " Pull down the nests, and the rooks will flee away."   And in a single day those nests of impurity and hypocrisy which had stood for ages were ravaged and swept away.

The queen, violently incensed at these outrages, vowed that she would raze the city of Perth to the ground, and sow its foundations with salt, in sign of perpetual desolation.   She collected an army of considerable force, and appeared in its neighbourhood in a few days.   The citizens shut the gates, and sent letters to the queen regent, the nobility, and " to the generation of Antichrist, the pestilent prelates, and their shavelings within Scotland."   These letters proved that the lords of the congregation were prepared to meet her.   Seeing the determination and force of the people, she was artful enough to come to terms of peace, and accomplish what she could by dissimulation.

A war of religion now began.   It is always distressing, and deeply to be deplored, to see Reformers taking up the carnal weapons of the world in their defence, and for the moment laying aside the sword of the Spirit.   But the cry to arms by the queen led the Reformers to utter the same cry in self-defence ;

* M'Crie, p. 127 ; Wylie, vol. iii., p. 491.

and in that age they thought that it was as lawful to follow the example of Joshua and David as of Peter and Paul. But the Lord in mercy interposed, and removed the queen dowager by death. This took place in the Castle of Edinburgh, on the 10th of June, 1560. Her decease was the **death-blow to French influence** in Scottish affairs, and happily resulted in the emancipation of the nation from a foreign yoke. The way was now fully open for the establishment of the Reformation. The nation, through the wonderful preaching of Knox during the previous fifteen months, was ready to throw off the Papal yoke, and abolish its jurisdiction in the land.

THE PAPACY ABOLISHED BY ACT OF PARLIAMENT.

Parliament was convened early in the month of August, 1560, and the voice of the three estates assembled, was to determine the question of religion. All men looked forward to this convention as one of the most important that had ever been held since Scotland became a nation. We can only give the results. The estates of the realm authoritatively decreed the suppression of the Roman hierarchy, and the establishment of the Protestant faith. A short confession, or summary, of Christian doctrine, had been drawn up by Knox and his associates, which was read in audience of the whole Parliament, and by the estates thereof ratified and approved, " as wholesome and sound doctrine, grounded on the infallible Word of God." The great victory was won. The enthusiasm of the assembly was at the highest, and the venerable Lord Lindsay rose and declared that he could say with Simeon of old : " Lord, now lettest thou Thy servant depart in peace, for mine eyes have seen Thy salvation."

Immediately after the ground had been cleared for the erection of a new ecclesiastical edifice, Knox was ready with the plan of the Reformed Church in what is known as " **The First Book of Discipline.**" The constitution of the Church, as set forth in this symbolic book, is strictly Presbyterian. It recognises four classes of ordinary and permanent office-bearers—the minister, the doctor, the elder, and the deacon. 1, Ministers, who preach to the congregation. 2, Doctors, who expound Scripture to students in seminaries and universities. 3, Elders, who are associated with the ministers in ruling the congregation. 4, Deacons, who manage money matters, and care for the poor. Then there are four courts—the Kirk-session, the Presbytery, the Provincial Synod, and the General Assembly.

The success of the Reform movement was now decided. Parliament had declared Protestantism to be the national faith, and Knox was ready with the fashion of the new Church and the creed of its members. But he entirely overlooks—like all the other Reformers—the doctrine of the Church of God, as taught by our Lord and His apostles, and frames a constitution according to human wisdom, though he no doubt thought it was in accordance with the Word of God.   The consequences of this mistake, as we have already seen, are set forth in the Lord's address to the Church in Sardis.   But we cannot speak too highly of those thirty-four years of faithful testimony to the truth at an immense expense of suffering and blood.   And the Lord greatly blessed the preaching of the Gospel.   Nearly the whole national mind was gained over to the new teaching during that period, and the altars and idols of superstition were destroyed throughout the land amidst the acclamations of the people.*

From this time, down to the **Revolution in 1688,** the Presbyterians were greatly oppressed and persecuted by the faithless and deceitful Stuarts, who wished to establish Episcopacy instead of Presbytery in Scotland.   But the history of these stirring times falls not within our plan.

We must now briefly glance at the effects of the Reformation in England.

* For many interesting details of this period, see Dr. Lorimer's " History of the Scottish Reformation ; " Spottiswood's " History," 3 vols.; Wylie's " Protestantism ; " M'Crie's " Life of Knox ; " Knox's " Original History."

CHAPTER LIV

The Reformation in England

FROM the times of Wycliffe, the great English Reformer, the Lord preserved a remnant in England, who witnessed for the truth, and who testified against the doctrines and superstition of Rome. We found many of the descendants of the Lollards, or followers of Wycliffe, in the western districts of Scotland, who were prepared to receive the new doctrines of the continental divines. So it was in England. There were many, very many, among the humbler classes, who still held to the doctrines taught by their great chief ; but they were compelled to hide themselves among the humbler ranks of the people, and to hold their meetings in secret. " They lived unknown, till persecution dragged them into the light, and chased them up to Heaven." The least whisper of dissent from Holy Mother Church was visited with the severest penalties. As an instance of this, six men and a woman were brought to the **stake at Coventry,** in the year 1519, for teaching their children the Lord's Prayer, the ten commandments, and the apostles' creed in the vulgar tongue.

Such were the scenes of daily occurrence in England, shortly before the Reformation. The priests were, as the apostle says, like " grievous wolves, not sparing the flock." **Richard Hun,** an honest tradesman in London, though still in the Romish communion, was a diligent student of his Bible, and a truly pious man. At the death of one of his children, the priest required of him an exhorbitant fee, which Hun refused to pay, and for which he was summoned before the legate's court. Animated by that public spirit which characterises his countrymen, he felt indignant that an Englishman should be cited before a foreign tribunal, and lodged an accusation against the priest under the act of *Præmunire.* Such boldness—most extraordinary at that time —exasperated the clergy beyond all bounds. " Such boldness," they said, " must be severely checked, or every layman will dare to resist the priest." Hun was accused of heresy, and thrown into the Lollards' Tower of St. Paul's, and left there with an iron collar round his neck, attached to which was a heavy chain which he could scarcely drag across his prison floor.

When brought before his judges no proof of heresy could be brought against him, and it was observed with astonishment " that he had his beads in prison with him." His persecutors were now in a great dilemma. To set him at liberty would proclaim their own defeat ; and who could stop the Reformers if the

priests were to be so easily resisted ? Three of their agents
undertook to extricate the holy fathers from their difficulties.
At midnight those men, one of them the bellringer, conducted
the others with a light to Hun's cell. They fell upon him,
strangled him, and then, putting his own belt round his neck,
they suspended the lifeless body by an iron ring in the wall ; and
thus the turnkey found him in the morning. "The priests have
murdered him," was the general cry in London, and demanded
an inquest to be held on his body. Marks of violence being found
on his person, and traces of blood in his cell, the jury concluded
that he had been murdered ; besides, two of the three criminals
were so conscience-stricken that they confessed their guilt. The
priests were now in a greater dilemma than ever. What was to
be done ? This would be a serious blow to them unless they
could somehow justify themselves. The house of Hun was
searched, a Bible was found in it, and it was Wycliffe's translation. This was enough. He was condemned as a heretic, his
body was dug up and burnt in Smithfield. But all this rather
exposed than screened their guilt. The case was brought before
Parliament ; Hun's character was vindicated, the priests were
charged with the crime of murder, and restitution of his goods
had to be made to his family. But through the influence of
Wolsey the criminals were not punished.

THE MARTYRDOM OF JOHN BROWN.

Although the clergy had been unfortunate in the affair of Hun,
and exposed themselves to shame and reproach, they were by no
means discouraged in their cruel course of persecution. There
were many sufferers and martyrs about this time, according to
our English martyrologist.

In the spring of 1517—the year in which Luther nailed his
theses to the Church door—**John Brown** of Ashford, an intelligent
Christian, happened to seat himself beside a priest in the Gravesend passage-boat. "Dost thou know who I am ? " said the
priest, in the most haughty manner. "No, sir," said Brown.
"Well then, thou must know that I am a priest ; you are too
near me." "Indeed, sir ! Are you a parson, or vicar, or lady's
chaplain ? "   "No ; I am a *soul-priest* ; I sing mass to save
souls." "Do you, sir," rejoined Brown ; "that is well done.
And can you tell me where you find the soul when you begin the
mass ? " "I cannot," said the priest. "And where do you leave
it, pray, when the mass is ended ? "   "I do not know," said the
priest. "What ! " continued Brown, "you do not know where
you find the soul or where you leave it, and yet you say that you
save it ! " "Go thy ways," said the priest angrily ; "thou art
a heretic, and I will be even with thee."

As soon as the priest landed at Gravesend, he rode off to

Canterbury, and denounced Brown to the archbishop. In three days after this conversation, as Brown sat at dinner with his family, the officers of Warham entered, dragged the man from his house, tied him on horseback, and rode off quickly. The heart-rending cries of his wife and children were of no avail. The primate's officers were too well acquainted with such tears and cries to be moved to pity. Brown was thrown into prison, and there he lay forty days, during which time his family knew not where he was, or what had been done to him. At the end of that time he was brought up for trial before the Archbishop of Canterbury, and the Bishop of Rochester. He was required to retract his " blasphemy." " Christ was once offered," said Brown, " to bear the sins of many, and it is by this sacrifice we are saved, not by the repetitions of the priests." At this reply the archbishop made a sign to the executioners, who immediately took off the shoes and stockings of the pious Christian, and placed his bare feet on a pan of burning coals. This heartless cruelty was in direct violation of the English laws, which forbade torture to be inflicted on any subject of the crown, but the clergy thought themselves above the laws. " Confess the efficacy of the mass," cried the two bishops to the sufferer. " If I deny my Lord upon earth," he replied, " He will deny me before His Father in Heaven." The flesh was burnt off the soles of his feet even to the bones, and still John Brown remained firm and unshaken. The bishops feeling their utter weakness in the presence of Divine strength, ordered him to be **burnt alive**—the last act of human cruelty.

The martyr was led back to Ashford. The servant of the family happening to be out when he arrived, saw him, and running back, rushed into the house, exclaiming, " I have seen him ! I have seen him ! " His poor wife hastened to see him. He was so tightly bound in the stocks that he could hardly move even his head, in speaking to his wife. She sat down beside him : his features were changed by suffering ; her tears and distress must remain for ever untold. He thanked the Lord for sustaining him under the torture, and for enabling him to confess his faith in the blessed Lord Jesus ; and exhorted his good wife, Elizabeth, to continue as she had begun—to love the Lord, for He is good, and to bring up the children for Him.

The following morning, being Whitsunday, he was taken out of the stocks and bound to the stake. His wife, his daughter Alice, and his other children, with some friends, gathered round the faggots to receive his farewell blessing. He sang a hymn while the flames were playing around him, but feeling that the fire had nearly done its work, he breathed out the prayer of his Lord and Master : " Father, into Thy hands I commend my spirit," adding, " Thou hast redeemed me, O God of truth."

The martyr was now silent ; but redoubled cries of anguish rent the air. His wife and daughter seemed as if they would lose their senses. The spectators moved with compassion, deeply sympathised with the distracted family, but scowled with indignation on the executioners. "Come," said Chilton, a brutal officer, "let us cast the heretic's children into the fire, lest they, too, should become heretics." So saying, he rushed towards Alice, but the maiden ran off, screaming with fright, and escaped the ruffian."*

Such were the servants of the archbishop, and such the heart-rending scenes in England, down to the time of Luther, and the reign of Henry VIII, to which we must now turn.

HENRY VIII.

From the rival claims of York and Lancaster the succession to the English throne had been a matter of fierce contention for many years. The struggle of the opposing factions amongst the nobility, known in history by the term " **The Wars of the Roses,**" broke out about the time when Gutenberg's labours at the printing press began, and greatly hindered the peaceful triumph of the arts and literature. The country was deeply affected in all its interests by these civil wars. Commerce was reduced to its lowest state ; ignorance covered the land, and true piety had scarcely any existence, except amongst the despised and persecuted Lollards.†

Such was the condition of things when **Henry VIII** ascended the throne in 1509. Uniting in his person the claims of the rival houses of York and Lancaster, he received the devotion of both. Everything seemed to favour the young monarch, and give hope of a peaceful and popular reign. His father, Henry VII, had successfully founded the Tudor dynasty, left him with a people outwardly quiet, and an exchequer overflowing with what would now amount to ten or twelve millions of gold. He was young—about eighteen—said to be "majestic in port, eminently handsome, and rioting in health and spirits." His manners were frank and open, and being most accomplished in all the manly exercises of the time, he became the idol of the nation. His marriage and coronation were followed by a constant succession of gaieties and amusements on the most expensive plan, which rapidly reduced the treasures accumulated by his parsimonious father.

Henry had also a taste for letters. He delighted in the society of scholars, and lavished upon them his patronage. Having been destined by his father for the Church, and educated accordingly, his naturally vigorous mind had been greatly improved

* For details, see Foxe's " Book of Martyrs," vol. ii., folio ed. pp. 7-14.
† " Universal History," vol. vi., p. 27.

by education, so that in mental accomplishments he far exceeded the princes of/ his age. The new study of revived classical literature had for some time been much cultivated in England. This was not the Reformation, but it exposed the ignorance of the clergy, and prepared the public mind for the approaching change. The priests were now as opposed to the scholars as to the heretics. They railed against the invention of printing, the manufacture of paper, and the introduction of such heathenish words as nominatives and adverbs : they were all of Satan, and sources of heresy—but, as the king favoured the most illustrious of scholars, it was not so easy to have them murdered or burnt as poor Hun and Brown.

But of all the learned men now in England, the one they hated most was **Erasmus.** He could not endure—as we have already seen in the course of our history—the greed, the gluttony, and the ignorance of the monks. He had often levelled against them his keenest shafts, and his most pungent satire. He had also indulged in some of his witty sarcasms against the Bishop of St. Asaph ; and, though he was a favourite at court, he must be banished, if he cannot be burnt. The bishops set to work accordingly. Erasmus, seeing their intentions, and true to his nature, left the country. This event was overruled by a gracious providence in the most blessed way. He went straight to Basle, and published his **Greek and Latin New Testament.** Copies were straightway despatched to London, Oxford, and Cambridge, where they were received with great enthusiasm. The priests had thought to maintain the darkness by driving away the master of letters, but his departure was the means of restoring to England the light of eternal truth—the pure Gospel of the Lord Jesus Christ. Before Luther had posted up his theses, the Holy Scriptures were circulated in England. Thus was the Reformation chiefly accomplished by the Word of God. There the Person and glory of Christ are revealed as the Saviour of sinners ; salvation through faith in His precious blood, and oneness with Him through the indwelling of the Holy Ghost.

."The Reformation in England," says D'Aubigné, " perhaps to a greater extent than that of the continent, was **effected by the Word of God.** Those great individualities we met with in Germany, Switzerland, and France—men like Luther, Zwingle, and Calvin—do not appear in England ; but Holy Scripture is widely circulated. What brought light into the British Isles subsequently to the year 1517, and on a more extended scale after the year 1526, was the Word—the invisible power—of the living God. The religion of the Anglo-Saxon race—a race called more than any other to circulate the oracles of God throughout the world—is particularly distinguished for its Biblical character."*

* " History of the Reformation," vol. v., p. 199.

THOMAS WOLSEY.

Just as everything seemed tending to the rapid advancement of the Reformation, a powerful priest, **Thomas Wolsey,** appeared on the scene, who, for a time, hindered its progress.

This remarkable man, according to tradition, was the son of a wealthy butcher in Ipswich, and born in the year 1471. He seems to have been designed for the Church from an early age, and was trained at Magdalen College, Oxford. About the year 1500 he was appointed chaplain to Henry VII through the influence of Fox, Bishop of Winchester. The diligence and capacity for business which he displayed soon attracted the attention of the old king, who rewarded him with the valuable deanery of Lincoln. He was equally successful iu gaining the favour of the son, Henry VIII. Although twenty years older than his new master, he adapted himself to his youth and all its tendencies. He was no ascetic, though a priest ; and vice, it is said, never hung her head in his presence. He was so clever, accommodating, and unscrupulous, that he could be gay or grave, as best served the purpose of his ambition. He gradually gained such an influence over the mind of Henry, that he virtually became the ruler of the realm. Wealth, honours, offices— civil and ecclesiastical—flowed in upon him rapidly. He was created Bishop of Tournay, and raised to the Sees of Lincoln and York in the year 1514, and the following year he received a cardinal's hat, with the office of Lord Chancellor.

His enormous wealth, gathered from so many sources, both at home and abroad, enabled him to maintain his elevated position with more than **regal splendour.** "Whenever he appeared in public, two priests, the tallest and comeliest that could be found, carried before him huge silver crosses, one to mark his dignity as archbishop, the other as Papal legate. Chamberlains, gentlemen, pages, serjeants, chaplains, choristers, clerks, cupbearers, cooks, and other domestics—to the number of more than five hundred—among whom were nine or ten lords, and the stateliest yeomen of the country—filled his palace. He generally wore a dress of scarlet velvet and silk, with hat and gloves of the same colour. His shoes were embroidered with gold and silver, inlaid with pearls and precious stones." But with all this pomp and grandeur, his capacity for business was great, and seemed to enlarge with the elevation of his rank, and the increase of his offices. He patronised learning, sympathised with the literary inclinations of Henry, while in matters of state he was the most profound counsellor in the English court, though too often swayed by his absorbing ambition.*

Thus it was permitted of the Lord that the Church of Rome, the mother of harlots, should be illustrated in the man who ruled

* D'Aubigné, vol. v., p. 184 ; Wylie, vol. iii., p. 355 ; " Universal History," vol. vi., p. 32.

in Church and State, and was arrayed in all the worldly glory spoken of in Revelation 17. It was a kind of Papacy in England : he only wanted the triple crown ; and the English people were to witness the kind of glory the Papacy ever valued, before it sank and disappeared from the land.

THE REFORMATION BEGUN.

The elevation of such a prince of Rome, who was now to take a share in domestic and foreign politics, even greater than that of Henry himself, could not be favourable to the Reformation. The priests, emboldened by this display of Papal power, determined to make a stand against the scholars of the Reformation. But it was too late to effect much, though heresy was still severely punished. The eve of the Reformation had arrived. Men's minds were disturbed ; the Papacy had lost its traditional hold upon the conscience and affections of the people, and the New Testament which Erasmus had given to England was doing a greater work than all the teachers or doctors in the land. Names so dear to every Christian's heart, and so famous in English history now come before us.

Thomas Bilney, a student at Trinity College, Cambridge, hearing some friends speak one day of the New Testament of Erasmus, made haste to procure a copy. It was strictly forbidden by the Catholics, but was sold secretly. Bilney opened the book which he had been told was the source of all heresy— his eyes caught these words : " This is a faithful saying, and worthy of all acceptation, that Christ Jesus came into the world to save sinners, of whom I am chief." He laid down his book, and meditated on the astonishing words. " What," he exclaimed, " St. Paul the chief of sinners, and yet St. Paul is sure of being saved ! " The Holy Spirit shed a Divine light on the sacred page, revealed Christ and His salvation to his soul, so that he at once began to preach Christ to others. He was the blessed instrument in God's hands in bringing many to the knowledge of Christ, among whom was the celebrated Hugh Latimer.

William Tyndale, from the valley of the Severn—who afterwards translated the Bible into English—was at this time a student at Oxford. He had the reputation of being an extremely virtuous young man of spotless character, and fond of sacred literature. He obtained the book which was then attracting so much attention, and God used it to the conversion of his soul. He began almost immediately to give public lectures on the Gospel of Christ, and the way of salvation through faith in Him ; but this being more than Oxford could yet bear, he left, and joined the dear evangelist, Bilney at Cambridge.

John Fryth, from Sevenoaks, was distinguished among the students of King's college for the quickness of his understanding, and the integrity of his life. He was brought to the knowledge of Christ by means of Tyndale; and these three young students, completely emancipated from the yoke of Rome by the Word of God alone, were amongst the earliest preachers of the doctrines of the Reformation, and ultimately were honoured of God with the crown of martyrdom. It was especially laid on the heart of Tyndale to translate the Holy Scriptures into the English tongue; but finding no convenience for this blessed work in England, he retired to the continent, and, settling at Antwerp, he there published a translation of the New Testament about the year 1527.

THE WORKS OF LUTHER REACH ENGLAND.

At the very time when God's Spirit was working so manifestly in the universities, the writings of Luther had entered the kingdom and were being widely circulated among the people. The noble stand which the monk had made at the Diet of Worms was much talked of, and awakened a deep interest in his writings. There was no small stir among the clergy; the bishops held a council to deliberate on what was to be done. The **bull of Leo against Luther** was sent to England; and Wolsey also issued a bull of his own against him. The bull of Leo which gave a description of Luther's perverse opinions was nailed to the Church door, while Wolsey's was read aloud during high mass. The cardinal issued orders at the same time to the bishops to seize all heretical books, and books containing Martin Luther's errors; and to give notice in all the Churches, that any person having such books, and failing to deliver them up within fifteen days would incur the pain of excommunication. But this was not all; the cardinal-legate, in great pomp, proceeded to St. Paul's and publicly burnt the arch-heretic's book.

The principal result of these proceedings, as some say, with the publication of Luther's alleged errors on the doors of the Cathedrals and Churches, was to advertise his works, awaken the slumbering interest of the English people, and prepare them for the more fearless profession of the doctrines of the Reformation. The bishops had taken counsel to arrest the progress of the Gospel; but in this, as in many other cases, the efforts of adversaries only accelerated the speed of the great work, and the puny wrath of men was turned to the praise of the Lord.

HENRY AND LUTHER.

When the writings of Luther were commanding such general attention, the king stood forward as the champion of the Church in the character of a polemic. Henry was at this time a bigoted enemy to the principles of the Reformation, and greatly incensed against Luther for treating with contempt his favourite author,

Thomas Aquinas. But Luther, nothing daunted by his royal antagonist, and in no wise convinced by his royal logic, soon replied to him in his usual style, plainly showing that, in his defence of the great principles of the Reformation, he was no respecter of persons.*

THE ROYAL MARRIAGES.

It is not difficult to discern, at this moment, the overruling hand of a Divine Providence in the marvellous changes which were taking place, and how little man at his best estate is to be trusted. The same gallant Henry that showed so much zeal for the Roman See, and was rewarded with the titles, " Most Christian King ; **Defender of the Faith,**" etc., in a short time denies the Pope's authority, renounces his supremacy, and withdraws his kingdom from the obedience of the Pontifical jurisdiction. And the same double policy of the Catholics that turned the mind of Henry, caused the downfall of Wolsey. Rome lost both—Henry and Wolsey—and the Reformation, indirectly greatly gained. But the events which led to these results have been so minutely related by all our historians, that we may fairly suppose the reader to be acquainted with them.

The quarrel between the King and the Pope first arose on the subject of the royal marriages. Arthur, the eldest son of Henry VII, was married to **Catherine,** daughter of Ferdinand and Isabella, and died without issue six months afterwards. The shrewd money-loving father-in-law, that he might preserve the advantages of the Spanish alliance, and retain her dowry of *two hundred thousand ducats*, proposed her marriage with Henry, his second son, now Prince of Wales. Some of the bishops were opposed to the union, as contrary to the laws of God, others favoured it ; but to settle the question, a bull was obtained from Julius II to sanction it, and the marriage took place soon after Henry's accession to the throne. For seventeen years no question appears to have arisen as to the validity of this union. Of five children—three sons and two daughters—only Mary survived the period of infancy.

One of the many reasons suggested for the king's doubts as to the lawfulness of his marriage was the loss of his children. He began to think that it was the judgment of God for marrying his brother's widow. But it is more generally believed that the origin of his doubts was the passion he had formed for **Ann Boleyn.** The great question of " the divorce " was first mooted about the year 1527, and it soon became the source of the most important results in both Church and State, and to the nation at large. The Pope was appealed to for a bull pronouncing the marriage of Henry and Catherine to be unlawful, and a dispen-

* See vol. ii., p. 654.

sation for King Henry to marry again. The Pope was now in a great perplexity. If he declared the marriage of the royal pair to be unlawful, he would thereby affirm to all Christendom that his *infallible* predecessor, Julius II, had made a mistake in declaring it to be lawful. Still, the artful Pope, who was most anxious to oblige the king of England, would have had little difficulty in making that straight ; but the armies of the powerful Charles—nephew to Catherine—were then in Italy, and he was indignant at the repudiation of his aunt.

This complication of interests led to the most shameful artifices and intrigues on the part of the Papal court, in which the double dealing of Wolsey—who had been promised the tiara by Charles if he threw difficulties in the way of the divorce—being discovered by the king, led to his disgrace and ignominious end. For seven long years the Pope, by his diplomatic strategy, kept the impetuous Henry waiting, which shows, on the other side, the immense hold which the word of a Pope had upon the mind of an absolute monarch. Driven to extremities, Henry resolved to take the law into his own hands, and **entirely abolish the Pope's power in England.** " In 1534 an Act of Parliament was passed with very little opposition, which put an end to the Papal authority, as well as to the various payments of whatever kind which had hitherto been made by the laity or clergy to the See of Rome."*

THE PERSECUTION BEGINS.

The king very prudently, demanded and obtained the sanction of the higher clergy to the great changes he was introducing into the ecclesiastical constitution of England. The bishops were greatly embarrassed. " If we recognise the king as supreme head of the Church of England," said they, " we overthrow the Pope." But they were obliged to submit to all his enactments or fall under his displeasure. To atone for their cowardly submission to Henry, and sacrificing the Pope, they resolved on kindling afresh the fires of persecution, which had been languishing during the latter years of Wolsey's reign. The evangelical preachers were becoming more numerous, Lutheranism was rapidly gaining ground, the leaders must be burnt.

" Your highness," said the bishops to the king, " one time defended the Church with your pen, when you were only a member of it ; now that you are its supreme head, your majesty should crush its enemies, and so shall your merits exceed all praise." Before giving Henry's reply to this insidious flattery, it is necessary to state that, although the alterations of the king had done much for the overthrow of the Papal power in England, they

* Marsden's "Dict. of Churches," p. 213 ; Miss Strickland's "Queens of England," vol. iv.; Fuller's "Church History of Britain," vol. ii.; "Universal History," vol. vi. chap. 4 ; Burnet's "History of the Reformation," vol. i., part 1.

had done nothing as yet for the deliverance of the persecuted Reformers. Henry had no intention at this time of proceeding further with the Reformation, though the steps which he had taken were overruled by God for the advancement of that great movement. The act which acknowledged the king's supremacy declared that, " they did not hereby intend to vary from Christ's Church about the articles of the Catholic faith of Christendom, or in any other things, declared by the Scriptures, and the Word of God to be necessary for their salvation."

As Henry had now broken with the Pope, and the fidelity of the clergy was not much to be trusted, he felt the necessity of uniting more closely with them ; and as he greatly delighted in his title, " Defender of the Faith," he consented to hand over the disciples of the heretic Luther to the priests. Thus an agreement was made between **the king and the clergy** of the most infamous character that ever darkened the pages of history. The king gave them authority to imprison and burn the Reformers, provided they would assist him in resuming the power usurped by the Pope. This was enough ; the priests would agree to anything, swear to anything, if only authority were given them to burn the heretics. The bishops immediately began to hunt down the friends of the Gospel—the holy men of God.

We regret being unable, from want of space, to give details of **the martyrs** of this period, but they are to be found in many histories,* and sure we are their record is on high ; and if the reader is a believer in the Gospel, which was then called heresy, he will meet them on the morning of the first resurrection. This is the sure and certain hope of all true believers. " For the Lord himself shall descend from Heaven with a shout, with the voice of the archangel, and with the trump of God : and the dead in Christ shall rise first. Then we which are alive and remain shall be caught up together with them in the clouds, to meet the Lord in the air ; and so shall we ever be with the Lord " (1 Thess. 4. 16, 17). Nothing can be plainer than these words of eternal truth. The Church, which is His body, is complete, the Lord Himself comes for her ; she hears His voice, whether in the caverns of the grave or alive upon the earth, and ascends in her chariot of clouds ; He meets her in the air, and conducts her to the house of many mansions—the home of love which He has prepared for the bride of His heart. Brightly, amidst the myriad hosts of Heaven, will shine on that day, the noble army of martyrs. But all will be perfect, absolutely perfect, as Christ Himself is perfect, and the joy of one will be the common joy of all ; for all will be like Christ, the perfect reflection of His glory.

* See Foxe's " Book of Martyrs," vol. ii., folio ed.; Strype's " Memorials of the Reformation ; " D'Aubigné's " Luther," vol. v.; " Calvin," vol. iv.

The prisons, the stakes, the faggots, as well as the tedious sick chamber, will all be forgotten on that day, save to speak of the grace which enabled us in some measure to glorify Him. Neither will it be an undistinguishable mass, for we shall know each other, and the links which had been formed on earth by the Holy Ghost shall remain unbroken for ever. Such is the bright and blessed future for which we wait, we long, we pray ; but we know He is too faithful to come before the right time. And this is the future of all who believe in Jesus—the feeblest as well as the strongest. All who come to Jesus now are received : He rejects none. His mournful complaint is, " Ye will not come to me that ye might have life." " Him that cometh to Me I will in no wise cast out " (John 5. 40 ; 6. 37).

The names of Bilney, Byfield, Tewkesbury, Barnes, Bainham, Fryth, and many others, who suffered martyrdom about this time, have become familiar as the **first Reformers in England.** But it was difficult for any honest man to escape persecution at this period of our history. The Reformers suffered as heretics, and many of the Papists as traitors. Those who refused to take the oath of supremacy were condemned as guilty of high treason. The aged Dr. Fisher, Bishop of Rochester, nearly eighty, and Sir Thomas More, late Lord Chancellor, styled the Erasmus of England, were condemned and executed in 1534 for refusing to acknowledge Henry as supreme head of the Church. Neither age, service, learning, nor virtue were respected by the cruel and vindictive tyrant. Just about this time, when scaffolds, blocks, and stakes were rapidly multiplying in the land, one of Queen Anne's maids of honour attracted the attention, and excited the guilty passion of the king. But as there was no ground for pleading a divorce in the case of Anne Boleyn, he resolved to clear his way, as one has said, by the axe, to a new marriage with **Jane Seymour.** Pretending to suspect her fidelity, the monster threw her into the Tower. She was denied even the help of counsel on her trial, and found guilty by judges who were bound to bend before the tyranny of their master. The beautiful, and, as many say, the virtuous, Anne Boleyn, was beheaded on May 19th, 1536, and Henry and Jane Seymour were married on the day following.

THE SUPPRESSION OF MONASTERIES.

Henry had been excommunicated by the Pope ; his subjects absolved from their allegiance ; Charles V might invade his kingdom, and avenge the cause of his royal aunt, Catherine : and should there be a Popish rebellion, the whole fraternity of monks would flock to the standard of revolt. The king was no doubt moved by such considerations and fears to make an end of the monasteries, and appropriate their wealth before the danger arose. His prime minister, **Sir Thomas Cromwell**, a favourer of the Reformation, and an energetic man, was authorised by his master to appoint a commission to visit the abbeys, monasteries, nunneries, and universities of the kingdom, and report the condition of these foundations. The result was overwhelming. In place of obedience, poverty, and charity, which these religious houses were established to exemplify, they had raised themselves above the laws of the land, besides rolling in wealth ; and, as to their practices, we leave them in the original histories. Bishop Burnet says : " I have seen an extract of a part of this report, concerning one hundred and forty-four houses, that contain abominations in it equal to any that were in Sodom."*

The king and the Parliament, on hearing the report of the commissioners, resolved on their suppression. The lesser and greater monasteries amounted in number to six hundred and forty-five, while their possessions were valued at one-fifth of the kingdom—" at least one-fifth of the soil of England was in the hands of the monks." Besides the enormous wealth which fell to the crown, from the abolition of the religious houses, the king seized the rich shrine of Thomas à Becket at Canterbury, and his name as a saint was ordered to be erased from the calendar. The monks and nuns were turned adrift to shift for themselves, which caused great confusion and distress throughout the land. **Cranmer and Latimer** pleaded that part of the confiscated property should be devoted to the founding of hospitals for the sick and the poor, and institutions for the cultivation of learning ; but the king and his courtiers had little to spare for such purposes. As Tyndale quaintly says : " The counsels were taken not of a pure heart and love of the truth, but to avenge themselves, and to eat the harlot's flesh, and suck the marrow of her bones."

THE SIX ARTICLES.

But, notwithstanding this apparent Reformation, Henry was a thorough Romanist at heart. He maintained the doctrines of Rome, while he abolished the authority of the Roman Pontiff in his kingdom. Under the influence of Gardiner and Bonner, two bigoted Papists, six articles were enacted by the king and his Parliament, usually termed the " **bloody statute.**" It condemned to death all who opposed the doctrine of transubstantiation, auricular confession, vows of chastity, and private masses ; and all who supported the marriage of the clergy, and the giving of the cup to the laity. This creed was thoroughly Roman. Cranmer used all his influence, and even risked the king's displeasure, to prevent its passing, but all in vain. The Romish party was still powerful, and the king's temper became more

* " History of the Reformation," part i., book iii., p. 334.

violent than ever. Latimer, now Bishop of Worcester, was thrown into prison, and hundreds soon followed him. The prisons of London were crowded with all sorts of persons suspected of heresy. Papists were hung for denying the supremacy, and men and women were burnt in great numbers for denying transubstantiation. Commissioners were appointed to carry out the act, and who could escape ? If a man was an honest Papist, he denied the king's supremacy, and if he was an honest Protestant, he denied the real presence. The number that died by the hand of the executioner, during the reign of Henry VIII could not be credited in our day. Some say **seventy-two thousand.***

THE TRUE SOURCE OF THE REFORMATION.

There are writers, we know, who ascribe the Reformation in England to the enactments of the king ; but we think this a great mistake. That mighty movement flowed from a purer source than the murderous heart of Henry. Besides, he was a Romanist, to the end of his days ; and bequeathed large sums to be spent in saying masses for the repose of his soul. The work throughout was evidently of God, and by means of evangelists and His own Holy Word.

We have already seen the learned men of England in possession of the New Testament in Greek and Latin ; but the common people—unless they had Wycliffe's translation—must receive the knowledge of the truth through preachers—such as Bilney, Latimer, and others. **William Tyndale,** a man chosen of God, translated the Greek into English at Antwerp, and sent thousands of his New Testament to England, concealed in vessels coming to our ports. Sometimes they were seized and burned, but many escaped detection, and were widely circulated. The whole Bible in the English of that day, translated by Tyndale, with the assistance of **Miles Coverdale,** appeared in 1535, dedicated to the king, being the first edition of the Scriptures published by royal authority. Probably through the influence of Cranmer, Henry ordered the free sale of the Bible, and a copy in Latin and English to be provided for every Parish Church in the realm, and chained to a pillar or a desk in the choir, that any man might have access to it and read it. " I rejoice," wrote Cranmer to Cromwell, " to see this day of Reformation now risen in England, since the light of God's Word doth shine over it without a cloud."

England had now thrown off the tyranny of Rome, abolished the whole monastic system, and re-established the authority of Scripture. Still, the Reformation made no great progress during the remainder of Henry's life. The fabric of Roman traditions had fallen, and the foundation of a new edifice was laid in restor-

* Wylie's " History of Protestantism," vol. iii., p. 401.

ing the Bible to the people ; but much patience, toil, and suffering had to be endured before the building could be completed

THE REIGN OF EDWARD VI.

On the death of Henry, in 1547, the English Reformation assumed an entirely different aspect. **Edward VI,** the child of Henry's third wife, Jane Seymour, was acknowledged King of England, January 28, 1547, when only nine years old. His coronation took place in February, when the friends of the Gospel were released from prison, the statutes of the " six articles " were abolished ; many returned from exile, and the ranks of the Reformers were greatly recruited. When the procession was about to move from the Abbey of Westminster to the Palace, three swords were brought to be carried before the newly crowned king, emblematic of his three kingdoms. Seeing this, the king observed, " There lacks yet one." On his nobles inquiring what it was, he answered, " The Bible ; " adding, " that book is the sword of the spirit, and is to be preferred before those. It ought in all right to govern us ; without it we are nothing. He that rules without it is not to be called God's minister, or a king." The Bible was brought, and carried reverently in the procession.

The natural gifts of Edward, it is said, were such as to raise him far above the ordinary conditions of childhood. His father had wisely provided him with pious teachers, who were also friends of the Gospel. Numerous letters written by the precocious prince in Latin and French, before he was ten years old, are still extant. **Catherine Parr,** the sixth wife of his father, said to be a lady of great virtue and intelligence, carefully watched over his training.

During the brief reign of Edward, every encouragement was given to the diffusion of the English Bible. Though his reign extended to little more than seven years, no fewer than eleven editions of the Bible and six of the New Testament were published. Various improvements were also introduced in the mode of conducting divine service. Images were ordered to be removed from the Churches, prayers were no longer to be offered for the dead, auricular confession and transubstantiation were declared to be unscriptural, the clergy were permitted to marry, and the service was ordered to be performed in English in place of Latin. Articles of religion were also agreed upon in convocation ; they were forty-two in number. In the reign of Elizabeth, they were reduced to thirty-nine, which continue, as then revised, to be the standard of the English Church. The liturgy was revised, and re-revised, chiefly by Cranmer and Ridley—after consulting Bucer and Martyr—known as the " **First and Second Book of Edward VI,**" and was duly ratified by the king and the Parliament, and came into use in 1552. It was substantially the Book of Common Prayer now in use.

While these works of Reform were being carried on with great vigour, the pious King Edward died, in his sixteenth year, July 6th, 1553 ; and with his premature death a night of terrible darkness surrounded the Reformation in England. His last prayer was : " O my Lord God, bless my people, and save Thine inheritance. O Lord God, save Thy chosen people of England. O Lord God, defend this realm from Popery, and maintain Thy true religion, that I and my people may praise Thy holy Name, for Jesus Christ, His sake." During this short reign, we may say, the Reformation was established, and Protestantism had assumed, in all essential points, the form in which we find it to-day. " When Henry VIII descended into the tomb in 1547, England was little better than a field of ruins ; the colossal fragments of that ancient fabric, which the terrible blows of the king had shivered to pieces, lay all about ; and before these obstructions could be removed—time-honoured maxims exploded, inveterate prejudices rooted up, the dense ignorance of all classes dispelled— and the building of the new edifice begun, a generation, it would have been said, must pass away."* Yet in six short years the work proceeded with such rapidity, that the ancient faith, which for a thousand years had stood firm and been held sacred, had passed away for ever.

THE REIGN OF MARY.

The **Princess Mary** ascended the throne in July, 1553. She inherited from her mother, Catherine of Arragon, a determined hatred of the Protestant religion, and a strong attachment to the Roman Catholic faith. Her first acts were to repeal the laws of her father and brother in favour of Reform and against the Pope and Popish worship. Gardiner and Bonner were released from the Tower, and the leaders of the Reformation—Cranmer, Hooper, Coverdale, Rogers, and others—were sent to occupy their vacant prisons. Meanwhile Cardinal Pole arrived from Italy, with full powers from the Pope to receive the kingdom of England into the Roman pale. Persecution commenced, and all men apprehended a terrible storm. " A thousand of the Reformers," says Marsden, " including five bishops, many noblemen, fifty dignitaries of the Church, and others whose position in society might render them obnoxious, hurried their departure and fled abroad—chiefly to Geneva, Basle, and Zurich, where the Reformed religion was now established." The year 1555 has been termed the one of burning and blood.

Rogers, Vicar of St. Sepulchre's, who had been the associate of Tyndale and Coverdale in the translation of the Scriptures,

* " History of Protestantism," vol. iii., p. 418 ; " Faiths of the World," vol. i., p. 825 ; Marsden's " Churches," p. 227.

was the first to suffer. As he was being led to Smithfield, he saw his wife in the crowd waiting to see him. She had an infant in her arms, and ten children around her. He could only bid them all farewell with a look of faith and love. A pardon was offered him when he reached the faggots if he would recant. " That which I have preached," he said firmly, " will I seal with my blood." " Thou art a heretic," said the sheriff. " That shall be known at the last day," responded the martyr. The torch was applied, the flames rose around him, and with hands raised to Heaven he bore with perfect calmness the torture until they dropped into the fire. So died John Rogers, the proto-martyr of the Marian persecution.

Hooper, late Bishop of Gloucester, was burnt alive in front of his own Cathedral. It was a market day, and a crowd of not less than seven thousand had assembled to witness the last moments of one so greatly beloved. His enemies, fearing the power of his eloquence, forbade him to speak, and threatened if he did to cut out his tongue. But it is said that the meekness, the more than usual serenity, of his countenance, and the courage with which he endured his prolonged and awful sufferings, bore nobler testimony to his cause than any words he could have uttered. He was much in prayer, and probably the greater part of the seven thousand were in tears. " To say nothing of his piety," says another historian, " and the cause for which he suffered, he was a noble specimen of the true English character ; a man of transparent honesty, of dauntless courage, of unshaken constancy, and of warm affections and a loving heart." His last words were, " Lord Jesus, receive my spirit." Within a few days after Hooper's death, Saunders was burnt at Coventry ; Dr. Taylor at Hadleigh, in Suffolk ; Ferrar, Bishop of St. David's, at Carmarthen, Wales. All these were clergymen.

Fires were thus kindled in all parts of England in order to strike a wider terror into the hearts of the people, and deter them by these terrible examples from siding with the Reformers. But they had just the opposite effect. Men could easily contrast the mild treatment of the Papists under the reign of Edward, and the cruelties practised on innocent men under the reign of Mary. Barbarous as the nation then was, and educationally Catholic, it was shocked beyond measure with the severities of the court of Mary ; especially when the council issued an order to the sheriffs of the different counties to exact a promise from the martyrs to make no speeches at the stake—otherwise to cut out their tongues. Thus were kindred and friends deprived of the last and sacred words of the dying. Even the most rigid Papists pretended to be ashamed of these savage proceedings when they saw their effect upon the nation. Undying hatred of the Church which encouraged such atrocities took the place of superstitious reverence. The hearts of the people by thousands and tens of thousands were moved by sympathy to take part with the oppressed.

In the summer of this year of horrors, **Brandford,** Prebendary of St. Paul's, was burnt at Smithfield, together with an apprentice, a lad of nineteen ; and many others whom we cannot name. But we must briefly notice three familiar and honoured names in the martyrology of England.

RIDLEY, LATIMER, AND CRANMER.

Having been examined by the queen's commissioners at Oxford on the charge of heresy, they were condemned to be burnt as obstinate heretics. They were old, learned, and greatly esteemed as ministers of Christ ; **Latimer** was eighty-four, and had been one of the most eloquent preachers in England. They were sent back to prison, where they were detained nearly twelve months, the sentence of death hanging over them. On October, 1555, an order was issued for the execution of **Ridley** and Latimer. They were led to the city ditch, over against Balliol College. After spending a few moments in prayer, they were fastened to the stake. The torch was first applied to the faggots around Ridley. Then dear old Latimer addressed his companion in words still fresh, after three centuries, as on the day on which they were uttered : " BE OF GOOD COMFORT, MASTER RIDLEY, AND PLAY THE MAN ; WE SHALL THIS DAY LIGHT SUCH A CANDLE, BY GOD'S GRACE, IN ENGLAND, AS I TRUST SHALL NEVER BE PUT OUT." They both leaned forward as if to embrace the flames— the chariot of fire that was to carry them to Heaven—their happy souls soon departed to be for ever with the Lord. Quietly have they been reposing on that heart of eternal love these three hundred years, and there they will rest until the morning of the first resurrection, when the sleeping dust of God's redeemed shall be raised, and their bodies fashioned like unto Christ's body of glory, " according to the working whereby He is able even to subdue all things unto Himself " (Phil. 3. 21).

Cranmer was still in prison. Having acted so prominent a part under two monarchs, Henry and Edward, and in both Church and State, he must be made to drink the bitterest dregs of humiliation ; besides, he had voted for the divorce, the unpardonable sin in Mary's eyes. He was visited by the most accomplished of the Romish party, and treated with courtesy. They professed a sincere desire to prolong his life for future service, and hinted that he might have a quiet sphere in the country. His gentle spirit, his age, his failing courage, caused him to give way, and he fell into a disgraceful dissimulation by the arts of his seducers, and signed the submission required of him. The Catholics gloated over the humiliation of their victim, and hoped thereby to inflict a deadly wound on the Reformation. But Mary and Cardinal Pole had no thought of pardoning him. Instructions were secretly sent down to Oxford to prepare for his execution. On the morning of the 21st of March, 1556, the venerable archbishop, meanly habited, was led in solemn procession to St. Mary's Church. Meanwhile grace had wrought deeply in the heart of Cranmer. He was truly penitent, his soul was restored, and fully prepared to make a bold confession of his faith. He was placed on a raised platform in front of the pulpit ; Dr. Cole preached a sermon, as usual on such occasions. " He," says Foxe, " that was late archbishop, metropolitan and primate of England, and the king's privy councillor, being now in a bare and ragged gown, and ill-favouredly clothed, with an old and square cap, exposed to the contempt of all men, did admonish men, not only of his own calamity, but also of their state and fortune. More than twenty several times the tears did gush out abundantly, dropping down marvellously from his fatherly face."

MARTYRDOM OF CRANMER.

Sermon being ended, Dr. Cole asked him to clear himself of all suspicion of heresy, by making a public confession. " I will do so," said Cranmer, " and that with a good will." He rose up and addressed the vast concourse, declaring his abhorrence of the Romish doctrines, and expressing his steadfast adherence to the Protestant faith. " And now," he said, " I come to the great thing that is troubling my conscience, more than anything that I ever did or said in my whole life. And forasmuch, as **my hand offended,** writing contrary to my heart, my hand shall therefore first be punished ; for, may I come to the fire, it shall be first burned." Hardly had he uttered the words, when the priests, filled with fury at hearing a confession contrary to what they expected, dragged him tumultuously to the stake. It was already set up on the spot where Latimer and Ridley had suffered. As soon as the flames approached him, holding his right hand in the hottest of the fire, he exclaimed, " That unworthy right hand ! " and there he kept it till it was consumed, repeatedly exclaiming, " That unworthy right hand ! " His constancy amazed his persecutors. He stood in the midst of the flames unmoved as the stake to which he was bound. His last words were those familiar to so many martyrs, and first uttered by the noblest of all martyrs : " Lord Jesus, receive my spirit." And in a few moments his happy soul, released from all its cares and troubles, joined his companions in the paradise of God. " Absent from the body, present with the Lord " (2 Cor. 5. 8).

Within three years (from 1555 to 1558) according to the historians of the time, **two hundred and eighty-four martyrs suffered by fire,** while many perished in prison from hunger and ill-usage. " Over all England," says one, " from the eastern counties to Wales on the west, and from the midland shires to the shores of the English Channel, blazed those baleful fires. Both sexes, and all ages and conditions, the boy of eight and the man of eighty, were dragged to the stake and burnt, sometimes singly, at other times in dozens. Just two days before the death of the queen, five martyrs were burnt in one fire at Canterbury." The news of her death filled the country with rejoicings. It is said that bonfires were lighted, that the people setting tables in the street, and bringing forth bread and wine, " did eat, drink, and rejoice." Thus was fulfilled the saying of the wise king : " When it goeth well with the righteous, the city rejoiceth ; and when the wicked perish there is shouting. By the blessing of the upright the city is exalted ; but it is overthrown by the mouth of the wicked " (Prov. 11. 10, 11). The world, notwithstanding the native enmity of the heart, bears its testimony to consistent godliness, both in princes and people ; and what a testimony against wickedness when the death of a wicked ruler is matter of national exultation ! So it was on the death of Mary ; there was the shout of joy throughout the whole land. And such was the joy of Rome on the death of Nero ; and of France on the death of Robespierre. And such shall it be at last when God shall judge the harlot, and avenge the blood of His saints at her hand. Then Heaven shall rejoice, and shout its loud Alleluia ! Alleluia ! (Rev. 18., 19).

On the same day that Mary breathed her last—November 17th, 1558—died **Cardinal Pole,** her guilty counsellor. The system of Jezebel, reared at the cost of so much blood, fell with these two, never to be restored. Mary's zeal for Rome had been fired into fanaticism by her marriage with Philip II of Spain ; and her three advisers—the bigoted Gardiner, the brutal Bonner, and the sanguinary Pole—led her to believe that in burning her Protestant subjects she was doing the will of God. When mourning the cold-heartedness of Philip, who rarely came to see her, Pole assured her that the estrangement of her husband was God's displeasure for her leniency towards the Amalekites : then a few more were sacrificed to bring over the gloomy bigot ; but Philip cared not to come, which, with other things, in the great mercy of God to this afflicted nation, hastened her to the grave in the forty-third year of her age, and in the sixth of her reign.*

* For minute details of the persecutions, see Foxe's " Book of Martyrs ; " Froude's " History of England ; " Fuller's " Church History ; " Burnet's " History of the Reformation ; " Wylie's " History of Protestantism."

CHAPTER LV

The Reign of Elizabeth

In 1558 the princess **Elizabeth,** daughter of Ann Boleyn, ascended the throne in the twenty-fifth year of her age. Her accession changed everything. The terrible gloom which the reign of the " bloody Mary " had spread over the land instantly passed away. Every steeple in town and country sent forth its merry peal ; the prison doors were opened, and men whom Mary had left to be burnt were set at liberty. All the laws which had been passed in the reign of Mary for the restoration of Popery were repealed, and the English service was again introduced. Her conduct in relation to the Reformation—the great question of the age— was such as to preclude all hope of the restoration of Popery, though she had a strong leaning to Romish ceremonies herself, and her public measures fell short of that complete removal of abuses which many desired to see effected. The Puritan party strongly objected to the habits and vestments commanded to be worn, nor did they think the prayer book itself free from super- stition. This led to a great schism in the Church, and occasioned a painful controversy, which lasted from the early days of Elizabeth to the restoration of Charles II. But we can only briefly refer to its commencement.

THE PURITANS.

" Among the first," says Marsden, " who introduced into England the controversy which soon afterwards ripened into Puritanism, was the martyr, **Bishop Hooper.** He had lived some time abroad, and was the friend of Bullinger and Gaulter—the two leaders of the Protestant cause in Germany and Switzerland. Returning from his exile in the days of Edward VI, his piety and talents were at once appreciated, and he was nominated to the See of Gloucester. But his conscience was embarrassed ; and in his person a contest began, which has never since been stilled. He demurred to the robes in which the Episcopal investiture usually took place." Hooper, with many of the exiles, had contracted a love for the severely simple style of worship which existed in the Reformed Churches on the Continent, and led them to complain that the Reformation in England was left in an imperfect state : many abuses, both in worship and discipline being still retained.

Hooper begged to decline the bishopric, or be admitted without the usual ceremonials. Through the influence of Peter Martyr and Bucer, then professors of divinity at Oxford and Cambridge, he at length consented to use the vestments at his consecration, and to preach in them, once at least, before the court. It is not certain that he ever wore them afterwards. But the controversy was now begun ; the elevated position of Hooper and his popular eloquence kept it alive. Some of the greatest names in the Church of England of that day became friendly to the Reform pleaded for by the Puritans. Many refused to be consecrated in robes worn by the bishops of the Church of Rome, and which they regarded as the badge of Antichrist. Elizabeth, though opposed to Popery, was resolved, notwithstanding, to retain as much show and pomp in religious matters as might be possible. From this time the court party and the Puritan party became more decidedly opposed to each other. An order was issued by the queen, that exact uniformity should be maintained in all external rites and ceremonies. This was followed by another, requiring immediate uniformity in the vestments on pain of prohibition from preaching and deprivation from office. Matters were now brought to a crisis ; multitudes of Godly ministers were ejected from their Churches, and forbidden to preach anywhere else. All hopes of further reform in the Church being now at an end, the suspended ministers formed themselves into a body distinct fron the Church of England, which they regarded as only half reformed. Elizabeth was enraged, and threatened them with her royal displeasure ; but in the face of persecution the Puritans, or *Nonconformists*, as they were now sometimes called, rapidly increased. The famous Thomas Cartwright, with three hundred more, threw off their surplices in one day within the walls of one college.*

During the reign of the **House of Stuart,** the tide of persecution ran high and strong, and the Puritans, deprived of all hopes of redress, fled in great numbers to the Continent. After the accession of Charles I fresh ceremonies were introduced by Laud, and additional cruelties were inflicted on the Nonconformists. Emigration now seemed their only hope. A body of Puritans embarked as exiles, landed on the western shores of the Atlantic, and formed a settlement in New England. This colony of the " **Pilgrim Fathers** " soon received vast accessions ; and the desire for emigration became so great, and the numbers leaving so many, that the Government became alarmed, and stopped by royal warrant eight vessels when they were on the point of sailing from the Thames with emigrants to New England. On board were ejected ministers of high standing, and men of influence and rank, among whom were Oliver Cromwell, Hampden, Hesselrig, Lord Brook, and Lord Saye. The circumstances which followed this disembarkation are so remarkable, that we

* " Faiths of the World," vol. ii., p. 725.

PRELACY RESTORED WITH POPISH CEREMONIALS 1031

are compelled to pause and wonder. The overruling providence of God is very manifest. There is only One who knows the end from the beginning, and blessed are all they that put their trust in Him. Man knows not the future, and can neither make provision for his need nor against approaching danger. In 1642—five years after the vessels were arrested—through the oppression of Charles and his Popish ways, the sword was drawn, and the war began, which ended in the subversion of his throne, his tragical execution, and the establishment of the Commonwealth under the protectorate of Cromwell.

Puritanism, properly so-called, became extinct under the Commonwealth. The vestments being generally laid aside, the ground of contention was removed. But the later Puritans went farther than the Hoopers and Cartwrights, and contended not only against the forms and vestments, but against the constitution of the Church of England ; and these immediately became two great parties—PRESBYTERIANS and INDEPENDENTS.

CHARLES II AND JAMES II.

After the restoration of Charles II the prelacy was restored with all its Popish ceremonials. On May 19, 1662, the following act was passed : " That all who had not received Episcopal ordination should be re-ordained by bishops. That every minister should, on or before the 24th of August following declare his unfeigned assent and consent to everything contained in the Book of Common Prayer, on pain of being deprived of his benefice," etc., etc. " The dreaded day arrived. Great anxiety was felt as to whether the Reformation was to stand or fall in England. But the grace of God triumphed, and the enemy was defeated. Two thousand ministers, rather than submit to the act of uniformity, surrendered their livings, and left their parsonages. Thus were the most faithful and able ministers of the Church of England cast out, ignominiously reduced to great poverty, and provoked by spiteful usage " (Burnet).

Charles II died in 1685, and his brother, the Duke of York, ascended the throne as **James II.** Although suspected of being a Papist, he was allowed to take possession of the crown in peace and quietness. But his true character and intentions soon appeared. Being surrounded with Jesuits as his advisers, edict followed edict, the tendency of which was the overthrow of the laws and institutions of the realm, and to restore Popery in all its power and completeness. One of these edicts, which was ordered to be read during divine service in all the Churches, hastened the final struggle. Several of the bishops, and a vast number of the clergy refused to read it. Seven bishops were summoned before the ecclesiastical commission, and sent to the Tower by the notorious Judge Jeffreys. But the heart of the nation was too soundly Protestant to submit long to such tyrrany. The bishops were tried at Westminster and acquitted. The hall rang with shouts of joy, and the crowd rushing to the streets crying, " Not guilty ! Not guilty ! " All London soon caught the flying joy ; but James, agitated and troubled, heard in these sounds the mutterings of the coming storm.

The disgraceful conduct of Charles and James, and the atrocious cruelties of **Jeffreys** in England, and of Claverhouse in Scotland, most thoroughly convinced all parties that if the slightest vestige of liberty was to be preserved, decisive measures must be adopted. A majority of the nobility favoured the intervention of William, Prince of Orange, son-in-law to James, and the next heir to the throne. Invitations were sent to the Hague, messengers were despatched, all entreating him to come over and mediate between the king and his subjects, and if necessary, to employ more stringent measures. Having duly considered the various aspects of this great enterprise, and prepared for it, he sailed under the English banner, with the motto : " For the Protestant Religion and Liberties of England," and landed at Brixham, in Torbay, on the 5th of November, 1688. In the meantime James fled, being fully aware of the universal feeling of disaffection existing amongst his subjects. He scarcely made any show of opposition.

THE REVOLUTION OF 1688.

A national convention was summoned, the throne was declared vacant by the abdication of James, and the crown was settled on the Prince and Princess of Orange. " This was the triumph," says Wylie, " not of English Protestantism only ; it was the triumph of the Protestantism of all Christendom. . . . It was the revival, not less of the Scotch Covenanters, whose torn and blood-stained flag, upheld at the latter end of their struggle by only a few laymen, was soon to be crowned with victory."*

Thus was the **Great Revolution of 1688** accomplished without tumult or bloodshed. The ignominious flight of James and his queen to France, relieved the ruling powers from all perplexities, and facilitated the arrangement of affairs connected with the Act of Settlement. Bills were speedily passed for the relief of the Protestants, and for securing the civil and religious liberties of the English people. William, who had been brought up a Calvinist, was strongly inclined to favour dissenters ; but several of the bishops and many of the clergy contending for the divine right of kings, refused to take the required oaths to the new Government, and became a troublesome faction, afterwards known by the term Nonjurors. In Catholic Ireland, and among

* " History of Protestantism," vol. iii., p. 624 ; " Universal History," vol. vi., p. 288.

the Popish Clans of the Highlands of Scotland, there were strong factions who favoured the House of Stuart.

In Ireland, Tyrconnel raised an army of Catholics, and was joined by James from France, with a fleet of fourteen vessels, and well supplied by Louis with men, money, and arms. Several battles were fought before the country was subdued. **The Siege of Derry** is one of the most memorable in history; but the famous Battle of the Boyne, fought on July 1st, 1690, closed the dispute. James, finding all was lost, escaped once more to France, where he solaced himself with a devotion almost monastic, and which made even his Catholic friends laugh at him, as a man who had thrown away three kingdoms for a mass.

In Scotland Viscount Dundee, the notorious **Claverhouse,** succeeded in raising a considerable body of Highlanders in favour of their dethroned monarch. The English army, under the command of General Mackay, met Dundee and the clans at the pass of Killiecrankie, where a serious engagement took place. The battle went against the army of William, but the cause of James suffered an irreparable loss in the death of Claverhouse. He was killed when on tip-toe in his stirrups urging on his men to the charge. The rallying power was now gone, and the Popish clans laid down their arms, and gradually submitted to the authority of William.

THE PROTESTANT SUCCESSION.

The reign of William is especially worthy of our notice, because he placed the throne of the United Kingdom on a thoroughly Protestant foundation. It was provided in the **Bill of Rights,** " not only that every person in communion with the Church of Rome, or marrying a Papist, shall for ever be incapable of the crown, but also that in case of any British sovereign's apostasy to Popery, the people shall be absolved from their allegiance, and the next heir shall immediately succeed, if a Protestant, just as if the royal personage reconciled to the Church of Rome, or marrying a Papist, had actually died." This famous bill immediately followed the Act of Settlement in 1689.

The English Church, we may say, is the same now as it was in the time of William. The *Episcopalians* are the reigning party, and number among their adherents the royal family, the principal part of the nobility, and the greatest part of the people. The foundation of the Presbyterian Establishment in Scotland was also firmly laid about the same time, by an Act of the Scottish Parliament which ratified the "**Westminster Confession of Faith**," as the creed of that Church.*

The unbounded liberty which the British subject enjoys of publishing his opinions without restraint, and of worshipping

* Mosheim, vol. iv., pp. 297-378; Cunningham, vol. ii., p. 285; " Universal History," vol. vi., p. 294.

God according to the dictates of his own conscience, enlightened by the truth as it is in Jesus, naturally causes various sects to arise, and controversies respecting things pertaining to religion to be perpetuated. Many of these may be most interesting to the student of ecclesiastical history; but we have already exceeded our limits, and can do little more than notice the names of the leading seceders whose followers now form large sections of the professing Church, with whom we are familiar.

EBENEZER ERSKINE.

The Church of Scotland in her early days allowed no latitude of belief within her pale. We speak of what she was, not alas! of what has disturbed her communion of late years. Her creed descends to the minutest particulars, and the slightest deviation from it was immediately canvassed and strictly dealt with according to that creed. The following remarks of Cunningham the historian, and one of her ministers, we fully accept as to what she has been, but not as to what she is at the present time. "All her ministers speak precisely the same things. The mind of each one presents a perfect impression of the Westminster divines. Notwithstanding the independence of the Scotch intellect, it has seldom been exercised upon forms of faith. Notwithstanding the free scope of its metaphysics, the region of theology has been carefully avoided. Notwithstanding the schisms which have taken place, heresy has never been able to lift up her head. . . . But notwithstanding this marvellous uniformity of faith, the Church judicatories have required, in a few instances, to deal with heresy."

In the year 1732, a controversy arose about the settlement of ministers in vacant parishes. The Assembly passed an act to the effect that, if the planting of a parish devolved upon the Presbytery, from the patron not availing himself of his right, the call was to proceed from the heritors and elders. **Ebenezer Erskine,** a grave and spiritual man, but energetic and always on the popular side of public questions, strongly opposed the act. He advocated the free choice and election of the minister by the members. "What difference," he exclaimed in the debate, "does a piece of land make between man and man in the affairs of Christ's kingdom which is not of this world? We must have the faith of our Lord Jesus Christ without respect of persons." Many of the most spiritual sympathised with him, and several joined him in his protest. The case was carried from court to court; but the Assembly would not yield, and the protestors would not yield, and so the secession took place. But the Lord overruled it for the revival of religion, the spread of the truth, and the blessing of precious souls.

These few seceders, four or five in number, immediately constituted themselves into a Presbytery, and commenced publishing and preaching in separation from the Established Church. This was the small beginning of the Secession Church, afterwards known as **United Presbyterian**, which estimate its adherents at half a million.*

JOHN WESLEY.

In England, things were in a very low condition in the establishment, as they were in Scotland. There had been a great reaction since the time of the Puritans. The people had thrown off the restraints of Puritanism, or, rather, of Christianity, and returned to their games and pleasures. They soon sank into their former ignorance and worldliness. But the Lord in great mercy, just about this time, was preparing His chosen servants for the revival of His work, for the spread of the truth, and for the preaching of His Gospel, which would reach the hearts and consciences of men in every sphere of life.

Samuel Wesley, the father of the celebrated **John and Charles Wesley,** was of Puritanical descent, and marrying a daughter of Dr. Annesley—one of the ejected ministers—the mother came from an eminent Nonconformist family. When the revolution was effected, Mr. Wesley was the first who wrote in favour of that great national change, and dedicated his work to Queen Mary, who rewarded him with the rectory of Epworth in Lincolnshire. Here John, their second son, the founder of the Methodists, was born in June, 1703. After receiving an early education at Charterhouse school, he proceeded to Christchurch, Oxford, where his brother Charles, who was several years younger, joined him in 1727. From reading such books as Thomas à Kempis' " Imitation of Christ," and Jeremy Taylor's " Rules of Holy Living and Dying," they became extremely troubled about the salvation of their souls ; but were dark as midnight as to the simple Gospel—the way of salvation through faith in the Lord Jesus Christ. Having been baptised, and received the sacrament, they thought, as they had been taught, and as almost every one else believed at that time, that they could only hope to be saved by persisting in good works to the end of their days. This they tried, as Luther and Calvin had done before them ; but, so far from being satisfied, they became every day more and more miserable. The God of all grace had touched their hearts, and created a void which nothing could fill but the knowledge of Christ in His Person and finished work.

In this troubled state of soul the Wesleys, with two or three others, held private meetings during the week for the promotion of personal piety, and rigidly observed all the rules prescribed by the University statutes. The strictness of their lives, and the

* Cunningham, vol. ii., p. 383 ; Thomson's " History of the Secession Church ; " Fraser's " Life of Ebenezer Erskine."

regularity of their habits, brought down upon them the contempt and scorn of their godless fellow-students, who called them " Bible Moths," " Methodists," and " The Holy Club."

GEORGE WHITEFIELD.

Just about this time, a young man from Gloucester—as earnest and sincere as themselves, joined the little community—**George Whitefield.** He was descended from a respectable family ; but his father, who was a wine merchant, ultimately kept the Bell Inn at Gloucester. There the future great preacher was born in 1714. For some time before meeting with the Wesleys, he had been the subject of much anxiety on matters of religion, and, like the Wesleys, he had been greatly perplexed by Thomas à Kempis, and also by Law's " Serious Call." But as we cannot pursue in detail the deep exercises through which they passed, and their subsequent course, we would only add that, ere long, they were led, by God's Holy Spirit, and the plain truths of Scripture, to know the Gospel for their own peace and joy, and to preach it to others.

Being clergymen of the Church of England, they were privileged to preach in the Churches this new Gospel—immediate pardon and salvation through faith in Christ, without works of human merit. But this was too simple and too Scriptural to be tolerated ; and in a short time almost every pulpit in England was closed against them. Thus driven outside, they were compelled to preach in the open air, and thereby inaugurated open-air preaching which has since become so common. In Moorfields, on Kennington Common, and such like places they preached in towns and country to audiences numbering from ten to twenty thousand. By the grace of God these " **twin apostles** " of England—Wesley and Whitefield—continued faithful and devoted to the end of their career.

They were used of God to rescue the English people from the depths of moral darkness, leading thousands both in this country and in America, to the feet of Jesus. Men of all ranks acknowledged the force of their appeals—colliers and carpenters, ploughmen and philosophers ; and many of the nobility yielded their hearts to the power of the truth. But their record is on high, and there the fruits of their labours shall abide throughout eternity. Whitefield died in America in 1770 ; and Wesley in London in 1791, in the eighty-eighth year of his age.*

REVIVAL AT CAMBUSLANG.

The eighteenth century was the period of great awakenings and great revivals in different countries and of a different character in each place. In the spring of 1742 strange symptoms of a

---

* See, for details, " The Story of John Wesley," by Frances Bevan ; " Life and Labours of George Whitefield."

religious revival began to appear at Cambuslang, in Lanarkshire, Scotland. **Mr. M'Culloch,** the parish minister, is spoken of as a godly man, but nothing remarkable as a preacher. Some of his parishioners began to call upon him at the manse, in deep concern about the state of their souls. This was something entirely new and unexpected. But there was evidently a growing desire for the Word of God, which resulted in a number of the parishioners signing a request for a weekly lecture in addition to the usual Sabbath-day services. One evening in the month of February, he happened to exclaim : " Who hath believed our report, and to whom is the arm of the Lord revealed ? " upon which some persons in the meeting cried aloud in great distress because of their sins. From this evening such scenes became common. And now the people desired to have preaching every evening. Other ministers came to assist, and crowds gathered round the preachers on every occasion. Men and women were violently agitated ; clasping their hands, smiting their breasts in great agony of mind. Others, as in a transport of joy, shouting, " He is come ! I have got Him, and will not let Him go ! " And there were others who seemed to be so full of the Spirit, and so supremely happy that they exclaimed : " Now, Lord, let Thy servant depart in peace, for mine eyes have seen Thy salvation."

As on all such marvellous visitations of the Holy Spirit, multitudes from all parts crowded to see the Lord's great work. During the month of August, when the Sacrament of the Supper was dispensed, about thirty thousand people were gathered together, and fourteen ministers were engaged in preaching on the green, and in dispensing the elements to one company after another inside the Church. George Whitefield was one of the ministers, and appointed to preach in the evening. The tent stood on the margin of a little stream ; in front of this rose a green bank in the form of an amphitheatre. About ten o'clock at night Whitefield rose to give the last address for the day. It was indeed nature's temple, as the preacher observed, built by God Himself for so great a concourse to worship in. As his deep voice in impassioned eloquence rolled over the vast multitude, it was answered by sighs and sobs, and soon the tens of thousands were melted in tears.

The minister, Mr. M'Culloch, in speaking of this gracious visitation nine years afterwards, had to lament many back-sliders ; but still he spoke of hundreds who had been truly converted.

At **Kilsyth,** and other places the work of God's Spirit was very similar. We can only give one short extract from a letter under date May 16th, 1742. " The Lord has shot His arrows very thick into the hearts of His enemies this day, not for their destruction, but that they might fall under Him. There was a great cry of awakened sinners this day; there have been seven and twenty awakened; all of them under so great agonies as we conceive those mentioned in Acts 2; besides others who were carried away by their friends whose names I have not got; I have dealt with them all this evening, as also Mr. Oughterson for a while, having sent for him. O praise the Lord, and pray much for us, and tell everybody to praise Him for His mercy to us, and that He will stay a long time with us after this sort."*

SUNDAY SCHOOLS.

It is generally known that the vast operations of the Sunday-school system, which have been so beneficial in their results for nearly a hundred years, commenced with a young man in Gloucester. **Robert Raikes,** the founder of Sunday Schools, was born in 1735. His father was a printer, and conductor of the *Gloucester Journal*, who, after giving his son a liberal education, brought him up to his own business, in which after a time he succeeded his father. The events of his life present nothing beyond those of an industrious tradesman in general; and but for his benevolent pity for the prisoners in Gloucester jail, and for the ignorant and neglected children of his native city, his name and memory might have sunk into the grave with himself.

He was struck with the number of wretched children whom he found in the suburbs and in the streets, especially on Sunday, and determined to make an effort at some improvement. He first found three or four decent women in the neighbourhood, who were capable of teaching children to read, to each of whom he agreed to give a shilling for the day's employment, and then induced the children to come to the school. The success was great; many of the children were not only eager to learn to read, but, on being presented with New Testaments, they began of their own accord to frequent places of worship. At first he found many of the children were unwilling to come on account of their clothes not being good enough; but he assured such that " clean hands, clean faces, and combed hair" were all that was required at school. The good effects of this new work were so evident, that in a short time Sunday Schools were established in all directions; and each succeeding generation has developed more fully the wide extent and the blessed results of the Sunday School system.

Most probably the thoughts of Mr. Raikes in the good work he was doing did not extend beyond the immediate objects of his benevolence. But great results in the things of God depend not upon our plans or human display. The man of faith reckons upon God, and he can afford to be unobtrusive, unostentatious, and quiet in his work, leaving consequences with Him. Mr. Raikes

* The above sketch of the work at Cambuslang is taken from Cunningham's " History of the Scotch Church," vol. ii., p. 460. For lengthy and minute details, see " Historical Recollections of Revivals," etc., by Dr. Gillies. This book gives an account of the remarkable periods of the success of the Gospel from the first to the nineteenth century.

is a happy illustration of what may be done by personal influence, and by taking up the work which the Master may have placed before our eyes, instead of waiting for the sanction of others, or a formal introduction to what others are doing. Individual responsibility is the true principle of Christ's servant, and he must watch against every arrangement, or co-operation, that would take him off the ground of faith.

Mr. Raikes had the satisfaction before his death on April 5th, 1811, of seeing his first humble endeavours become the most efficient means of educating the children of the poor throughout the kingdom.*

FOREIGN MISSIONS.

At the Reformation in the sixteenth century, as we have already seen, the light of the Gospel spread rapidly among the nations of Europe; and many at that time, fired with a holy zeal for the wider spread of the truth, sent missionaries to foreign parts. Among the first of these were the Swiss, the Swedes, the Dutch, and the Moravians. Many of them were exposed to great sufferings, and, in some instances, were very unsuccessful.

The **Baptist Missionary Society** seems to have taken the lead in the missionary enterprise in this country, and no doubt, by its example, aroused other Churches to their responsibility in reference to the benighted heathen. In October, 1792, a few Baptist ministers assembled at Kettering, in Northamptonshire, united in constituting a Society for the Propagation of the Gospel among the Heathen. **William Carey,** then a Baptist minister in Leicestershire, was the chief mover in this new society. He afterwards went to India as a missionary, and became famous for the acquisition of Eastern languages. Soon after the publication of the New Testament in the Bengali language, translated by Mr. Carey, he was appointed by the Marquis of Wellesley, the British Governor-General, teacher of the Bengali and Sanskrit languages in the new college of Fort-William. The labours of Messrs. Carey, Marshman, and Ward, in India, have often been written, and are generally known. To Dr. Carey, it is said, belongs the honour of having awakened the zeal of the Church in the important work of foreign missions.

In 1795 the **London Missionary Society** was formed. This Institution for the propagation of the Gospel among the heathen, was composed of Christians of various denominations. The spread of the truth, irrespective of all denominational distinctions, was its motto. The institution of this society on so broad a scale was everywhere hailed as a new era in the Christian Church. Its attention was immediately turned to the islands of the South Seas.

In 1799 the **Church Missionary Society** was formed, consisting

* Knight's " Dictionary of Biography."

of members of the Church of England. It sent a mission to the Susoo country, in the neighbourhood of Sierra Leone.

In 1796 the **Scottish Missionary Society** was formed in Edinburgh, and commenced its operations by a mission to the Foulah country, in the neighbourhood of Sierra Leone.

In 1812 the familiar names of Judson, Newell, Hull, and others, sailed under the auspices of " The **American Board for Foreign Missions,**" for Calcutta. They laboured in many parts of the eastern world.

In 1786 several **Wesleyan ministers** sailed as missionaries from England for Nova Scotia ; but, after encountering a succession of storms, the captain directed his course for the West Indies. Having reached Antigua, and finding the inhabitants favourable, they resolved to attempt the establishment of a mission in the West Indies. Such were the circumstances, under the overruling providence of God, which led the Methodists to turn their attention to the heathen, and to adopt measures for the diffusion of Christianity among them.*

Surely we can thank God with full hearts for all these societies. For a number of years they have been scattering the blessings of Christianity among many tribes and tongues, where darkness reigned. The light and life of the Gospel have been carried to millions who were sitting in the region and shadow of death. The rise and fall of empires, the achievement of great victories, the discovery and civilisation of new countries, the improvements of the arts and sciences, are but as nothing compared with the diffusion of the Gospel throughout the world, which brings " glory to God in the highest, peace on earth, and good will toward men " (Luke 2. 14).

May the Lord greatly bless both our home and foreign missions, and give good success to the arduous labours of the Sunday School, that His Name may be glorified, and multitudes of precious souls eternally saved. And may He keep both reader and writer near Himself until we see His face, hear His voice, and be for ever in the full enjoyment of His love and glory.

* For minute particulars and details of the formation and history of Missionary Societies, from the Reformation to the present time, see Dr. Brown's " History," 3 vols. octavo.

CHAPTER LVI

The Last Fifty Years

A FEW SUPPLEMENTARY PAPERS BY WM. HOSTE, B.A.

THROUGHOUT our Lord's ministry a threefold leaven was at work in Jewry, that of the Pharisees, Sadducees, and Herodians. They represented respectively religious tradition, religious scepticism, and worldly compromise. There was also a fourth category, the godly remnant, who received the Lord Jesus as Messiah. These currents of thought are recognised in the last four " Apocalyptic " messages to the Churches of Asia. They have continued down the centuries, and in the last fifty years have increased in volume and intensity.

In the first chapter of Revelation these **Seven Churches** are contemplated as golden candlesticks, each a testimony formed by Christ for God through His Spirit, but in the following two chapters they are seen in the place of responsibility. Here failure has come in and evil doctrine and practice are allowed. We have to do now especially with the last four, which continue to the end. *Thyatira* suffers Jezebel to continue her abominations and the evil blossoms eventually into the Papacy and her daughter Churches. *Sardis*, instead of strengthening the things which were ready to die, becomes the progenitor of the dead-alive religious systems, represented by unregenerate Protestantism and political dissent, parents of that evil progeny, the Higher Criticism and Modernism. There is, however, a faithful remnant in *Sardis*, which becomes *Philadelphia*, represented in later years by " the Evangelical Revival ; " all down the centuries there have been those who have " kept His Word and not denied His Name "—a godly remnant, not seldom persecuted as heretics by the religious world, but known to God, such as the Albigenses, the poor men of Lyons—known to-day as the Waldenses, the Reformers, the Puritans, the Wesley and Whitefield Revivals, in fact every evangelical denomination which, however far their departure to-day from the Word of God, did in their origin represent a definite movement of the Spirit for the revival of His people, or the recovery of some special truth of His Word. *Laodicea* marks the closing phase of the Church's history as a collective witness for God and is characterised not by doctrinal error or moral lapse, but by luke-warmness and self-satisfaction. Christ has morally lost His place in their midst, (He is seen outside the door of the Assembly), the secret of all declension, individual or collective.

RELIGIOUS TRADITION.

The last fifty years has inherited these movements, and we see them running on parallel lines to-day, each holding on its course, to a great extent uninfluenced by the others. The year 1870 was marked by the Vatican Council, convened by Pius IX, to enforce the dogma of **Papal infallibility.** It had long been held that a Papal decree ratified by the Universal Roman Episcopate partook of the nature of infallibility. But this was a new departure, engineered by the Jesuits, and only adopted in the face of strong opposition among Romanists themselves. The dogma does not mean that any Pope claims to be personally infallible, but that when speaking *ex-cathedra*, as the representative of the whole Church his decrees are such. Satan's aim is always to exalt man and " cast Christ down from His excellency." If, as the Psalmist truly says, " All men are liars," and so fallible, how can the representative of a company of such be infallible ? There is only one who is infallible—Christ who is the Truth, and His Spirit conveys the truth to us through the Word.

The history of the Papacy, for the claim is retrospective, is surely sufficient answer to the Papal claim. Her enemies have pointed to the events which followed as the Divine commentary thereon. The pressure of the Franco-Prussian War led to the withdrawal of the French garrison from Rome, the capture of the City by Victor Emmanuel and the loss of the temporal power. The Pope has ever since called himself as a protest the " **Prisoner of the Vatican.**" Though the Roman Curia has never ceased to resent the loss of the temporal power, it may well be doubted whether the change from a petty state to a world-wide spiritual sovereignty has not increased rather than diminished her influence in the world—at any rate it humbled her, though she has never humbled herself or abated her claims, spiritual or temporal.

Cardinal Manning, one of the most zealous promoters of the dogma of Infallibility, was also an open and zealous champion for the " conversion " of England, but did much to break down the natural British antipathy to Rome, by the active part he took in temperance and social reform and by his frequent appearances on interdenominational platforms.

Rome is like the sea, losing ground here, she encroaches there. She has certainly lost ground in France and Italy and other Roman Catholic countries (though even there she is said to have once more gained ground since the Great War), but she has gained in other lands, in our own not least. Much spade-work has been done of the sapping and mining kind, and popular feeling has greatly changed. The old distrust and dread of Rome has given way to indifference and even to a kind of admiration. A great worldly system, as she is, naturally appeals to the heart of unregenerate man. To-day Rome is carrying on an active propaganda at the street corners in London and elsewhere through various societies, and in these degenerate days will often get more hearers than the Gospel preacher.

Whether she has gained much ground in England by direct " perversion " may be doubted. The **division of England** in 1850, by a Papal edict, into Roman Catholic Sees under an Archbishop of Westminster, provoked great Protestant opposition, and the Ecclesiastical Titles Bill was passed declaring such an edict null and void, but it fell into disuse, and in 1871 was repealed. There was no opposition in 1878 when Scotland was partitioned off into Roman dioceses.

There has been a great increase in England in Roman Catholic building property, convents, etc., and numbers of adherents from abroad, especially since 1906, when the " **Concordat** " was denounced by the French Government under M. Combes, and the Religious Congregation dispersed, but there again the Roman Catholic Church gained in moral weight what she lost in money payments. Had she limited herself all through to her professed religious role, and not interfered in politics, the French Government would have left her alone. Though Rome may not have gained greatly by direct perversion, there can be no doubt she has gained enormously by the Ritualistic movement. In a Roman Catholic paper, *The Ransom*, appears the following words : " As to conversions (to Romanism) it is well known that nine out of every dozen are the direct result of ritualistic teaching. It is God's will (!) apparently that this extraordinary movement or revolution in the Anglican Church shall be one of the means used in the gradual, almost insensible extension to the whole English people of Catholic doctrine."

Since the publication of the " **Tracts for the Times,**" in 1830, great changes have passed over our land. It is affirmed by those who ought to know, that many ritualistic clergy of to-day are ordained Romish priests, with a dispensation to remain in the Anglican Communion. As one of them writes :* " The work now going on in England is an earnest and carefully organised attempt on the part of a rapidly increasing body of priests and laymen to bring the National Church and the country at large up to the full standard of Catholic faith and practice and eventually to plead for her union with the Church of Rome." In another Romanising work, " Essays on Reunion," we read : " The first great hindrance that is before us arises from the Protestantism of England. Till this is removed the reunion of our Church, as the Church of England with either Greek or Latin Churches is absolutely hopeless."

* In " Union Review," organ of the Association for the Promotion of the Union of Christendom, vol. v., p. 432.

That this may long continue so, is the prayer of every enlightened soul.   In 1921, Anglican orders were recognised by the Greek Church, but such recognition is still refused by Rome. There can be little doubt that the whole Ritualistic movement is largely Jesuitical, not only in method, but in actual fact.

THE JESUITS.

De Sanctis,* a convert to the faith of Christ, once holding, among other high offices at Rome, that of Official Theological Censor of the "Inquisition," writes : "Despite all the persecution they (the Jesuits) have met with, they have not abandoned England, where there are a greater number of Jesuits than in Italy ; there are Jesuits in all classes of Society, in Parliament, among the English clergy, among the Protestant laity, even in the highest stations."

The movement passed through a period of persecution and scandals.   The exposure of "The Priest in Absolution" caused widespread indignation, prosecutions were initiated against some prominent Romanisers, but as we shall see the line of least resistance was followed in the judgments delivered, and law and right were politely ignored.   In 1859, the **English Church Union** was formed to further the Romanising movement and protect the law-breakers.   This led to the formation of the "Church Association," in 1865, to reassert Protestant doctrine and practice, but how could the true cause of Christ be advanced by appeals to the law-courts ?   The Church of England carried in herself the seeds of dissolution.   The teaching of baptismal regeneration in her formularies can only be got rid of by special pleading.   The only remedy is separation from the evil.

The decision in the celebrated **Gorham case,** though it seemed in favour of the Evangelical party, was really a curse in disguise. Had the Privy Council supported Bishop Philpotts in his plea that the true and only doctrine of the Church of England is "baptismal regeneration," the Evangelicals must have left in a body and formed a "Church" on a more Scriptural basis. At least they would have cleared themselves from complicity with openly unsound doctrine.   As it was, this opportunist decision, a mere juggling with words, has ever since given them the *locus standi*, which truth denies to them.

However, what the Evangelicals seemed to gain by the Gorham decision they lost by the **Bennett Judgment,** in 1872, which really legalised "transubstantiation," though that word was not used.   There was the opportunity for the Evangelicals to follow the splendid example of the Scotch Seceders of 1843, but nothing effectual was attempted.

In 1877 another opportunity occurred.   The **Ridsdale Judg-**

* " Popery and Jesuitism in Rome," p. 128.

ment practically legalised the Eastward or Sacrificial position of the celebrant at the Holy Communion. But the Evangelicals remained passive. And then in 1890 occurred the prosecution of Dr. King, the Bishop of Lincoln, as a man no doubt most pious and earnest, but as thorough-going a Romaniser as existed. He was practically acquitted by his fellow-bishops of all serious illegality, except on one or two minor points, and their decision was confirmed in 1892 by the highest court of appeal. Surely then the Lord's people in the Church of England might have seen that their place was not within, but outside a Church where illegality and opportunism ruled, not law and truth, and much less the Word of God, to which indeed no appeal could be made. But only a very few had the energy " to obey God rather than man."

EVANGELICAL DEGENERACY.

Since then things have gone from bad to worse. On every side now may be seen " Churches " in some cases once evangelical, and built with evangelical money, turned into mass-houses, their ministers " sacrificing " and confessional-haunting " priests." The indignation once felt has given way to acquiescence. The scandals of the eighties have become the common-places of this century.

The movement continues to spread and intensify. Only lately unofficial meetings for conference have come to light between Anglican clergymen, accredited by the Archbishops of Canterbury and York, and representatives of the Romish Church, an ominous sign when taken with the determined effort to Romanise officially the formularies and prayer-book of the Established Church.

The movement has even spread, incredible as it may appear, doubtless under the same Jesuitical management, to the non-conformist bodies, and a notorious dissenting and ritualistic " priest," practising extreme Romish ceremonial and auricular confession in the bosom of the Congregational Denomination, boasts that he has between 300 and 400 dissenting " priests " on his list of associates.

We may be sure of two things : First, were Rome to regain her old place in our land, she would show herself the same as ever, an opponent of the Gospel of the grace of God, hostile to, if not a burner of, Holy Scriptures, and a determined enemy of civil and religious liberty ; and, secondly, when the reunion of Christendom does take place, as it surely will, it will be manifested in its final form as " The Great Whore ; Mystery Babylon," to be destroyed later by the Beast and his ten-kingdomed confederacy.

The various worldly religious systems, however much they may seem to differ, are in essence one in their **exaltation of** man—Pope, cardinals, archbishops, bishops, priests, dissenting ministers and theological professors, and their hatred of the Christ of God and His salvation by grace alone. When we examine the tenets of the Ritualist we are face to face with a system as legal as Sinai, and, in all but names and phrases, not really more Christian. The work of Christ as a true atonement, fully meeting all the claims of God and placing the believer, as justified and accepted, in the presence of God, is unknown. The idea of sacrifice is associated with the Eucharistic offering, rather than with Calvary, which, according to their teaching, needs to be repeated, and so is really as powerless as the Jewish sacrifices (Heb. 10). The Cross is viewed more as the instrument of our Lord's passion, than the finished work accomplished there. Salvation by works, prayers, fastings, and discipline is the rule, and grace is unknown. The Church replaces Christ, tradition the Bible; baptismal regeneration and the "Sacrament," personal faith in Christ.

Many Ritualists are most earnest and sincere men, ultimately trusting in Christ for final acceptance ; but they have "fallen from grace," and are frankly on legal ground ; Ritualism being essentially the old Judaising heresy which afflicted the Galatian and other of the early Churches. The Ritualist is essentially Roman in all but name ; Jezebel was allowed to prophecy, now she reigns.

MODERNISM.

Meanwhile another movement has been spreading throughout the professing Churches, permeating like leaven every department of religious life. It is known as "**Modernism**," or "**Higher Criticism.**" The name is misleading ; the thing is as old as the Christian Era, indeed as Eden. Satan has a snare for every type of mind ; for the superstitious, Romanism and Ritualism ; for the Rationalistic, Modernism. The Ritualist makes God's Word void by his traditions, the Rationalist by his reasonings.

The word "Modernism" comes from the Rationalistic movement in the Church of Rome, with which such names as the Abbé Loizy and Father Tyrrell were associated. The movement in its outward expression was speedily crushed, but the act remains, and, in spite of the Roman claim to unity of doctrine, the thing itself is no doubt still widely prevalent in the Romish Church.

Though Modernism, in its latter day sense as the Higher Criticism, arose in France, its spiritual home is Germany. Dr. Colenso, of Natal, had the unenviable claim of being the harbinger of the movement in England. His neo-critical works on the Pentateuch and Joshua extending over a period of seventeen years (1861-79), created a storm of controversy. But he is now almost forgotten. His attack failed pitifully.

The Higher Critics of to-day go far beyond his wildest fancies, and they are failing, too—though one claim of theirs impresses the public. They speak as though they had a monopoly of scholarship. They are fond of repeating that their conclusions are " the inevitable finding of scholarships " or are such as are " universally recognised by scholars." Such a conviction, however mistaken, must be very reassuring. But it is not accurate. God has been pleased to raise up from the ranks of His people competent champions for His truth. Would it be reasonable to deny " **Scholarship** " to such men as Drs. W. L. Baxter, James Orr, Green, Moller, Sir William Ramsay ? Are men like Drs. M. G. Kyle, R. D. Wilson, of the U.S.A., to be refused the name of scholars ? Could no one worthy of such a description be found among the authors of " Lex Mosaica," Professor Sayce, Canon Rawlinson, Canon Girdlestone, Bishop Valpy Trench, Chancellor Lias, Dr. Stanley Leathes, Dr. R. Sinker, and Dean Wace ? Is the taunt levelled at the Higher Critical school altogether without foundation, that they fail to take serious notice of works on the conservative side ? It has, for instance, been seriously questioned whether " Sanctuary and Sacrifice " (Dr. W. L. Baxter), " The Unity of the Pentateuch " (A. H. Finn), " Early Religion of Israel " (Dr. J. Robertson), " The Higher Critics and the Verdict of the Monuments " (Dr. A. H. Sayce) have been adequately answered.* There are some good people who seem to love peace at any price. What they would have done in the martyr days is a great mystery. They seem to mistake liberality for charity and tolerance of evil for brotherly-kindness. They deprecate all controversy. " **Don't defend the Bible**," is their slogan. Well, we do not believe that the Bible needs defence. All the critics in the world will never destroy one verse, but we do fear lest " the faith of some be overthrown " (2 Tim. 2. 18).

One would suppose that the findings of the Higher Critics, so subversive as they are of the Foundations of the Faith, would only be put forward with reluctance and sorrow under the pressure of inexorable proofs. But this is not the case. If the Higher Critics do feel regret at having to wreck the Faith of the ages, they are successful in concealing it. Their reasonings, too, are very subjective, and the linguistic argument on which they lay so much weight is declared by such scholars as Erdmans, Harold Wiener, and R. D. Wilson (of Princeton, U.S.A.) to be precarious and false. Their theories, moreover, far from displaying the stability which soundness imparts, succeed one another with a vertiginous celerity.

The " **document** " **theory** of Eichorn was succeeded by the

---

* For information on the subject, see " The Higher Criticism," by R. Sinker, D.D., and " Jonah's Critics Criticized," by W. Hoste, B.A.

"Supplement" theory of De Wette; that by what was some-times known as the "crystallization hypothesis" of Ewald and Hupfield. That again was superseded by what is now the dominant theory in Britain, the scheme of Kuenen and Well-hausen. This has been challenged by the newer school of Maurice Vernes and others, and König himself protests against the treatment of the Hebrew Scriptures by Wellhausen. Should not this contradictory testimony of the "scholars" give room for pause?

The publication of "**Essays and Reviews**," mostly by digni-taries of the Church of England, marked an epoch in the develop-ment of this movement. It stepped into the light. The work was censured by nearly all the bishops on the bench, and formally by Convocation in 1860. The excitement and controversy raised by such a book only emphasizes the serious progress of this leaven in later years. The "Essays" would now be regarded as the commonplaces of religious thought, and by many even as hopelessly behind the times. One of the essayists eventually became Archbishop of Canterbury.

Probably few circumstances have contributed more to the spread of the movement than the appointment of Drs. S. R. Driver and T. K. Cheyne (who had both been members of the Old Testament Revision Committee), the former in 1883 as Regius Professor of Hebrew at Oxford, the other two years later as "Oriel Professor of Interpretation of Holy Scripture." To those who were repelled by the extreme vagaries of the Oriel Professor, the more conservative, but scarcely less deadly handling of the Scriptures by the Regius Professor (Dr. Driver) made appeal. The influence of these men was felt not only within the pale of their own Church, but practically among all sections of dissent. The venerable Canon Christopher of Oxford, in his kindness of heart, thought it a great triumph when he prevailed on these two Higher Critics to be present at his annual C.M.S. breakfast. It may be that that very fact led C.M.S. men to read their writings, and thus contributed to the spread of their evil doctrine in the Society as it is to-day.

EVOLUTION.

The appearance of **Darwin's "Origin of Species,"** in 1859, and later "The Descent of Man," exercised a profound influence in the succeeding decades of the past century. These ideas com-pletely fascinated the scientific world as a theory, and that greater world, the pseudo-scientific, as a scientific fact, and was popularised by the cheaper press for whom and its readers it became as unquestionable as gravitation, and the very hall-mark of the enlightened mind. But for the true scientist it never outgrew the stage of a working hypothesis, which held the field in default of some more plausible explanation. Darwinism and the Evolutionary Theory it professes to explain are certainly an attack on the Creatorship of God. "Darwin," according to Haekel, "had provided an 'Anti-Genesis,' and won a conclusive victory over the mythical superannuated Biblical accounts." There can be no doubt that the whole tendency of the hypothesis has been, as in its author, so in its adherents, to darken faith and obscure the authority of the Scriptures. Darwinism is now largely discredited.

"Natural selection" was an important plank in the original theory, and Dubois-Reymond speaks* thus of it : "We seem to have the sensation, in holding to this doctrine, of a man hopelessly sinking, who is grasping a single plank that keeps him above water." This plank had to be superseded by Darwin himself with another, "sexual selection." But that could not prevent its foundering. Wilser has said :† "He is no scientist who has not settled accounts with Darwinism." But then we are told "**Evolution**" still holds good. But if its explanation be gone, how can it be scientific to hold what no one can prove or explain ?

Yet we need not be surprised at all this. In the perennial conflict between truth and evil ; one lie must succeed another till the cup of iniquity is full. Then the truth will shine forth and be recognised as it already is by all subject to God and His Word.

This leaven has permeated the Churches, national and free, at home, leading to the federation of the latter on a basis mainly of unbelief. It has lately been publicly stated in a well-known‡ American journal, by a prominent Nonconformist minister of London, "that the National Free Church Council of Great Britain, by its acceptance of the Presidential Statement of Dr. G. can no longer be regarded as an evangelical movement . . . but is to-day a body of ministers and Churches having for its object the express purpose of ignoring and denying the very fundamentals of the Christian Faith." Not only so, but it has attacked the mission field. A great change has taken place regarding the whole missionary question.

MISSION WORK.

Forty years ago the godly and devoted men who went forth as missionaries were subjects of ridicule to many even in the religious world. To-day the enemy has sown his tares—**Missionary work** has become quite fashionable. The mission field is overrun with men of the Modernist school, who preach "another gospel." Bible Leagues and Unions have been formed in China and India, not as might be expected to combat the false systems of heathen-

* "Modern Science and Christianity," Bettex. p. 147.
† Idem (footnote).
‡ "The King's Business," Nov., 1924, by Dr. E.A.C.

dom, but the negations of Modernist colleagues. Missions to missionaries are sadly needed to-day. The Home Committees in many cases either cannot or will not interfere ; they are too often tainted with the same virus.

The heathen are encouraged in their unholy faiths by the denials of so-called Christian professors and missionaries. A great change has come over even evangelical work, as for instance the Church Missionary Society. Its founders were men who would have died for the faith ; their successors deny it, for they explicitly refuse to accept the utterances of Christ Himself, and virtually charge Him, who is the Truth and who only spake as the Father gave Him commandment, with ignorance and obscurantism. All honour to those faithful men, who have shaken off the dust of their feet against her, and have founded the "**Bible Church Missionary Society**," on the old well-tried evangelical lines. And what a spectacle is presented by the Established Church ! High dignitaries, men who have* at, to them, the most solemn moments of their lives, affirmed their "unfeigned belief in all the Canonical Scriptures of the Old and New Testament," and later promised "with all faithful diligence, to banish and drive away all erroneous and strange doctrines contrary to God's Word," are found shamelessly vieing with one another as to who can go furthest in denials of such vital truths as the "Virgin birth," the Resurrection of the body, the veracity of Christ, in order to keep abreast of modern thought and placate the scientific world. Certainly the path of ecclesiastical preferment to-day leads by the way of lawlessness, either to the formularies of the Church or to the Fundamentals of the Faith.

THE CONTINENTAL CHURCHES.

Modernism has wrought havoc in the **Protestant Churches** of the Continent, and the faithful few have been too weak to raise an effective protest, but in the United States and Canada it is otherwise. There the champions of the truth are waging a good warfare for Christ and His Word, and are even carrying the war into the enemy's country, ably supported by such Christian journals as *The Sunday School Times* of Philadelphia, *The Free Presbyterian Magazine*, *The King's Business*, etc., and the Modernists are posing as martyrs. But this is not permissible. No one denies to any other man the right to believe or disbelieve, to teach or deny what he likes, but he must not profess, at his appointment to a post, to hold one set of beliefs, and claim the right to change them subsequently without notice. On what principle of righteousness should a man accept payment to preach certain specific doctrines, and insist later on his right to preach the opposite ?

* See Services for the Ordering of Deacons and Priests and Consecration of Bishops, "Book of Common Prayer."

At home God is raising up able men, not only among scholars of the first rank, but among Bible students, teachers, and writers who are taught of the Spirit how to use His Sword. The "**Bible League**," the "**Baptist Bible Union**," the "**Victoria Institute**," and other such bodies are all bearing their part in the good warfare, in sure and certain hope of final victory for "we can do nothing against the truth but for the truth." But as long as Modernism holds our Theological and Missionary Colleges, what hope of better things can there be ? The testimony is poisoned at its source.

UNSCRIPTURAL CULTS.

Along with Modernism all systems of unbelief or misbelief flourish. **Spiritism** has made great progress in all civilised lands. It is supposed to show the survival of the soul, but its votaries are dupes of demons, as their teaching proves, which is both antibiblical and antichristian. Other kindred systems such as Christian Science, Millennial Dawnism, Seventh-day Adventism, Annihilationism, and Universalism spread and increase and slay their thousands. Many true children of God are ensnared by false holiness teachings and such mistaken views as Pentecostalism and the Tongues Movement. Claims to powers of Faith-healing are advanced on all sides, which, if tested by the Holy Scriptures and the New Testament pattern leave little doubt of their spurious character ; but the religious world is gulled and loves to have it so. Alas, the whole course of the Church of God is strewn with wrecks from these and other false systems. Let him that thinketh he standeth, take heed lest he fall !

But are we to be surprised at such things ? We are warned to expect them. We are in the last days, and such were to be difficult. The Word is clear : " Evil men and seducers shall wax worse and worse, deceiving and being deceived. But continue thou in the things that thou hast learned, knowing of whom thou hast learned them, and that from a child thou hast known the Holy Scriptures which are able to make thee wise unto salvation, through faith which is in Christ Jesus. All Scripture is given by inspiration of God and is profitable for doctrine, for reproof, for correction, for instruction in righteousness that the man of God may be perfect, thoroughly furnished unto all good works."

THE EVANGELICAL REVIVAL.

We now turn from the workings of man's mind, whether religious or rationalistic, to the workings of the Spirit of God, corresponding to the Church of Philadelphia. Three things marked this Church, a "little strength," a "holding fast the Word of Christ," and "faithfulness to His Name." This is exemplified in the **Modern Evangelical Revival,** beginning in the eighteenth century with the " Methodist " movement under

Wesley and Whitefield. Man's work is in contrast with God's. It is big like the great tree of Matthew 13, and is so far popular with the world, but it cares not for Christ or His Word.

The last half century has been the heir to the **Revivals of '59** and the succeeding years. Beginning in Ireland, they radiated throughout the world. They naturally prepared the way for the wave of evangelistic and philanthropic activities of the seventies, which centred largely round the visits of the American evangelists, **Moody and Sankey,** beginning in 1873 and continuing at intervals during the following decade. D. L. Moody was born at Northfield, U.S.A., in 1837. Chicago was the first scene of his mission labours. In 1870 he was joined by Ira D. Sankey, three years his junior. Together they held numerous missions in America, and then in all parts of Great Britain and Ireland, amidst universal interest and blessing. Such buildings as the Opera House and Agricultural Hall, besides immense buildings specially erected in London, being crowded weeks on end. Perhaps not since the Whitefield days had such gatherings been known.

A characteristic of the last half of the nineteenth century has been the enterprises for God initiated by individual Christians, usually " **laymen,**" and quite outside the influence and favour of ecclesiastical circles. Such have been the Tower Hamlets Mission founded in the East End of London by Frederick Charrington, the Mildmay Mission to the Jews founded by John Wilkinson, Fegan's Homes, Quarrier's Homes, Miss Daniels' Soldiers' Homes ; Dame Agnes Weston's work in the Navy ; also such world-wide movements as the Blue Ribbon Temperance Mission of R. Booth, and the " Christian Endeavour Society " of Dr. Clarke, both of the U.S.A.

Comparatively few Evangelical Christians in the early eighties did not wear the **blue ribbon,** and later the C.E. badge became very familiar. Anything denominated by a ribbon or a badge has its day of popularity, but like all other earthly fashions, passes away.

ORPHANAGES.

Though the **Ashley Down Orphan Homes** go back nearly ninety years they continue to occupy no unimportant place in the testimony for God in the world. George Müller was born in Prussia, in 1805. Converted to God when a theological student at Halle, at the age of twenty, he soon after came to London to prepare for mission work among the Jews, but his course was ordered otherwise. The Orphanages were opened in 1836, not only as a work of mercy, but primarily as a testimony to the faithfulness of God. It was of course not George Müller who originated the idea of trusting God for temporal supplies, but the Homes under his care and his successors have been in a special way a demonstration by God of His living faithfulness, and an encouragement to others of His servants to venture out on the same path. But living by faith is not limited to temporal supplies. When Paul wrote of " living by faith of the Son of God " he spoke not merely as an apostle, but as a Christian. All such are called to this path. It may sometimes be easier to trust God for Heaven than for the next loaf or a new coat, though these things ought not so to be. From 1836 up to George Müller's death in 1898, a period of sixty-two years, over £988,000 were received for the building of the Homes and the support of the orphans. During the twenty-six years which have elapsed since, not very far short of the same amount has been contributed, namely over £816,000. Besides this, a total of over £312,000 have been received and distributed for the maintenance of mission work at home and abroad, making a total of over £2,000,117 received, without appeal to man, but only to the living God in the Name of Jesus Christ. Surely this is an encouragement to writer and reader to trust in God " at all times," " with all our heart " and " evermore."

Y.M.C.A.—RISE AND DECLINE.

Another name that has left its mark " writ large " on the closing decades of last century was **Sir George Williams**, the founder of the **Y.M.C.A.** Little could the business clerk from Dulverton have thought when in 1846 he opened a room for young City men in St. Paul's Churchyard, that he was starting a movement destined to be a help to thousands in peace, and nothing less than a national asset in the Great War, as universal caterer for our soldiers, though, as far as the Gospel went, if report be true, " the fine gold had become dim."

In 1880, Sir George, in conjunction with other Christian men, bought Exeter Hall at a cost of £25,000, which became not only the Central Quarters of the Y.M.C.A., but a rallying ground for evangelical workers and societies, for which in the popular eye it stood. When he died his sons presented his house to the Association in his memory, and the present building on that site forms the Central Y.M.C.A. in Tottenham Court Road. The present-day departures of the Association, Christian Alliance of Women and Girls, with many notable exceptions, from the old standards and its surrender to the Modernist spirit would have filled the founder with grief and dismay. The same retrograde movement has been painfully manifested in the Y.W.C.A., and has led to the formation of a New Association on the old well-known Bible lines. These Associations carried in themselves the principle of their own disintegration in that at any moment the membership might and generally did find itself in a minority. It was the " associates " who had to be catered for, and the

Y.M.C.A. henceforth, instead of " sticking to its last," began to rival the world at its own amusements. If the Church becomes worldly to gain the world, it is the world that has gained the Church. As long as the leaders were spiritual, they averted the catastrophe, but when they became worldly and opportunist the disaster was inevitable.

The same process has taken place in the Y.W.C.A., not so much on the side of Modernism, as of worldly method. The idea of true Evangelism is to take out of the world a people for God's Name, not to make a number of worldlings more respectable or even to make a better world.

The present day is a day of testing for works and principles ; what is of God will stand, the rest will be carried away in the current of apostasy, and become a bit of the world going on to judgment.

Two other names may be mentioned here. They began works in a humble way in faith in God, and became of world-wide importance. One was Dr. Barnardo and the other William Booth, the " General " of the Salvation Army.

DR. BARNARDO'S HOMES.

The work of **Dr. Barnardo** was begun in 1866, owing to what was humanly-speaking a chance discovery of the otherwise incredible conditions under which many poor slum boys were existing in the East of London. In 1873 a village home was opened at Ilford for training girls. The Young Helpers' League was formed in 1891. Emigration to Canada and other British Colonies has formed a large and successful feature of the work. Only two per cent have failed to make good. Religious training and Gospel effort have always had a good place in this work, but there has been no claim in this case that the enormous outlay has been met " without appeal to man."

THE SALVATION ARMY.

It was in 1865 that **William Booth** took his stand on the Mile End Waste to fulfil his part of responsibility towards the lost of the East End. The work continued for thirteen years as the Christian Mission, and it was only in 1878 that it finally took shape as a military religious system, entitled " The Salvation Army." The founder was born in Nottingham, in 1829, and in 1850 was a Methodist Minister there till 1861, when he moved to London. The Army at first met with great opposition in this and other countries, but its social work went far to break this down, and to-day it is recognised as occupying a definite niche in the national life, and the offence of the " red jersey " may be said to have ceased at all events in the home lands (whether for the better or worse we will not assert). The world can appreciate " labours of love," but " works of faith " are to them worse than folly. The works of faith singled out by the Spirit of God in James 2, from the Old Testament story where the sacrifice of Isaac and the reception of the spies by Rahab, the one in the eyes of the world child-murder, the other a base betrayal of country.

The Army operates to-day in 79 countries and colonies, with 13,577 corps and subposts. It is not for us to laud to the skies or deprecate severely the work of any of the Lord's servants. " Judge nothing before the time." Every man's work shall be tried of what sort it is. But even now it may be asked by what right administrative and executive authority over men in the things of God can Scripturally be vested in women, or by what authority a dedication service replaces the initatory rite of baptism or a holiness-meeting the Lord's Supper. On the other hand, we must rejoice that doubtless by means of this great organisation multitudes have heard of Christ who might otherwise have lived and died without it. It has been said that God has many different moulds, and only uses them once.

METROPOLITAN TABERNACLE.

While Booth and Barnardo were consolidating their efforts, and even years before, a preacher had been drawing great crowds in London, who, had he lived in early days' might have been known as Charles " Chrysostom," and who by the printed sermon and volume became a world-wide witness for the Gospel of the grace of God. Born in 1834, at Kelvedon, Essex, the son of an Independent Minister, **Charles Haddon Spurgeon**, already at the age of sixteen a lay-preacher at Cambridge, became later Baptist Pastor at Waterbeach. In 1854 he. too. gravitated to London, and it may be quoted as a testimony to his extraordinary gift that as a young man of twenty-three, he was chosen to address an audience of 23,000 people at the Crystal Palace, on the day of National Humiliation during the Indian Mutiny. The great Metropolitan Tabernacle, to hold 6,000, was finished in 1861, where he continued for thirty years to attract large crowds. The Tabernacle became a Mecca for Evangelical pilgrims from all parts of the world. In 1856 Spurgeon founded the Pastors' College, and the Stockwell Orphanage in 1867. Besides his wekly sermons and his monthly *Sword and Trowel*, he gave the world more than a hundred volumes. In 1887 he withdrew from the Baptist Union on account of what he considered to be their connivance with down-grade preachers and teachers. He had previously left the "**Evangelical Alliance**," because their membership included so many Evangelical clergymen, who, while denying baptismal regeneration in word, continued to teach it in their Church catechism and formularies. When he left the Baptist Union he found his chief supporters among the so-called "brethren," towards whom he had up till then displayed but little sympathy. He passed away in 1892, at the premature age of fifty-eight, leaving a name to be remembered. Thousands will rise and call him blessed. His sermons, reprinted or published for the first time have continued to have a wide circulation. He has been followed at the Tabernacle by an "apostolic succession" of men, his inferiors, as was almost inevitable, in gift, but faithful to the truths he held dear.

BIBLE AND OTHER SOCIETIES.

A characteristic of the period under review has been the rise of the undenominational Society or Mission. Perhaps it would be more correct to term this interdenominational or pan-denominational. It did not mean that Christians had any intention of giving up their denominational position, that they held to as strongly as ever, but that they recognised the common bond of Christian unity above and beyond the sectarian differences. This spirit had already found expression in such great organisations as the **British and Foreign Bible Society**, formed in 1804, the London City Mission founded in the thirties, the Ragged School Movement begun a little later, and was further manifested in the formation of the Evangelical Alliance in 1845-46, an alliance not of Churches, but of individual Christians of any country, holding "the views commonly called Evangelical," laid down by the Alliance on a definite ninefold doctrinal basis. They have held a series of international congresses in various capitals—London, Paris, Berlin, Geneva, New York, etc. Its organ is *Evangelical Christendom*. The Evangelical Section of the Church of England led the van in this movement of reunion. A common reproach against the Evangelicals was that they put the individual before the "Church." This is true, if by Church is meant an ecclesiastical organisation, but not, if the thought be of a spiritual organism, embracing all true members of Christ. They called this the "Invisible Church," and so, of course, it is as a whole ; but surely the Christianity of the individual should not be invisible. Should not all such endeavour to keep the Unity of the Spirit by recognising one another, and coming together as members of their Risen Head to His Name alone. The united "**Week of Prayer**" at each New Year was an expression of this desire, but the question was sometimes put in a friendly way afterwards, "Why if you can come together as Christians for the first week of the year, should that Name not suffice for the remaining fifty-one ? " In the seventies and eighties the Evangelical party in the Church of England were a power in the land. Dr. J. C. Ryle, of Liverpool, exercised wide influence by his writings and as an outspoken leader of

Evangelical thought, and in a more general sense as Christian teachers the names of Drs. Lightfoot, Westcott, and Moule, all afterwards in succession Bishops of Durham, stand out pre-eminently; Canon Christopher was holding the fort at Oxford; Canon Hoare, Sholto Douglas, afterwards Lord Blythswood, and men of their stamp were pillars of Evangelical truth; and such names as the Bevans, Dennys, Lord Shaftesbury, were household words in the eighties.

THE REVISION OF THE SCRIPTURES.

The name of Westcott attaches itself naturally to **the Revised Version** of the New Testament, in which he, along with Dr. Hort, took a predominant part. The Revision of the Authorised Version was based on a previous revision of the Greek Text, based to a large extent on the great Uncials Sinaiticus and Vaticanus, for which they (Drs. Westcott and Hort) had, as some* believe, an exaggerated predilection. Copies of this Greek Text were distributed among the Company of Revisers on the eve of their first sitting, and no doubt exercised a strong influence on the ultimate result. Had the Revisers attempted less, they would have accomplished more. The resultant version, while confessedly introducing many useful changes, went far beyond its mandate, and is generally considered by judges to be woefully inferior to the Authorised Version as an English translation. Even its admirers now sorrowfully admit it will never replace that version. This was followed three years later by that of the Old Testament. Warned by the hostile reception accorded to the New Testament Revision, the revisers were in this case far more conservative. The Church Missionary Society had not then allowed itself to be contaminated by the Modernist virus. The Ritualistic movement was only gradually fighting its way to the front. Neo-Evangelism, with its feeble grasp of the old distinctively evangelical truths, the total depravity of man, and the Atonement, as a necessity if the holy claims of God were to be met, was not then exercising its deadening influence. Now you may read of such an anomaly as a " liberal-evangelical " bishop, and there are " neo-evangelicals " to-day who would sooner doubt the utterances of our Lord than believe in the story of Jonah.

MILDMAY, KESWICK, AND OTHER CONFERENCES.

Another movement may be noticed, that of Christians of various denominations coming together for days to Conference. The **Mildmay Conference** may be considered the parent of many similar gatherings. It was initiated by William Pennefather, Vicar of Mildmay, and continued for a long series of years under

* *e.g.*, Drs. Scrivener and Burgon no less authorities in their way than the other two scholars mentioned.

the leadership of the founder, Sir Arthur Blackwood, Permanent Secretary of the Post Office ; Captain Moreton, John Mathieson, Lord Polwarth, Lord Kintore, and others. At these conferences the truths of the oneness of the body and the headship of Christ were realised in a marked degree with corresponding joy in the members, and it may be questioned whether any series of conferences since have preserved such a high level of spirituality and sound doctrine as those conferences during the seventies and early eighties. There were giants in those days. The Bonars, Grattan Guinness, Webb-Peploe, Evan Hopkins, Charles Fox, were household words.

This Conference has been superseded by **Keswick.** Their motto is, " *All one in Christ Jesus.*" Quite apart from its distinctive " higher-life " teachings, these conventions have been a means of refreshment to multitudes. Christ has been presented as the sufficient source to the believer, according to his faith, of sanctification, as well as justification. There is always a danger of a movement, a scheme of doctrine, a place gradually superseding Christ. Then the blessing, like Cherith's brook, dries up. Keswick has set loose and directed a considerable force of missionary enthusiasm, and many of her lovers have carried the Gospel to the ends of the earth, the South African General Mission, the Ceylon General Mission, and other similar organisations have drunk largely of her spirit.

Again, it seems a matter for regret that where this unity is recognised, and no other Name but Christ permitted for the duration of a conference, other names should have to be recognised next day on the return home. What a contrast for men who have been preaching high doctrine on a convention platform to have to descend to the conventionalities of denominational routine ! Reports of the Keswick Movement are given in various journals. Among other religious journals that have exercised a good evangelical influence might be mentioned, *The Christian*, a champion of every good cause ; *The Record* ; *The English Churchman*, voicing different wings of the Evangelicals ; *The Witness*, standing for " All the Word of God for all the People of God." These have continued to uphold the banner of the truth in their respective circles.

CHRISTIAN JOURNALISM.

The last fifty years have witnessed a notable advance in Christian, as in worldly journalism of every periodicity, form and spiritual note, including an ever increasing number of missionary magazines. In fact, there is a danger of the Bible being ousted by books and papers about the Bible, and missionary work being hampered by the supposed necessity of continually recording its successes. Any account of the nineteenth century would be defective which failed to record the important services of the **Seventh Earl of Shaftesbury,** already referred to, to the Church of Christ. God has His trophies of grace from the highest as from the lowest strata of Society ; the former need that grace no less than the latter.

God early marked out young Lord Ashley as His own. Born in London in 1801, he owed, it is said, his earliest and deepest religious impressions to a faithful old servant. At twenty-eight he entered Parliament for Bath, and was a Lord of the Admiralty in 1834-35. As a " Member " he was instrumental in passing a number of philanthropic measures for the betterment of conditions in mines and for the restriction of hours of labour, and of the age limit of children workers. He amended and extended the Factory Acts, and was largely instrumental in effecting as a Lunacy Commissioner (1831-85) a complete reform of the Lunacy Acts. In 1843 he threw himself into the Ragged School movement, and indeed no movement for the social, moral, evangelistic good of the needy classes failed to find his cordial and able support. Such works as the London City Mission, the Bible· Society, the Y.M.C.A., owed much to his influence, which indeed was great everywhere, even in the Cabinet of his relative Lord Palmerston, as regards his ecclesiastical appointments, and a number of excellent prelates nominated during his Premierships were known as " Shaftesbury's bishops." It is said that Queen Victoria and the Prince Consort sought his counsel. He was an out and out Evangelical openly opposed to Ritualism, Rationalism, and Socialism, a friend of good men wherever found, a champion of every noble cause. But what was it made him to differ ? Only the grace of God. He was a sinner saved by grace, and his position was merely a talent entrusted to him to be used for God.

The same can be said of other noble sinners besides the old Countess of Huntington, who was thankful, as has often been recorded, for the letter " M," for otherwise the " not many noble " of Corinthians would have read " not any noble." Among these we might mention Lords Lynhurst, Selbourne, **Cairns,** Hatherly, and **Halsbury**—all Lord Chancellors of comparatively later years. Those who hold that only the weak-minded can be evangelicals might find in the fact just noted food for thought.

SPECIAL MISSIONS AND MOVEMENTS.

Other names might be mentioned, among many others such stalwart soldiers of the Cross as **Brownlow North,** Henry Varley, Reginald Radcliffe. Two other names deserve more than a passing reference, neither prominent in the world of politics or even philanthrophy, but both having left a deep mark in the spiritual life of a certain strongly evangelical circle of their time.

I refer to Lord Congleton and **Lord Radstock**, the former through his connection with a very real movement of the Spirit of God among His people, the latter for his evangelistic witness in divers countries among all classes. The movement with which **Lord Congleton** was connected from its commencement has, in spite of the failures, and they have been many and humiliating, of its leaders, made the whole Church its debtor by its influence for God during the last ninety years. But to be indebted and that involuntarily, to a person does not guarantee love to that person, and it must be admitted that the attitude of these reformers to their fellow-Christians has not always been such as to beget love. The so-called " **brethren** " **movement** has not lacked its critics and detractors, but few spiritual persons would deny that it has been an honest attempt to return to the Holy Scriptures, and has in measure acted as a salt of the earth to hold in check the apostasy of Christendom.

Its rise about 1830 practically synchronised with that of the High Church Movement already referred to Possibly the connection between the two may not be far to seek, the one intended by unseen powers to counteract the other—as Jesuitism the Reformation. This movement began in a very informal way. The Lord knew what He would do, but it did not follow the chief actors did. It is an anachronism to read back into their minds that they were " fleeing from the corruption of Christendom back to primitive simplicity." Men like **Anthony Norris Groves,** J. G. Bellett, Dr. Cronin, Lord Congleton, to limit ourselves to Dublin—though the movement seems to have been " in the air " in various places—were, with the exception of Cronin, who was a Congregationalist, laymen of the Established Church, and mostly High Churchmen at that. **J. N. Darby,** who came in later, was a clergyman of decidedly high-church convictions and practices, disclaiming the name of Protestant, practising strict fastings, holding apostolic succession, and utterly opposed to the Erastianism of the Low Church party in Ireland, who would appeal to the State in their conflicts with the Roman Catholic Church. The union of Church and State he held to be Babylonish.

There was no idea in the minds of Groves and his fellow-seekers after truth, of forming a new " Church " or of leaving their " Church," but it kept dawning on them that certain things were by the Scriptures permissible, that till then had been forbidden by the Churches, and that certain things these had regarded as indispensable, such as human ordination to preach the Gospel or administer the Sacraments, were after all not insisted on in the Scriptures. Why should they not as Christians meet as the early disciples did, to break bread every Lord's day **in remembrance of their Lord** ?

It is clear that when once men get fairly launched on the principle that only Scriptural permissions and prohibitions count they will sail far and discover a new world.   Everything must go that has not a " thus saith the Lord."   It has been said by critics " that with the brethren the garnered experience of eighteen Christian centuries counted for nothing."   But at least two experiences seem to have counted, and the first was, to how serious a departure a small deflection from the Word of God may lead ; and, secondly, how heavy a burden a slight addition to that Word may become !   It is easy to see the difference between this and the High Church methods.   These Dublin believers and their fellow-disciples went back straight to the New Testament.   They did not stop to inquire, " What saith Rome ? " or " What think the Fathers ? "   But, " What saith the Holy Ghost through His apostles and prophets ? "   The Tractarians, too, would go back to primitive use, but it was a laborious plod back on foot through the dark ages, and always via Rome, where so many stuck fast.   Some got back as far as the Fathers, but few if any to apostolic precedent or precept.   It was apparently too much to hope that we could ever agree as to what the early disciples professed and practised.

"A RETURN TO THE WORD OF GOD."

Here was a living principle, the basis of every true revival that ever has taken place, a return to the Word of God.   No wonder men of spiritual light and leading were profoundly influenced.   It has been asked, " Which of all the smaller sects of Christendom has enrolled among its enthusiastic adherents such men as John Nelson Darby and Francis William Newman (brother of the Cardinal), George Müller and Anthony Norris Groves ; Benjamin Wills Newton and Samuel Prideaux Tregelles," and we might add William Kelly of Guernsey, and Robert Chapman of Barnstaple.   But " let no man glory in men ! "   What had these that they had not received ?

Though this movement, like Tractarianism, was not in its origin the work of any one outstanding man, there can be little question which of the above exercised the greatest influence (perhaps some will say for evil as well as good) on its subsequent development.

J. N. Darby was born in London, in 1800, a few months before Cardinal Newman, and a year before Lord Shaftesbury.   He was educated at Westminster School, otherwise he was thoroughly Irish.   At the age of fifteen he entered at Trinity College, Dublin, and in 1819 graduated there as Classical Gold Medallist, no mean testimony to his scholarship, which has been belittled by some, and is quite in harmony with the phenomenal gifts for languages he afterwards displayed, and used so signally in the service of Christ. Like J. G. Bellett, he was called to the bar, but soon yielded to another call, and was ordained deacon and priest in the Church of Ireland ; and as late as 1834, though he had by then formed close connections with those " breaking bread," he had not completely separated from the Church of Ireland. The movement began in an irregular, indefinite way. Lord Congleton, then John Parnell, was among the first to break bread on the pattern of the early Church, and continued faithful to the end of a long life to the earliest and simplest principles of the testimony.

Another point of contact between those known as " brethren " and the Tractarians was that they both went further than the individual to **the truth of the Church** ; but the Church of the Tractarian was a Christianised world, that of the " brethren " would ideally include all the true believers in every place.

We need not trace the subsequent history of this movement which has ramified through every part of the world, new and old, and especially of the British Empire—Canada, South Africa, and the Antipodes, and the United States of America. But so far from its being a merely Anglo-Saxon movement, it has spread in France, Germany, and Switzerland, and it is said that there are to-day in Russia more assemblies of simple believers than in the British Isles, whilst there is scarcely a country but quite a number of companies assemble on these simple principles of the New Testament.

Wherever God has been counted on, and Christ given His true place in the midst of His people, and His Word carried out in dependence on the Holy Spirit, worship to the Father and blessing to souls has resulted ; but where there has been a glorying in position, an ignoring of other Christians, and an attempt to arrogate a claim to be " the Church of God " there has been failure and division. To attempt to form a world-wide organisation and call it " the expression of the body of Christ " seems to ignore the vast number of His members who are not in your circle, and virtually to form a new body. To claim to be anything but a remnant testimony is to ignore the failure of the Church as a united witness for God ; and to set up a central authority, whose decisions are to be accepted throughout the World, is to create a condition of unstable equilibrium, and reduce " division " to a fine art.

Division has not only been peculiar to the so-called "brethren." Methodists, Baptists, Presbyterians, Rome itself, have been divided, but they did not start with the watchword, " The unity of all the people of God," nor were their divisions carried out as some others have been, on the plea of " *Keeping* the Unity of the Spirit."

But while the failure must with shame and humiliation be

admitted, it must not be exaggerated. To gloat as some would-be historians have done over the divisions of " brethren," as though they were the sum and substance of the movement, would be like making the contentions of Acts 15. 2, 7, 39, or Galatians 2, typical of apostolic relations, or mistaking a diary of the Marburg squabbles for a history of the Reformation.

The historian who makes his history consist of a series of battles is out of date.

We may be sure the day of Christ will have a story of blessing, as well as of battles to reveal to the praise and glory of His grace. All that is of Christ and His Spirit will remain, all that is merely of man will be consumed.

By the grace of God the movement now under review has stood for the **Headship of Christ** and the oneness of the body, the presence of the Spirit, and the priesthood of all believers, the integrity of God's Word, and the Gospel of the grace of God to every creature, and God has in His infinite condescension honoured their testimony by lip and pen.

But to claim for this movement, as some have done, to represent " Philadelphia," is to ignore the sovereignty of God and belittle every movement of the Spirit outside of it, in other words, to fail to see the wood for the trees, or to take the part for the whole.

The local Church is not a monarchy, even less is it a democracy, but a theocracy. The liberty of the Spirit is not liberty for every one or any one to do as they like, but for the Holy Spirit to do as He likes. Open ministry does not make every one capable of ministering the Word or preaching the Gospel, but leaves those free to do so whom the Lord has called and qualified. God has made many of these simple believers " gifts " of the ascended Christ, though for the most part unknown in the schools of men, to the whole Church by their writings, especially in the form of **Notes on the Scriptures** of Studies of Prophecy. Works such as the " Notes on the Pentateuch " of C.H.M., or " The Moral Glory of our Lord Jesus Christ," by J. G. Bellett, or the works of Darby, Kelly, Müller, or Robert Chapman, for instance, are found in many an Evangelical library outside their immediate circle. They have also produced many excellent·tract writers and tract distributers.

MISSIONS IN MANY LANDS.

God has also in His great grace raised up and sent forth from their ranks large numbers as witnesses in foreign lands. In 1829, **A. N. Groves** in dependence on God alone, started to Bagdad at the head of a small missionary expedition, and since then hundreds more have gone forth in the same way, " taking nothing of the Gentiles." He was soon followed by Francis Newman

and Lord Congleton (John Parnell as he then was), and Dr.
Cronin before alluded to. They did not stay long, and Groves
himself was led soon after to leave Bagdad for India, where he
spent many years of self-sacrificing labour. Judged by the
standards of men, his life was a failure. His self-supporting
mission proved a fiasco, the converts were few, and though some
became devoted men of faith and missionaries to their own
people, he left very little to show for all his labour. But
" weighed in the balances of the sanctuary," it was no doubt a
precious and fruitful service. He not only ministered the truth
to fellow-missionaries of " the household of faith," but his
devoted life was a picture lesson to encourage others in the same
path, and his apparent failure became the starting point for
others who followed where he had " blazed " the way. Space
will not allow us to follow the development of the work in India
and many other lands. The *Missionary Echo*, since known as
Echoes of Service, appeared first in 1872, containing in the
numbers of that year letters from thirty to forty servants of
Christ in foreign lands. Such countries as China (represented
now by nearly a hundred missionaries), North and Central Africa
(represented by over 180), and the Spanish-speaking countries
of South America (represented by over 100 workers) were not
mentioned at all in that first number.

At the present date, to the glory of God be it said, over 800
from the above source alone are known in various countries of
the world, and these are but a small part of those who have gone
forth in obedience to their Lord's command, not to mention
that missionary Church *par excellence*, the Moravians. These
call for the practical fellowship of their brethren in the homeland. It is needless to refer to such names as Martyn, Carey,
Moffat, Livingstone, Patteson, Paton, Mackay, Hudson
Taylor, Arnot, Crawford, in the history of Missions, they " being
dead yet speak." They went forth, but devoted men at home
" held the ropes." We cannot refrain from mentioning here in
this connection the names of Bickersteth, Wigram, Stock, in
connection with the C.M.S., and those of Robert Chapman, Dr.
Maclean, and Huntingdon Stone, less widely known in the
religious world, but succourers of many of the Lord's servants
by counsel, correspondence, and practical fellowship. They
were remarkable men by their gifts and outstanding ability,
but more so by their spiritual graces and devotion to the cause
of Christ. It may be said of them as was carved on Darby's
grave, " Unknown, yet well-known."

CONTINENTAL MISSIONS.

The other name, already noted, that played a great part
during nearly half a century in definite spiritual work among

saint and sinner at home and in foreign lands, such as Switzerland, France, Sweden, and Russia, was the fourth **Baron Radstock.** He used to say that when he resigned his Colonelcy of the London Volunteers, he lost his last shred of respectability in the eyes of the world. He built Eccleston Hall in the eighties, and later opened the Victoria Homes for homeless seamen.

His zeal for individual dealing was so great that it was said of him that he " button-holed the world." He died in Paris early in the century, still in harness when over eighty. Perhaps the most unique ministry of his long life for God was his Gospel campaigns in St. Petersburg, in 1874, and the three successive winters, when the Spirit of God moved in a remarkable way in a most unlikely sphere, the highest circles of that sceptical and pleasure-loving city. The meetings were very simple in character. Gospel meetings and Bible readings held in drawing rooms, and God worked in a wonderful way, and such men as Col. Pashkoff, of the Imperial Guard, Count Bobrinsky, at one time Minister of the Interior, Count Korff, to name only a few, were brought to Christ. When Lord Radstock's visits ceased, the work only intensified, the converts carrying it on not only in St. Petersburg, in their mansions and palaces, but on their country estates, where many of their retainers heard the Gospel and believed.

The work was further strengthened and developed by visits from George Müller, Reginald Radcliffe, and **Dr. Baedeker,** another convert of Lord Radstock. All this was stopped when Pobiedonostzeff became Procurator of the Holy Synod. He takes his place among the great persecutors of history. It has been gravely stated that even the persecutions of the Roman Emperors were not more severe and widespread than those of Pobiedonostzeff during his reign of twenty-five years. He resigned in 1905, and died soon after. The aristocratic movement was easily dealt with. The leaders were expelled.

But there was another work for God which could not thus be dealt with, the **Stundist** (from *stunde*, an hour, the time their meetings lasted), which was essentially a peasant movement. It was started by a feeble testimony of German settlers, but spread among the Russian Moujiks. There was a measure of liberty in the reign of Alexander II, and the Gospel had free course and was glorified over wide areas ; but when Alexander III succeeded his father, who had died at the hands of the Nihilists, this liberty was withdrawn. But in spite of fire and sword and imprisonment and Siberian exile, the work of the Spirit continued. The difference between Rome and the Greek Church is, that while the former forbids its members to read the Bible, the latter forbids them to follow it. They may read it, but they must not leave the Orthodox fold. As a matter of fact the price of a Bible in Russia is prohibitive for any but the well-to-do.

The work in Russia has continued to this day, and since the war, in spite of **Red Soviet** prohibitions and persecutions, has developed marvellously. It has been said that nothing since the Reformation can compare to the present work of God in Poland and Russia. Thousands have been converted, and hundreds of simple Christian Assemblies have been formed. No doubt this work was in part prepared by the widespread distribution of the Word of God by Dr. Baedeker travelling through the length and breadth of the land in the eighties and nineties, with the help of the British and Foreign Bible Society, and every facility from the Russian Government.

Meanwhile other similar movements on a much smaller scale had been taking place in other parts of Europe. The fall of the Empire in France gave new liberty to the servants of Christ. Paris became open to Gospel preaching. **Dr. M'All** and others took advantage of this and halls were opened in all parts of the city, and many trophies were won to Christ. So the work continues with wonderful perseverance to the present day, though not perhaps in the same freshness and power that marked those early days.

Even **Spain** tasted for a brief space a small measure of religious liberty, and a number of earnest and godly men from our shores pressed in as witnesses for the Gospel; and even among Spaniards, men like Matamores rose up as bold witnesses for Christ, but the reign of liberty was brief. Still the testimony for the Gospel has continued with the blessing of God in spite of much priestly opposition and every possible restriction, short of absolute prohibition on behalf of the authorities, who were ever ready to play into the hands of the priests.

In **Italy** the work initiated by Count Guiccardini, and T. P. Rossetti, of Vasto, cousin of the poet Dante Gabriel Rossetti, continued. The priests had lost much of their old prestige and power. But it was a saying among the Evangelists who had laboured in the early days of fierce opposition, that there was more power in the Word, more true conversion work then, than in the easier days of greater liberty.

The natural evolution of Roman Catholic countries is toward infidelity, and an infidel who has been through Romanism is harder to win for Christ than a pious Romanist, who has at any rate a certain fear of God, and faith in the fundamental truths of Christianity. Countries left high and dry by Romanism are not " white unto the harvest," any more than land reclaimed from the sea.

CHINA INLAND MISSION.

The last visit of Moody and Sankey, in 1883, had a lasting influence on foreign missions because of the interest created by their visit to Cambridge and Oxford and other Universities, especially the first named. In a visit there in 1883 many under-graduates were converted to Christ, and a number were led to yield themselves to God or His service. Several young men of good social position and training volunteered for mission work in China in connection with the China Inland Mission, founded in 1865 by **Dr. Hudson Taylor,** already a missionary in China. The definite object before him was the occupying for God of all the interior provinces of China. Hitherto missionary work had been confined to the Treaty Ports, or at most to the provinces bordering on the sea. Hudson Taylor, along with another remarkable man, a Scotch Presbyterian missionary, William Burns, had already launched out from time to time into the interior at the risk of their lives. Now he felt the time had arrived to make a systematic effort to occupy the inland provinces for Christ.

The C.I.M. was founded on the lines of, " Expect great things from God, attempt great things for God." At the time of its founding, five missionaries, the nucleus of the future mission, had already gone forth. By 1875 these had increased to 51. In 1885 the young men above referred to started out. They were known as " **the Cambridge Seven.**" Their going forth made a great stir. They held farewell meetings all through the country. The subject of foreign missions was brought before the educated young men of Great Britain as never before. Many were con-verted to God and consecrated to the service of Christ. A number volunteered for service abroad ; a great volume of prayer went up for mission work, and for the " seven " in particular. Nearly forty years have elapsed, and now be it said to the glory of a prayer-hearing, faithful God, six of the seven are yet alive. Three are still in China. One of them succeeded Hudson Taylor as Director of the C.I.M., another founded a mission in Central Africa, and all are still seeking to work for God.

At the close of 1923 there were in China, 6562 missionaries and wives of such, occupying 1038 stations and 6482 out-stations. These missionaries represented about 100 societies, of which one, the C.I.M., had enrolled as many as 1101, and there are besides, a number unconnected with any Society, working chiefly in Kiangsi, Shantung, Northern Chili and South Mongolia.

Modernism is doing its deadly work in China as elsewhere. Education, too often takes the place of the Gospel and the moral raising of the nation, as a whole, is frankly substituted as an aim, for individual conversion. However, the faith-dream of Hudson Taylor has been realised, and the Gospel is now systematically preached in all the nineteen provinces of China proper.

BRITISH AND FOREIGN BIBLE SOCIETY.

This brief reference to foreign missions ought not to close without a grateful reference to that great nursing mother of missionary work, the British and Foreign Bible Society. Voltaire's foolish prophecy that in a hundred years the Bible would only exist in museums has been stultified in a marked degree by the Society as in numerous other ways, for in France alone 196,856 copies of the Scriptures in whole or in part were circulated in 1923. Voltaire died in 1778 ; by 31st March, 1923, that is, 145 years later, the total circulation through the Bible Society alone (and she does not give, but sells her copies), had been during the 119 years of its existence, more than three hundred and thirty-six million copies, in whole or in part, all *outside* museums. The total income for the same period had been £19,662,420, which indeed shows that " God is greater than His foes." The number of languages in which the Society has published, or circulated at least some portion of God's Word, is 558. All this is apart from the work of other Bible Societies, such as the National Bible Society of Scotland, the Trinitarian Bible Society, the Scripture Gift Mission, Pocket Testament League, etc., the circulation by means of which can only be reckoned by tens of millions. Not only so, but it continues in spite of all the negations and criticisms of unbelief, a message of light, and life, salvation and comfort to a dead, lost, heavy-laden world. Whatever the colour of skin may be, the blood is the same, and the need of the heart is the same, and that need Christ alone can fill.

MOVEMENTS AMONG THE YOUNG.

Another encouraging sign which may be mentioned here is the Sunday School and **Missionary Study Class** movements, to inform the young concerning foreign missions. The **Children's Special Service Mission** has left its mark on the present generation in definite conversion work among boys and girls of the more educated classes, not reached by Sunday Schools, with its Beach services, its missions to Public School boys, and its literature for the young—translated into French, German, Italian, and other languages. Nor should Band of Hope work, Church Lads' Brigades, perhaps we should add the Scout Movement founded on a religious basis, pass unnoticed. But how great the tendency in all such movements to lose sight of a spiritual ideal and drift world-ward.

THE WELSH REVIVAL.

No account of God's work in this century could omit a reference to the Welsh " Revival " of 1904, though of course " Revival " is a misnomer. The term applies to the people of God, but we use it here in default of a better and briefer. If we are constantly reminded of the sovereignty of God's ways, in working where, when, and by whom He wills, it would be difficult to find a more remarkable example than the said " Revival," when one looks at a group of those whom God used to stir Wales to its depths and far beyond Wales, the whole Evangelical world—a few young men and women, of humble origin, slender educational advantages, and with no financial or ecclesiastical backing. Wales had been deeply moved in 1859, and still more deeply was this the case in 1904. No doubt the Revival was characterised by extravagances ; much, if tested by that " Word which endureth for ever," was disorderly, fleshly, and spurious. Where God operates, Satan imitates. The same Spring that brings forth flowers, breeds thistles, but the flowers are not rejected for that, nor do they smell less sweet. There was certainly alloy in the Welsh " Revival," but there was much gold, too. The one whom God used to start and lead the movement was early noted for an intense love for the Bible and prayer, and more than this, for a habit of spending hours at a time in silent communion with God. Perhaps no notable servant of God, from Paul to Luther, and from Luther downwards, but has been characterised by this in a greater or less degree. It is said that often in the midst of the " Revival " meetings, when large congregations were longing to hear him speak, the young " Revivalist " would be praying silently during most of the meeting in some corner of the chapel.

Evan Roberts was born in1878, at the village of Bwlchymynydd, outside the little seaport of Loughor, in South Wales. The Revival began in the very place in which he had been born and bred and known for years as a boy-miner. That he should attempt a Revival there was frankly ascribed by his friends to mental derangement (though no saner letters were ever written than those by Evan Roberts at that very crisis), but that such an attempt should succeed is no small argument for the Divine power at the back of it. The Revival began then on his own doorstep, but it spread far and wide in Wales, to the blessing of thousands. The Liverpool Mission followed. This was a further test. Could the Revival flourish in an English atmosphere ? The answer was as triumphant as ever. But perhaps the work in Anglesea surpassed everything seen in Liverpool or in South Wales. The whole life of the island was turned upside down during the month that the mission was there. One reproach against the work was that hymn singing supplanted Scripture reading. Certainly there was great need for the Word of God to stabilise the work and its results. But the Cross of Christ was the basis of the preaching of the Revivalist. He would say : " There is nothing like the Cross of our Lord Jesus Christ to melt the hardest heart." All who heard or have read Evan Roberts' address to 10,000 persons in the Carnarvon Pavilion, on the " **Name of Jesus**," would wish that more like it could be heard everywhere to-day. No wonder the Spirit of God blessed such a testimony to the Person and work of Christ. A great dependence on the Spirit and much prayer for His presence and power were characteristic of the leaders. We have been so clearly taught not to pray for the Spirit to come, which would be to ignore the great fact of Pentecost, that we have sometimes forgotten that we do need the daily ministry of the Holy Spirit, for which we may well pray in faith (Gal. 3. 5 ; Eph. 3. 16). The liberty of the Spirit is often counterfeited by the liberty of the flesh, even where no Spirit of Revival is apparent. In Wales sometimes hymns would interrupt the current of the testimony. Singing had in the judgment of many too large a part. Evan Roberts was not unaware of this. He is reported to have said to Dr. Sanday of Oxford : " Where there is much singing, there is little saving." Professed conversions were numbered by tens of thousands. " The Lord knoweth them that are His," and perhaps He reckons as His own many whom others would exclude for their ignorance, or who would exclude themselves for their failures. It has been said that nowhere is Gospel preaching so barren in results as in the very valleys, most deeply affected by the " Revival." This is somewhat disconcerting, but may be accounted for in part by the fact that true converts do not need to be converted again, and such a visitation as the Welsh Revival would leave spurious converts and hardened sinners harder than ever, but still one would hope that the real converts would come forward in numbers. A very stale reproach, brought at Corinth even against the Apostle Paul, though without the least foundation, and falsely brought against many a servant of Christ since, that he was " making a gain of them," could hardly have been brought against Evan Roberts. He gave away all he had, and arrived at Liverpool for his mission there, and that of set purpose, so well off that had he needed a penny to use for an illustration, he would have been obliged, like his Master, to borrow one. He would never allow a collection to be taken, nor could he be accused of making merchandise of the people, for apparently he had not even a hymn book to sell.

INDIFFERENTISM.

The last phase of Church history to which reference should be made corresponds with Laodicea. This Church has been highly favoured as the object of apostolic prayers (Col. 2. 1), as the recipient of apostolic epistles (Col. 4. 16), probably as the scene of apostolic labours. It was characterised neither by moral disorder nor doctrinal error. As far as we know, Scriptural order was enforced, the ordinances observed, and everything going on with machine-like regularity. Indeed everything seems to have been in its place—except the centre. Christ, instead of being in the midst, as no doubt they boasted He was, was outside the door. Laodicea is Philadelphia cooled down to lukewarm point. She is self-satisfied and full of indifference. This is not an atmosphere conducive to revivals of any kind.

The **War of 1870** had another effect beyond those already noted. It revealed an appalling condition of indifference, especially among men in such lands as France and Italy. Christianity they thought they had tried, but it was a counterfeit. They had tried Romanism, a very different thing, and found it wanting. The growth of Modernism has only added to this, with its denial of the Fall and of Judgment to come. If there be no Fall, there is nothing to be saved out of ; and if no Judgment, nothing to be saved from. Indifference in the world to the claims of God, indifference in the Churches to the needs of the world, are increasing. Men are indeed " lovers of pleasure rather than lovers of God." The open neglect of the Lord's day has become general. The introduction of motor service has fostered this. Men no longer remain in London or other cities on the Sunday if they can get away to the country or seaside, and there throw off all pretence of the fear of God. The **Great War** did for a time modify this state of things. Men were brought face to face with the stern facts of danger, wounds, and death. Many unaccustomed to take God into account, much less publicly to acknowledge His overruling providence, did even in the daily press acknowledge His hand in the war. Surely when peace was attained men would turn and seek His face.

THE LEAGUE OF NATIONS.

A great revival was predicted. A new condition of things would be introduced. But these hopes were not realised. The world had other projects. " War was to end war." The world was to be made " safe for democracy." Man had earned " a good time " and must have it. A sort of Millennium was about to break. But all but the desire for pleasure has past. The air is full of war and rumours of war. Perhaps the world was never less safe for anybody than to-day. Men's hearts are failing them for fear. The pathetic little prophecies in the daily papers of the imminence of better times are usually belied in the next morning's issue. But Christ is still the only hope for a lost world, and in spite of indifference God continues to work by His Spirit. Still, widespread effort is being put forward in the Homeland in Gospel tents, caravans, hired cinemas, and halls to reach those who will not darken the doors of " religious " buildings. At the time of the Armistice a wave of blessing in the Gospel broke on many towns and countrysides of East Anglia. It was nothing short of a " Revival." The same is being experienced in North Ireland as a very real and present fact. We may quote words spoken at Chicago, in June, 1924, by a delegate of the Irish

Wesleyan Conference to the General Conference of the Methodist Episcopal Church.

GREAT CHANGES IN IRELAND.

One event has taken place since the War which would have made the ears of Englishmen to tingle during the long years of the Home Rule Agitation—the granting of a separate Parliament to Ireland and the establishment of the "**Irish Free State**," including all Ireland, except "the six counties" of Northern Ireland. They, too, have a Parliament, but retain their connection with Great Britain. Whether Home-Rule has proved to be Rome-Rule, to the extent anticipated, is not certain, but if not, it would be from political reasons. Rome and religious liberty can only be incompatibles.

"Ireland had become a butcher's shop. The nightly lullaby by which we went to sleep was rifle fire. Statesmen and all of us had done all we could to make Ireland seem again a Christian country. All seems in vain. We cried in our shame and agony to God to save us. He answered with a Revival. When the Revival came the shooting ceased. Men who had destroyed their neighbours' property confessed their offences and paid, or are paying month by month, for the damage they had done. Outlawed debts were paid or are being paid. Drunkards and drunkards' homes are transformed. It is perfectly easy to win men to Christ. The Churches will not hold the people crowding into them."* This is not a solitary testimony. Credible witness is borne by eye-witnesses to the number and reality of well-attested cases of conversion, and that of no ordinary kind. Shipwrights, tramwaymen, political Protestants are brought under the power of the Word.

That which has spoken peace to Ulster would speak peace to Europe. That which has saved Irishmen would save Bolsheviks ; not the blood of their victims, but the blood of Calvary. That which Ulster has, China, India, Africa, South America need. What Ulster has, lukewarm Laodicean Christendom needs. "JESUS Christ, and Him crucified." The world's only redeeming Name, humanity's only saving Gospel, a fallen race's only hope. What Ulster has the world may have : not revolution, but revival ; not the sword, but the Cross.

One characteristic of these last days to which attention may be called is the increase of "**Faith-Healing**" cults, really only another symptom of the materialism of the age. It is not the Church that offers the highest spiritual advantages which wins the suffrages of the religious world, but the Church which makes the most sensational claims to powers of bodily healing and to physical manifestations. Such passages as Mark 16. 17, 18 are

* Quoted from the *Indian Christian*, July, 1924.

freely quoted in justification, but whereas our Lord's promises to His early disciples' faith, " in His Name," were unconditional, and included, besides the powers referred to, " taking up serpents " and drinking poison with impunity, as well as casting out demons, and that, invariably and indisputably in response to " the Name of Christ," the results, as offered by these cults, only belong to specially "consecrated " men, are only granted to special faith, and can with difficulty be produced, still less proved genuine.

While the **Non-Conformist Churches** have been drawing closer to one another in these latter times, and **Union** is in the air, and indeed is an accomplished fact in the case of the greater Methodist and Presbyterian Churches in England, the differences in the Established Church have become more acute than ever, and she presents the spectacle of a house not only divided against itself, but in an advanced state of decomposition.

The revision of **the Prayer-Book** has been mooted on and off for the last twenty years. The lawlessness of the Ritualist and the doctrinal aberrations of the Broad Church party, calling themselves now " Modern Churchmen," had long been a scandal. Why did not the bishops refuse to license or give preferment to all unfaithful to the rubrics and standards of the Church? That would have been an *argumentum ad hominem* which all would have understood. They pursued a very different policy ; the way of lawlessness proved the path of preferment, and the only ones who were ignored and ostracized were the *old* Evangelicals, who were faithful to their trust. But however much the bishops might prefer weakly to follow the line of least resistance, they could not but feel it made them play a sorry figure before the world. How could the matter be set right ? How could the lawless become law-abiding ? A way was discovered. The law must be changed, and what had been unlawful made lawful. On this principle the revised Prayer Book was planned. and introduced. Twice it was presented to the House of Commons and twice rejected : that is, in December, 1927, and again, with certain modifications, on **June 14th, 1928,** by majorities of **33** and **46** respectively. Had the book become law it must have meant the secession of many true Evangelicals. They would at last have been forced definitely to throw off an " unequal yoke." Can, then, the rejection of the revised Prayer Book, however desirable on general grounds, be regarded as an unmixed blessing?

Midst all the turmoil in Nations, in the world, and in the Churches, we may conclude by asking—

WHAT IS THE HOPE OF THE CHURCH ?

Is it the gradual and world-wide introduction of a better state of things—a worldly Millennium of peace and prosperity, but without the rightful King ?   Is it the conversion of the world, or even a general " Revival ? "   None of these things, but the return of Christ ; and to this response the ardent desire and expectations of large numbers of the Lord's people.   It has been said by a certain historian and critic of the movement already referred to as " the brethren," that " it is clear now that ' brethrenism ' took shape under the influence of a delusion " (*i.e.*, of the immediate return of the Saviour).   In judging, however, of such matters, we do well to remember the words of the Lord : " Judge not according to the appearance, but judge righteous judgment."   Faith itself is a delusion to the unbeliever, but " the evidence of things not seen " to the man of faith. The Spirit, by Peter, warns believers : " Be not ignorant of this one thing, that one day is with the Lord as a thousand years, and a thousand years as one day."   Did not our Lord leave His apostles under this " delusion " when He said : " I will come again and receive you unto Myself ? "   Did not Christianity by the same showing take shape under the influence of the same " delusion ? "   Surely our Lord intended His Church to be always expecting His immediate return.   Was it " a delusion " that they took Him at His Word ?   It ought to be enough as answer to quote two verses out of many, one from the first letter of Paul, the other the closing words of the Bible.   " Ye turned to God from idols, to serve the living and true God, and *to wait for His Son from Heaven* " (1 Thess. 1. 9, 10). and, " He which testifieth these things saith, *Surely I come quickly, Amen.*   Even so come, Lord Jesus " (Apoc. 22. 20).

Appendix A. Page 198.

The blasphemous doctrine of Arius was an offshoot of Gnosticism, perhaps the least offensive in appearance, but directly and inevitably destructive of the personal glory of the Son as God, and hence overthrowing the basis of redemption. Modern Unitarianism denies the Lord Jesus to be more than man, and thus even His supernatural birth of the Virgin Mary, though Socinus asserted the singular modification of such an exaltation after His resurrection as constituted Him an adequate Object of Divine worship. Arius seemed to approach the truth on the side of His pre-existence before He came into the world, owned that He, the Son of God, made the universe, but maintained that He was Himself created, though the very first and highest of creatures. It was not the Sabellian denial of distinct personality, but the refusal to the Son, and of course to the Spirit, of true, proper, essential, and eternal Deity.

Not only is Arianism fundamentally inconsistent with the place given to the Son from first to last throughout Scripture, as well as with the infinite work of reconciliation and new creation, for which the old creation furnished but the occasion, but it is distinctly refuted beforehand by many passages of Holy Writ. A few of these it may be well here to cite. He who, when born of woman, was named Jesus, the Spirit of God declares (John 1. 1-3) to be in the beginning the Word who was with God and was God. "All things were made by Him; and without Him was not anything made that was made." Impossible to conceive a stronger testimony to His uncreated subsistence, to His distinct personality when He was with God before creation, and to His divine nature. He is here spoken of as the Word, the correlate of which is not the Father, but God (and thus leaving room for the Holy Spirit); but, lest His own consubstantiality should be overlooked, He is carefully and at once declared to be God.* Go back beyond time and the creature, as far as one may in thought, "in the beginning was the Word." The language is most precise; He was in the beginning with God, not ἐγίνετο, "He was," in the sense of coming into being or caused to be, but ἦν, "He was," in His own absolute being. All things ἐγίνετο, "came into being" through Him. He was the Creator so completely that St. John adds, "and without Him not one thing came into being which is come into being." On the other hand, when the incarnation is stated in verse 14, the language is, "The Word was made flesh," not ἦν but ἐγίνετο. Further, when come among men, He is described as "the only begotten Son 'who is' (ὁ ὢν, not merely who *was*) in the bosom of the Father"—language unintelligible and misleading unless to show that His manhood in no way detracted from His Deity, and that the infinite nearness of the Son with the Father ever subsists.

Again, Romans 9. 5 is a rich and precise expression of Christ's underivative and supreme Godhead, equally with the Father and the Spirit. "Christ came, who is over all, God blessed for ever. Amen." The efforts of heterodox critics bear witness to the all-importance of the truth, which they vainly essay to shake by unnatural efforts which betray the dissatisfaction of their authors. There is no such emphatic prediction of

---

* The absence of the article here is necessarily due to the fact that Θεός is the predicate of ὁ Λόγος, in no way to an inferior sense of His Godhead, which would contradict the context itself. Indeed, if the article had been inserted, it would be the grossest heterodoxy, because its effect would be to deny that the Father and the Spirit are God by excluding all but the Word from Godhead.

supreme Deity in the Bible : not of course that the Father and the Holy Spirit are not co-equal, but because the humiliation of the Son in incarnation and the death of the Cross made it fitting that the fullest assertion of Divine supremacy should be used of Him.

Next, the apostle says of Christ, "Who is the image of the invisible God, the firstborn of every creature ; for by Him were all things created, that are in Heaven and that are on earth, visible and invisible, whether thrones, or dominions, or principalities, or powers : all things were created by Him and for Him ; and He is before all things, and by Him all things subsist" (Col. 1. 15-17). The reveries of the Gnostics are here anticipatively cut off ; for Christ is shown to have been chief of all creation, *because* He was Creator, and this of the highest invisible beings as well as of the visible : all things are said to have been created for Him as well as by Him ; and as He is before all, so all subsist together in virtue of Him.

The only other passage I need now refer to is Hebrews 1, where the apostle illustrates the fulness of Christ's Person, among other Old Testament Scriptures, by Psalms 45 and 102. In the former He is addressed as God and anointed as man ; in the latter He is owned as Jehovah, the Creator, after He is heard pouring out His affliction as the rejected Messiah of Jehovah.

It is impossible then to accept the Bible without rejecting Arianism as a heinous libel against Christ and the truth ; for it is not more certain that He became a man than that He was God before creation, Himself the Creator, the Son, and Jehovah.—*From unpublished MSS. of W. Kelly.*

Appendix B.   Page 201.

The Eastern Churches from an early period observed the festival of Easter in commemoration of the *crucifixion* of Christ, which answered to the Jewish Passover, on the fourteenth day of the month. This may have arisen from the fact that in the East there were many Jewish converts. The Western Churches observed the festival in commemoration of the *resurrection*. This difference as to the day gave rise to a long and fierce controversy. But after much contention between the Eastern and Western Churches, it was ordained by the council of Nice to be observed in commemoration of the resurrection throughout the whole of Christendom. Thus, Easter-day is the Sunday following the fourteenth day of the paschal moon which happens upon or next after the 21st of March : so that, if the said fourteenth day be a Sunday, it is not that Sunday but the next. It may be any Sunday of the five weeks which commence with March 22nd and end with April 25th.

General Index

	PAGE
ABBEY, Jedburgh	512
— Paisley	513
Abbeys in Scotland,	512
Abolition of Mass,	781
Abuses, Articles Concerning,	708
Acts, Transitional	109
Administration of Alva,	894
Age of Miracles and Visions,	378
Albigenses, The	303, 456
Albigensian Persecution,	461
Alpine Regions,	543
America, Discovery of	883
American Board of Foreign Missions,	1040
Anabaptists, The	658, 679
Anglo-Saxon,	390
Anointing,	416
Apologists, The	149
Apology, The	705
— for the Confession,	718
Apostasy of Otho,	436
Apostle, Name of	41
Apostles, Married	64
— The Twelve	41
Apostleship of Paul,	37
Apostolic Council,	60
— Fathers,	151
Appeal of the Princes,	674
— unto Cæsar,	105
Arabs,	327
Archeteles,	754
Arian Controversy,	196
Arianism,	197, 1074
Army of the Confederates,	848
Articles Concerning Abuses,	708
— of Faith,	708
— of Smalcald,	723
Arundel, Constitutions of	564
Asceticism,	232
Ascetics, First Society of	229
Assemblies,	163
Assembly of Baden,	776
Association of the Nobles,	890
Augsburg, Diet of	697
Augustine in England,	257
Augustinian Convent,	618
Augustinians,	752
Auricular Confession,	416
Auto de Fé,	490
BABYLON of Revelation 17,	422
Banner of Lucerne,	806

	PAGE
Baptism, Christian,	219
— Infant,	223
— Regenerating Waters of	307
— Variations of	218
Baptist Bible Union,	1051
— Missionary Society,	1039
Barbarians,	235
Barbaric Invaders,	213
Barbarities of Simon and Arnold,	472
Barnardo's Homes,	1054
Battle of Askelon,	363
— of Aussig,	589
— of Cappel,	815
— of Muret,	475
Benedictines, The	496
Bennett Judgment, The	1044
Bible Church Missionary Society,	1050
— English Version,	558
— First Printed,	595
— First Printed in England,	596
— German	652
— in Bohemia	591
— in French,	928
— Latin Vulgate	594
— League,	1051
— Restored to the Nation,	994
— Revised Version,	1057
— Rome's Opposition to	596
— Translations,	559
Bigotry, Effect of	897
Bill of Rights,	1033
Bishop in Early Times,	156
Black Plague, The	551
Blockage of the Five-Cantons,	810
Bloody Statute, The	1021
Bohemia, Reformation in	568
Bohemian Scholars,	571
— War,	585
Boniface, Death of	532
Border War,	993
Born of Water,	224
Brethren Movement, The	1060
British and Foreign Bible Society,	1056, 1067
Bulgarians,	302
Bull of Innocent VIII,	545
— of Leo,	640, 1016
Bulls, Papal	421
Burning of Beziers,	465
— of Heretics,	562
— of Rome,	120, 348

	PAGE
CÆSAR, Appeal to	105
Cæsar's Court,	111
— Household,	111
Calamities of Languedoc,	481
— of Rome,	234
Caliphs, The	285
Calling in of the Gentiles,	25
Calvin Society,	920
Calvinism,	921
Calvinistic Congregations in France,	951
Cambridge Seven, The	1067
Canon Law in England,	392
Canterbury Monks,	444
Capital of Islam,	284
Capture of Constantinople,	593
Carthusians, The	498
Catechisms, Luther's	698
Cathari, The	543
Catholic Church,	203
— Indignation,	809
Celebacy,	236
Celtic Element,	512
Ceremonies and Rights,	336
Chain of Witnesses,	453
Chair of St. Peter,	310
Charlemagne, Wars of	303
Children's Special Service Mission,	1068
China Inland Mission,	1066
Christ, Ascension of	19
Christian Endeavour Society,	1052
— Journalism,	1058
Christianity, Altered Position	163
— in Germany,	272
— in Ireland,	509
— in Scotland,	511
— Papal	663
— Rapid Progress of	131
— Spread of	263, 517
— under Gratian,	211
Church at Beginning of Sixteenth Century,	610
— Body of Christ,	110
— Building Spirit Revived,	326
— Catholic	203
— Christ only Builder,	9
— Courts,	952
— Condition of	173
— Doctrine of	39
— Dutch Reformed	896
— Effects of Royal Favour,	192
— Effect of Worldliness,	167
— First Missionaries of	40
— First Reformed in France,	951
— Foundation of	8
— Government, Divine Principles of	13

	PAGE
Church, Greek,	248
— in Arms,	482
— in Britain,	255
— in Ireland,	510
— in Rome,	121
— in Spain,	884
— Irish Presbyterian	982
— Internal History of	150, 218
— Missionary Society,	1039
— of God,	24
— Reception into	16
— Rock Foundation of	7
— Second Period of History,	139
— True Character Disappears,	194
— Truth of	1062
— Union with State,	190
Churches, Christian	164
— Continental	1050
— Lutheran	655
— The Seven of Revelation,	3, 1041
Circumcision,	73, 97
Cistercian Monasteries,	374
Cistercians, The	498
Civil Commotions,	573
— War, Great	341
— War in Germany,	434
Clerical Independence,	334
Clericalism,	150
Clergy and Laity,	154
— Effect of Wealth on	514
— Lord's Dealings with	164
— New Order of	154
— Position and Character of	226
Close of First 1000 Years,	325
Colossians,	111
Concordat of Worms,	372
Condemnation of Huss,	580
Confederacy,	802
Confederates, Army of	848
— of Zurich,	768
Conference of Baden,	785
— of Berne,	788
— of Marburg,	683
Confession, Auricular,	416
— Form of	418
Confessional, Origin of,	417
Confession of Augsburg,	696
Conquest of Damietta,	523
Conquests of Innocent,	430
Constantine, Conversion of	185
— Edict of	187
— Head of Church,	191
Constitutions of Clarendon,	397
Consubstantiation,	658, 677
Continental Churches,	1050
— Missions,	1064
Corinthians I,	91
— II,	93

	PAGE
Corpus Christi, ...	702
Council at Jerusalem, ..	73
— of Arles, ...	209
— of Basle, ...	589
— of Blood, ...	894
— of Bologna, ...	694
— of Bourges, ...	479
— of Constance, ..	570, 584
— of Milan, ...	209
— of Nice, ..	200, 294
— of Pisa, ...	568
— of the Lateran, ..	381, 476
— of Toulouse, ..: ..	485
— of Trent, ...	842, 961
— of Tyre, ...	204
— of Zurich, ...	814
Creed, The New	858
Crusades, The	353
— Reflections on	369
— The Home, ...	464
Culdees, The	271, 511
DANES, Ferocious Nation of	330
Dark Year of 1560, ...	547
Dawn of Light in Dark Ages,	383
Day of Pentecost, ...	18
Deacons, Seven	28
Decay of Empire, ...	149
Decline and Fall of Roman	
Empire, ...	213
Defender of the Faith,	654, 1017
Descent of Holy Spirit, ..	20
Dictates of Gregory, ..	335
Diet, Helvetic	741
— of Augsburg,	695, 719, 857
— of Nuremberg, ...	655
— of Spires, ...	660, 674
— of Worms,..	642
Dioceses, Origin of	156
Diocletian, Acts of	174
Disciples Persecuted and	
Scattered, ...	30
Discovery of America, ..	883
Disputations at Zurich, ..	756
Dissolution of the League, ..	852
Division of England,.. ..	1043
Documentary Theory, ..	1047
Dominicans, ...	500, 752
Donation of Matilda, ..	371
Donatistic Controversy, ..	196
Downfall of Images, ..	769
— of Jerusalem, ...	122
Dutch Reformed Church, ..	896
EARTHQUAKES, ...	165
Easter, ...	1075
Edict of Constantine, ..	187
Edicts, The	175
	PAGE
Education, Revival of ..	316
Elders of Ephesus, ...	95
Election by Lot, ...	65
Emperor Deposed by Pope,..	340
End of the World, Supposed	323
England and the Papacy, ..	549
— Augustine in	257
— Crown Offered to France,	447
— Romish Hierarchy in ..	258
— Saxons in	256
— Surrendered to Rome, ..	448
— Under the Ban, ...	445
English Law and Custom, ..	391
Ephesians, ...	111
Ephesian, Condition of Church,	136
Epistles of Ignatius, ...	135
Established Church, ...	499
Ethiopian Eunuch, ...	33
Eucharist, The	685
Evangelical Alliance, ..	1055
Evolution, ...	1048
Exiles, Italian	881
Extreme Unction, ...	414
FATHERS, The ..	134, 151
Feast of St. Bartholomew, ..	956
Fegan's Homes, ...	1052
Female Recluses, ...	231
Ferocious Danes, ...	330
Feudal Hierarchical System,	309
Final Contest Between Pagan-	
ism and Christianity, ..	170
First Bible Printed, ..	595
— Book of Discipline, ..	1007
— Buildings for Christians,	163
— Council of Church, ..	73
— Covenant, ...	1004
— Crusade, ...	357
— Day of Week, ...	95
— Edict, ...	175
— False Step—Confederacy,	802
— Legal Persecution, ..	122
— Martyr, ...	27
— Martyrs of France, ..	932
— Martyr of Swiss Reforma-	
tion, ...	766
— Missionaries, ...	40
— Missionary Journey, ..	69
— Papal Jubilee, ...	628
— Paper Mill in England, ..	595
— Period of Church History,	136
— Persecution Under Em-	
perors, ...	121
— Preachers in Scotland, ..	267
— Thousand Years, Close of	325
Foreign Missions, ...	1039
Formula of Concord,.. ..	691
Fornication, ...	423

PAGE

Franciscans, ... 503, 752
French Protestantism, . 960
Friars, The Preaching .. 504
From Asia to Europe, .. 78

GALATIANS, ... 94
General Persecution, .. 115
Gentiles Brought into Blessing, 25
German Peasants, ..., 657
Germans Treated as Con-
quered, ... 855
Giant Heresy, .. 843
Gnosticism, ... 171, 1074
Golden Year, ... 629
Gorham Case,.. 1044
Great Civil War, ... 341
Great is Diana, ... 92
Greek and Latin New Testa-
ment, ... 606, 1013
Greek Church, ... 248
Guilt of the Sovereign, .. 440
Gunpowder Plot, ... 871

HAIL Mary, ... 405
Headship of Christ, ... 1063
Hebrews, ... 112
Helvetic Diet, ... 741
Henricians, ... 455
Henry and Bertha Crowned, 346
— at Conosa,.. 343
Heresiarch, John Huss as a .. 581
— Wycliffe as a 554
Heresy, ... 882
Heretics, Crusade against .. 547
— Statute for Burning .. 562
Hermits, Early 505
Herodian Line of Kings, .. 46
Herodians, ... 47
Higher Criticism, ... 1046
Historians, Mistakes of .. 2
Hohenstaufen, House of .. 432
Holy Ghost, Descent of .. 20
— Presence of 43
Holy Land, ... 31
— Vessel, ... 410
Home Crusade, ... 464
Hospitallers, The 370
House of Savoy; 545
— of Stuart, ... 1030
Huguenots, The 948
Humiliation of Pontiff, .. 531
Hundred Grievances, .. 656
Huss, Condemnation of .. 580

ICONOCLASM, ... 287
Idolatry, ...: 289
Idols Destroyed, ... 797
Image Worship, ... 289

PAGE

Immaculate Conception, The 507
Imperial Sovereignty in Rome
Abolished, ... 428
Impostures, ... 908
Indifferentism, ... 1069
Individual Opinion, .. 668
— Responsibility, ... 153
Indulgences, ... 419
— Sale of 630, 739
Infant Baptism, ... 223
— Communion, ... 226
Innocent's Demand of John, 448
Inquisition, The 471
— Application of Torture, .. 488
— Established as Ritual, .. 486
— Established at Lanquedoc, 484
— History of 486
— Internal Proceedings, .. 487
Institutes of Christian Re-
ligion, ... 914
Interim, The 857
Investitures, ... 338
Iona Missionaries, ... 268
Ireland, Great Changes in .. 1072
Islam, Religion of 282
Isle of Saints, ... 265
Italian Exiles, ... 881

JAILER at Philippi, .. 80
Jerome, Execution of .. 584
Jerusalem and Samaria United, 32
— Downfall of 122
— Made over to Christians, 526
Jesuits, .. 229, 868, 1044
John, King, and the Papacy, 442
Journalism, Christian, .. 1058
Judaism, ... 170
Judgment, Hand of Lord in .. 179
— of Sigismund, ... 578
Justification by Faith, .. 668

KESWICK Convention, .. 1058
Kingdom of Heaven, .. 11
King of Ireland, ... 981
King's Penance, ... 400
Knights Templars, ... 370
Koran, The 282

LABARUM, The 190
Laity, Origin of Clergy and .. 154
Last Words of the Acts, .. 109
Lateran, Council of the 381, 472
Latin Vulgate Bible, .. 594
League of Nations, ... 1071
— of Smalcald, ... 723
Letters of Melanchthon and
Luther, ... 710
— of Trajan, ... 128
Literary Men,.. 537

	PAGE
Literature, Revival of	327
Lollards, The	561
Lombards, The	253, 274
London Missionary Society,	1039
Low Countries, The	889
Luther and German Bible,	652
— at Worms,	641
— Conversion of	619
— Nails his Thesis,	633
— Precursors of	598
Lutheran Churches,	655, 671
— Heretics,	752
Lutheranism,	626, 894
Lutherans Burnt Alive,	944
MAGNA CHARTA,	449
Manicheans,	297
Man of Sin Foreshadowed,	278
Mariolatry,	240, 405
Martyrdom of Arnold,	387
— of Cyprian,	169
— of Huss,	580
— of Ignatius,	133
— of James,	50, 61
— of Jerome,	584
— of John Brown,	1010
— of Justin,	141
— of Lord Cobham,	566
— of Patrick Hamilton,	987
— of Paul,	117
— of Polycarp,	142
— of Ruteman,	778
— of Stephen,	30
— of the Wriths,	778
— of Wishart,	997
Martyrs of France,	932
— of Scotland,	985
Mary Worship,	240, 405
Mass, Abolition of	781
Massacre of Rora,	969
Mediators Appointed,	714
Mendicants, Apostasy of the	506
Mercy of the Gospel,	792
Metropolitan Bishop,	157
Metropolitan Tabernacle,	1055
Mildmay Conference,	1057
— Mission to the Jews,	1052
Ministry,	153
Mission of Columba,	265
Missionaries, First	40
Missionary Study Class,	1068
— Work,	1049
— Zeal of the Benedictines,	497
Missions in Many Lands,	1063
Modernism,	1046
Mohammed's Successors,	285
Mohammedanism and Romanism,	286
	PAGE
Monasteries,	230
Monastic Orders,	504
— Rules,	494
Monasticism,	226, 374
Monk Superior,	266
Monks, Ancient and Modern,	491
— of Canterbury,	444
Monothelites,	287
Moody and Sankey,	1052
Moravians, The	590
Mosheim's Sad Summary,	313
Mother of God,	405
Muller's Orphanage,	1052
NAZARITE'S Vow,	100
Nestorians,	239, 296
New Creed,	858
— Order of Clergy,	154
— Order of Things,	68
— Testament,	597
— Testament, Tyndal's,	825
Nice, Second Council of	294
Nicene Creed,	201
Nicolaitanism,	183
Northern Nations,	318
Northmen,	322
Number Seven,	3
Number Twelve,	41
Nunneries,	231
Nuns,	504, 784
ORIENTALISM,	170
Origin of Species,	1048
Orphanages,	1052
PÆDOBAPTISTS,	225
Paganism,	170
Papacy Abolished,	1007
— England and the	550
— One Grand Object,	274
— Transition Period,	273
Papal Ambition,	432
— and Imperial Rights,	372
— Army Defeated,	588
— Authority,	422
— Bulls,	421
— Forgery,	310
— Infallibility,	1042
— Jubilee, First	628
— Period, Commencement of	247
— Power, Decline of	522
— Scheme of Aggrandisement,	273
— System,	295, 515
Paper Manufactured,	594
Parable of Tares,	12
Pardon System,	631
Pastoral Epistles,	112
Paul, Apostleship of	37

	PAGE
Paul, Life of	66, 118
Paulicians, ...	296, 453
Peace of Ratisbon, ..	.. 725
— Offering Procession,	.. 944
Pecuniary Payments,	.. 420
Pelagian Heresy, ..	.. 237
Pentecost, Feast of ..	.. 18
Pepin's Plot, ..	.. 276
Pergamos Period, ..	182, 241
Persecuted and Scattered,	30
Persecution, First Legal,	.. 122
— First under Emperors,	.. 121
— General	.. 165
— in Africa, ..	.. 160
— in Asia, ...	.. 139
— in France, ..	143, 930
— of Christians, ..	.. 879
— of Waldenses, ..	544, 973
— under Decius, ..	.. 165
— under Diocletian,..	.. 192
Peter's First Appeal to Jews,	22
Peter, Preaching and Miracles	
of	44
Petrobrussians, ..	.. 454
Pharisees, ...	.. 103
Philemon, ...	.. 111
Philippians, ...	.. 111
Picts and Scots, ..	.. 256
Pilate's Staircase, ..	.. 626
Pilgrim Fathers, ..	.. 1030
Pilgrimages, ...	.. 407
Placards, The ..	.. 941
Plague of Dundee, ..	.. 996
Platonism, ...	.. 160
Pontiff, Humiliation of	.. 531
Pontifical Glory, ..	.. 422
Pope, ...	.. 5
Popery and Mankind,	.. 609
— as a System, ..	.. 515
— History of ..	.. 519
— Life Blood of ..	.. 520
— Real Character of	.. 895
Pope's Legate in France,	.. 439
— Missionaries, ..	.. 307
Popes of Avignon, ..	.. 533
Pope's Power in England	
Abolished, ..	.. 1018
Popish Priesthood, ..	.. 405
— Refutation, ..	.. 713
Popular Tumults, ..	.. 1006
Pragmatic Sanction, ..	.. 529
Prayer, Power of ..	.. 148
Preaching Friars, ..	.. 504
Presbyterianism, ..	.. 982
Presence of Holy Spirit, ..	43
Pretensions of Rome, ..	244
Priesthood of all Believers,	155
Priest's Authority, ..	.. 414

	PAGE
Printing Invented, ...	594
Prisoner of the Vatican, ..	1042
Processions and Martyrdoms,	944
Propagation of the Faith, ..	966
Prophet Joel, ...	23
Proscription Roll, ...	991
Protection of Holy See, ..	277
Protest, The	662
Protestant Succession, ..	1033
— Systems, ...	666
Protestantism, ...	664
— French, ...	960
— Mistakes of	801
— Rise of	654
— Wrong Ecclesiastically, ..	667
Protestants, ...	662
— Calamities of	867
— First Operations of ..	850
— Meetings of	675
— Perplexities of	708
— The Origin of Term ..	662
Providential Dispensation, ..	726
Publicans, ...	56
Publications of Zwingle, ..	753
Purgatory, ...	313, 410
Puritanism, ...	1031
QUARRIER'S Homes, ..	1052
Queen of Heaven, ...	406
RAGE of the King, ..	440
Real Presence, The ..	331, 677
Reception, Principle of ..	16
Recess of Augsburg, ...	864
Recess, The	718
Recluses, Female, ...	231
Reconciliation, Attempts at	811
Red Soviet, ...	1066
Reform Doctrines, Rapid	
Spread of	939
Reformation and Denmark,	875
— and Henry VIII, ..	654
— and Italy, ...	876
— and Spain, ...	882
— and Sweden, ...	873
— Approaching Dawn of ..	509
— Events Adverse to ..	657
— Forerunners of	536
— General Progress,	653, 781
— in British Isles, ...	778
— in Basle, ...	794
— in Berne, ...	783
— in Bohemia, ...	568
— in England, ...	1009
— in France, ...	923
— in Danger, ...	812
— in Germany, 608, 673, 771, 823	

	PAGE
Reformation in Germany, Effect on Europe,	873
— in Ireland,	978
— in Lausanne,	908
— in Scotland,	988
— in Spain Suppressed,	884
— in Switzerland, 728, 771,	899
— in Zurich,	751
— of Brissonnet,	928
— Political Chiefs of	659
— Rising Sun of	598
Reign of Gratian,	211
— of Hadrian,	135
— of Severus,	159
— of Antonines,	135
— of Trajan,	126
Relic Worship,	409
Religion in Scotland,	983
Religious Tradition,	1042
Republic of the Grisons,	881
Resolutions of Luther,	635
Resurrection of Christ,	19
Retributive Justice,	945
Return to Word of God,	1060
Revelation, Threefold Division	3
Revised Version of Bible,	1057
Revival at Cambuslang,	1036
— in Wales,	1068
— of 1859,	1052
— of Church-Building,	326
— of Education,	316
— of Letters by Arabs,	327
— of Literature,	327
Revolution in Germany,	863
— in 1688,	1032
Ridsdale Judgment,	1044
Rites and Ceremonies,	237
Ritualism, Influence of	237
Roman Colony,	78
— Empire, Decay of	149
— Empire Decline and Fall,	213
— Jews,	109
— Pontiff,	230
Romans,	94
Rome, Burning of	120, 348
— Calamities of	234
— Early Rulers,	120
— Thousandth Year of	165
ROMISH CHURCH, DOCTRINES AND PRACTICE,	403
Auricular Confession,	416
Bulls,	421
Confessional, The	417
Encroachments in England,	390
Extreme Unction,	414
Hierarchy in England,	258
Imperial Sovereignty,	428
Indulgences,	419

	PAGE
ROMISH CHURCH, DOCTRINES AND PRACTICE :	
Inquisition,	471, 484
Mary Worship,	405
Missionaries,	518
Opposition to Bible,	596
Papal Ambition,	432
Papal and Imperial Rights,	372
Pardon System,	631
Pilgrimages,	407
Pretensions,	244
Priesthood,	405
Purgatory,	410
Real Presence,	677
Relic Worship,	409
Rosary, The	406
Saint Worship,	407
Sale of Indulgences,	630
Seven Sacraments,	403
Superstitions,	404
Theology,	403
Transubstantiation,	403
Universal Monarch,	424
Weapons of Warfare,	774
SACRAMENTARIAN Question,	658, 677, 799
Sacraments,	403
Sacred Heart,	408
— Places,	353
Sadducees,	103
Saint Worship,	407
Sale of Indulgences,	630, 739
Salvation Army,	1054
Sanhedrim,	103
Sardis, Condition of Church,	664
Savoy, House of	545
Saxons in England,	256
Saxony, House of	432
Schism, The Great	380
Scholarship,	1047
Schoolmen, The	542
Schools of Learning,	536
Scotland, First Preachers in	267
— Wealth of Abbeys in	512
Scots, The	256
Scottish Martyrs,	985
— Missionary Society,	1040
Scriptures Suppressed,	175
Seamless Coat,	410
Second Council of Nice,	294
Seven Churches of Asia,	3, 1041
— Deacons,	28
Siege of Antioch,	361
—·of Basle,	795
— of Beziers,	465
— of Carcassonne,	466
— of Derry,	1033

	PAGE		PAGE
Siege of Jerusalem,	362	Treaty of Ratisbon,	823
— of Nicæa,	360	Trial of Lord Cobham,	564
— of Toulouse,	473	Triumph of Gospel in Samaria,	31
Sigismund, Judgment of	578	— of Truth and Righteousness	896
Simoniacal Heresy,	337	Two Hundred, The	760
Simony,	336	— Popes Murdered,	333
Six Articles, The	1021	Tyndal's New Testament,	825
Slaughter and Burning of			
Beziers,	465	UNION of Church and State,	190
Slavonians,	319	Unitarianism,	1074
Smalcald War,	845	United Brethren, The	590
Smyrna, Church of,	138	— Presbyterianism,	1035
Soldiers' Homes,	1052	Unity, Proposal for	689
Sons of Constantine,	207	Universal Monarch,	424
Sorbonne, The	938	Universities of Oxford, Cam-	
Sovereign Pontiff,	304	bridge and Paris Founded,	536
Spanish Exiles,	887	Upon this Rock,	8
Spiritism,	1051		
Spirits in Prison,	411	VAUDOIS The	456, 976
Spread of the Truth,	571	Vicar of Christ,	279
Stephen's Address,	27	Victoria Institute,	1051
St. Paul's Cathedral,	555	Victories of the Taborites,	587
Student Movement,	1065	Virgin Resolution,	660
Stundists, The	1065		
Sunday Schools,	1038	WALDENSES, The 456, 542, 964,	
Supererogation,	419		973
Superstitions of Rome,	404	Waldensian Missionaries,	546
Suppression of Monasteries,	1017	— Persecutions,	544
Swiss Reformers,	754	Wars of Charlemagne,	303
Syrians,	239	— of Extermination,	965
		— of Religion,	953
TABORITES, Victories of the	587	— of the Roses,	1012
Tares among Wheat,	13	— of 1560,	965
Tartars,	353, 518	— of 1870,	1071
Temporisers, The	940	Wealth, Effect on Clergy,	514
Theologians,	538	— of Abbeys in Scotland,	512
Theses of Zwingle,	757	Week of Prayer,	1056
Third General Council,	241	Wesleyan Missionaries,	1040
Throne of Saxony,	966	Westminster Confession,	1033
Thundering Legion, The	148	What is the Hope of the Church?	1073
Thyatira Period,	243	Woman of Revelation 17,	423
Timothy I,	114	Worldliness in Church,	166
Titus,	114	Worship of Images,	762
Titus at Troas,	93	Writings of Luther,	877
To the Lions,	139	— of the Fathers,	134
To the Unknown God,	84	Wycliffe, a Heresiarch,	554
Toleration, Proposal for	689	— and the Bible,	558
Tombs of Peter and Paul,	628	— and the Government,	553
Torture, Application of	488	— and the Papal Bulls,	556
Tower Hamlets Mission,	1052	Wycliffites,	555
Tracts for the Times,	1043		
Transubstantiation, 403, 658, 677		YEAR of Placards,	941
Treaty between Pope and		Year of Terror,	324
Emperor,	844	Y.M.C.A.,	1053
— of Cappel,	807		
— of Paris,	481	ZEALOTS, The	62
— of Passau,	864	Zwingle's Policy,	808

Index of Persons

	PAGE
ABELARD, Peter, ...	382
Acquila and Priscilla, ..	90
Acquinas, Thomas,	507, 540
Adrian IV, ...	387
Adrian VI, ...	655
Agabus, ...	96
Agrippa, ...	104
Alaric, ...	233
Albert, Jeanne d'	946
Alesius, ...	989
Alexander, ...	828
Alexander of Ephesus,	115, 163
Alexander III, ...	390
Alexander of Jerusalem, ..	168
Alfred, King .. ,. ..	559
Almeric, ...	469
Alva, Duke of	892
Amadeus II, Victor	973
Ambrose, ...	217, 231
Ananias and Sapphira, ..	16
Anastasius, ...	240
Andrew, Apostle	48
Anjou, Baron of	443
Anne, the Good Queen ..	572
Anne, Queen	976
Anne Boleyn, ...	1017
Anselm, ...	331, 383
Antipas, ...	183
Antony, ...	227
Apollonius, ...	158
Apollos, ...	89
Aquinas, Thomas, ...	1017
Arcadius, ...	233
Arius, ...	197, 1074
Arnaud, Henri, ...	975
Arnold of Brescia, ..	385, 472
Arragon, King of, ...	475
Arran, Earl of	993
Astolphe, ...	277
Athanasius, ...	202
Attila, ...	234
Augustine, .. 238, 257, 496
Augustine, Bishop of Hippo,	410
Aurelius, Marcus	136
BABDY, John	563
Babylas, ...	168
Bacon, Roger, ...	539
Baedeker, Dr. L. W. ..	1065
Balaam, ...	245
Ba...arossa, ...	367
Bar-jesus, .. ,. ,.	71

	PAGE
Barnabas, Apostle	69
Barnabas, Father, ...	151
Barnardo, Dr.	1054
Bartholomew, Apostle ..	55
—Bartholomew, Monk ..	361
Basil, Bishop of Cæsarea, ..	221
Bavaria, Duke of	707
Beaton, Archbishop, ..	986
Beaton, Cardinal	990
Becket, Thomas à ..	394, 979
Beda, Noel	931
Bede, The Venerable 256, 327, 559
Benedict, ...	262, 492
Benedict XIII, ...	568
Berengar, ...	383
Bernard of Clairvaux,	365, 373
Berquin, Louis	936
Bilney, Thomas	1015
Blanche of Castile, ..	480
Blandia, ...	145
Blauser, Andrew, ...	750
Blaurer, Thomas, ...	750
Boanerges, ...	50
Boccaccio, ...	537
Bodenskein, Andrew ..	679
Bonaventura, ..	507, 540
Boniface, ...	273
Boniface VIII, ...	529
Booth, General Wm... ..	1054
Botheric, ...	215
Brandford, ...	1026
Brissonnet, William	925
Brown, George, ...	979
Brown, John	1010
Brueys, Peter de	454
Bullinger, Henry ..	740, 822
CAJETAN, Cardinal Thomas 635,	
	828
Caliph Omar, ...	286
Cairns, Lord	1059
Calixtus, ...	372
Calvin, ... 729, 909, 1003
Campbell, John	983
Campeggio, Lorenzo, 659, 710, 328
Capito, ...	729
Carbeas, ...	302
Carey, Wm.	1039
Carlstadt, Dr. Andrew,	651, 679
Catherine de Medici, ..	940
Catherine of Bora, ..	772, 836
Caxton, William .. ,,	596

1085

	PAGE
Celestine II,	382
Celestius,	238
Celsus,	149
Chancellor of Treves,	644
Charlemagne,	275, 303
Charles II,	1031
Charles of Anjou,	528
Charles of Spain,	889
Charles V, of Germany	639
Chatelain, Dean	935
Chaucer,	537
Chicheley, Henry,	567
Chrysostom,	222
Claudius Lysias,	101
Claudius,	454
Claverhouse,	1033
Clement,	151
Clement the Scot,	321
Clement VI,	659
Clement VII,	828
Clovis,	236
Cobham, Lord	564
Coligny, Admiral	954
Columba,	265, 511
Columbanus,	266
Columbus,	883
Commodus,	158
Congleton, Lord	1060
Constans,	207
Constantia,	202
Constantine (Son),	207
Constantine, Sylvanus	297
Constantine the Great,	182, 593
Constantius,	207
Cornelius,	25
Coverdale, Miles,	1022
Cranmer,	1021
Crescens,	115
Cromer, George	979
Cromwell, Oliver	971
Cromwell, Sir Thomas	1021
Cyprian,	167, 221
Cyril,	241
DAMARIS,	85
Damiano, Peter	333
Dante,	537
Darby, J. N.	1060
Darwin,	1048
D'Aubigné,	728
Decius,	165
Demus,	115
De Sanctis,	1044
Diocletian,	173
Dionysius,	85, 167
Dioscurus,	168
Dominic,	333, 463, 498
Domitian,	125
Donatus,	196
Drithelm,	412
Du Bourg,	943
Dunbar, Cardinal,	998
Duns Scotus,	541
ECK, Doctor	637, 662
Eck, John of	829
Edelfrid,	259
Edward III,	553
Edward VI,	981, 1023
Eichorn,	1047
Elector of Saxony,	714
Elizabeth, Queen	880, 959, 982, 1029
Eloisa,	384
Elymas the Sorcerer,	70
Englehardt, Dr.	782
Epaphras,	110
Epicursus,	85
Erasmus,	604, 798, 828, 1013
Erastus,	115
Erigena, John Scott	322
Erskine, Ebenezer	1034
Ethelbert,	257
Ethiopian Eunuch,	33
Eugene III,	365
Eusebius,	203
Eutyches,	242
FABER, John	742, 785
Fabian,	168
Farel, William	729, 899, 949
Faust, John	595
Felix,	104
Festus,	104
Forrest, Henry	988
Fouquet,	477
Francis I,	947
Francis II,	952
Francis of Angouleme,	924
Francis, St.	503
Frederick Barbarossa,	389
Frederick I of Germany,	367
Frederick II,	438, 524
Frederick the Wise,	674
Froben, John	877
Froment,	905
Fryth, John	1015
GALERIUS,	174
Gall, St.	267, 729
Gallio,	88
Garcia, Juan	884
Gastaldo,	966
George, Duke of Saxony	620
George, Squire,	651
Gianavello, Joshua	968

	PAGE
Gibbard, Bishop	351
Godfrey of Bouillon,	359
Gordian,	165
Gratian,	211
Gregory,	208
Gregory Nazianzen,	221
Gregory the Great,	247
Gregory II,	291
Gregory III,	293
Gregory VII,	332
Gregory IX,	524
Gregory XII,	568
Grey, John de	444
Grostete, Robert	538
Groves, Anthony Norris	1060
Guiscard, Robert	347
Guise, Duke of	956
Guises, The Two	952
Gutenberg, John	595
HADRIAN,	135, 304
Haller, Berthold,	748
Halsbury, Lord	1059
Hamilton, Patrick	985
Hausschein, John	744
Harding, Stephen	374
Hedio, Caspar	748
Helena,	195, 295
Hennuyer, John	958
Henry, Monk of Cluny,	455
Henry II,	400, 948
Henry IV,	338, 562
Henry V,	370, 564
Henry VI, of Germany,	428
Henry VIII, 402, 654, 859, 979,1012	
Herod Agrippa,	45
Herod the Great,	46
Hildebrand,	332
Hoffman, Conrad	763
Honorius,	233
Honorius III,	479, 522
Hooper, Bishop of Gloucester,	1025
Hottinger,	766
Hun, Richard	1009
Huss, John	572
Hutten, Ulric von	603
IGNATIUS,	133, 151
Ignatius Loyola,	869
Innocent II,	380
Innocent III,	422, 517
Innocent VIII,	545
Irenaeus,	154, 219
Irene,	294
Isidore,	312
JAGELLO,	518
James, Apostle	49

	PAGE
James, Son of Alphæus,	59
James II,	1031
James V,	991
Jeffreys, Judge,	1032
Jerome,	231, 582
Jezebel,	244
Joanna, Papess,	314
Joel,	23
John, Apostle..	51
John, Elector of Saxony,	714, 827
John, King	442, 550
John Mark,	70
John of Chlum,	578
John of Eck,	829
John of Wesalia	601
Josephus,	124
Jovian,	209
Juda, Leo	729, 744, 761
Jude, Apostle	63
Julian,	209
Justin Martyr,	141
Justinian,	250
Justus,	729
KEYSER, James,	804
Kilian, St.	272
Kirsner, Conrad	746
Knox, John	516, 950, 1000
Koefflin, Wolfgang Fabricus	746
LANFRANC,	331, 383
Lange, John	619
Latimer,	1021
Leclerc, John	933
Lefevre, James	900
Leo the Great,	249
Leo III,	289
Leo X,	630
Leonides,	160
Leonis, Peter	380
Licinus,	187
Lindsay, Sir David	991
Lodi, Bishop of	568
Logie, Gawin,	989
Lothario de' Conti,	426
Louis the Pious,	317, 873
Louis XI,	368
Louis XIV,	972
Loyola, Ignatius	869
Luke,	79, 115
Luther, Martin	542, 611, 829
Luther, John	611
Lydia,	79
M'ALL, Dr.	1066
M'Culloch,	1037
Manning,	1042
Mansefield, Counts of	830

	PAGE		PAGE
Marcus Aurelius, ...	136	Pandulph, ...	450
Margaret of Angouleme, ..	926	Papess Joanna, ...	314
Margaret, Queen of Scotland,	331	Paris, Matthew	507
Markwald, ...	429	Parr, Catherine	1023
Martin V, ...	571, 585	Paschal, Lewis, ...	547
Mary of Guise, ...	1002	Patrick, St.	263, 509
Mary, Queen	981	Paul, Apostle 10, 37, 66 to 118
Matilda, ...	343, 371	Paul, Father	706
Matthew, ...	56	Pelagius, ...	238
Matthias, ...	64	Pepin, ...	275
Maurice of Saxony, ...	851	Perpetua, ...	160
Maximin, ...	163, 180	Pertinax, ...	159
Maxwell, Lord	994	Peter, Apostle ..	11, 42
Melanchthon, Philip	638	Peter, Cardinal of St. Mary,	439
Melito, ...	140	Peter de Brueys	454
Meyer, ...	783	Peter of Castelnau, ...	462
Mill, Walter	1005	Peter the Hermit, ...	354
Millon, Bartholomew ..	942	Peter the Lombard, ...	536
Miltitz, Charles von ..	636	Peter Waldo, ...	457
Milton, ...	971	Petrarch, ...	537
Mohammed, ...	281	Philip, Apostle	53
Mohammed II, ...	593	Philip Augustus, ..	367, 434
Montfort, Simon de	477	Philip, Emperor	165
Moody, D. L.	1052	Philip, Evangelist	96
Müller, George, ...	1052	Philip, Landgrave of Hesse,	673
Munzer, Thomas, ...	652	Philip of France, ...	447
Myconius, Oswald	749	Philip the Fair, ...	529
		Pianessa, Marquess of ..	967
NAPOLEON, ...	976	Pius IV, ...	962
Nathaniel, ...	53	Plato, ...	85
Nazianzen, Gregory ..	221	Pliny the Younger, ...	127
Neander, ...	219	Pole, Cardinal	1028
Nerva, ...	126	Polycarp, ...	142
Nestorius, ...	239	Pothinus, ...	144
Nicholas I, ...	301	Priscilla, ...	86
Nicholas V, ...	594	Procopius, ...	588
Ninian, St.	267	Publius, ...	108
Nogaret, ...	531	Pucci, Antonio, ...	742
North, Brownlow	1059		
Nugnez, Fernando	885	RADCLIFFE, Reginald ..	1059
		Radstock, Fourth Baron, ..	1065
ŒCOLAMPADIUS, ..	680, 744	Radstock, Lord	1060
Œlbi, ...	807	Raikes, Robert	1038
Œxlin, ...	755	Raymond VI, ...	460
Olave, King of Sweden, ..	329	Raymond, Roger	465
Oldcastle, Sir John	575	Reinhart, Anna	772
Omar, Caliph	286	Reuchlin, ...	604
O'Neill, ...	980	Reust, Mark	757
Onesiphorus, ...	116	Richard I, ...	367, 434
Origen, ...	172, 220	Richard the Lion-Hearted, ..	442
Oswald, ...	268	Ridley, ...	1026
Oswy, ...	269	Robert, Evan	1069
Otho, ...	433	Rogers of St. Sepulchres, ..	1024
Othingar, ...	329	Ruteman, ...	777
PACHOMIUS, ...	230	ST. AUGUSTINE, ...	496
Palatine, Count	704	St. Benedict, ...	492
Paleario, Antonio	879	St. Bernard, ...	365

	PAGE
St. Boniface,	273
St. Dominic,	498
St. Francis,	503
St. Gall,	267, 729
St. Jerome,	213
St. Kilian,	272
St. Ninian,	267
St. Patrick,	263, 509
Saladin,	366
Samson, Bernardin	739
Saul of Tarsus,	17, 35
Sautree, William	563
Savonarola, Jerome	598
Savoy, Duke of	972
Scotus, Duns	541
Seaton, Alexander,	989
Servetus, Michael	918
Severus,	159
Seymour, Jane	1020
Shaftesbury, Seventh Earl of	1059
Sigfred, Archdeacon	329
Sigismund,	570
Silas or Silvanus,	76, 87
Simon de Montfort,	466
Simon Zelotes,	62
Socrates,	85
Spurgeon, Charles H.	1055
Squire George	650
Staupitz, John	620
Stephen, King	392
Stephen, Martyr,	27
Stephen of Hungary,	329
Swabia, Duke of	429
Sylvanus,	289
Sylvester II,	328
TACITUS,	120
Taylor, Dr. Hudson	1067
Tertullian,	149, 220
Tetzel, John	632
Theodora,	299
Theodoric,	234
Theodosius,	212, 486
Thomas, Apostle	57
Timothy,	76, 87
Timur-Bec,	518
Titelmann,	892
Titus,	93
Titus, Son of Vespasian,	125
Torquemada,	490
Toulouse, Count of	469
Trajan,	126

	PAGE
Treves, Chancellor of	644
Trophimus,	115
Tychicus,	110
Tyndal, William	1015, 1022
ULPHILUS,	235
Ulric von Hutten,	603
Urban, Pope	355
Urban V,	553
Ursula,	613
Unwan,	329
VALENS,	210
Valentinian,	210
Valerian,	169
Varley, Henry	1059
Vespasian, Emperor	125
Vettius,	144
Viret, Peter	906
WALDO, Peter	457
Walt, Joachim von	750
Wenceslaus, King	574
Wesalia, John of	601
Wesley, Charles	1035
Wesley, John	1035
Wessalus, John	602
Whitefield, George	1036
William of Champeaux,	377
William of Ockham,	541
William, Prince of Orange,	983
William the Conqueror,	323, 391
William the Silent,	896
William III,	976
Williams, Sir George	1053
Willibrord,	272
Winfrid,	273
Wishart, George,	514, 995
Wittenbach, Thomas,	729
Wolsey,	1014
Writh, Adrian	775
Wycliffe, John	549
Wyss, Urban,	754
ZACHARY,	275, 294
Zebedee,	49
Zenghis,	364
Zeno,	85
Ziska,	586
Zwingle, Anna	818
Zwingle, Ulric von	678, 731, 752, 818

Index to Places

	PAGE
ACRE,	628
Africa,	160
Aigle,	901
Alexandria,	202
Altenburg,	637
America,	883
Anagni,	532
Angrogna, Valley of	965
Antioch,	47, 70, 89, 214, 361
Antioch in Pisidia,	71
Apii Forum,	108
Arles,	209
Asia,	139, 273
Asia Minor,	114
Askelon,	363
Athens,	83
Augsburg,	635, 695, 719, 857
Aussig,	589
Austria,	802
Avignon,	533
BADEN,	776, 785
Basle,	589, 731, 794
Bearn, Kingdom of	946
Berea,	82
Berne,	783
Beziers,	465
Bohemia,	568
Bologna,	694
Bourges,	479
Bouvines,	438
Bremen,	861
Bremgarten,	740, 822
Bright Valley,	377
Britain,	163, 253
Bulgaria,	319
Byzantium,	247
CÆSAREA,	45
Calabria,	546, 964
Cambridge,	536
Canosa,	343
Canterbury,	444
Cantons, The Five	802
Cappel,	807
Carcassonne,	466
Carthage,	160
Cenchrea,	88
Cibossa,	298
Citeaux,	374
Clairvaux,	376
Clarendon,	397

	PAGE
Coburg,	700
Constance,	570
Constantinople,	247, 593
Corinth,	86, 94, 114
Crete,	114
DAMASCUS,	67
Damietta,	523
Denmark,	330, 873
'Derry,	1033
Dijon	439
Dorylium,	360
Dundee,	996
EAST LOTHIAN,	997
Einsidlen,	733
Eisleben,	830
Eisnach,	613
England,	256, 320, 390, 445, 549
Ephesus,	4, 88, 91, 137
Erfurt,	614
Europe,	78
FRAISSINIERE,	545
France,	143, 439, 923, 1066
France, South of	453
GENEVA,	903, 974
Germany,	272, 608, 673, 823, 863
Glaris,	732
Glastonbury,	506
Greece,	114
HAMBURG,	861
Heidelburg,	634
Holland,	888
Holy Land,	31
Hungary,	329
INGOLDSTADT,	850
Iona,	268
Ireland,	263, 320, 509, 978, 1072
Italy,	113, 343, 876, 1066
JEDBURGH,	512
Jerusalem,	32, 67, 89, 122, 362, 526
Judæa,	114
KESWICK,	1058
Kilpatrick,	263
Kilsyth,	1037
Kincavil,	986
Konigsfeldt,	784

	PAGE
LANGUEDOC,	481, 549
Laodicea,	5
Lausanne,	908
Lavaur,	473
Lindisfarne,	269
Lucern,	769, 806
Lutterworth,	554
MACEDONIA,	92
Magdeburg,	612
Malta,	107
Marburg,	676
Mar's Hill,	84
Meaux,	928
Mecca,	282
Medina,	283
Melita,	107
Metz,	435
Milan,	209
Mildmay,	1057
Miletum,	114
Miletus,	95
Montbeliard,	901
Muret,	475
NARBONNE,	476
Nerac,	932
Netherlands,	888
Neuchatel,	902
Neufchatel,	916
Nicæa,	360
Nice,	200, 294
Nicomedia,	176
Nicopolis,	114
Northumbria,	268
Norway,	329
Norwich,	451
Noyon,	910
Nuremberg,	655
OXFORD,	536
PAISLEY,	513
Paris,	481, 536, 913
Passau,	864
Patara,	96
Patmos,	52
Pergamos,	4, 182
Philadelphia,	5

	PAGE
Philippi,	79
Piedmont,	544
Pisa,	568
Poland,	518
Pragela,	544
RATISBON,	725, 823
Rhodes,	96
Rome,	48, 97, 108, 120, 625
Rora, Valley of	965
Runnymede,	450
Russia,	1065
ST. ANDREWS,	998
Samaria,	31
Sardis,	5, 664
Saxony,	432
Scotland,	267, 320, 511, 983
Sicily,	428
Smalcald,	723
Smyrna,	4, 138
Spain,	113, 882, 1066
Spires,	342, 660, 674
Stamheim,	774
Strasburg,	916
Sweden,	329, 873, 1065
Switzerland,	728, 801, 899, 1065
TARSUS,	66
Thessalonica,	82
Thurgau,	774
Thyatira,	5, 243
Tockenburg,	731
Toulouse,	469, 473, 485
Trent,	842, 961
Troas,	93, 114
Tyre,	96, 204
ULM,	848
Ulster,	982
WALES,	1068
Wartburg,	650
Wittemburg,	624, 651, 832
Worcester,	451
Worms,	340, 372, 641
ZUG,	821
Zurich,	735, 751, 811